Alberta Butterflies

C.D. Bird

G.J. Hilchie

N.G. Kondla

E.M. Pike

F.A.H. Sperling

The Provincial Museum of Alberta
Edmonton, Alberta
1995

Canadian Cataloguing in Publication Data

Main entry under title:

Alberta Butterflies

Includes bibliographical references and index.
ISBN 0-7732-1672-3

1. Butterflies--Alberta--Identification. 2. Butterflies--Alberta--Geographical distribution. 3. Butterflies--Alberta. I. Bird, C.D. (Charles Durham), 1932-
II. Provincial Museum of Alberta.
QL552.A62 1995   595.78'9'097123   C95-910388-0

Cover photos by John Acorn; front — *Celastrina ladon* (Lycaenidae); title inset — *Lycaeides melissa* (Lycaenidae); spine — *Boloria selene* (Nymphalidae).

Printed in Canada

Foreword

Nearly wanton destruction is being wreaked on planet Earth by a human population whose growth is virtually out of control, a situation exacerbated by corporate and personal greed. Those who understand the magnitude and long-range consequences of environmental degradation have prevailed upon national governments to attempt appropriate action to conserve as many of the presently living species as possible. These species and their interactions represent the extant biodiversity of the planet. The principal result of the action of concerned and responsible citizens has been the United Nations Convention on Biodiversity, which Canada ratified in December, 1992.

Alberta Butterflies is a book about one small but striking segment of biodiversity — the 181 species and subspecies of butterflies (about 1.5% of the world fauna of this insect group) whose geographical ranges extend into or are confined to the province. As the authors point out in the Introduction, "the first step to concern about living things is knowing they exist." This book is dedicated to that end. In a more general context, it is a step in fulfilling Canada's responsibility in meeting its commitment to the terms of the Convention on Biodiversity.

The culmination of long years of hard work and thought in the field, laboratory and museum by five dedicated biologists, *Alberta Butterflies* is a triumph, both scientific and artistic, in which Albertans can take pride. The book is a triumph of cooperation and compromise among the authors, each of whom brought to the project special talents, ideas and interests in addition to their collective overriding interest in butterflies.

Alberta Butterflies is a triumph as well of cooperation between the authors and those institutions in Alberta and elsewhere, charged with the care and preservation of samples of biodiversity: the Canadian National Collection of Insects, Biological Resources Division, Agriculture Canada; Alberta's university biology departments with their collections of biological specimens; and the Provincial Museum of Alberta. A.T. Finnamore, curator of Invertebrate Zoology in the Provincial Museum, was instrumental in bringing the work to fruition.

Publications such as *Alberta Butterflies* are constructed not only with the personal knowledge acquired by the authors, but also with that accumulated through the efforts of specialists of previous generations. Such debt to the past is acknowledged in a section about biographical history, with succinct, vibrant verbal sketches of the authors' surprisingly numerous predecessors, many of whom were Albertans. So, the book treats a segment of human history, as well as natural history.

Butterflies are a part of an ecological web including flowering plants. This special and complex relationship has provided much of the driving force for evolution in both groups. *Alberta Butterflies* gives due recognition to the importance of this plant-butterfly relationship by supplying informative notes and an illustration of the principal food plant associated with each butterfly species — a distinctive if not unique feature of this book.

Alberta Butterflies appeals on etymological as well as entomological grounds. Aware that the formal and seemingly ponderous Latin and latinized names of genera and species are likely to be troublesome to those not versed in the classics, the authors begin treatment of each genus and species with a section entitled "Etymology." This gives the English translation or derivation of each name. Thus, *Alberta Butterflies* is a source of information about words that one does not encounter in daily conversation.

Alberta Butterflies is a model for similar publications which might address other groups of insects which live in Alberta and contribute to the richness of the environment we enjoy. Would that we had persons with the interest and will to do work comparable to that of Bird, Hilchie, Kondla, Pike and Sperling. Perhaps this book will provide the needed stimulation — a torch of scholarship and learning that lights the way.

George E. Ball
Professor Emeritus
Department of Biological Sciences
University of Alberta

Dedication

To our parents and children of all ages.

This book is dedicated to parents whose children never outgrew their fascination with insects and remain enthralled by the diversity of insect life.

Acknowledgments

This book was made possible through generous support from the Provincial Museum of Alberta (Alberta Community Development); the Friends of the Provincial Museum of Alberta Society; the Recreation, Parks and Wildlife Foundation (now Alberta Sport, Recreation, Parks and Wildlife Foundation of Alberta Community Development); Human Resources Development Canada; and the Department of Biological Sciences of the University of Alberta.

Alberta Butterflies is the result of the efforts of a great many people, who, in spite of their idiosyncrasies, persevered to achieve a common goal. Special thanks are extended to staff of the Provincial Museum of Alberta, especially Albert T. Finnamore (Invertebrate Zoology) for his support of this project, management of the manuscript production, and without whom it may never have come to fruition. The publication team at the Provincial Museum (W. Bruce McGillivray, Assistant Director; James A. Burns, Quaternary Paleontology; and Mark Steinhilber, Ichthyology and Publications) spent countless hours massaging the manuscript to give it a professional look and editing it to make it accessible to a wide-range of readers. Carolyn Lilgert (Exhibit Services, Provincial Museum) provided a cover design. We thank Glen P. Semenchuk, Federation of Alberta Naturalists, for assistance in obtaining support to complete and publish the book. Heather Proctor, Department of Biology, Queen's University, Kingston, Ontario, provided initial editing, standardized species treatments, and wrote much of the introductory chapter. Simon Pollard, Department of Zoology, University of Canterbury, Christchurch, New Zealand, produced most of the technical photographs of pinned butterflies. Jack S. Scott produced the technical photographs of several species. Mary-francis Daly was indispensable in electronic layout, file organization, and handling the innumerable editorial changes resulting from a project of this complexity. Milton Fredlund produced the ink illustrations which grace the pages of the text. Wendy Johnson of Johnson Cartographics Inc. produced the map design and distribution maps. Michael Ward, Department of Classics, University of Alberta, assisted with derivation of scientific names. We also thank Douglas Stenrue for layout design, Paul Hansen for electronic recording of locality data used in map production, and James Taylor for database design. Marcia Caamano, Janet Cameron, Lauren Guertin, William Schimeck and Bob Wong acted as project assistants during the manuscript production phase. Thanks are also extended to Patricia Anderson, Doug Nicholl and Maurice Rosseau of Human Resources Development Canada, Edmonton, for their assistance and support under the UI Section 25 program.

We wish to thank the many people who supplied data and hours or years of companionship while studying butterflies throughout Alberta. Thanks are extended to John and Bertha Carr of Calgary, Alberta, wonderful beetle collectors who picked up thousands of butterflies over the years in all regions of the province and who accompanied several of the authors on many collecting trips. Special thanks are extended to S.S. Shigematsu for providing an impressive number of butterfly records from Alberta, especially from the southern regions.

We wish to thank the following people for sharing unpublished information or allowing access to collections containing Alberta butterflies: J. Acorn, P. Allen, R.L. Anderson, G. Anweiler, K. Avery, G.E. Ball, J. Belicek, J.W. Case, C. Ferris, E. Fuller, B.J. Godwin, L.P. Grey, M. Grinnell, C. Guppy, S. Harris, R. Hooper, D.L. Johnson, J. Lake, D.L. Larson, D. Lawrie, J.S. Legge, R. Lein, D. Macauley, I. Mackenzie, H. Mandzie, R. Moon, J. Nordin, W. Nordstrom, H.W. Pinel, J. Reichel, J.D. Reist, A. Rupp, C. Schmidt, J.H. Shepard, S.S. Shigematsu, W.W. Smith, T.W. Thormin, D.L. Threatful, E. Williams, and R. Woodley.

The following museums and institutions were used to acquire data for this book: Biological Resources Division, Centre for Land and Biological Resources Research, Agriculture Canada, Ottawa; Olds College, Olds, Alberta; Provincial Museum of Alberta, for loan of specimens used in photography; Strickland Museum, Department of

Entomology (now merged with the Department of Biological Sciences), University of Alberta, for making the Bowman collection available for loan of specimens used in photography; University of Calgary; and the Northern Forestry Research Centre, Edmonton.

Special thanks must also be given to our wives, Ann Bird, Carol Hilchie, Trudy Kondla, Betty Pike and Janet Haley-Sperling. In addition to accepting the many long days and nights we spent while preparing this book, these ladies have humoured and tolerated us in so many ways, from tagging along into mosquito and blackfly-infested bogs, persevering on arduous mountain treks, to baking in prairie badlands, all in pursuit of Alberta butterflies.

Contents

Introduction to Butterfly Study in Alberta

1

Butterflies have long fascinated humanity. In ancient Greece butterflies symbolized Psyche, the human soul. Christian iconographers found the metamorphosis of caterpillar to chrysalid to winged adult symbolic of earthly life, death and the resurrection of the soul. In the South Pacific, a dying Solomon Islander would tell members of his family whether he intended to transform his spirit into a butterfly or a bird; the species would be held sacred and protected after his death. Babies in the Blackfoot Indian tribe of North America were put to bed with butterfly tokens tied into their hair to make them sleep, as butterflies were thought to bring dreams. In British folklore, depending on their number, colour and the time of year, butterflies could presage health, wealth or imminent death. The great poets have all paid tribute to them, and the English language itself is rife with butterfly phrases — "social butterfly," "butterflies in the stomach" and "to break a butterfly on a wheel," to name but a few. Today they symbolize the beauty and fragility of wild places, and butterflies rank second only to birds as popular subjects of nature study.

Why are so many people fascinated, if not obsessed, with butterflies? Part of the reason is certainly the beauty and variety of their wing patterns. Another factor is the relative ease of study. Butterflies are large, diurnal species that are easy to see (if not to capture!). They are diverse enough to be interesting, but not so overwhelmingly species-rich as to make the goal of "learning all about butterflies" impossible. How people choose to study butterflies is also varied; one may be a butterfly collector, a "lister," or an observer of their habits or life histories. In fact, non-professionals can do a great deal to further our knowledge of butterfly biology. We have 181 species and subspecies in Alberta, and for many of them little is known about their distributions, host plant preferences, mating behaviour, and sometimes even what their caterpillars look like.

Alberta Butterflies began in the late 1960s when John Legge (a geologist) and Charles Bird (Professor of Botany, University of Calgary, now retired) discussed the project and established a plan to complete the work. A short time later, John moved to Colorado leaving Charley with the entire project.

Over the next few years, butterfly data were gathered from museum collections, both private and public, from naturalists, and anyone willing to cooperate with the effort. Many young butterfly enthusiasts were approached by Charley in the ensuing years. By 1971, four of these young collectors were making yearly data contributions to the project and continued to do so. Charley retired from the University of Calgary and moved to a farm near Buffalo Lake where limited resources placed the feasibility of the project in doubt.

In response to these limited resources, Norbert Kondla was invited to join the project; his enthusiasm and knowledge of our butterfly fauna proved a boon. In 1984, invitations to join the project were extended to Gerald Hilchie, Felix Sperling and Edward (Ted) Pike. All three hold graduate degrees in entomology from the University of Alberta. Their experience and training in entomology, their love of butterflies and extensive data gathering for the book made them natural choices.

By 1985 the group of authors divided a manuscript, produced by Charley, into broad subjects with each tackling those sections in which they felt most competent. Although each author worked on a particular section of the book, all sections were circulated among the other authors and the book written through a team approach. Initial responsibility was as follows: Charley was to compile information on the history of butterfly study in Alberta. Norbert coordinated the project, did species treatments for Hesperiidae, some Nymphalidae, mapping, and the introductory section on morphology. Gerald did species treatments for most Satyridae, larval food plants, larval stages, treatment of species expected to occur in Alberta, derivation of species names and some introductory sections. Felix produced species treatments for the Papilionidae and Pieridae, introductory sections on species concepts, population dynamics, nomenclature and taxonomy. Ted produced species treatments for Lycaenidae, most Nymphalidae, some Satyridae and introductory sections on studying and collecting butterflies.

During the ensuing years, growing families, job changes and relocations all contributed to increasing strain on the project. Gerald took the role of interim editor, compiling, editing and typing the manuscript sections as they were completed. In 1992 the authors reached an agreement with the Provincial Museum of Alberta whereby Museum resources would be used to assist in completion of the manuscript and ultimately publish Alberta Butterflies. Gerald worked closely with the Provincial Museum acting as liaison with authors while Albert Finnamore (Invertebrate Zoology, Provincial Museum of Alberta) assumed responsibility for the production of maps, photography, illustrations, editing and layout for the electronic version of the manuscript that resulted in this volume.

This book is aimed at the enthusiastic naturalist and the professional entomologist alike. For the first time, comprehensive distribution and host plant records for Alberta butterflies are assembled in one source. All species and subspecies recorded in Alberta are included, as well as those whose ranges border on our province. Much of this information is unpublished records amassed by the five authors from decades of collecting and observations. Compared to the usual method of leafing through pages of photographic plates to find a photograph that matches the specimen, the pictorial keys in this book make it easy to identify butterflies. Each species and, where required, subspecies, sex, or colour variant is illustrated with high quality, life-sized photographs produced by professional photographers. Introductory chapters cover biographies of historical and contemporary collectors in Alberta, techniques of butterfly study, habitats, adult morphology, taxonomy, natural history and evolution. The remaining chapters deal with the species of Alberta butterflies. Each species is treated in sections on appearance, behaviour, larval food plants, distribution and flight times. Both common and scientific names are provided, and great effort has gone into explaining the etymological origin of these names — a subject almost as fascinating as butterflies themselves. Finally, for the serious student, there is a bibliography on Alberta butterflies.

How to Use This Book

This book is designed to enable anyone to identify all the butterflies known to occur in Alberta. Many identifying characteristics are difficult to observe except on fresh, undamaged, well mounted specimens. For accurate determinations, mounted specimens are always preferable to field observations.

Keys to families, genera and species have been provided to assist identification of specimens. Begin with the key to families. Once the family has been identified, proceed to the key to the genera. If the genus has been ascertained, the next step is to use the species key to identify the specimen. Not all species are easily identified. In some instances, identification to the generic level may be all that is possible. As your experience with butterflies increases you will become better at noting the subtle characteristics that distinguish some species. More experienced workers may find the family or genus keys to be unnecessary. Keys are presented as a series of numbered choices termed couplets (nos. **1** and **2** on accompanying diagram). Start with couplet 1. The choices are presented as 1a or 1b. Select the choice that *best fits* the specimen by comparing it to both the written description and corresponding pictures. The specimens in the pictures may not look like your specimen but one of the choices will contain a character, indicated by the arrow(s), that is present on your specimen. Once the best choice has been made, follow the lines in the picture key to the next couplet or, in the text key, go to the couplet number indicated at the end of your choice. Pictorial and text couplets are associated with each other and have the

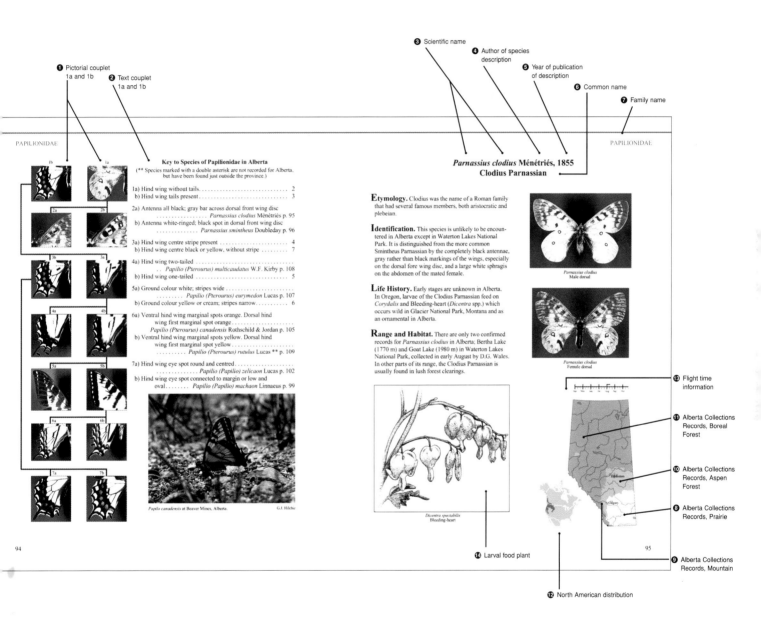

❶ Pictorial couplet 1a and 1b

❷ Text couplet 1a and 1b

❸ Scientific name

❹ Author of species description

❺ Year of publication of description

❻ Common name

❼ Family name

PAPILIONIDAE

Key to Species of Papilionidae in Alberta
(** Species marked with a double asterisk are not recorded for Alberta, but have been found just outside the province.)

1a) Hind wing without tails. 2
b) Hind wing tails present 3

2a) Antenna all black; gray bar across dorsal front wing disc
. . . . *Parnassius clodius* Ménétriés p. 95
b) Antenna white-ringed; black spot in dorsal front wing disc
. . . . *Parnassius smintheus* Doubleday p. 96

3a) Hind wing centre stripe present 4
b) Hind wing centre black or yellow, without stripe 7

4a) Hind wing two-tailed . . . .
. . *Papilio (Pterourus) multicaudatus* W.F. Kirby p. 108
b) Hind wing one-tailed 5

5a) Ground colour white; stripes wide . . . .
. . . . *Papilio (Pterourus) eurymedon* Lucas p. 107
b) Ground colour yellow or cream; stripes narrow 6

6a) Ventral hind wing marginal spots orange. Dorsal hind
wing first marginal spot orange. . . . .
Papilio (Pterourus) canadensis Rothschild & Jordan p. 105
b) Ventral hind wing marginal spots yellow. Dorsal hind
wing first marginal spot yellow . . . .
. . . . *Papilio (Pterourus) rutulus* Lucas ** p. 109

7a) Hind wing eye spot round and centred. . . . .
. . . . *Papilio (Papilio) zelicaon* Lucas p. 102
b) Hind wing eye spot connected to margin or low and
oval. . . . . *Papilio (Papilio) machaon* Linnaeus p. 99

Papilio canadensis at Beaver Mines, Alberta.

G.J. Hilchie

94

PAPILIONIDAE

***Parnassius clodius* Ménétriés, 1855**
Clodius Parnassian

Etymology. Clodius was the name of a Roman family that had several famous members, both aristocratic and plebeian.

Identification. This species is unlikely to be encountered in Alberta except in Waterton Lakes National Park. It is distinguished from the more common Smintheus Parnassian by the completely black antennae, gray rather than black markings of the wings, especially on the dorsal fore wing disc, and a large white sphragis on the abdomen of the mated female.

Life History. Early stages are unknown in Alberta. In Oregon, larvae of the Clodius Parnassian feed on *Corydalis* and Bleeding-heart (*Dicentra* spp.) which occurs wild in Glacier National Park, Montana and as an ornamental in Alberta.

Range and Habitat. There are only two confirmed records for *Parnassius clodius* in Alberta; Bertha Lake (1770 m) and Goat Lake (1980 m) in Waterton Lakes National Park, collected in early August by D.G. Wales. In other parts of its range, the Clodius Parnassian is usually found in lush forest clearings.

Parnassius clodius
Male dorsal

Parnassius clodius
Female dorsal

Dicentra spectabilis
Bleeding-heart

❸ Flight time information

❶ Alberta Collections Records, Boreal Forest

❿ Alberta Collections Records, Aspen Forest

❽ Alberta Collections Records, Prairie

❾ Alberta Collections Records, Mountain

❹ Larval food plant

❷ North American distribution

95

3

same couplet numbers. If no line leads from your choice in the pictorial key, then you have identified the specimen. Refer to your choice in the associated text key for the name of the specimen and a page reference to a family, another key or to a species.

Each species treatment begins with the scientific name (**3**) and common name (**6**) for the species. The scientific name (*in italics*) is followed by the author (**4**) of the species and the year in which the species description was first published (**5**). Parentheses around the author, for instance, *Nymphalis antiopa* (Linnaeus), indicate the species *antiopa* is now placed in a different genus than that originally published by Linnaeus. Square brackets around the year of publication indicate the date of publication is in doubt.

A paragraph on Etymology provides an explanation of the origin and derivation of the scientific name. The Identification paragraph offers several diagnostic characters that should be used to confirm the species identification. Although it may be possible to identify species just from this written description, we recommend use of the keys. This section generally compares a species to others with which it may be confused. The Life History paragraph reviews the knowledge of the life cycle, from egg through caterpillar to adult, especially for Alberta. Range and Habitat for Alberta and North America are indicated in a final paragraph. Illustrations of larvae (caterpillars) or food plants (**14**) often accompany the text. Most species of butterflies do not have any known larval food plant records in Alberta. Plants known to be food sources in other parts of the distribution of

the species are often used in the text illustrations. Food plant illustrations should be considered Alberta records only if stated specifically in the text.

A map of the Albertan and North American distributions for each butterfly species is provided. Map colours refer to the biomes of Alberta (Prairie (**8**) - yellow, Aspen Parkland (**10**) - green, Boreal Forest (**11**) - blue, Mountains (**9**) - purple), the North American distribution is inset (**12**). Black dots on the Alberta map indicate collection records in the province. The Albertan distribution is often based on relatively few records. Confirmation of range extensions are of interest and records should be forwarded to the Invertebrate Zoology Program, Provincial Museum of Alberta, 12845-102 Avenue, Edmonton, Alberta T5N OM6. Flight times are indicated on the scale above the map (**13**). Solid blocks on the flight time scale indicate main flight period while a thin horizontal bar indicates the range of possible flight times.

We hope that this book will further awareness of Alberta butterflies for both their physical beauty and ecological requirements. As butterflies are such popular objects of study we are sensitive to changes in their abundance. It is not surprising that most invertebrates on endangered species lists are butterflies, or that the Xerces Society — a group dedicated to the conservation of invertebrates — chose to name itself after a species of butterfly driven extinct by human activities. The first step to concern about living things is knowing they exist; *Alberta Butterflies* provides the information needed to start one leg of this journey.

Biographical History of Butterfly Study in Alberta

The first record of butterflies in Alberta dates from 1844 when a naturalist collecting plants for Lord Derby of England also gathered a few butterflies. Since then, the number of amateur and professional naturalists who have contributed to our knowledge of butterflies in this province has grown enormously. The information in this book was gleaned from the records of almost 300 collectors, but the true total is undoubtedly much higher. The following account highlights the activities and achievements of major researchers presented in order from the earliest to the most recent; however, it should not be viewed as a complete historical review as we were unable to include all collectors. But even with this selective history it is clear that there has been a great deal of interaction and communication among the butterfly enthusiasts of Alberta.

Thomas Drummond, a botanist, served as assistant naturalist on the Second Land Arctic Expedition under the command of Captain John Franklin. Drummond reached Cumberland House, Saskatchewan, on June 18, 1825, remained there until August 20, then journeyed on to Edmonton and eventually to the area near present-day Jasper. He spent most of the next summer in that area, especially near Rock Lake, where he stayed from June 15 to July 23. The English entomologist William Kirby described a number of insects based on collections made on the above expedition, but it appears that the butterflies Kirby described (*Incisalia augustinus augustinus*, *Celastrina ladon lucia* and *Erebia discoidalis discoidalis*) were collected in Saskatchewan. Thus, although Drummond may have collected butterflies while in Alberta, we have no record to this effect.

Edward Burke appears to be the first person to have made a documented collection in Alberta. He spent the summer of 1844 in the same area where Thomas Drummond collected plants and even used the same Indian guide. Burke collected botanical specimens and "a small box of butterflies" for Lord Derby of England. Six of these were later described by Edward Doubleday. The modern names of the six are *Parnassius smintheus*, *Euchloe creusa*, *Boloria astarte*, *Euphydryas anicia*, *Erebia disa mancinus* and *Oeneis chryxus*. After Burke, there was an 18-year gap in butterfly collecting activity in Alberta.

In 1862, with the encouragement of naturalist R.W. Kennicott, who left her a net and pins, **Christina Ross,** wife of the Hudson's Bay Company factor at Fort Simpson, Northwest Territories, collected a large number of butterflies and sent them to W.H. Edwards of Coalburgh, West Virginia. Included was a new species from Mountain Rapids, Slave River, in extreme northern Alberta that Edwards named *Colias christina* in her honour.

Another twenty-one years elapsed before there was a record of further collecting in Alberta. **J. Gamble Geddes** (1850-1896), first a banker then aide-de-camp and private secretary to J.B. Robinson, Lieutenant-Governor of Ontario, devoted much of his leisure time to collecting insects. He visited Alberta in the summer of 1883, the same year that the Canadian Pacific Railway reached Calgary. The butterflies he collected were sent to W.H. Edwards for identification. They included three taxa that Edwards described as new: *Argynnis lais* (now *Speyeria electa lais*) and *Lycaena afra* (now regarded as a synonym of *Glaucopsyche lygdamus couperi*) from Red Deer, and *Chrysophanus florus* (now *Epidemia dorcas florus*) near Lundbreck. In the same year, Geddes published the first list of Alberta butterflies ("Diurnal Lepidoptera Collected in the Northwest Territory and the Rocky Mountains") in the *Canadian Entomologist*. He collected in Alberta again in 1884 and found a few more species. One of these he referred to as *Melitaea geddesii* Edwards (nov. sp.) but the name was never officially published. Another, which was collected at Kicking Horse Pass, Alberta, was described by Strecker in 1885 as *Colias meadii elis*. Geddes eventually sold his collection to the Dominion Government.

5

John Macoun (1831-1920) was a botanist with the Canadian Government from 1877 to 1912 and made a number of trips to Alberta. Although plants were his main concern he had wide interests and often collected butterflies. Specimens he took at Morley and Kananaskis in June, 1885, and in the Cypress Hills in 1894 are in Agriculture Canada's Canadian National Collection in Ottawa. *Oeneis macounii*, which he collected at Nipigon, Ontario, was named in his honour.

James M. Macoun (ca. 1863-1920), son of John Macoun (above), worked with the Geological Survey of Canada in the Peace River area of Alberta during the summer of 1893 and made a small collection near the town of Peace River. He also spent time in Banff and may have collected there. The specimens are now in the Canadian National Collection.

Thomas E. Bean (1844-1931) was born in England. He emigrated with his wife and family to Galena, Illinois, and later found employment as a telegrapher with the Canadian Pacific Railway. He collected extensively at Laggan (now Lake Louise), Alberta and produced a number of publications. His finds included six new butterflies, *Boloria alberta, Colias nastes streckeri* Grum-Grshimaïlo, *Colias pelidne minisni* Bean, *Euphydryas editha beani, Oeneis melissa beanii* and *Speyeria electa beani*, and at least twelve new species of moths. Bean returned to Galena, Illinois, in 1895 and his collection was later purchased by C.F. dos Passos.

William J. Holland was the well-known author of "The Moth Book" (1903) and "The Butterfly Book" (1898) and director of the Carnegie Museum, Pittsburg, Pennsylvania. While on a trip in 1887 on the Canadian Pacific Railway from Winnipeg, Manitoba, to Victoria, British Columbia, he made a collection at Canmore. The ten butterfly species he captured there are reported in a paper published in the *Canadian Entomologist* in 1888.

In 1890, **Henry H. Lyman** and **H.K. Burrison** travelled the Canadian Pacific Railway from Quebec to western Canada. Both collected butterflies at Banff. On his return home, Lyman collected an unknown skipper at Regina, Saskatchewan, and described it as *Pamphila manitoba* var. *assiniboia* (now *Hesperia comma assiniboia*). The Lyman Entomological Museum and Research Laboratory, on the Macdonald Campus of McGill University, was named in Lyman's honour.

In 1892, **Elizabeth Taylor** collected butterflies at various places while on a trip down the Athabasca, Slave and Mackenzie rivers to Fort McPherson. The eighteen species she found were reported by A.G. Butler in 1893 and are in the British Museum.

Thomas N. Willing (1858-1920) came from Ontario in 1879, homesteaded in 1881 on what is now part of Calgary, then farmed near Olds. On the recommendation of James Fletcher, he became Inspector of Weeds and Game Guardian in Saskatchewan in 1899, and subsequently Professor of Natural History at the University of Saskatchewan in 1911. Butterfly specimens in the Canadian National Collection show that he collected in the Calgary area in 1894, Olds from 1895 to 1898, Lethbridge in 1899 and 1904, and Fort Macleod, St. Albert and Calgary in 1904. He knew Wolley-Dod and was active in early natural history activities in the province. Willing's Alberta collections resulted in the naming in whole or in part, of four moth taxa and one butterfly form, *Glaucopsyche lygdamus couperi* form *mcdunnoughi* Gunder.

Arthur Hudson lived near, and often collected with, Wolley-Dod from 1895 to 1910. In 1895 Wolley-Dod wrote "I have a fellow worker about nine miles further west, near the head of Pine Creek, by the name of Mr. Arthur Hudson, a keen observer, and, I believe, the only entomologist beside myself who has ever collected here for a whole season, and between us we are almost daily increasing the list of macrolepidoptera found around Calgary."

James Fletcher (1852-1908) was appointed Honorary Entomologist to the Dominion Department of Agriculture in 1883 and was Dominion Entomologist from 1884 until his death in 1908. Fletcher established contact with over 400 insect enthusiasts throughout Canada. He played a key role in encouraging amateurs to carry out research on insects by identifying specimens, corresponding, and often visiting individuals on annual trips from 1893 to 1907. He was compiler of the *Entomological Record* of the Entomological Society of Ontario from 1901 to 1908. This publication played a unique role in promoting interest in entomology by including notes on interesting discoveries, names of specialists who would identify specimens, and names and addresses of subscribers so contact could be made between those of similar interest. Fletcher was interested in butterflies, as well as other insects, and the Canadian National Collection includes specimens he collected in Alberta from 1895 to 1907.

F.H. Wolley-Dod, 1914.

The Wolley-Dod house, 1914, located southwest of Calgary at the head of Pine Creek.

The 1914 photos by W.H.T. Tams were obtained by J. Franclemont (Cornell University) from Tams in 1968. They were obtained by F.A.H. Sperling from Franclemont in 1988.

The Wolley-Dod House, 1994.   F.A.H. Sperling

Frederic Hova Wolley-Dod (1871-1919) collected moths and butterflies in the Calgary area from 1893 to 1917. He was a true amateur in the sense of E.H. Strickland (i.e. ,"one of those who pursue a definite line of action simply for the love of so doing; certainly with no suggestion of financial gain and, usually at considerable cost to themselves"). Wolley-Dod, a well educated and independently wealthy English gentleman, arrived by train at Calgary in early 1893. He brought with him a collection of three to four thousand British moths and butterflies and a strong desire to work with Alberta species. Wolley-Dod lived for two years on the ranch of his brother Arthur near the mouth of Fish Creek, then moved to a ranch 28 km southwest of Calgary at the head of Pine Creek. Except for four trips to a ranch near Dorothy and five trips to the mountains in the Banff and Lake Louise areas, almost all of his Alberta collections were from these two locations. In his first spring in Alberta he collected specimens of an *Oeneis* that he did not know. A specialist in the group, Henry J. Elwes of Cheltenham, England, and President of the Entomological Society of London, visited him in July of that year, saw the material, and later described a new species, *Oeneis alberta*. Three other butterflies were described

on the basis of material he collected: *Chrysophanus arethusa* (now *Lycaena phlaeas arethusa*) by himself; and *Argynnis nevadensis calgariana* (now *Speyeria callippe calgariana*) and *Papilio machaon dodi* by J. McDunnough. Over 60 of the moths he collected turned out to be new species, including five he described himself. Wolley-Dod published the first comprehensive list of Alberta butterflies and moths and followed it up with a number of additions and corrections. He was in close touch with other Albertans interested in Lepidoptera, as well as world experts, and visited a number of the major U.S. and European museums. When at the British Museum in 1912 he met W.H.T. Tams and asked Tams to become his entomological assistant. Tams agreed, arrived about a year later, and was soon collecting, setting, arranging and cataloguing specimens. Tams returned to England in 1917 and was appointed Curator of Lepidoptera at the British Museum. Wolley-Dod joined the army in 1917 and died in Macedonia on July 24, 1919. His death came at the peak of his scientific career. The fact that he was largely self-trained and self-motivated in entomology is a reminder to all that capable amateurs can do much. His specimens are now in the Canadian National Collection.

Norman Bethune Sanson (1861-1949) came west in 1885 as a member of the Queen's Own Regiment to put down the Riel Rebellion. He stayed in Calgary until 1892, when he moved to Banff to work in its sanatorium. With the opening of the Banff Museum he was Curator from 1896-1931. Sanson collected many natural history specimens during this time. The 585 labelled skipper and butterfly specimens now in the University of Calgary collection make up 71 different taxa. Most of these were from Banff or Sulphur Mountain; for the latter collections Sanson climbed 1065 m to the top of that mountain 815 times in order to take weather readings. The Sanson collection includes a small number of specimens from other Alberta collectors — J. Macoun, T.E. Bean and J. Fletcher — and it is likely that Sanson was personally acquainted with these people.

Percy B. Gregson farmed near Blackfalds and was interested in many aspects of natural history, especially fleas and other insects. He was President of the Northwest (Canada) Entomological Society in 1899, and lectured about insects, weeds and agriculture. Many of his collections are referred to in Wolley-Dod's list of the macrolepidoptera of Alberta, and he contributed to the *Entomological Record* of the Entomological Society of Alberta from its inception in 1901 to 1904. A nephew of his, J.D. Gregson, became an expert on ticks and biting flies, and collected some butterflies in Alberta.

Merritt Cary (1880-1918) and **Edward A. Preble** of the U.S. Biological Survey spent the summer of 1903 collecting animals and butterflies along the Athabasca, Slave and Mackenzie rivers. Cary started collecting butterflies at Edmonton on May 10, reached Smith Portage on June 13, and collected in the province again from August 5-25. His Smith Portage collections included type material of *Oeneis chryxus caryi* which was named in his honour.

Kenneth Bowman (1875-1955) was born in Durham, England, and came to Alberta in 1904. He ranched briefly at Pine Lake, southeast of Red Deer, then in 1906 moved to Edmonton where he became a chartered accountant. He cultivated a keen interest in natural history, especially in Lepidoptera. His first Alberta collections were in 1904 and 1905 at Blackfalds. From 1907 to 1909 he collected mainly in Edmonton, but from then on he managed to collect in a number of places each year. His accounting work often took him to the Jasper-Pocahontas,

Nordegg and Hillcrest-Blairmore areas, from where he gathered many specimens. In 1919, he updated Wolley-Dod's list and published an "Annotated Checklist of the Macrolepidoptera of Alberta." Additions and corrections were regularly made to this, from 1921 to 1944. Then in 1951, with help from E.H. Strickland, he brought out a further update in "An Annotated List of the Lepidoptera of Alberta." The latter contained over 1800 taxa, roughly twice the number in the former, with most additions being microlepidoptera. More of a collector and compiler than a taxonomist, Bowman seldom described anything new, with the exception of *Colias eurytheme alberta*. Bowman's extensive and meticulously prepared collection was deposited at the University of Alberta.

Mary de la Beach-Nicholl, or simply Mary Nicholl, of Bridgend, South Wales, was an aristocratic woman with a serious interest in insects, especially butterflies and moths. After her six children had grown up, she went on extensive collecting trips. In 1904, at the age of 57, this petite English lady travelled to western Canada. She visited Wolley-Dod at his ranch in late May, then travelled to Banff and on into the Yoho area, British Columbia, where she met John Macoun. She returned to Alberta in mid-July, collected in the Lake Louise area with Wolley-Dod, visited Mount Assiniboine and the Simpson River in British Columbia, and returned to the Banff area in the last half of August. The next year she collected in the Okanagan area of British Columbia. In 1907 she returned again to the Alberta mountains and spent the summer collecting from Bow Lake to the Alexandra River. Her guide on many of these trips was James Simpson, a well known outfitter. Among the Alberta material she collected was *Boloria eunomia nichollae*, which Barnes and Benjamin named in her honour, and three new moths. Her collection was eventually deposited in the British Museum.

C.B.D. Garrett was a keen collector of moths and butterflies in the Didsbury, Fallen Timber Creek and Calgary areas from 1904 to 1908. In 1922 he was an insect pest investigator in Banff. He made numerous butterfly collections there from May 25 to September 20, according to specimens in the Canadian National Collection and in the Los Angeles County Museum. J.D. Gunder, who named *Speyeria zerene garretti* in his honour, bought his collection around 1931.

John Braithwaite Wallis born in Erith, England, in 1877, moved to Manitoba in 1893, where he worked on farms for three years before becoming a teacher. He developed a serious interest in natural history through contact with fellow enthusiasts in Manitoba. He gradually confined his interests to insects, especially Odonata, Lepidoptera and Coleoptera, then finally to water beetles and tiger beetles. Wallis collected butterflies in Alberta in Banff (1907, 1915), Lethbridge (1909, 1912) and Lake Louise (1915). He knew Wolley-Dod and worked with him on two papers; he was sole author of "A Colour Key to the Manitoban Butterflies" (1927) and many papers on Coleoptera.

C.H. Young, known for his life history studies of various insects and his interest in microlepidoptera, made a few collections of butterflies along the Red Deer River while travelling with the ornithologist P.A. Taverner in 1917, and many at Waterton Lakes National Park in 1922 and 1923. His specimens are in the Canadian National Collection.

Frederick Stephen Carr (1881-1934) moved from Ontario to teach school at Innisfail from 1904-1909 and Edmonton from 1909-1919, then was a school inspector until his death. He moved to Medicine Hat in 1921. Seriously interested in beetles, Carr amassed a vast collection of Alberta species and published the first list of the beetles of the province. Though his main bent was beetles he made a few collections of butterflies in the Medicine Hat and Cypress Hills areas. His collection of around 100,000 insect specimens was donated to the University of Alberta in 1939. His son John and daughter-in-law Bertha have continued in his footsteps and have made many beetle and butterfly collections.

Richard John Fitch (1886-1961), the son of one-time President of the British Entomological Society Edward A. Fitch, began collecting Lepidoptera as a boy. He brought this interest with him when he left Malden, Essex, for Canada in 1905. He homesteaded southwest of Lloydminster. Fitch started collecting again in 1921 and was at it in earnest by 1930. He developed a small business selling butterflies and some moths and sent specimens to many individuals in North America and elsewhere. Although most of his collections were made on or close to his farm, because his mailing address was given as "Rivercourse via Lloydminster, Saskatchewan,"

many who received specimens from him believed they were from Saskatchewan. Specimens that Fitch collected served as type material of two butterfly subspecies: *Boloria toddi jenistae* Stallings and Turner and *Erebia epipsodea freemani*.

Gaylord C. Hall made a butterfly collecting trip to British Columbia in July, and Alberta in August, of 1921. He described *Cercyonis pegala ino* based on material he took at Calgary.

James Halliday McDunnough (1877-1962) was a systematist who specialized in moths and butterflies. Author of some 313 papers, he was employed by the Entomological Branch of the Canadian Department of Agriculture for most of his professional life. He made extensive collections of Lepidoptera in Alberta from 1921-1923, especially in Waterton Lakes National Park in 1923, but also in Nordegg (1921), Lethbridge (1923, 1928, 1933), Moraine Lake (1923), Jasper (1923, 1926, 1933) and Banff (1923). He collected with Kenneth Bowman in Nordegg in 1921 and in Waterton in 1923. McDunnough described three butterflies based on Alberta material: *Speyeria callippe calgariana* (type locality, head of Pine Creek), *Coenonympha inornata benjamini* (type locality, Waterton Lakes), and *Papilio machaon dodi* (type locality, Dorothy). J.D. Gunder named *Papilio zelicaon* ab. *mcdunnoughi* (type locality, Waterton Lakes) after McDunnough. Most of McDunnough's specimens are in the Canadian National Collection.

Edgar H. Strickland, born in England in 1889, joined the Federal Department of Agriculture in Lethbridge in 1913 to initiate studies on the control of the pale western cutworm, a noctuid moth. F.H. Wolley-Dod, by that time recognized for his taxonomic knowledge of the local noctuid moths, helped Strickland sort out his identification problems. Strickland founded the Department of Entomology of the University of Alberta in 1922. He was the lone entomologist for 23 years until Brian Hocking arrived in 1946. Strickland emphasized economic entomology, built up the University insect collection, and published lists of the insects known to occur in the province. The University collection contains a number of butterflies collected by Strickland in Waterton (1923, 1924) and Milk River (1930).

J.H. Pepper, while employed by the Federal Department of Agriculture in Lethbridge, made numerous collections of butterflies and skippers in southern Alberta in 1929 and 1930. The specimens are now in the Canadian National Collection.

Jack F. May came to Manitoba in the early 1920s, became a forest ranger, and then a park warden, when the Riding Mountains became a national park. From his home base in Kelwood, Manitoba, May made numerous collections of local butterflies and moths and soon developed a sideline of selling and exchanging specimens with interested collectors and taxonomists. Many of his butterflies were purchased by Frank H. Chermock and J.D. Gunder and the two named a number of new subspecies and forms on the basis of this material. Jack, in company with his wife Marjorie and son John, made numerous collections in the Alberta mountains in 1929, 1930 and 1933. The Mays visited End Mountain (near Exshaw), Banff, the Lake Louise area and Jasper. *Parnassius phoebus manitobaensis* Bryk and Eisner (type locality, End Mountain, Manitoba) was described on the basis of May material, but J. McDunnough pointed out that not only was *manitobaensis* really *P. phoebus smintheus*, but that End Mountain was in Alberta, not Manitoba. May exhibited his collection of insects at various fairs and, after leaving government service, began a travelling exhibition in the United States. John May was Curator of the May Natural History Museum, near Colorado Springs, Colorado.

F. Martin Brown, a teacher in Colorado Springs, Colorado, was co-author of "Colorado Butterflies," (with D. Eff and B. Rotger), "Butterflies of the Rocky Mountain States" (with C.D. Ferris) and "A Catalogue/Checklist of the Butterflies of America North of Mexico" (with L.D. Miller) as well as many papers on systematics and biogeography. He visited Alberta in 1934 and collected butterflies at a number of places in Banff National Park.

George S. Walley, an employee of the Entomology Research Institute who specialized in the taxonomy of parasitic wasps, made numerous collections of butterflies in Alberta in 1938. His collections from Magrath, Lethbridge, Moraine Lake, the Lake Louise area and Banff are now in the Canadian National Collection.

Paul F. Bruggemann (1890-1974) moved from Germany to Canada in 1926 and settled near Lloydminster, Alberta. He worked for a number of years as a farm labourer and later established a small business repairing automobiles and farm machinery. His scientific interest in Lepidoptera appears to have originated in part from discussions with Richard Fitch, who lived nearby. He started collecting butterflies in 1938 and by 1940 was at it in earnest, visiting Cold Lake, Primrose Lake, Big Gulley, Streamstown, Lloydminster, Blackfoot Hills, Blackfoot Coulee, Frog Lake and Battle River in Alberta and Onion Lake and the Harlan area in Saskatchewan. He later took part in the Northern Insect Survey from 1949-1954 and had various jobs in Ottawa, including a ten-year stint as editor of the journal *Arctic*.

Art W. Rupp, a geologist living in Priddis, was born in Didsbury in 1928. He started collecting there in 1938 and continued sporadically until 1970. Most of his collections are from Didsbury, Edmonton, Calgary and Medicine Hat. Rupp's collection also contains specimens from Texas, Florida, Holland, and Qatar in the Middle East.

A.R. Brooks was an assistant on the Federal Government research on wire worms from 1936 to 1939. He made many collections of butterflies at Blackfoot Coulee in 1940, apparently with P.F. Bruggemann and Kenneth Bowman. These are now housed in the Canadian National Collection along with others he made in Alberta at Frank (1952), Elkwater (1952) and Orion (1955).

C.L. Neilson, who later carried out work on parasitic wasps and on the control of insects and ticks in livestock, collected butterflies at several locations in the Peace River country in 1940. The specimens are now in the Canadian National Collection.

Steve Sunao Shigematsu was born in 1909 in Vancouver, British Columbia. He received most of his formal education in Japan but on his return to Canada developed natural history interests with the encouragement of Professor G.J. Spencer and Dr. John Davidson of the University of British Columbia. He was an active collector of both plants and insects. However, anti-Japanese feelings at the start of the Second World War resulted in his relocation to Raymond, Alberta, and his collection was damaged extensively and eventually destroyed. Shigematsu started collecting again at Raymond and commenced a series of excellent paintings of the local butterflies. His work as a carpenter kept him mainly in the Raymond and Lethbridge areas and most of his collections were from these areas. During holidays in the mountains he collected numerous specimens.

Gordon A. Hobbs (1916-1977), an authority on leaf-cutter bees and bumblebees at the Agriculture Canada Research Station, Lethbridge, collected butterflies across southern Alberta from 1945 to 1963. His specimens are in the Research Station Collection.

William Hovanitz of California was the author of several papers on the biology of *Colias* butterflies. His research led him to collect in Alberta in 1950 and 1964.

Douglas F. Hardwick, an entomologist with Agriculture Canada, made extensive collections of butterflies at Manyberries, Elkwater, Lost River Coulee and Wild Horse in 1951. One of his collections from Lost River was the first Canadian find of *Pyrgus scriptura*.

Brian Hocking was born in London, England, in 1914 and trained at Imperial College. During the Second World War, he served as an entomologist with the Indian Army. He joined the Department of Entomology at the University of Alberta in 1946 and became its head in 1954. Hocking was an expert on biting flies but also collected butterflies and other insects. His butterfly specimens in the University collection date from 1949 to 1956 and are from a number of central Alberta locations.

Charles D. Bird collected butterflies in Manitoba in the 1940s and early 1950s. He worked for the Northern Insect Survey during the summers of 1951 (Bathurst Inlet, N.W.T.), 1952 (Churchill, Manitoba) and 1953 (Herschel Island, N.W.T.); and for Forest Entomology (Red Rock Lake, Manitoba) during the summers of 1954 and 1955. He ranched near Buffalo Lake and is now retired and living in Erskine. His Manitoba collections were donated to the American Museum of Natural History and the Canadian National Collection. His first Alberta collections were at Moraine Lake in 1950 but he did not collect in the province again until 1961 and not in earnest until 1971. He taught botany at the University of Calgary from 1966 to 1979, and while there started work on the present book in 1970. He is the author of some 200 scientific papers, many of them on bryophytes and lichens, and in 1977 received the Loran Goulden Award in recognition of outstanding contributions to Alberta natural history.

Both **W.J. Brown**, an Agriculture Canada expert on the taxonomy of leaf beetles, and **George E. Ball**, a beetle taxonomist and for many years chairman of the Department of Entomology at the University of Alberta, made numerous collections of butterflies at Fort McMurray in 1953. Brown also made butterfly collections in Banff National Park in 1955.

Kenneth Richards, of the Agriculture Canada Research Station in Lethbridge, made frequent collections of butterflies in southeastern Alberta from 1954 to 1962. The specimens are in the Research Station Collection.

Colin W. Wyatt (1909-1975) of Farnham, England, was a keen butterfly collector. He collected extensively in the Banff area in 1954 and later named *Oeneis jutta chermocki* based on material he had collected.

Robert L. Anderson, Curator of Lepidoptera at the Riveredge Foundation for many years, was born in 1916 in Omaha, Nebraska. He became interested in butterflies through Richard Heitzman and collected around Kansas City while in his teens. Anderson came to Calgary in 1947 and collected in southwestern Alberta from 1950 to 1970. His collection was sold to Riveredge Foundation and the Riveredge Collection was later donated to the Provincial Museum of Alberta.

R. Coyles, **J.R. McGillis** and **G.E. Shewell** worked out of a camp at Eisenhower (Castle) Junction for the Entomology Branch of Agriculture Canada in the summer of 1955. All of them collected butterflies as well as other insects for deposit in the Canadian National Collection. Collection locations were Highwood Pass, Seebe and Banff National Park.

E.E. Sterns made an extensive collection of butterflies in the ecologically interesting southeastern corner of Alberta. The specimens are now in the Canadian National Collection.

Nicholas W. Van Veen, of Calgary and Banff, was President of the Entomological Society of Alberta in the early 1960s. He collected butterflies, mainly in the mountains of southwestern Alberta, from 1956 to 1964. Some of his specimens went to the Riveredge Foundation, together with those of Robert Anderson.

David Larson did his Ph.D. on the water beetles of Alberta, and is now with Memorial University, St. John's, Newfoundland. An avid collector, he gathered many butterfly specimens in Alberta prior to moving east. In 1967, with his wife Margaret, he made an extensive and important collection of the insects of Waterton Lakes National Park.

John Watson collected butterflies in the Rocky Mountains and Cypress Hills of southern Alberta from 1959 to 1961. His specimens are now in the University of Calgary collection.

John A. Legge, a retired geologist, lived for many years in the Calgary area before residing in Boulder, Colorado. He built up a good collection of local and arctic butterflies and was known for his well reasoned taxonomic opinions. Most of his Alberta material is from the foothills and mountains and was taken between 1960 and 1972. John often collected with his son J. Allan Legge, Jr.

A.I.W. Mackenzie of Calgary has an excellent collection of Alberta butterflies that he gathered from 1959 to 1965. Most of the specimens are from the mountains; others are from Calgary, Munson Ferry and the Cypress Hills.

Ronald R. Hooper, a pastor from Fort Qu'Appelle, Saskatchewan, and author of the book "Butterflies of Saskatchewan" (1973), has collected mainly in that province. He did, however, gather a few specimens in southern Alberta in 1963 and 1964.

Edward C. McMackin, then a school teacher in Calgary, now in British Columbia, made numerous collections of butterflies and moths in southern Alberta from 1965 to 1973.

Ross Moon was a keen butterfly collector from 1964 to 1969. His specimens, mainly from the Calgary area and the mountains to the west, were donated to the University of Calgary in late 1973.

Don G. Wales, then a teaching assistant in the Biology Department of the University of Calgary and now teaching at Red Deer College, made a small collection of Alberta butterflies in 1965 and deposited them in the University of Calgary Collection. In 1967 and 1968 he gathered butterflies as part of a report on the insects of Waterton Lakes National Park. The specimens are now in the Park collection.

In 1981, **B.J. (Buck) Godwin**, instructor at Olds College, was presented the Norman Criddle Award of the Entomological Society of Canada. This award had only been given once before and is in recognition of the "contribution of an outstanding non-professional entomologist to the furtherance of entomology in Canada." Godwin is a top-notch teacher, instilling enthusiasm, curiosity and the desire to learn in his students. The insect collections his entomology students are required to make have provided many valuable data, as the butterflies in these collections have been made available for research for the present book. Collections go back to 1965 and many students, too numerous to mention, are represented. A specimen of *Polygonia interrogationis* collected near Lloydminster by Joe Smith, Godwin's student, was a provincial first.

C.S. Guppy, of Vancouver, has made butterfly collections in the Alberta Rocky Mountains since the mid-1960s.

Gerald J. Hilchie was born in Calgary in 1953. He received a B.Sc. from the University of Calgary in 1975 and an M.Sc. in Entomology from the University of Alberta in 1978. Hilchie is a partner in Ryan and Hilchie Consultants Ltd, and also works for the Department of Biological Sciences, University of Alberta. A keen collector, he has wide-ranging interests and has published on butterflies, wasps and beetles. He started collecting seriously in 1970 and has built up an outstanding personal collection. Much of his Alberta material is from the southern half of the province. Two summers, 1978 and 1979, were spent in the Fort McMurray area with James K. Ryan conducting an insect survey for the Alberta Oil Sands Environmental Research Program. Many butterflies were collected. Hilchie and Kenneth Avery made a provincial first by discovering *Erebia magdalena* at Adams Lookout in Willmore Wilderness Park.

Felix A.H. Sperling grew up on a farm near Bragg Creek and attended high school at Springbank, west of Calgary. He enrolled at the University of Alberta in 1975, where he obtained a B.Sc. in zoology and an M.Sc. in entomology. An avid butterfly collector since 1969, he has collected in most parts of the province. Much of his pinned material is in the Canadian National Collection in Ottawa. He worked in Colorado during the summers of 1977 and 1978, and was the co-discoverer of *Boloria acrocnema*, a Colorado butterfly that is now officially listed as endangered. His M.Sc. thesis research was on the evolution of the *Papilio machaon* group in western Canada, and included the description of *Papilio machaon pikei*. He completed a Ph.D. on *Papilio* evolution at Cornell University, Ithaca, New York in 1991, and for the next three years developed DNA-based diagnostics for pest insect complexes at the University of Ottawa. He now has a faculty appointment at the University of California at Berkeley.

A. Gordon Edmund of Toronto collected butterflies in Alberta from 1967-1970 and in 1975. The material, from the interesting southeast corner and the mountains, is in Edmund's private collection.

David M. Shackleton, now with the University of British Columbia, obtained his Ph.D. in Biology from the University of Calgary. While in Alberta he collected butterflies in Elk Island National Park in 1967, Calgary in 1969 and the Panther Pass area in Banff National Park in 1970.

Jon H. Shepard of Nelson, British Columbia, has been working for some time on a book of the butterflies of British Columbia. He is the author of a paper that established that, in 1894, Edward Burke was the first definite collector of Alberta butterflies. Shepard collected several thousand butterflies over two years along the Kananaskis and Forestry Trunk Road in Alberta, and continues to make sporadic collecting trips into Alberta.

Edward (Ted) M. Pike was born in Calgary in 1954. He obtained B.Sc. and M.Sc. degrees in entomology at the University of Alberta, writing his thesis on the distribution of Alberta's alpine butterflies. He taught school at Fairview and there made an extensive study of the butterflies of the Peace River area. Pike is a keen collector and from a youthful start in 1966 has built a large collection of Alberta butterflies, especially from the mountains. His special interest is the genus *Boloria* and he is credited with the first provincial find of *B. improba* (Butler) which he discovered on Prospect Mountain. Pike co-authored the first Alberta report of the skipper *Amblyscirtes oslari*. During the 1970s and 1980s Ted Pike, Gerald Hilchie and Felix Sperling went on many collecting trips together and even lived in the same apartment building in the late 1970s. Ted has

recently received a Ph.D. from the University of Calgary and has published extensively on fossil insects preserved in Cretaceous amber.

A.W. Thomas, now with the Canadian Forest Service in New Brunswick, made an extensive collection of butterflies in the vicinity of the R.B. Miller Biological Station at Gorge Creek in 1969.

Peter Kuchar carried out Ph.D. research on plant ecology of the Bald Hills in Jasper National Park in 1969 and 1970, making the first butterfly collections for that seldom studied area. Many of the specimens were later donated to the University of Calgary.

Clifford D. Ferris, born in Philadelphia in 1935, has been with the University of Wyoming since 1968 and was president of the Lepidopterists' Society in 1986. Ferris is a keen collector and taxonomist and is the author or co-author of many publications including "Butterflies of the Rocky Mountain States" (with F.M. Brown). He has collected butterflies in Alberta since the early 1970s.

Peter Allen of Calgary collected butterflies from 1971 to 1976 while he, together with his father Des and mother Elizabeth, was studying the fauna of natural areas in Calgary. He also made numerous collections in the mountains.

Norbert George Kondla, a keen naturalist since 1963, became interested in butterflies in 1971. Since then he has travelled extensively through the province in pursuit of butterflies and has added *Incisalia mossii schryveri, Euphydryas editha hutchinsi* and *Celastrina ladon nigrescens* to the provincial list. A graduate of the University of Calgary, Kondla has pursued diverse careers since 1965, primarily in the natural resource and environmental management fields. He is presently working as a manager with the British Columbia Ministry of Forests in McBride, British Columbia. In addition to government reports, consultants' reports and papers on other natural history topics, he has published a number of papers documenting the butterfly fauna of various regions of the province and clarified the type localities of a number of species. Norbert also assembled a comprehensive bibliography of Alberta butterflies, compiled detailed distribution maps of all Alberta butterflies and clarified the status in Alberta of difficult groups such as *Erynnis, Phyciodes, Colias* and *Speyeria*.

Harold W. Pinel earned a B.Sc. degree at the University of Calgary, then found employment as a naturalist with Calgary Parks and Recreation. Pinel is a knowledgeable birder and botanist. He is well known for the natural history courses he teaches and co-ordinates at the Inglewood Bird Sanctuary. Pinel was the editor of *Calgary's Natural Areas*. He became interested in butterflies in 1971 and has collected more-or-less continuously ever since. He has written several papers documenting the butterfly fauna of different areas of the province.

David L. Threatful, formerly of Revelstoke and now of Richmond, British Columbia, made many collections in the Rocky Mountains of Alberta from 1971 to 1974. He made a special study of the butterflies of Mount Revelstoke and Glacier National Parks in British Columbia.

John H. Acorn received his B.Sc. in zoology at the University of Alberta and his M.Sc. in entomology at the same institution, where his thesis dealt with tiger beetle biology. Acorn has collected Alberta butterflies since the 1970s and is actively involved in encouraging interest in butterflies, including organizing the first Canada Day Butterfly Count in Lethbridge in 1993. Acorn's excellent photographs illustrate his 1993 guidebook *Butterflies of Alberta*.

James W. Case did a Ph.D. on the effect of sulphur effluents on lichens in the Peace River country. He collected butterflies in that region from 1972 to 1977 and published the first paper on the species of that area.

Lionel Paul Grey, a specialist on the taxonomy of the species of the genus *Speyeria*, made numerous butterfly collections in southwestern Alberta in 1973 and 1975.

J. Derek Johnson did M.Sc. studies at the University of Calgary and then joined the staff of the Canadian Forestry Service in Edmonton. He obtained numerous butterfly specimens in 1974, especially from previously uncollected Ram Mountain.

Wayne W. Smith, a Calgarian and ardent field naturalist, built up an interesting collection of butterflies from 1974 to 1977. These were later donated to the University of Calgary. His material from the Milk River-Lost River area and from northeastern Alberta are of special interest, as they include the first provincial records of *Limenitis weidemeyerii* (Pinhorn Grazing Reserve, Lost River and Writing-on-Stone Provincial Park) and of *Poanes hobomok* (Cold Lake).

M. Ross Lein, an ornithologist with the University of Calgary, started collecting butterflies in 1975 and has made frequent collections in the mountains of southwestern Alberta.

Terry W. Thormin of the Provincial Museum of Alberta in Edmonton has been interested in butterflies since the mid-1970s and has often collected in the province. His collection of the skipper, *Polites rhesus* (near Pendant d'Oreille) was a first for Alberta, as was his collection of *Coenonympha ochracea mackenziei* (south of Fort Smith).

James D. Reist received a B.Sc. from the University of Calgary, an M.Sc. from the University of Alberta and entered Ph.D. studies at the University of Toronto. Reist made numerous butterfly collections in Alberta from 1975 to 1977, among them the first documented Alberta report of *Incisalia niphon clarki* (near Clyde).

Jens Roland did his M.Sc. (University of British Columbia) on *Colias* in the Kananaskis region. He is now on the faculty of the University of Alberta and researching dispersal patterns in mountain butterfly species.

Butterfly Habitats in Alberta

Natural Habitats

More than 170 species of butterflies and skippers can be found or are expected to occur in Alberta. Each species has a unique distribution and at most 70 species can be found at any one locality. Despite this variation, several common patterns can be discerned across the province. These correspond reasonably well to habitat types based on vegetation analysis.

For the purposes of this book Alberta is considered to contain four major Natural Regions: (1) grasslands dominating the southeastern part of the province, and also occurring as small remnants along the Peace River; (2) the aspen parkland occupying the transition area between grasslands and the boreal region; (3) vast boreal forest zones extending through northern and central Alberta; and (4) the Cordilleran region encompassing the Rocky Mountains and foothills of the west, as well as the Cypress Hills. For a detailed description of the Natural Regions of Alberta, the reader is referred to Strong and Leggatt (1981).

Alberta grasslands are characterized by high summer temperatures and low precipitation. Butterfly diversity is highest in the relatively moist spring. Typical grassland species include Uhler's Arctic (*Oeneis uhleri*), Alberta Arctic (*Oeneis alberta*), Olympia Marble (*Euchloe olympia*) and Dotted Blue (*Euphilotes enoptes*) in the spring, and Riding's Satyr (*Neominois ridingsii*) and Silver-spotted Skipper (*Epargyreus clarus*) in the summer. Sages (*Artemisia* spp.) are among the few plants that remain lush throughout the growing season, and the Artemisia Swallowtail (*Papilio machaon dodi*), whose larvae feed on it, is one of the few species that does not feed on agricultural plants yet is able to complete two generations per year in this region.

At higher altitudes to the west, precipitation increases, allowing diverse montane and subalpine vegetation to grow on the foothills and mountain slopes. Species characterizing these habitats include the Draco Skipper (*Polites draco*), Sara Orange Tip (*Anthocharis sara*), Smintheus Parnassian (*Parnassius smintheus*), Chryxus Arctic (*Oeneis chryxus*) and Anicia Checkerspot (*Euphydryas anicia*). Above the treeline, there is a suite

of butterflies that is able to cope with strong winds, long winters and cool summers. Typical alpine butterflies include species like the Nastes Sulphur (*Colias nastes*), Melissa Arctic (*Oeneis melissa*), Astarte Fritillary (*Boloria astarte*) and Lustrous Copper (*Lycaena cuprea*).

In northern and central Alberta, summers are wet and winters are long and bitterly cold. Virtually all of the boreal region is covered by conifer-dominated forest. In the more well drained areas toward the foothills and in the Swan Hills, pines and aspens are common and butterflies like the Canadian Tiger Swallowtail (*Papilio canadensis*), Christina Sulphur (*Colias christina*), Macoun's Arctic (*Oeneis macounii*), Red-disked Alpine (*Erebia discoidalis*) and Compton's Tortoise Shell (*Nymphalis vaualbum*) are characteristic. Poorly drained, boggy areas have a separate suite of butterflies, including the Jutta Arctic (*Oeneis jutta*), Frigga Fritillary (*Boloria frigga*), Disa Alpine (*Erebia disa*), Giant Sulphur (*Colias gigantea*) and Cranberry Blue (*Plebejus optilete*).

Parkland habitat has a floral and faunal composition that is intermediate between grassland and boreal forest to the north, and grassland and Cordilleran habitats to the west. Characterized by groves of aspen trees interspersed with grassy meadows, the parkland zone now contains the highest density of human habitation. Common butterfly species include the Meadow Fritillary (*Boloria bellona*), Northwestern Fritillary (*Speyeria electa*), Rustic Blue (*Plebejus rusticus*), Spring Azure (*Celastrina ladon*), Persius Duskywing (*Erynnis persius*) and Canadian Tiger Swallowtail (*Papilio canadensis*), though these species are by no means restricted to this zone.

Human-Made Habitats

Human horticultural activities sometimes provide habitats for certain butterfly species. Most familiar of these is the introduced Cabbage Butterfly, *Pieris rapae*, which can be a pest in commercial or domestic gardens where members of its host plant family Cruciferae are grown. (Crucifers include cabbage, broccoli and brussels sprouts.) Most butterfly visitors are benign and can be encouraged to frequent home gardens if host plants for caterpillars or flowering plants for adult nectaring are provided (see "Butterfly Study").

Local Ecology

Ecological preferences are probably the most important factors determining where particular butterflies are found. Unless a species is migratory, like the Monarch (*Danaus plexippus*), it cannot persist in an area unless all its ecological requirements are met. For example, the Artemisia Swallowtail (*Papilio machaon dodi*) is a strong flier but is rarely found far from dry, eroding riverbanks or roadcuts. These are the kinds of sites that have healthy patches of Tarragon (*Artemisia dracunculus*), the larval host plant of *P. m. dodi*. Tarragon, but not the butterfly, can also be found in dry, overgrazed pastures. *P. m. dodi* also needs patches of flowers for adults to sip nectar, as well as geographic prominences like high riverbanks that act as mate-finding sites.

Many areas with apparently perfect host plants, nectar sources and prominent river banks still don't have colonies of *P. m. dodi*. The answer to this puzzle almost certainly lies in the vagaries of the recent past. Tarragon is an early successional plant and perhaps a particular host plant patch only recently came into existence after a heavy flood eroded that riverbank, causing it to slump and expose fresh soil. Perhaps there was a healthy colony of *P. m. dodi* there only a few years ago, but parasites wiped out the colony. Or perhaps a drought recently decimated plants and insects alike, leaving the few remaining caterpillars to fall prey to random forays by generalist predators.

If any of these scenarios is true then it will only be a matter of time before wandering *P. m. dodi* females find the site and start another colony. Large, unoccupied sites that are close to healthy populations of *P. m. dodi* should be recolonized relatively quickly. Small, isolated sites will probably have to wait longer. In any case, the geographic range of *P. m. dodi* will be a mosaic of small populations, always changing on a small scale but more stable as a metapopulation.

Glaciation

Even large-scale patterns are likely to change over hundreds or thousands of years. Glaciers have swept across Alberta several times in the last two million years, scraping all life from the landscape. The only possible survivors were a few alpine-adapted species on isolated mountaintop refugia.

The most recent glaciation, the Late Wisconsin, reached its peak only 18,000 years ago. Alberta was completely iced over from about 20,000 to 12,000 years ago according to recent evidence although the Cypress Hills were not covered by ice. Thus, any life in these areas would certainly have had a very severe climate to contend with.

Most Alberta butterfly species survived the Late Wisconsin glaciation south of the ice, in forested regions to the east, grassland and alpine regions in the west, and a band of tundra habitat at the margin of the ice. Some alpine tundra butterflies also survived the last glaciation to the north of the ice sheets, in a large refugium in Alaska and Yukon Territory called Beringia. This refugium was characterized by dry, grassy "steppe" tundra, rather than the more boggy tundra that currently dominates the Beringian region.

In many cases, the preglacial ranges of butterfly species were bisected by ice. Separate populations were isolated for thousands of years. These populations continued to evolve during this time, often in divergent ways that reflected differences in their new surroundings. *Papilio machaon* must have been subjected to several divisions of this sort. Now the species is composed of many ecological races, or subspecies, whose habitat preferences reflect the history of ecological change in North America.

When the ice melted after the glaciation, it happened rapidly. Meltwater lakes covered large parts of Alberta for hundreds of years. Large glacial rivers cut wide valleys through southern Alberta. Then the torrent calmed into the trickling creeks that now meander through the coulees. In central and northern Alberta, the debris left behind in stagnant ice formed a legacy of hills and potholes.

Boreal butterflies and colonizing plants followed the ice northward and westward. Butterflies like the Artemisia Swallowtail (*Papilio machaon hudsonianus*), Frigga Fritillary (*Boloria frigga*), Disa Alpine (*Erebia disa*) and Jutta Arctic (*Oeneis jutta*), now grace the spruce woods and bogs of northern and central Alberta.

The Rocky Mountains received migrants from both the north and the south. The northern contingent, derived from Beringia, includes the Dingy Arctic Fritillary (*Boloria improba*) and Napaea Fritillary (*Boloria napaea*). These species are now restricted to the alpine zone of the northern Rocky Mountains in Alberta. The southern Cordilleran contingent includes a number of alpine butterflies such as the Astarte Fritillary (*Boloria astarte*) and Alberta Fritillary (*Boloria alberta*), as well as subalpine and montane species like the Anise Swallowtail (*Papilio zelicaon*), Smintheus Parnassian (*Parnassius smintheus*), Northern Marble (*Euchloe creusa*), Sara Orange Tip (*Anthocharis sara*) and Northern Checkerspot (*Charidryas palla*).

In several cases, subalpine or montane butterflies moving northward encountered closely related species or subspecies moving westward in boreal habitats. The Western Pine Elfin (*Incisalia eryphon*) and Eastern

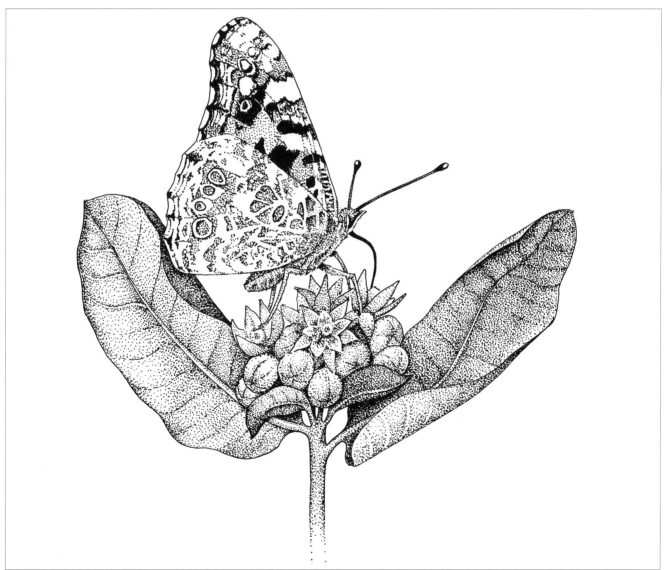

Vanessa cardui feeding on milkweed.

17

Pine Elfin (*Incisalia niphon*) may be hybridizing along a wide zone of contact, as are the Hoary Comma (*Polygonia gracilis*) and Zephyr (*Polygonia zephyrus*). The Anise Swallowtail (*Papilio zelicaon*) and Artemisia Swallowtail (*Papilio machaon hudsonianus*) formed a series of persistent hybrid populations in central Alberta. Trans-mountain encounters also occur; White Admirals (*Limenitis arthemis*) and Lorquin's Admirals (*L. lorquini*) hybridize in the Crowsnest Pass to Castle River area.

Hypsithermal

The warming trend after the last glaciation continued steadily until 9000 to 6000 years ago, during a period called the hypsithermal. Climate between 6000 and 9000 years ago was much hotter and drier than at present, allowing a substantially greater expansion of grassland habitats.

The Peace River grasslands were connected to the southern Alberta grasslands during the hypsithermal. Now isolated by 400 km of boreal forest, Peace River grassland endemics include the Uhler's Arctic (*Oeneis uhleri*), Alberta Arctic (*Oeneis alberta*), Gorgone Checkerspot (*Charidryas gorgone*), Northern Checkerspot (*Charidryas palla*), Coral Hairstreak (*Harkenclenus titus*), Striped Hairstreak (*Satyrium liparops*), Great Spangled Fritillary (*Speyeria cybele*) and Artemisia Swallowtail (*Papilio machaon pikei*). Most of these species are now slightly darker than their southern counterparts, but still show clear relationships with grassland butterflies in southern Alberta. Only *P. m. pikei* appears to have originally been derived from *Papilio machaon* populations to the north, or perhaps even from populations in southern British Columbia.

In the Rocky Mountains, the hypsithermal probably drove alpine habitats to higher elevations, severing connections between mountaintops and interrupting range expansions along the crest of the Rocky Mountains. Forests on the Cypress Hills became isolated from the Rocky Mountains by a sea of grassland, but retained some distinctive Cordilleran butterflies like the Anicia Checkerspot (*Euphydryas anicia*).

Some butterflies from eastern deciduous forests may also have spread to Alberta during recent warm periods. The Question Mark (*Polygonia interrogationis*) and Hobomok Skipper (*Poanes hobomok*) are now found on the eastern edge of the parkland zone in Alberta.

The colonization of Alberta continues. In southwestern Alberta there are regular incursions through the mountain passes by British Columbian species like the Pine White (*Neophasia menapia*) and Pale Swallowtail (*Papilio eurymedon*). Some butterflies from Montana also slip into Alberta, including the montane Two-tailed Swallowtail (*Papilio multicaudatus*) and the prairie Weidemeyer's Admiral (*Limenitis weidemeyerii*). The Cabbage Butterfly (*Pieris rapae*) arrived in Alberta only about 100 years ago, after being introduced into North America from Europe. The European Skipper (*Thymelicus lineola*) was similarly introduced but arrived in Alberta in the 1980s. Other species are regularly found in the province but cannot survive the winter in Alberta, including the Monarch (*Danaus plexippus*), Painted Lady (*Vanessa cardui*), West Coast Lady (*Vanessa annabella*), and California Tortoise Shell (*Nymphalis californica*).

The composition of butterfly species in Alberta reflects the workings of a melange of factors. The ghosts of ancient cataclysms haunt every butterfly as it flits among flowers. Local climatic and vegetational factors channel it relentlessly. The random minutiae of everyday life provide spice.

Evolution, Life History, Ecology and Behaviour

Evolution of the Lepidoptera

The evolutionary history of the Order Lepidoptera (moths, skippers and butterflies) is closely tied to that of flowering plants, which first appeared approximately 100 million years ago. It seems likely that the specialized tube-like mouthparts of butterflies and moths evolved to suck up the sugary nectar produced by flowers. Even before the proboscis evolved, however, ancient lepidopterans were probably feeding on flowers, albeit eating pollen rather than nectar. Evidence for this can be seen in adults of a primitive family of moths, the Micropterigidae, which feed on pollen and still have chewing rather than sucking mouthparts. The Lepidoptera probably evolved from ancestors that looked like present-day caddisflies (Order Trichoptera). The overall appearance and the tent-winged resting position of many moths are similar to those of caddisflies (Fig.1) and larvae of both orders also have similar body forms. Within the Lepidoptera, skippers (superfamily Hesperioidea) and butterflies (superfamily Papilionoidea) are very closely related to each other (Fig. 2) and together with another small family of nocturnal lepidopterans (the Hedylidae) are considered "butterflies" in the broad sense. Moths, on the other hand, are not such a unified group. Two rather distantly related groups are lumped into the moth category (Fig. 3), one of which is actually more closely related to butterflies than to other moths! Among other things, butterflies share the characteristics of clubbed antennae and their wings lack the frenulum and retinaculum that hook most moth wings together. Moving forward in evolutionary time, with regard to the origin of the North American lepidopteran fauna, the closest relatives of our butterflies and moths are found in Europe and Northern Asia. Only a few genera of butterflies have migrated north from places of origin in Central and South America (e.g., *Phyciodes, Satyrium* and *Neophasia*). Finally, there are some species that have been introduced to North America through human activities, including the occasionally pestilent Cabbage Butterfly (*Pieris rapae*; see also "Butterfly Habitats in Alberta").

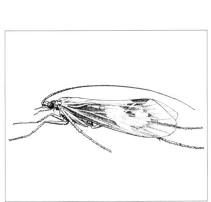

Figure 1. Caddisfly

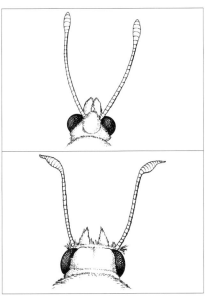

Figure 2. top - Superfamily Papilionoidea
bottom - Superfamily Hesperioidea

Figure 3. Moth

Life Cycle

Butterflies are holometabolous insects, meaning that their life cycle includes egg, larva, pupa and adult, with each stage being very different from the others (Fig. 4). In brief, a tiny larva (called a caterpillar) hatches from an egg laid on or near its food plant. The caterpillar is essentially an eating machine that may increase its weight up to 10,000-fold before pupating. After four to five moults, the caterpillar enters the pupal stage in which its larval tissues are reorganized into those of an adult. The winged adult that emerges from the pupal case has reproduction as its main objective, and most of an adult butterfly's characteristics are concerned with finding mates, producing offspring, or living long enough to do either of these. Secondarily, the adult is also the stage that migrates or disperses to colonize new areas. Throughout its life cycle a butterfly must deal with unfavourable temperatures, finding food, and avoiding parasites and predators. Below, the trials and tribulations of each life history stage are discussed in detail.

Egg: Butterfly eggs are usually less than 1 mm wide, and may have smooth, ribbed or pitted eggshells. Often, but not always, the egg's colour provides good camouflage by blending in with the background. Female butterflies can lay up to several hundred eggs although very rarely are all eggs deposited at once. Rather, they are deposited singly (sometimes even only one per plant), cemented to leaves or buds of the larval food plant. Some butterflies deposit eggs in groups of 5 to 100, depending on the species. A few do not attach their eggs to host plants at all, but scatter them on the ground near the larval food plant or on other species of plants nearby (e.g., *Parnassius, Speyeria*). This scattering may protect the eggs from the attention of parasitic wasps that lay their own eggs within those of the butterfly. In a few species, winter is passed in the egg stage.

Larva: Newly hatched caterpillars are very small, at most a few millimetres in length. Caterpillars have well developed heads with powerful chewing mouthparts, and most have a worm-like cylindrical body with three pairs of legs on the thoracic segments and stubby prolegs on several abdominal segments (Fig. 5). Some lycaenid larvae are flattened and slug-like, however, and legs may be greatly reduced.

Upon hatching, the caterpillars of many species eat their empty eggshells as their first meals and then move on to feed on their host plants. In species in which eggs are laid away from the larval food plant, caterpillars crawl to the food plants after hatching. Butterfly larvae can be broadly classified as solitary or communal, depending on whether they feed alone or in groups. Usually, species that deposit eggs singly have solitary caterpillars while those that deposit eggs in large clutches have communal caterpillars. These latter species are mainly members of the nymphalid subfamily Nymphalinae (e.g., *Euphydryas, Chlosyne, Phyciodes* and *Nymphalis*). Communal larvae frequently live together in silken nests, whereas solitary ones may remain exposed on the plant surface or in small shelters between leaves (e.g., most skippers).

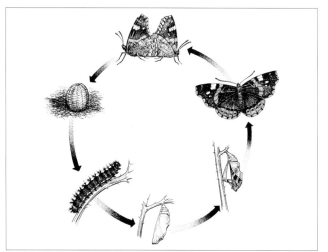

Figure 4. Butterfly life cycle

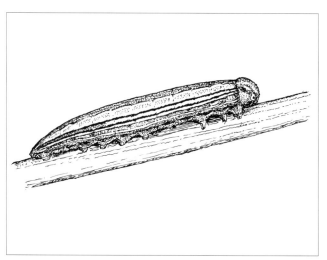

Figure 5. Larval stage

With the exception of a few predatory lycaenid species, butterfly larvae are herbivores. Caterpillars are choosy about what plants they eat, usually limiting their food plants to members of one genus or order, and sometimes to a few closely related species. They have good reason to be particular, as plants try to defend themselves against defoliating insects by producing toxic chemicals. However, chemicals that would kill larvae of some butterfly species can be detoxified by those of others, which safely use these plants as feeding sites. Some even store plant chemicals in their bodies where they serve as protection for both the caterpillar and later, the adult. For example, the wings and bodies of adult Monarch butterflies (*Danaus plexippus*) contain cardiac glycosides from the milkweeds they ate as larvae. These chemicals can cause extreme discomfort and vomiting in any bird or mammal foolish enough to attack these insects. Unpleasant-tasting caterpillars such as those of the Monarch are often brightly coloured to warn potential predators of their nasty flavour.

As well as gaining protection from predators by using plant chemicals, caterpillars have a variety of other defences. Tubercles, spines and bristles on the caterpillar's skin may make it difficult for a predator to swallow. Cryptic colouration is a common way to avoid being seen, but once detected, caterpillars of many species attempt to startle predators. Swallowtail caterpillars rear up, exposing the dark eye-like patches on the thoracic segments and everting foul-smelling tubes called osmeteria

(Fig. 6). The caterpillars of many lycaenids, especially blues and hairstreaks, have glands that produce a sugary nectar very attractive to ants. The attention of these pugnacious social insects provides protection against many predators. But despite their many defences, most butterfly larvae fall prey to a host of predators including mites, spiders, insects, rodents and birds. Caterpillars are especially at risk of being parasitized by wasps or flies (Fig. 7), or of being stricken with bacterial or viral diseases.

Larval life may continue for weeks, months, or up to two years. After going through four or five moults, and often passing winter in a state of diapause, the now much larger caterpillar is ready to pupate.

Pupa: When a caterpillar is ready to pupate, it moves from its feeding or overwintering site to a place suitable for pupation. This may be a twig, a rolled-up leaf, beneath loose bark or under rocks, or even among leaf litter on the ground (e.g., *Parnassius*). The last larval skin splits and the soft-skinned pupa wriggles free. After several hours the pupal skin hardens and becomes an immobile, water-tight case. Although all skippers and the "true" butterfly *Parnassius* are similar to moths in that they spin silken cocoons in which to pupate, the pupae (or "chrysalids") of other butterflies are exposed and naked. Chrysalids of some butterflies (e.g., Danaidae, Nymphalidae, some Satyridae) are attached to leaves or twigs by the cremaster, a spiny process at the posterior

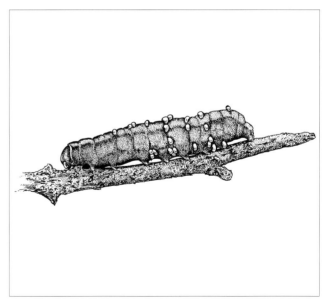

Figure 6. Swallowtail larva in defensive posture with osmeteria exposed.　　　Figure 7. Butterfly larva attacked by wasp parasitoids.

of the body, and hang head downwards (Fig. 8). In other groups (Lycaenidae, Pieridae, Papilionidae) the chrysalid is attached by the cremaster but is held upright by a silken girdle spun by the caterpillar prior to pupation (Fig. 9). Pupae are usually cryptically coloured to blend in with their backgrounds. Some species overwinter as pupae, but for those that do not, the pupal stage typically lasts 8 to 14 days. Within the pupal case, the larval tissues are broken down and reorganized into the form of an adult butterfly.

Adult: Upon emergence from the pupal case, the butterfly's wings are small and moist. The new butterfly hangs upside down and pumps haemolymph into the wing veins to expand them, then slowly opens and closes the wings until they harden and dry. This is a critical period, for if its wings are not properly expanded the insect will be unable to fly. As well as expanding its wings, the newly emerged butterfly must connect the two halves of its proboscis, in essence zipping up its mouthparts.

Although adults do not grow, they require high-energy food to fuel their activities and keep them going. Even for females with eggs, most of the materials for the eggs have been gathered in the caterpillar stage. Although we tend to think of butterflies feeding only on flower nectar, they consume a variety of other substances including such surprising meals as tree sap, rotting fruit or fungus, pollen, bird droppings, dung and even carrion. Salts, especially sodium, are important in the manufacture of spermatophores. Butterflies are often observed on wet sand (mud puddling) where salts can be obtained.

The shared characteristics of butterfly food are that they are easily converted into sugar or fat and that they are sufficiently liquified to be sucked up. Sap feeders include the Mourning Cloak (*Nymphalis antiopa*) and *Polygonia* spp.; some Satyridae imbibe only water (many *Oeneis*).

Most butterflies, however, do get their energy from nectar. Flowers benefit from butterfly visits because the hungry insects inadvertently act as pollinators. As butterflies have good vision, flowers pollinated by butterflies tend to use colour rather than scent to attract them. Most butterfly flowers are yellow, white, blue, pink or purple and may also contain ultraviolet patterns. The nectary of a butterfly-pollinated flower is found at the base of a long corolla tube where it cannot be reached by insects with shorter tongues. There is a rough correlation between the length of the proboscis of a species and that of the flower corollas they visit.

Even if a butterfly has enough energy, it cannot fly unless the temperature is right. In general, most butterflies cannot fly when the air temperature is much below 16°C or above 38°C. Because they are cold-blooded (i.e., cannot metabolically control their internal temperature), butterflies regulate their body temperature through a variety of behaviours. Aspects of behavioural thermoregulation include wing orientation to the sun, abdominal raising or lowering, and moving into or out of the shade. If a butterfly needs to warm up, it will move into a sunny area and orient its wings to expose the maximum area to the sun's rays. Such basking postures may be dorsal, in which the butterfly perches with its wings spread (Fig. 10), or lateral, in which the wings are

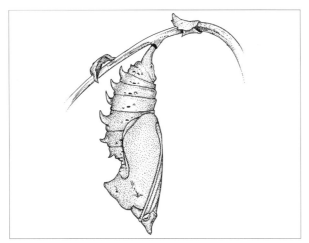

Figure 8. Nymphalid pupa

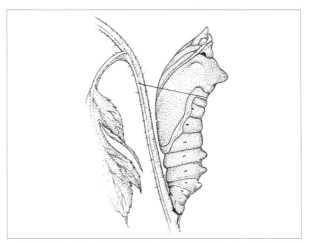

Figure 9. Papilionid pupa

Figure 10. Basking butterfly
Nymphalis antiopa, the Mourning Cloak

closed and oriented perpendicular to the sun's rays. Colour patterns on wings are often designed to increase efficiency of basking, usually with the darkest markings near the wing bases to maximize heat absorption at the sites of muscle attachments. As well, many species show altitudinal or seasonal variation in the darkness of wings, with more dark scales and hair in cooler habitats or seasons (e.g., Mead's Sulphur, *Colias meadii*). At night or during cool or cloudy weather, butterflies rest in roosting sites beneath leaves, on plant stems or on flowers.

Adult butterflies are prey for many animals. Birds, rodents, amphibians, reptiles, spiders and many insects include butterflies in their diets. Butterflies can often escape in the air, as the direction of their fluttery, jerking flight is difficult for predators to anticipate. Wing patterns can also foil predators. Some butterflies have bright, flashing colours on the dorsal sides of their wings and dull patterns on their undersides. A bird chasing a flying butterfly fixes on the flashing colours and when the butterfly abruptly stops, perches, and folds its wings to hide the bright colours, it appears to have vanished. Cryptically coloured underwings are common in butterflies, allowing resting insects to blend in with their backgrounds. Wing shape and pattern in some nymphalids (e.g., Satyr Anglewing, *Polygonia satyrus* and Gray Comma, *P. progne*) make a resting butterfly look very much like a dead leaf. Wings can deceive in other ways. The false eyes and tails of swallowtails and hairstreaks may fool predators into attacking the wings rather than the heads of the butterflies. The black and orange Monarch (*Danaus plexippus*) displays its bright wing colours as a warning to predators that it is distasteful. Its wings are laden with cardiac glycosides, chemicals gathered when the butterfly was a larva feeding on milkweed. In areas where the Monarch is common, the palatable Viceroy (*Limenitis archippus*) gains some protection from predators by mimicking the poisonous butterfly.

Due to its ability to fly, the adult serves as the main dispersal stage in the butterfly life cycle. Travel is usually rather haphazard, with butterflies colonizing new habitats through irregular, one-way movement (emigration). Migration, on the other hand, refers to regular, two-way mass movement of individuals. In butterflies, migration is best illustrated by the Monarch (*Danaus plexippus*), although weaker two-way movements are suspected in other North American species such as the Mourning Cloak (*Nymphalis antiopa*) and the Red Admiral (*Vanessa atalanta*). The migratory pathway of Monarchs found in Alberta begins in a small overwintering area in Mexico. Mated butterflies move north in the spring, laying eggs en route. Butterflies from these eggs continue the northward progression and some individuals reach Alberta. In the southern part of Alberta, these Monarchs produce another generation of butterflies that migrates to California and Mexico in the fall.

Although much time is spent feeding, thermoregulating, avoiding predators, or dispersing, the raison d'être for an adult butterfly is reproduction. For males, this means finding and mating with as many females as possible. For females, it means mating and laying eggs in good sites for larval growth. How does an individual butterfly find a member of the opposite sex? In moths, which are nocturnal, the female typically sits in one place and produces attractive chemicals called pheromones that male moths can detect from a great distance. Butterflies, which are active in daylight, primarily use vision to recognize potential mates. But vision can operate over only short distances and so mate-seeking butterflies must first come within a few metres of another individual before visual recognition occurs.

Butterflies can be divided roughly into two groups depending on which mate-finding strategy is used. In perching species, a male stays in one place, making short investigative flights whenever something vaguely like a female flies past. Thus it is up to the female to reach the general vicinity of a male. Perching species include all hairstreaks and coppers, most nymphalids and skippers, some satyrids and a few swallowtails. In patrolling species, males fly almost constantly, resting for brief periods for refreshment. Again, anything that looks like a female is checked out. Patrollers include most satyrids, blues and swallowtails, a few nymphalids and a few skippers. With close inspection, a combination of appearance (especially wing pattern) and behavioural cues informs the male whether he is chasing a female of the right species. It is this investigative behaviour of male butterflies that has given rise to the idea that males are territorial and aggressive. However, what appears to be aggressive battles between males is simply mistaken identity. Most perching species mate only at certain times of day, whereas patrollers typically mate at any time. Other differences between perchers and patrollers include: low population density of perchers and high for patrollers; perchers usually mate in a limited area of the overall habitat; perchers seldom mate in the same sites as larval host plants whereas patrollers usually do; patrollers sometimes locate females hidden nearby using pheromones, perchers rarely do. Additionally, newly emerged males of patrolling species often engage in a behaviour called puddling. Males gather to take up moisture at wet spots along stream margins, mud puddles, or places where a mammal has recently urinated. Sodium ions (salt) appear to be the cue for puddling. As females and males of perching species do not puddle it may be that sodium ions are vital for activities peculiar to patrolling males (e.g., greater need for temperature regulation) and for production of spermatophores.

One extraordinary modification of the perching category of mate-searching behaviour deserves mention. Hilltopping occurs when male butterflies gather on prominent peaks and newly emerged females fly to these rendezvous sites. Hilltopping appears to be especially common in rare or very dispersed species, and may be an adaptation to increase the probability of male and female encountering each other. Swallowtails of the *Papilio machaon* species-group are well known for this behaviour, but many other butterflies engage in hilltopping (e.g., Pahaska Skipper, *Hesperia pahaska* and Checkered White, *Pontia protodice*) as do many species of bees and flies. It must be remembered, however, that not every species can be easily categorized as patrolling, perching or hilltopping.

Once the male butterfly has contacted and recognized a female, he usually starts courtship by forcing the female to land while he flutters above her. In most species, the male then lands beside or behind the female and curves the tip of his abdomen towards hers. Pheromones play a larger role in butterfly courtship once males and females are close together. Males of many species have specialized scented scales called androconia whose perfume appears to encourage female receptivity. In some members of the Danainae the male actually showers the female with androconial scales as he hovers over her. If the female is interested in mating she allows the male to copulate by joining the tip of his abdomen to hers. If she is not receptive (e.g., if she has already been mated) she rejects the male by spreading or fluttering her wings or by moving the tip of her abdomen away. During copulation the male transfers an encapsulated packet of sperm (the spermatophore) to the female's spermatophore storage pouch (the bursa copulatrix). The sperm are transferred to another pouch called the spermatheca, leaving the spermatophore case behind. Depending on the species, mating may last 20 minutes to several hours, and females may mate once or several times. It is sometimes possible to determine the number of times a female has mated by counting the empty spermatophores in her bursa copulatrix. Male butterflies can also mate repeatedly, but after mating it may take several days for the male to produce another normal-sized spermatophore.

Eggs are fertilized one by one as they pass by the opening of the spermatheca. As mentioned above, female butterflies produce hundreds of eggs but usually lay them only one or a few at a time. The female first uses visual cues to locate suitable places for oviposition (egg-laying). Leaf-shape has been shown to be very important in oviposition site choice in many species. After landing on a piece of vegetation, the female samples it using taste receptors on her legs. Most species lay eggs on the larval host plant, but a few oviposit on plants nearby, or, in the case of *Parnassius*, in litter on the ground. If the normal host plant is unavailable, some butterflies can be induced to lay on bits of paper soaked in host plant extracts.

There is no parental care in butterflies, so after mating and laying eggs the adults have no more reason to live. Adult lifespan is usually only a few weeks, except for the few species that hibernate as adults (e.g., the Mourning Cloak, *Nymphalis antiopa*). Most of our Alberta species have one generation per year, while a few have two (e.g., Artemisia Swallowtail, *Papilio machaon*) and possibly more than three (the Cabbage Butterfly, *Pieris rapae*) . Populations of these species further south often have more generations than in Alberta, undoubtedly because of the longer growing season. More detailed descriptions of life cycles are provided with each species account.

Butterfly Study

To many people, the study of butterflies conjures up the movie image of an eccentric, oddly dressed person chasing across the countryside, oblivious to anything except capturing some rare specimen. The capture of specimens is often a necessary element, but butterfly study encompasses many other aspects.

Historically, the study of butterflies has been based on museum specimens. This is still a very important part of study, as it provides the basis for identification and classification. But this is only a part of the picture. Butterflies are living creatures that interact with their environment, with each other and with other organisms. Butterfly behaviour includes courtship, feeding, habitat selection, territoriality and predator evasion. Studies of butterflies may also focus on ecological interactions with host plants or with abiotic factors such as climate.

Butterfly Observation

The first requirement for successful butterfly watching is knowing where butterflies are likely to be found. Urban areas tend to be represented by few species, with the Cabbage Butterfly, *Pieris rapae*, and some *Colias* species prevailing. Natural parks in urban areas, river valleys, gullies, hillsides and ravines host a richer butterfly fauna with many species of blues, coppers, sulphurs, alpines, whites, swallowtails and nymphalids.

Once you get out of the city you find more interesting and diverse habitats. Hilltops on native prairie serve as aggregation sites for many species. Males congregate near the tops of hills during midday, waiting for females to pass by, then disperse down the slopes later in the day. Alpine meadows are even more interesting because they are home to many high-altitude butterfly species in addition to those transients that hilltop during midday. Swamps and marshes also harbour unique species that may not occur in other habitats. Other areas often rich in butterflies are transition zones, such as those where meadow meets forest, where grasslands are interspersed with thickets beside ravines and where floodplain vegetation abuts grasslands. Butterflies are creatures of warmth and sunshine. They seldom make an appearance on very cool or overcast days. Generally speaking, butterflies are on the wing from about 10:00 AM through to about 5:00 or 6:00 PM, depending on local weather conditions, with peak activity from about noon to 4:00 PM. The hotter the day, the earlier the start of flight and the longer it will last into the evening.

Many species have characteristic markings or behaviours and may be easily identified in the field. Others, such as many of the blues, coppers and elfins, require careful study of wing patterns for accurate identification. Even when you have a butterfly "in hand," it may not be identifiable to species if it has excessively worn wings. It is a good idea to have a magnifying glass for looking at wing patterns both in living butterflies in the field and for mounted specimens at home.

Butterflies may also be associated with certain types of vegetation within a habitat. Many butterflies are avid nectar feeders and frequent particular flowers. Thistle, milkweed and many types of legumes and composites are popular nectar stations. Some butterflies, like anglewings (*Polygonia* spp.) and nymphalids, are attracted to sap oozing from trees. Other species are rarely if ever associated with flowers or sap but get moisture from dew drops and damp ground (e.g., many satyrid spp.). To observe these butterflies it is sometimes necessary to flush them out of the grass.

Photographic Study

Photography is a popular method of studying butterflies as it does not depend on capturing and killing them. This is a preferred method in areas where collecting is prohibited (e.g., nature preserves, national and provincial parks). The thrill of the chase is still there and the challenge of getting a good photograph is usually greater than simply collecting a specimen.

Equipment used to photograph butterflies may be as simple or as elaborate as you can afford. One needs a camera that can be made to focus closely enough to have the butterfly fill the frame. Bodies of single lens reflex (SLR) cameras can be fitted with a variety of attachments to allow close-up photography. These include close-up rings and lenses, bellows, macro lenses, telephoto lenses, teleconverters and simple flash units to ring flashes, tripods and cables. If you use slow film (less than 100 ASA), you will definitely require a flash to get the best result. To get close enough to a butterfly, the photographer may use a variety of methods depending on the species. Bait stations attract some species, while sitting and waiting near a preferred flower may work for others. Some species must be stalked as their flight pattern is unpredictable. For that really fresh picture, many photographers rear the butterfly themselves and take photographs shortly after the adult emerges from the pupa. Others use a net and icebox, chilling the subject so that it holds still long enough to be posed and photographed.

Rearing and Life History Study

Rearing provides many opportunities to study and appreciate the life history of butterflies. As well, this is an area in which amateur lepidopterists can contribute a great deal. For many butterfly species we do not know exactly what the immatures look like or what their preferred food plants are, although we can often infer this information from what we know of similar species. Many children pick up caterpillars, pop them into a jar and watch what happens. Sometimes the caterpillars are diseased or neglected, and die. Some do manage to complete development to the great delight of their caretakers. For the more serious student of butterflies, higher levels of hygiene and care are required. Notes on food preferences, development times, parasitoids, and survivorship provide a guide to future care, and the data are potentially useful to professional entomologists. Photographs, cast skins and voucher specimens can serve to document development.

Especially for species whose immatures are unknown, females may be captured in an effort to induce them to lay eggs. This is usually more reliable than trying to find eggs, larvae or pupae of a given species in the field. To induce egg-laying, place captive females in a cage or container together with known or suspected larval host plants. A variety of plants may be introduced if the host is unknown. The appropriate container size varies depending on the species and space available. For many butterflies, placing the cage in a warm location that catches the morning sun helps to induce egg-laying. For other species, oviposition is stimulated with ample supplies of a nectar substitute (e.g., a 10% solution of honey in water) in tubes with cotton plugs. Every species is different and some may completely refuse to lay eggs in captivity.

Once eggs are obtained, either from nature or a captive female, they should be kept on or near their preferred host plant, either potted or as cuttings. In laboratories, where mass rearing of some types of Lepidoptera is done, disease is a major concern. Eggs are surface sterilized (usually with 3% to 10% bleach solution for three to fifteen minutes), then transferred to synthetic diets for rearing under sterile conditions. For home rearing, such a set-up is not required and may be difficult to manage without specialized equipment; however, it is still important to practise reasonable levels of hygiene to limit diseases. It is advisable to wash containers with a 10% bleach solution between rearings. Keeping the container well ventilated helps to reduce fungal and bacterial growth by allowing insect droppings (also called "frass") to dry out, but care should be taken to maintain a high enough humidity level to avoid stressing the larvae. Reusable containers include glass jars, plastic refrigerator containers and elaborate screened cages holding entire plants, or simple screened cages around plants in the field. Paper grocery bags or food packaging containers can serve as disposable rearing cages.

Under suitable conditions, the eggs will hatch in three to fifteen days, depending on the species. Some may not hatch due to infertility or obligatory diapause. First stage (instar) larvae often bear little resemblance to the mature larvae in markings, spines or colour, and often have different feeding behaviours. The duration of the larval period is dependent on temperature and food quality. Use of non-preferred host plants often results in slow growth, small size and increased larval mortality. Some species overwinter as larvae and development is arrested until a suitable chilling period has been completed. The same holds true for some pupae, which require winter chilling to break developmental diapause.

Mature larvae often leave the host plant to search for suitable places to pupate. In the field, this is the time when many larvae are found as they wander about in search of a sheltered spot. Pupation sites are species-dependent; some prefer to pupate on the host plant, others crawl under stones and some seek sheltered cracks in bark. If the pupa is healthy and not diapausing, adult emergence takes place after ten to twenty days, depending on the temperature.

If winter chilling is required, an unheated porch or garage may be used to break diapause. The insect usually needs to be kept cool for about three months. For some species, this period can be extended for over a year by placing the immatures in a refrigerator. However, survivorship drops sharply after a year, or if the storage container is allowed to dry out.

Collecting and Specimen Study

A butterfly collection is an important information filing and retrieval system. A collection may be made to show what butterflies were studied in the field, or how a species varies geographically. It may act as a catalogue of what

species are found in a particular area, or show the association of immature stages with the adults. Ethics of insect collecting are important. When collecting, do not take rare or endangered species or collect from nature sanctuaries or national and provincial parks without appropriate permits. In addition to having poor moral standards, violators are subject to prosecution by law. Do not collect more than your specific needs dictate; over-collection of some species may threaten their existence, especially if they exist in isolated colonies. Worn or

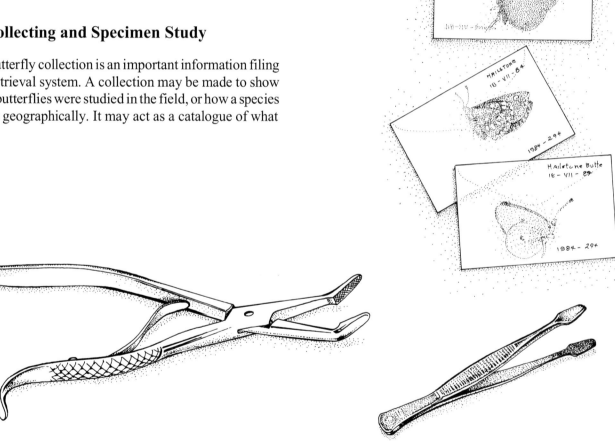

Figure 11. Collecting paraphernalia

damaged specimens should be released, unless they have special scientific value. Collecting butterflies from private land should be done with the permission of the land owner. Use respect when collecting; do not damage property, litter, or be a nuisance in any way; you and others may wish to come back some other time. Once collected, specimens should be provided with a full data label, stored in a location safe from pests and eventually incorporated into a collection. In the event one loses interest in the collection, donation to a public museum or university is a good alternative to throwing the specimens away, as your data may be used by other people studying butterflies.

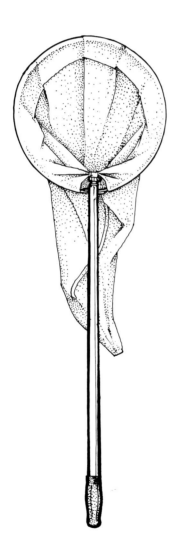

Figure 12. Butterfly net

Equipment

Times and technology have changed but in butterfly collecting many things have stayed the same. Field equipment still consists of a net and a storage or killing container. Much of the equipment is easily acquired or made at home. Exact size is less important than the principles of construction.

Net: The collecting net (Fig. 12) is often portrayed as the hallmark of a butterfly collector. There are almost as many variations in net styles as there are collectors. Most serious collectors adapt the design to suit particular requirements. Nets can be purchased from supply houses or made inexpensively from materials around the home.

A basic net is constructed of a stiff wire hoop about 30 to 45 cm in diameter (larger if desired). The ends are bent to an angle to fit in grooves on the handle and are fastened in place. Methods of fastening vary; a metal ring may be used to hold the ends in place, or a hose clamp, wire wrapping, cord wrapping, or various types of tape. The basic idea is that the net hoop is removable to allow replacement or repair of the net bag.

The handle may be made of a variety of materials, such as light-weight metal tubing, wood (be careful to get wood that does not splinter easily) or plastic. Length is a personal decision. The bag should be about 2.5 times longer than the hoop diameter and the closed end should be broadly rounded to reduce damage to the butterfly while in the net. It is a good idea to have a spare bag in the unfortunate circumstance that your net is torn on thorns, branches or fence wire. Material for the bag is usually a light open, double interlocking weave that prevents separation of strands in either direction. The bag is somewhat transparent and should offer minimal resistance to air flow. Polyester fabrics are more stable and will not break down as quickly as other fabrics when exposed to outside conditions, especially ultraviolet light.

Many strategies may be employed to capture butterflies. The first is site selection as explained under "Butterfly Observation." Go where butterflies like to be. Different species have different preferences. When a butterfly is found, it is best to stalk it; a spooked butterfly often leaves the area very quickly in an erratic flight pattern. Sweeping butterflies off flowers is very effective and positioning oneself in a flyway along a gully or on a hilltop allows the butterflies to come to you. However, if you wish to patrol an area, do so watching for any movement, then make a quick sweep if the butterfly is in the air, or flop the net down if the butterfly is on reasonably flat ground. Everyone develops his own style of capturing butterflies. If the butterfly has worn wings or turns out to be a species you do not want, release it unharmed.

Field storage and handling: Killing the butterfly may be accomplished by several methods, each with its own merits and drawbacks. A common method of killing small butterflies and stunning larger ones for handling is to pinch the thorax while the butterfly is restrained in a fold of the net. Care must be taken not to crush the butterfly or damage its wings. Once stunned, the butterfly may be transferred from the net to either an envelope or a killing jar. The envelope may be placed in a temporary storage container, to protect the specimen, or into a killing jar.

Use of killing jars may be a point of contention with regard to children. One of the classic killing jar designs uses cyanide, which is poisonous to humans. In Alberta this chemical is restricted and one requires a permit for its purchase and use. Information concerning regulations and permits may be obtained from Alberta Environmental Protection, Pesticide Chemicals Branch. A better solution is to forget about cyanide and use a less dangerous substance. Ethyl acetate is the poison of choice for many entomologists. It does not stiffen the specimens or induce colour changes. It may be difficult to obtain by the general public, although some drug stores will special order it.

A killing jar may be constructed from a wide-mouthed jar with some paper towels stuffed in the bottom, or may be more elaborate and have a layer of plaster of paris on the bottom. Some collectors prefer to use wood chips; the important parameter is that the material be absorbent. The killing agent is poured in and allowed to seep into the material lining the jar. The excess should be poured back into its original container to prevent wetting and matting of scales and hairs on the butterflies. An advantage of these "rechargeable" killing jars, as opposed to the permanent cyanide type, is that when the jar is not in use, it does not have any poison in it, thereby reducing the risk of accidental poisoning. All killing jars should clearly identify the killing agent and be labelled **POISON**.

There is a 100 kg killing jar that most people do have access to — their freezer. Specimens brought back from the field may be frozen and kept in storage until pinned; this may not work well on those species that overwinter as adults. Unfortunately, a freezer is difficult to take out in the field!

Larval collection is another aspect of butterfly collecting. Larvae may be collected as specimens for their own sake or as material for rearing to adulthood. Different methods need to be employed to collect larvae, as they tend to be inconspicuous and very localized. If host plants are known, careful examination may yield larvae or eggs. Heavy canvas beating nets or collecting sheets spread under the plants which are beaten may yield some specimens. In general, larvae tend to grip the host plant very tightly and are difficult to dislodge, except with violent shaking. Such larvae may be injured and rendered unsuitable for rearing.

Larvae may be killed and preserved by placing them directly in 70% ethanol. A variety of concoctions has been developed to aid in preservation of soft-bodied insects, including adding glycerin, acetic acid, formaldehyde (now in disuse), kerosene and other agents to the ethanol (Martin 1977). If ethanol is not readily available, 70% isopropyl alcohol (rubbing alcohol) may be used. It is important to change the liquid in the storage vial after a few months as various fats and other chemicals leach out and discolour the liquid. Large-bodied larvae may decompose and discolour before penetration of the preservative. To avoid this, you may inject them directly with preservative, or place them in hot preservative to speed penetration. Alternatively, larvae may be placed in the preservative, then frozen to prevent decomposition, while the preservative slowly penetrates over a period of several months. After preservation, the specimen may be stored at room temperature. Caterpillars may be stored for the long term in glass vials, complete with data tag(s), which are placed in a larger jar of alcohol. By topping up the large jar as required, desiccation of the smaller vials is prevented. Alcohol is poisonous and flammable (to below 30%). Containers with alcohol should be stored away from sources of heat and out of reach of children.

Care and preparation of specimens

Material freshly caught and killed is best suited for pinning. Sometimes this may be impossible or simply inconvenient. To store specimens, place them in an envelope while still fresh. Care should be taken to make sure that the wings are folded above the back and the antennae are tucked between the wings. All appropriate data should be written on the envelope.

Envelopes (Fig. 11) may be purchased or made. "No-glue" glassine envelopes used by stamp collectors come in a variety of sizes and are readily available at many stamp/coin shops in packs of one hundred or boxes of one thousand. Glassine triangles are sold for butterfly storage by many biological supply companies via mail order. Paper envelopes may be used, but they are less desirable because one cannot see the butterfly inside without opening the envelope. The advantage of using paper triangles is that they can be made anywhere out of most any bond paper. Avoid using coloured paper, or those with inks or dyes, as the dyes may run if placed in a relaxing chamber (see below).

Many butterfly collectors paper the butterfly after pinch immobilization in the net. The papered butterfly is immediately placed either into a killing jar, or a protective container of metal, cardboard, or plastic to reduce risk of crushing and further damage in the field. Pertinent data are written either on the envelope or a slip of paper which is kept with the butterfly. If specimens are not killed at the site of capture, they may be killed back at "camp" (or at home) using a killing jar or freezer.

For long-term storage, butterflies are allowed to dry out and are then placed in a larger pest-proof storage container. For storage of less than a few months, they may be stored frozen; this may eliminate the need for relaxing when being pinned (see below).

Pinning, display and storage

To pin butterflies for display, use of fresh material gives the best results. Dried material needs to be relaxed. A relaxing jar or container can be constructed from a small fish tank, battery jar, plastic freezer container or plastic bag. The traditional set-up uses a layer of clean sand or blotting paper (or other absorbent material, e.g., cotton rags). The material is dampened but not to the point of water pooling. Fibreglass or plastic window screen may be placed on top to keep the specimens out of contact with the water when placed in the container without the envelope. Data must be kept associated with the correct specimen.

An alternate method used by some lepidopterists is to place butterflies, while in the envelope, directly in the relaxing chamber, alternating with successive layers of moist cloths (or blotting paper) and layers of butterflies. This has the advantage of keeping the data with the butterfly but runs the risk of matting hairs and scales if the cloths are too moist. This method is suitable for use in almost any type of container including plastic bags.

A major problem with relaxing butterflies is the risk of specimens going mouldy. This is especially true if specimens are left in the chamber for more than twenty-four hours. To combat this problem a mould inhibitor may be added. Some people use paradichlorobenzene, others use Lysol. Ethyl acetate is very effective; just make sure the container has a chance to air out (preferably outside) before pinning the specimens. If your plans to mount up a number of specimens suddenly change, you can quickly stop the relaxing process without removing the specimens by placing the whole container in the freezer. When ready to spread the specimens, remove, allow to thaw, then proceed.

Pinning or mounting is done with the aid of a spreading board (Fig. 13). This may be purchased commercially or constructed from materials locally available. Certain aspects of design are important. The upper surface should be smooth and flat yet soft enough to readily accept pins. Materials frequently used include balsa or other soft wood, composition board, cork board or dense styrofoam. The surface may be perfectly flat or slightly inclined with the butterfly body sitting slightly lower than the wing tips. A groove slightly wider than the butterfly's body runs down the centre of the board.

At the base of the groove, there is another pinning surface to receive the pin which holds the butterfly's body.

Pins used in insect collections are a special type that may be purchased from supply houses. Insect pins come in a variety of thicknesses, from 000 to 7, and in different styles, from rolled brass heads and nylon heads to integral heads. The shafts may be black japanned spring steel or stainless steel. The most common ones used are sizes 2 and 3 black pins.

To spread a specimen, push an insect pin through the centre of the thorax, leaving about 10 mm from the thorax to the head of the pin. Care must be exercised to avoid rubbing off scales or damaging the wings. The pin is then pressed into the pinning surface at the bottom of the mounting board groove, adjusting the wing bases to line up with the top edge of the groove. Using the finest pin available (000 preferred), position the wings as shown in Figure 13. Place strips of stiff paper over the wings and pin to the top of the mounting board (glass-headed sewing pins work well). Position the antennae as desired. Make sure the data are kept with the butterfly, i.e., pinned beside the specimen. The specimen is allowed to dry for several days (or, if in a hurry, in a warm oven for a few hours, being careful not to over-heat). Remove the specimen very carefully, making sure all the extra pins are removed first, as butterflies are very fragile. Place a data label on the pin below the specimen.

Information recorded on a label should contain the minimum of: Locality (where the butterfly was collected); Date (when it was collected); Name (who collected it). Additional information describing eleva-tion, habitat and species name may be placed on the pin by placing additional labels below the locality label. Production of many labels, for either one date or locality, may be produced by a variety of methods. Modern technology has been a boon to label making for the amateur. Professional-looking labels can be made using a computer and a laser printer directly, or a typewriter and a reducing photocopier. Another method employed is a photograph of a typed page. The best labels for quality are made by offset printing, but this is also the most expensive route. For many people, using a fine pen and india ink produces suitable labels when written on good quality stiff paper.

Storage and display of specimens is up to the individ-ual collector. There are many types of display boxes. They range in size from a few centimetres square up to drawers over 60 cm square. Some have solid tops, others have glass or clear tops. Most butterfly collectors use clear-topped boxes to show off their specimens, usually in a drawer system. The sizes are not critical provided that the depth of the box is at least 40 mm from the top of the pinning surface to the underside of the lid.

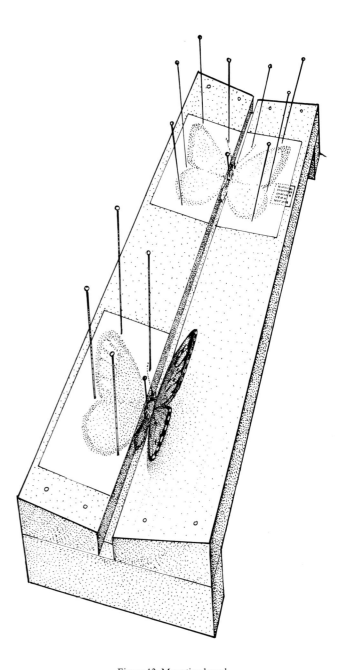

Figure 13. Mounting board

Riker mounts are sometimes used to display specimens. These shallow glass-fronted boxes may be hung on walls for display. They come in a variety of sizes and are about 20 mm deep. The insect pin in the butterfly must be removed after spreading, and the specimen is placed on the fibrefill backing.

Virtually all collections will suffer damage from unwanted insect visitors if not properly protected. These visitors include various dermestid beetles, carpet and museum beetles, merchant and sawtoothed grain beetles, book lice, and a host of other insects associated with human habitation. The first line of defence is to maintain a clean working environment. Next, the storage or display boxes should have tight-fitting dust seals restricting pest entry. Lastly, some sort of chemical deterrent or poison may be used to make the butterfly collection unattractive as food. Various chemicals have been employed, each having advantages and drawbacks. Paradichlorobenzene (moth crystals) may reduce entry, but is unlikely to kill dermestids if they do enter. Prolonged exposure to the fumes may cause liver damage in humans. Dichlorvos (No-Pest Strips) works well as a fumigant. Small pieces are cut off and a pin placed through the strip. Follow warnings on the packaging and avoid handling the material. This method is used by some large entomology museums. Caution must be exercised to avoid touching treated areas of the drawers. This method of pest control is not recommended for the casual home entomologist.

In the event that pests do break into a collection that is not chemically protected, destruction of the pests may be accomplished by placing the material into a freezer overnight (or outside if below -15°C in the winter); alternatively the collection may be fumigated using Dichlorvos strips, which can be removed after fumigation. The best method of all is prevention.

As a general rule, the collection should be stored in a cool, dry location away from bright light. Excessive humidity damages specimens by encouraging mould growth and causing sagging. Exposure to light results in fading of certain colours (especially reds). Storage container lids should be tight-fitting to physically exclude pests. If pests do show up in the collection, other forms of control (e.g., chemical) may be considered.

Butterfly Gardening in Alberta

The use of plants to attract wildlife, coupled with a trend toward "naturalized landscaping," has contributed to increasing demands for information on plants that can be used to attract butterflies. Plants that are attractive to butterflies fall into two categories, those that are used as nectar sources by the adults, and those that are used as larval food sources. Nectar plants include those plants bearing flowers that contain a nectar supply. They include many ornamental species used in flower gardens, but also include introduced species such as Dandelions (*Taraxacum officinale*).

Larval food plants can ensure a more constant supply of butterflies (and caterpillars) but the plants are generally less attractive in a garden setting. Larval food plants are more suited to "naturalized landscaping" where indigenous plants are used to develop scenic perspective. A certain amount of leaf damage is inevitable when larval food plants are successful in attracting butterflies. The female butterflies deposit eggs on the appropriate larval food plants which the caterpillars partially consume in development to butterflies. A further requirement for success of larval food plants is an insecticide-free (both chemical and biological) local environment.

Some knowledge of plants is necessary for use of larval food species as most of these plants are not available in garden centres. The scientific names for plants are used in the table on the following pages to assist access to further information on the plants. Common names for plants can be found in the appropriate butterfly species treatments. The greatest chances of success will be obtained by selecting plants that occur in your local area. These will attract butterflies whose larvae eat those plants. Plants should be relocated into situations that the butterflies would normally find them; for instance, plants found in shady areas should be placed in shady spots in the garden. Annual leaf litter should be left in place since many butterflies pupate, overwinter or lay eggs in litter surrounding the larval food plant. Success will also be enhanced by group plantings and proximity to natural areas; rural settings will generally have more success than urban settings.

Table 1 lists those plants which occur in Alberta (including indigenous, agricultural, ornamental and weed species) that are known to be nectar or larval food sources. Plant families are indicated with bold face type, plant genus and species names are italicised. Some butterfly larvae will consume any species in a family of plants, othersare restricted to a particular genus of plants and others eat only a single species of plant in Alberta. The numbers following each plant category (family, genus, species) refer to butterfly species found in Alberta that use those plants as a nectar or larval food source. Numbers of butterflies are referenced in the checklist at the end of this chapter. Nectar sources in the table below are indicated by "n" (e.g., n83) preceding the reference number to the butterfly species. Confirmed larval food sources in Alberta are indicated by an asterisk (e.g., *15) preceding the reference number to a butterfly species. Numbers without an asterisk or an "n" indicate larval food sources outside Alberta. Most species of butterflies in Alberta have no confirmed host plant (larval food plant) in the province. Host plant preference can change over the distribution range of a species but it is likely that the same host plant species or a close relative will be used in Alberta.

To use the following table, first determine the biome (Prairie, Aspen Parkland, Boreal, Mountain) in which a butterfly garden will be established. Biomes are colour coded on all distribution maps in the text. Move down the column until you come to a plant species you wish to use or to a butterfly species that occurs in the biome. For instance, if you wish to attract the Monarch Butterfly (*Danaus plexippus*, number 177) to a garden in southern Alberta, the table indicates that any species of *Asclepias* (milkweeds) can be used as a larval food source in the Prairie or Aspen Parkland biomes, but would not likely attract Monarchs in the Boreal or Mountain biomes, even though the plant may naturally occur there. The table is constructed to indicate only overlapping distribution ranges of plants and butterfly species. Further refinement to determine a butterfly's presence at an exact locality may be obtained by reference to the butterfly distribution maps.

Table 1. Butterfly Gardening Plant Cross Reference For Alberta.

Plant	Plant and Butterfly Occurrence			
	Prairie	Aspen Parkland	Boreal	Mountain
Amaranthaceae				
Amaranthus retroflexus L.	10			
Anacardiaceae				
Rhus L.	91	91		
Apocynaceae				
Apocynum L.		n148, 177		
Asclepiadaceae				
Asclepias L.	n25, n119, 177, n177	n119, 177, n177		
speciosa Torr.	n25, 177			
ovalifolia Dcne.		177		
Betulaceae				
Alnus Mill.	105	105	105	105
Betula L.	3, 105, 153	3, 105, 110, 140, 153	3, 105, 110, 140, 153	3, 105, 110, 140, 153
glandulosa			134	134
Boraginaceae	115	115, 149	115, 149	115, 149
Cannabinaceae				
Humulus L.	104	104	104	104
Caprifoliaceae				
Lonicera involucrata (Richards) Banks			150	150
*Symphoricarpos occidentali*s Hook.	76		150	150,76
Viburnum L.		91	91	91
Caryophyllaceae				
Silene acaulis L.				n135, n138
Chenopodiaceae				
Chenopodium album L.	10			
Compositae	n99, 115, n115, n118, n119, n120, n127, n133	115, n115, n118, n118, 120, n126, n127, n133, n140	115, n115, n118, n119, n120, n126, n127, n133, n135, n140	n69, n99, 115, n115, n118, n119, n120, n127, n133, n135, n140
Achillea millefolium L.				n69
Antennaria Gatern.		114		
Artemisia L.		114		
dracunculus L.		34	34	
Aster L.	n7, 141, 142, 143, n143, 144, n144, 145, 146	n7, 140, 141, 142, 143, n143, 144, n144, 145, 148	n7, 140, 142, 143, n143, 144, n144, 145, 146, 148	140, 142, 143, n143, 144, n144, 148
Chrysothamnus Nutt.	146			
Cirsium Mill.	n25, n38, 115, n115, n116, n117, n119, n129, n146, n152	115, n115, n116, n117, n119, n129, n146, n152	115, n115, n117, n119, n129, n152	n38, 115, n115, n116, n117, n119, n129, n152
Erigeron L.	n7	n7, n27, 148	n7, n27, 148	147, 148
Helianthus L.	113, 145	113, 145	113	113
Liatris punctata Hook.	n17	n17		

Table 1. continued

	Plant and Butterfly Occurrence			
	Prairie	**Aspen Parkland**	**Boreal**	**Mountain**
Lygodesmia juncea (Pursh) D. Don	n25			
Machaeranthera canescens (Pursh) A. Gray	*146			
Senecio L.	n17, n34, n144	n17, n34, n144	n17, n34, n144	n17, n34, n144
Solidago L.	n143	n70, n143	n70, n143	n70, n143
multiradia Ait.				147
Taraxacum officinale Weber	n35, n36	n35, n36	n35, n36	n35, n36
Cornaceae				
Cornus L.	91	91	91	91
Crassulaceae				
Sedum L.			n6, 118	n6, 118
lanceolatum Torr.				33, 85
Cruciferae	43, 46, 47, 50	43, 45, 46, 47, 50	43, 45, 46, 47, 50	43, 44, 46, 47, 50
Arabis L.	41, 49	45, 48, 49	41, 45, 48	48, 49
drummondi A. Gray			*47	*47
Brassica L.	42, 43, 46	42, 43, 46	42, 43, 46	43, 46
Draba L.		45, 48	45, 48	48
cana Rydb.				*48
Lepidium L.	42	42	42	
Sisymbrium L.	41		41	
Cyperaceae				
Carex L.	159, 161, 166, 170	159, 161, 164, 166, 169, 170, 174	157, 159, 161, 164, 166, 169, 170, 173, 174	159, 161, 164, 166, 169, 170, 173, 174
Eriophorum L.			174	174
Ericaceae		60, 78, 84, 95, 137	78, 84, 95, 137	60, 84, 95, 137
Arctostaphylos uva-ursi L.		84, 86, 137	84, 86, 137	84, 86, 137
Ledum groenlandicum Oeder			84, 95	84, 95
Rhododendron L.				106
Vaccinium L.		6, 59, 84, 91, 95, 102, 137	6, 58, 59, 84, 91, 95, 102, 137	6, 59, 60, 84, 91, 95, 102, 137
myrtillus L.		101		
Fumariaceae				
Corydalis Medic.				32
Dicentra Bernh.				32
Gramineae				
Agrostis L.	31	31	31	31
stolonifera L.	22, 31	22, 31	22, 31	22, 31
Avena L.	31, 161	31, 161	31, 161	31, 161
Bouteloua Lag.	16, 17	16,17		
gracilis (HBK) Lag.	15, 19, 30, 158	158		
Bromus L.	11, 17	11, 17	11, 17	11, 17
Calamagrostis Adans.	11	11	11	11
Festuca L.	17, 20, 172	17, 20, 23, 172	17, 23, 165, 172	17, 20, 23, 172
saximontana Rydb.		20		20
Hordeum vulgare L.				165

Table 1. continued

	Prairie	Aspen Parkland	Boreal	Mountain
Koeleria Pers.		20		20
macrantha (Ledeb.) J.A. Schultes f.	24	20, 23, 24	23	20, 23, 24
Panicum L	25	27	27	
Phleum pratense L.		14		
Poa L.	11, 12, 31, 162	11, 27, 31, 162	11, 27, 31, 162	11, 31, 162
pratensis L.	13, 22, 24, 159	13, 22, 23, 24, 159	13, 22, 23, 159, 165	13, 22, 23, 24, 159
Schizachyrium Nees	25			
Sitanion Raf.	20			20
Stipa L.	16, 17, 161	16, 17, 20, 161	16, 17, 161	17, 161
comata Trin. & Rupr.	17, 20	17, 20	17	17, 20
Grossulariaceae				
Ribes L.	105	103, 105, 109	105, 109	103, 105, 106
triste Pall.			107	
Hydrangeaceae				
Philadelphus L.			n75	
Juncaceae				
Juncus L.		174	174	174
Labiatae				
Monarda L.	119, 120, 129	120, 129		
Leguminosae	53, 89, n90, n96, 115, n129	62, n90, n96, 115, n129	55, 56, n90, n96, 115, n129	55, 56, n90, n96, 115, n129
Astragalus L.	1, *5, 90, 94, 96, 99, 100	1, *5, 90, 94, 96, 100	*5, 90, 94, 96, 100	*5, 90, 94, 96, 99, 100
crassicarpus Nutt.	4	4		
Glycyrrhiza lepidota (Nutt.) Pursh	*1, 96	*1, 96		
Hedysarum L.	n34, 94	n34, 94	n34, 94	n34, 94
sulphurescens Rydb.		*54		*54
Lathyrus L.		1, 2, 90, 95	2, 90, 95	2, 90, 95
Lotus corniculatus L.	100			100
Lupinus L.	5, 75, 93, 94, 95, 96, 98, 99, 100, 116			5, 75, 93, 94, 95, 96, 98, 99, 100, 116
argenteus Pursh	4			
Medicago sativa L.	2, n34, *51, 52, 96, n115, n117, n119, n120, n124	2, n34, *51, 52, 62, 96, n115, n117, n119, 120, n124	2, n34, *51, 52, 96, n115, n117, 119, 120	2, n34, *51, 52, 96, n115
Onobrychis viciifolia Scop.	*112	*112	*112	*112
Oxytropis D.C.	90, 96, 99	90, 96	90, 96	90, 96, 99
splendens Dougl. ex Hook			*57	*57
Petalostemon Michx.		62	64	64
Thermopsis R. Br.	5, 90	5, 90	90	90
rhombifolia (Nutt.) Richards	4	4	*54	*54
Trifolium L.	2, *51, 90, 97, 99, n115	2, *51, 62, 90, 97, n97, n115	2, *51, 90, 97, n97, n115	2, *51, 90, 97, n97, 99, n115
Vicia L.	2, 90, 94, 95	2, 90, 94, 95	2, 90, 94, 95	2, 90, 94, 95
Loranthaceae				
Arceuthobium Bieb.				82

Table 1. continued	Plant and Butterfly Occurrence			
	Prairie	**Aspen Parkland**	**Boreal**	**Mountain**
Malvaceae	9, 115, 116	115, 116	115	115, 116
Malva L.	7	7	7	
Sphaeralcea St. Hil.	7	7		
coccinea (Pursh) Rydb.	9			
Onagraceae				
Gayophytum racemosum T. & G.	71	71		
Pinaceae				40
Abies Mill.				40
Picea A. Dietr.				40
Pinus L.			88	40,88
banksiana Lamb.			87	
contorta Loudon			88	40, 88
Pseudotsuga menziesii (Mirb.) Franco				40
Tsuga Carr.				40
Plantaginaceae	149		149	149
Plantago L.			150	150
Polygonaceae				
Eriogonum Michx.	92, 100	100	100	69, 100
umbellatum Torr.				69, 81
Oxyria Hill				*63
digyna (L.) Hill				64
Polygonum L.	67, 71	67, 70, 71	67, 70, 71	63, 67, 70, 71
coccineum Muhl.	67	67		
viviparum L.			130, 131, 140	131, 140
Rumex. L.	65, 67, 68, 71, 73	65, 67, 70, 71, 73	67, 70, 71, 73	63, 65, 67, 70, 71, 73
pauciflorus Nutt.				*63
venosus Pursh	*68			
Portulacaceae				
Portulaca oleracea L.	118	118	118	
Primulaceae				
Androsace chamaejasme Host			102	102
septentrionalis L.	102	102	102	102
Dodecatheon L.		102		102
Ranunculaceae				
Thalictrum L.		131	131	131
Rhamnaceae				
Ceanothus L.				39,91.111
Rosaceae	78,89	78	78,89	89
Amelanchier alnifolia Nutt.	38, 74, 78, 154	74, 78	74, 78	38, 74
Crataegus L.	78	78		
Dryas L.			n138, n139	n138, n139
octopetala L.			138	138
Fragaria L.		6, n6	6, n6	6, n6
virginiana Duchesne		6	6	6

Table 1. continued

	Plant and Butterfly Occurrence			
	Prairie	**Aspen Parkland**	**Boreal**	**Mountain**
Potentilla L.	71	n6, 8, 70, n70, 71	n6, 8, 70, n70, 71	n6, 8, 70, n70, 71
diversifolia Lehm.		6		6
Prunus L.	38, 74, 91, 152	74, 91, 152	74, 91, 152	38, 39, 74, 91, 152, 155
virginiana L.	38, 74, 78	74, 78	74, 78	38, *39, 74
Rubus chamaemorus L.			6	
Salicaceae				
Populus L.	3, 112, 152, 153, 154	3, 112, 152, 153	3, 112, 152, 153	3, 112, 152, 153, 155
tremuloides Michx.	36, 110, 153	36, 110, 153	36, 110, 153	36, 110, 153, 155
Salix L.	3, 36, 105, 110, 112, 113, 152, 153, 154	3, 36, 61, 105, 110, 112, 113, 131, 134, 140, 152, 153	3, 36, 61, 105, 110, 112, 113, 131, 134, 135, 140, 152, 153	3, 36, 61, 105, 110, 112, 113, 131, 134, 135, 140, 152, 153, 155, 168
arctica Pallas			140	140
exigua Nutt.	76			76
Saxifragaceae				
Saxifraga bronchialis L.				139
oppositifolia L.				102
Scrophulariaccac				
Castilleja Mutis ex L.f.			149, 150	149, 150
Orthocarpus Nutt.			150	150
Pedicularis L.			150	150
Penstemon Mitch.	149		149	149
Ulmaceae				
Ulmus L.	103	103	103	
Umbelliferae	34, 35	34, 35	34, 35	34, 35
Angelica arguta Nutt.				*35
dawsoni S. Wats.				*35
genuflexa Nutt.			*35	
Heracleum lanatum Michx.	*35	*35	*35	*35
Lomatium dissectum (Nutt.) Mathias & Constance				*35
triternatum (Pursh) Coult. & Rose	*35			*35
Pastinaca sativa L.	35	35	35	35
Sium suave Walt.		*35	*35	
Urticaceae	116	116		116
Urtica L.	104, 113, 117	103, 104, 113, 117	104, 113, 117	104, 113, 117
Violaceae				
Viola L.	118, 119, 120, 121, 124, 132, 133	118, 119, 120, 121, 124, 131, 132, 133	118, 119, 120, 121, 124, 128, 131, 132, 133	118, 119, 120, 121, 124, 128, 131, 132, 133, 136
nuttalli Pursh	121	121		

n = nectar source.

* = confirmed host in Alberta.

Adult Morphology

In this section we describe the morphology of adult butterflies, as it is primarily adult anatomy that is used in the identification keys. Other life history stages (eggs, larvae and pupae) are described briefly in the Life History section of each species account.

Like all adult insects, butterflies have three major body sections: head, thorax and abdomen (Fig. 14). On the **head** are the primary sensory structures. The most obvious of these are the two enormous, multifaceted **eyes**. Because they are active during the day, butterflies rely much more on vision than do their nocturnal cousins, the moths. Butterflies see movement and colour very well, which allows them to find mates and food and to avoid predators (and lepidopterists!). In addition to the normal range of colours, butterflies can see beyond the range of human vision into the ultraviolet. Plants pollinated by butterflies often have ultraviolet patterns, and male whites and sulphurs (family Pieridae) have UV wing markings that they display when courting females. The next most obvious structures on a butterfly's head are the **antennae** (Fig. 15). Antennae have dual roles, as organs of olfaction (smell) and proprioception (balance). Butterflies whose antennae have been removed have difficulty maintaining their balance in flight. In advanced butterflies the tip of each antenna has a rounded knob, whereas in skippers (family Hesperiidae) each antenna has a drawn-out point on the tip. In contrast, moth antennae are usually thread-like in females and feathery in males. The head also bears the butterfly's mouth parts, the **proboscis** and the **palps**. The proboscis is a long tube, designed to suck fluids, that is kept neatly coiled when not in use. Two palps flank the base of the proboscis and act as organs of taste and touch. The length of the proboscis reflects the type of food taken by the butterfly. In species that feed on nectar, the proboscis is usually quite long, whereas in those that feed on sap, carrion or rotting fruit it is much shorter. Within the nectar-feeding group, proboscis length of a species often mirrors nectary length of the flowers most commonly visited.

The middle part of the body, the **thorax**, is made of three closely fused segments, each bearing a pair of **legs**. In three Albertan families (Nymphalidae, Satyridae and Danaidae), the front legs are much reduced in size and

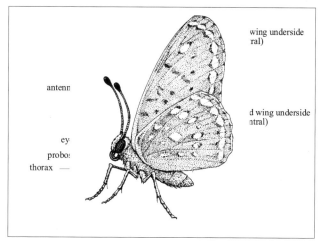

Figure 14. Anatomy of a butterfly.

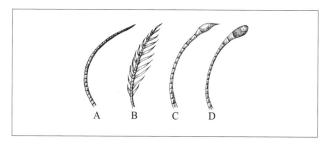

Figure 15. Antennae: A, Female moth. B, Male moth. C, Skipper, Hesperiidae. D, Butterfly

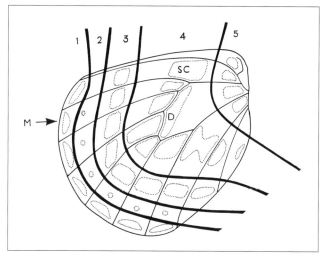

Figure 16. Hind wing regions: 1, marginal. 2, submarginal. 3, postmedian. 4, discal or median area. 5, basal. D, discal cell spot. M, wing margin. SC, subcostal spot of discal region

39

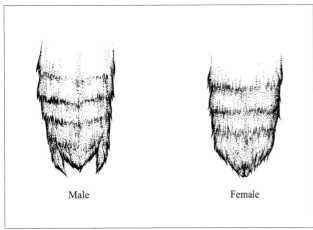

Figure 17. External genitalia

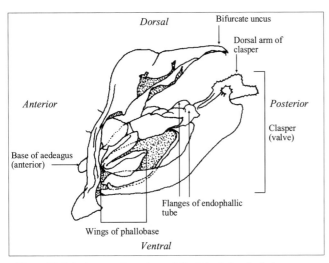

Figure 18. *Boloria eunomia*, male genitalia, lateral view. Left clasper removed to expose aedeagus and wings of phallobase (length 4.0 mm).

colour on butterfly wings. The markings usually differ between dorsal (upperside) and ventral (underside) aspects of an individual wing. The patterns are created by the microscopic scales that give the name to this order: **Lepidoptera** = "scaly wings."

There are two ways in which scales impart colour to butterfly wings. In most cases, scales get their colours from internal pigments. Sometimes these pigments are derived from chemicals collected from food plants by the larvae. Other butterflies have scales whose colour is derived not from pigments, but from ridges and air chambers within the scales that produce iridescent and metallic colours through the diffraction of light. This structural colouration is particularly spectacular in tropical butterflies of the genus *Morpho*, whose wings flash like bits of sky through the rainforest undergrowth. Scales may also be modified to disperse attractive scents; these paintbrush-shaped scales are called androconia and are confined to patches on the wings of males of several families (e.g., Hesperiidae, Satyridae, Danaidae). What functions do wing patterns serve? The beautiful colours are not for our benefit, but rather communicate an individual's species and sex to other butterflies, and in many cases also act to hide the butterfly from predators or to deter attack. For example, many butterflies have cryptically coloured underwings that make them appear like leaves when the wings are folded over the back. Bright eye spots on the hind wings may be flashed to frighten predators. Finally, in some species (e.g., the Monarch, *Danaus plexippus*) bright colours warn that the butterfly is distasteful and should be avoided. Wing patterns may vary within a species seasonally, geographically, or along an altitudinal gradient (see the earlier section "Evolution, Life History, Ecology and Behaviour").

are useless for walking. The tips of the third pair of legs bear organs of taste, which makes sense since butterflies walk on their food or oviposition sites. The **wings** are on the second and third thoracic segments and are crossed with **veins** whose interconnections form discrete **cells**. Veins and cells all have names, and differences in their shapes are useful for identifying species in keys. In some groups of butterflies, the hind wings have been divided into regions which are useful for species discrimination. These regions are illustrated in Figure 16. However, most important for identification, and most fascinating to us, are the often beautiful patterns of

The third section of the body, the **abdomen**, is composed of ten segments. Holes on the first seven segments called **spiracles** open into fine membranous tubes called **tracheae** that branch throughout the insect's body, transporting oxygen to all the cells. The abdomen also contains most of the digestive tract and the reproductive organs. The last two abdominal segments make up the external **genitalia**: males have a pair of **claspers**, and females have a pointed **ovipositor**. It is sometimes necessary to look at male genitalia to identify a butterfly to species (Figs. 17 and 18).

Butterfly Names:
Systematics, Taxonomy and Etymology

The study of how organisms are related to each other is called systematics. Within systematics, taxonomy refers to the description and ordering of organisms so that the system of words we use to classify them represents their interrelationships accurately. Etymology (not entomology which is the study of insects) is the study of word origins and often proves useful when trying to understand why an organism has the name it does. It is impossible to be a serious student of any group of organisms if you lack a basic understanding of systematics. This section serves as an introduction to the classification and naming of butterflies.

What is a species?

The most fundamental problem in systematics is the designation of species. Because humans naturally tend to recognize patterns in nature, we unconsciously develop a sense of what "species" are purely through observing or collecting the organisms around us. In fact, there is often a good correlation between folk and scientific classification systems, simply because the patterns we observe usually mirror the genetic relationships among organisms. But it is not always simple to recognize what constitutes a true species.

The determination of whether a particular population of organisms is a distinct species can be a fascinating exercise in problem solving. Several simple rules are widely accepted for delineating species among sexually reproducing organisms such as butterflies. 1. Different individuals produced from one mother are not considered to belong to different species. 2. Aberrations due to unusual environmental or developmental conditions should not be considered separate species. 3. If two whole populations from two separate geographic areas look different from each other, but are connected by a series of populations showing intermediate forms, then both populations still belong to the same species.

Unfortunately, it is more difficult to define what a species is than to say what it is not. Many biologists define species as those groups of organisms that successfully breed among themselves. For this reason, observations of matings in the field can be very important in establishing whether a particular group of butterflies is composed of one or two species. However, it may take a long time to find a reasonable number of such pairings. Lab matings may be easier to obtain, but

are not always meaningful, as butterflies often behave very differently in a lab compared to their natural environment. For these reasons, species are usually delimited by morphology alone, and it is typically assumed that any group of butterflies that has a continuous range of variation probably represents a single potentially interbreeding population.

There are some situations in which it is difficult to apply this definition. For example, two populations that are geographically separated and do not presently interbreed may still have the potential to do so. Since lab matings are both difficult to obtain and to interpret, what are the alternatives? One can only compare the degree of difference in appearance of habits between the two populations with the amount of variation found within any one of the populations. If the difference between the populations is relatively minor, then they are considered to belong to the same species. Such a situation can be found in *Erebia magdalena*, which has a population in the northern Rocky Mountains of Alberta and British Columbia that is isolated from a population in southern Montana.

It may also be difficult to know how to deal with two populations that occur in the same area and generally behave as separate species, but for which one can still find occasional hybrids. For such situations it may help to keep in mind that species are biological units; that is, populations with their own identity and integrity. If there is relatively little hybridization between populations and the distinctions between them appear to be maintained over generations, then they are considered two separate species. Some *Colias* species, as well as *Limenitis*, *Incisalia eryphon* and *Incisalia niphon*, hybridize with each other at the very edge of their ranges or in disturbed habitats, and yet maintain distinct biological identities. Among the most complex situations is that between *Papilio machaon* and *Papilio zelicaon*. These two species overlap but hybridize relatively little in the Peace River region and the prairies of southern Alberta, but have formed large hybrid populations in the forested regions between Calgary and the Swan Hills. Such "species" are a real challenge for the taxonomist to categorize, but are useful to biologists as examples of intermediate stages in the evolution of new species.

What's In a Name?

The main reason we give names to species is to communicate information about them. This transfer of information is accomplished at several levels. Each species name (e.g., *Papilio machaon*) includes a specific epithet (*machaon*), which is unique for each species in a genus. The species name also includes the name of the genus to which it belongs (*Papilio*). This portion immediately tclls the reader that *Papilio machaon* is also related to other species such as *Papilio zelicaon* and *Papilio canadensis*.

Subspecies names are constructed by adding a third portion to a species name (e.g., *Papilio machaon dodi*). These names are simply convenient ways of referring to consistently distinguishable geographic divisions of a species. Though two subspecies may merge into each other, the zone of intergradation should be much narrower than the ranges of the subspecies. If most specimens cannot be easily identified to subspecies without using a locality label, then there is little sense in using a subspecies name.

Some collectors use form names. Such names refer to distinctive genetic variants occurring infrequently in populations. Examples include the black wing morph of *Papilio machaon* and *Papilio zelicaon*, as well as the white female form of several *Colias* species. Form names can easily be overused and misused. Many collectors in the past described a plethora of such names and applied them to every trivial variant in their collection. However, form names can be useful if they are used in conjunction with simple genetic studies to determine their inheritance. Such studies have long been popular with plants, and there is even a field guide available for British Columbia (Griffiths and Ganders 1983). Very few genetic studies of this sort have been done for butterflies,

so there are many opportunities for people who like to rear butterflies to undertake real research.

A genus is a group of species. A genus should be strictly monophyletic, which means that all the species in a genus should have a single common ancestor, and all the species descended from that common ancestor are included. Species that should be included as part of a genus can be recognized because they share derived characteristics (e.g., morphology, behaviour) possessed by their common ancestor. A good way to visualize a genus is to imagine it as a branch on the family tree of life. Species would be the twigs that diverge nearer to the tip, and the common ancestor would be at the base of the branch. As any branch on such a family tree is itself part of the larger branch, there is some degree of arbitrariness in deciding where a branch, or genus, begins. The problem is usually dealt with by delineating genera as groups of species which are all clearly related to each other, but which have a substantial gap between themselves and other such groups.

Gaps may occur at several levels and practical reasons guide the decision to define a genus at a particular level. Some taxonomists prefer to include only a few very closely related species in each genus and to name many genera. For example, the genus *Papilio* is sometimes considered to include only *Papilio machaon*, *Papilio zelicaon* and a few other very closely related species, while *Papilio canadensis*, *Papilio multicaudatus* and their closest relatives are placed in a new genus *Pterourus*. Such a designation tells the reader what the very closest relatives are, but conveys no information on which species may be slightly more distantly related. On the other hand, broadly defined genera give information on more distant relationships, but not as much on the most immediate ones. If larger genera are used, then close relatives are often informally designated as species groups. Thus, *Papilio* in the broad sense includes the *Papilio machaon* group and the *Papilio glaucus* group.

Taxonomists are still in the process of discovering exactly how most species are related and are often still not in agreement among themselves. Broad definitions of genera mean that such disagreements are less likely to result in changes in generic names. As it is very confusing when names are constantly in flux, we have generally opted to use the more stable, broader genus names. Only those new names that are strongly supported in the scientific literature are adopted here.

Rules for Naming Species

The application of scientific names has a legalistic aspect as well as a biological component. To further the consistent application of taxonomic names, the International Commission of Zoological Nomenclature has established a variety of rules by which scientists abide. For example, all species names are composed of at least two parts, the genus name and the specific epithet, and these are latinized and written in italics or underlined to indicate their formal nature. The earliest published name receives priority and is the one which is used thereafter. This is a necessary convention because sometimes one species is redescribed and renamed several times, often because the describer was unaware of these previous names. If, for example, a species is described in 1908 by I.M. Wright as *Aus bus*, and again in 1912 by B. Wrongue as *Aus cus*, the 1908 name has priority. *Aus bus* and *A. cus* are called senior and junior synonyms, respectively. A synonymy is the history of the names that have been applied to a species and is often useful when doing research on butterflies. The person who describes and names a new species is called the author of that species. In the example above, the full name of the species is *Aus bus* Wright 1908, where the date indicates when the description was published. Sometimes further research indicates that the author assigned the species to the wrong genus, or that the genus should be given a different name; in this case, the author's name and date are presented in parentheses to indicate that the name of the species has changed since the author described it. For example, if research in 1995 shows that members of the genus *Aus* are merely modified *Dus*, then the proper representation of the species name would be *Dus bus* (Wright 1908).

Etymology

The amateur lepidopterist often finds scientific names intimidating and wonders why common names can not be used instead. The answer is simple — scientific names are universal and common names are not. A Mourning Cloak in North America is a Camberwell Beauty in England, but it is *Nymphalis antiopa* no matter where you are. Although scientific names sometimes appear to be a random conjunction of syllables, with a little knowledge of Greek and Latin you can often make sense of them. For example, the butterflies commonly known as anglewings belong to the genus *Polygonia*, which when translated means "many angles." The specific epithet for *Pieris rapae* means "turnip" and refers to the fact that caterpillars of this butterfly feed on leaves of turnips and their relatives. Unfortunately, lepidopterists often name species in a less sensible way, giving in to trends or the desire to honour relatives. A large number of butterflies are named after mythological characters, either classical Roman or Greek (e.g., *Limenitis arthemis* and *Charidryas gorgone*) or, for northern species, Norse characters (e.g., *Boloria frigga* and *Boloria freija*). Patronymic names may refer to a person's first (e.g., *Vanessa annabella*) or last (e.g., *Phyciodes batesii*) name. In our species descriptions we have attempted to explain the origin of each butterfly's name; however, we were sometimes stymied and the true explanation for a few names is still a mystery.

Pronunciation

There are two schools of pronunciation for scientific names. One holds that a name should be pronounced in the most euphonious way and the other that it should be pronounced in a way that makes the name's origin clear. For example, *Anthocharis* is composed of two Greek roots, *anthos* meaning "flower" and *charis* meaning "grace" or "beauty." Members of the first school might pronounce the genus with the accent on the "-tho-," whereas members of the second would maintain the integrity of the original roots by accenting "An-" and "-char-." Neither is necessarily the "right" way to pronounce *Anthocharis*.

Checklist of Alberta Butterflies

Family	Species	Page
HESPERIIDAE: Pyrginae	1 *Epargyreus clarus clarus* (Cramer)	80
	2 *Thorybes pylades* (Scudder)	92
	3 *Erynnis icelus* (Scudder & Burgess)	83
	4 *Erynnis afranius* (Lintner)	82
	5 *Erynnis persius borealis* (Cary) *Erynnis persius fredericki* H.R. Freeman	84
	6 *Pyrgus centaureae freija* (Warren) *Pyrgus centaureae loki* Evans	87
	7 *Pyrgus communis* (Grote)	89
	8 *Pyrgus ruralis* (Boisduval)	90
	9 *Pyrgus scriptura* (Boisduval)	91
	10 *Pholisora catullus* (Fabricius)**	86
Heteropterinae	11 *Carterocephalus palaemon mandan* (W.H. Edwards)	78
Hesperiinae	12 *Ancyloxypha numitor* (Fabricius)	60
	13 *Oarisma garita* (Reakirt)	69
	14 *Thymelicus lineola* (Ochsenheimer)	77
	15 *Hesperia uncas uncas* W.H. Edwards	68
	16 *Hesperia comma manitoba* (Scudder) *Hesperia comma assiniboia* (Lyman)	63
	17 *Hesperia leonardus pawnee* Dodge**	65
	18 *Hesperia pahaska pahaska* (Leussler)**	67
	19 *Hesperia nevada* (Scudder)	66
	20 *Polites rhesus* (W.H. Edwards)	75
	21 *Polites peckius* (W. Kirby)	74
	22 *Polites mystic mystic* (W.H. Edwards)	73
	23 *Polites draco* (W.H. Edwards)	72
	24 *Polites themistocles* (Latreille)	76
	25 *Atrytone logan* (W.H. Edwards)	61
	26 *Ochlodes sylvanoides napa* (W.H. Edwards)	70

HESPERIIDAE:		Page
Hesperiinae	27 *Poanes hobomok hobomok* (Harris)	71
	28 *Euphyes vestris* (Boisduval)**	62
	29 *Amblyscirtes simius* W.H. Edwards**	58
	30 *Amblyscirtes oslari* (Skinner)	57
	31 *Amblyscirtes vialis* (W.H. Edwards)	59
PAPILIONIDAE:		
Parnassiinae	32 *Parnassius clodius* Ménétriés	95
	33 *Parnassius smintheus* Doubleday	96
Papilioninae	34 *Papilio (Papilio) machaon hudsonianus* A.H. Clark *Papilio (Papilio) machaon dodi* McDunnough *Papilio (Papilio) machaon pikei* Sperling	99
	35 *Papilio (Papilio) zelicaon* Lucas	102
	36 *Papilio (Pterourus) canadensis* Rothschild & Jordan	105
	37 *Papilio (Pterourus) rutulus* Lucas**	109
	38 *Papilio (Pterourus) multicaudatus* W.F. Kirby	108
	39 *Papilio (Pterourus) eurymedon* Lucas	107
PIERIDAE:		
Pierinae	40 *Neophasia menapia menapia* (Felder & Felder)	115
	41 *Pontia sisymbrii flavitincta* (J.A. Comstock)	126
	42 *Pontia protodice* (Boisduval & Le Conte)	125
	43 *Pontia occidentalis occidentalis* (Reakirt)	123
	44 *Pieris marginalis* Scudder	117
	45 *Pieris oleracea* Harris	119
	46 *Pieris rapae* (Linnaeus)	121
Anthocharinae	47 *Euchloe ausonides mayi* (Hy. Edwards)	129
	48 *Euchloe creusa* (Doubleday)	131
	49 *Euchloe olympia* (W.H. Edwards)	132
	50 *Anthocharis sara stella* W.H. Edwards	128
Coliadinae	51 *Colias philodice* Godart	146
	52 *Colias eurytheme* Boisduval	138
	53 *Colias alexandra alexandra* W.H. Edwards	134

		Page
PIERIDAE: Coliadinae	54 *Colias christina christina* W.H. Edwards	136
	55 *Colias meadii elis* Strecker	142
	56 *Colias canadensis* Ferris	135
	57 *Colias nastes streckeri* Grum-Grschimaïlo	143
	58 *Colias palaeno chippewa* W.H. Edwards	144
	59 *Colias interior* Scudder	141
	60 *Colias pelidne skinneri* Barnes	145
	61 *Colias gigantea gigantea* Strecker *Colias gigantea harroweri* Klots	139
	62 *Zerene cesonia* (Stoll)	148
LYCAENIDAE: Lycaeninae	63 *Lycaena (Lycaena) phlaeas arethusa* (Wolley-Dod)	166
	64 *Lycaena (Lycaena) cuprea snowi* (W.H. Edwards)	165
	65 *Lycaena (Gaeides) dione* (Scudder)	163
	66 *Lycaena (Gaeides) editha* (Mead)**	162
	67 *Lycaena (Hyllolycaena) hyllus* (Cramer)	164
	68 *Lycaena (Chalceria) rubida sirius* (W.H. Edwards)	157
	69 *Lycaena (Chalceria) heteronea heteronea* Boisduval	156
	70 *Lycaena (Epidemia) dorcas dorcas* W. Kirby *Lycaena (Epidemia) dorcas florus* (W.H. Edwards)	158
	71 *Lycaena (Epidemia) helloides* (Boisduval)	159
	72 *Lycaena (Epidemia) nivalis* (Boisduval)**	161
	73 *Lycaena (Epidemia) mariposa penroseae* Field	160
Theclinae	74 *Harkenclenus titus immaculosus* (W.P. Comstock)	170
	75 *Satyrium fuliginosum semiluna* Klots	180
	76 *Satyrium acadicum montanensis* (Watson & W.P. Comstock) *Satyrium acadicum watrini* (Dufrane)	179
	77 *Satyrium sylvinum* (Boisduval)**	184
	78 *Satyrium liparops aliparops* (Michener & dos Passos) *Satyrium liparops fletcheri* (Michener & dos Passos)	181
	79 *Satyrium saepium* (Boisduval)**	183
	80 *Callophrys affinis* (W.H. Edwards)**	168
	81 *Callophrys sheridanii sheridanii* (W.H. Edwards)	169

		Page
LYCAENIDAE: Theclinae	82 *Mitoura spinetorum* (Hewitson)	178
	83 *Mitoura siva* (W.H. Edwards)**	177
	84 *Incisalia (Deciduphagus) augustinus augustinus* (Westwood)	172
	85 *Incisalia (Deciduphagus) mossii schryveri* Cross	173
	86 *Incisalia (Deciduphagus) polia obscura* Ferris & Fisher	174
	87 *Incisalia (Incisalia) niphon clarki* T.N. Freeman	176
	88 *Incisalia (Incisalia) eryphon eryphon* (Boisduval)	175
	89 *Strymon melinus franki* Field	185
Polyommatinae	90 *Everes amyntula albrighti* (Clench)	189
	91 *Celastrina ladon lucia* (W. Kirby) *Celastrina ladon nigrescens* (Fletcher)	186
	92 *Euphilotes enoptes ancilla* (Barnes & McDunnough)	188
	93 *Glaucopsyche piasus daunia* (W.H. Edwards)	193
	94 *Glaucopsyche lygdamus couperi* Grote *Glaucopsyche lygdamus oro* (Scudder)	191
	95 *Lycaeides idas* (Linnaeus)	194
	96 *Lycaeides melissa* (W.H. Edwards)	196
	97 *Plebejus (Plebejus) saepiolus amica* (W.H. Edwards)	203
	98 *Plebejus (Icaricia) icarioides* (Boisduval)	201
	99 *Plebejus (Icaricia) shasta* (W.H. Edwards)	202
	100 *Plebejus (Icaricia) acmon* (Westwood & Hewitson)	199
	101 *Plebejus (Vacciniina) optilete yukona* (Holland)	204
	102 *Plebejus (Agriades) rusticus megalo* (McDunnough) *Plebejus (Agriades) rusticus rusticus* (W.H. Edwards)	197
NYMPHALIDAE: Nymphalinae	103 *Polygonia interrogationis* (Fabricius)	222
	104 *Polygonia satyrus* (W.H. Edwards)	225
	105 *Polygonia faunus rusticus* (W.H. Edwards) *Polygonia faunus arcticus* Leussler	219
	106 *Polygonia zephyrus* (W.H. Edwards)	226
	107 *Polygonia gracilis* (Grote & Robinson)	221
	108 *Polygonia oreas silenus* (W.H. Edwards)	223
	109 *Polygonia progne* (Cramer)	224

NYMPHALIDAE: Nymphalinae	110 *Nymphalis vaualbum j-album* (Boisduval & Le Conte)	Page 218
	111 *Nymphalis californica* (Boisduval)	217
	112 *Nymphalis antiopa* (Linnaeus)	215
	113 *Aglais milberti milberti* (Godart)	214
	114 *Vanessa virginiensis* (Drury)	230
	115 *Vanessa cardui* (Linnaeus)	229
	116 *Vanessa annabella* (Field)	227
	117 *Vanessa atalanta rubria* (Fruhstorfer)	228
Argynninae	118 *Euptoieta claudia* (Cramer)	245
	119 *Speyeria cybele leto* (Behr) *Speyeria cybele pseudocarpenterii* (Chermock & Chermock)	253
	120 *Speyeria aphrodite manitoba* (Chermock & Chermock)	247
	121 *Speyeria edwardsii* (Reakirt)	254
	122 *Speyeria coronis* (Behr)**	252
	123 *Speyeria zerene garretti* (Gunder)	258
	124 *Speyeria callippe calgariana* (McDunnough) *Speyeria callippe semivirida* (McDunnough)	251
	125 *Speyeria egleis* (Behr)**	255
	126 *Speyeria atlantis hollandi* (Chermock & Chermock)	249
	127 *Speyeria electa beani* (Barnes & Benjamin) *Speyeria electa lais* (W.H. Edwards)	249
	128 *Speyeria hydaspe sakuntala* (Skinner)	256
	129 *Speyeria mormonia eurynome* (W.H. Edwards)	257
	130 *Boloria napaea alaskensis* (Holland)	243
	131 *Boloria eunomia dawsoni* (Barnes & McDunnough) *Boloria eunomia nichollae* (Barnes & Benjamin) *Boloria eunomia triclaris* (Hübner)	237
	132 *Boloria selene atrocostalis* (Huard)	244
	133 *Boloria bellona jenistae* D. Stallings & Turner	234
	134 *Boloria frigga saga* (Staudinger)	240
	135 *Boloria improba* (Butler)	241
	136 *Boloria epithore uslui* (Koçak)	236
	137 *Boloria freija freija* (Thunberg)	239
	138 *Boloria alberta* (W.H. Edwards)	232

NYMPHALIDAE Argynninae		Page
	139 *Boloria astarte astarte* (Doubleday)	233
	140 *Boloria chariclea* (Schneider)	235
	141 *Phyciodes tharos tharos* (Drury)	273
	142 *Phyciodes batesii lakota* Scott	270
	143 *Phyciodes cocyta* (Cramer)	271
	144 *Phyciodes pulchella* (Boisduval)	272
	145 *Charidryas gorgone carlota* (Reakirt)	263
	146 *Charidryas acastus* (W.H. Edwards)	261
	147 *Charidryas damoetas damoetas* (Skinner)	262
	148 *Charidryas palla* (Boisduval)	264
	149 *Euphydryas anicia anicia* (Doubleday)	265
	150 *Euphydryas editha beani* (Skinner) *Euphydryas editha hutchinsi* McDunnough	267
	151 *Euphydryas gillettii* (Barnes)	269
	152 *Limenitis (Basilarchia) archippus archippus* (Cramer)	275
	153 *Limenitis (Basilarchia) arthemis rubrofasciata* Barnes & McDunnough	276
	154 *Limenitis (Basilarchia) weidemeyerii oberfoelli* F.M. Brown	278
	155 *Limenitis (Basilarchia) lorquini burrisoni* Maynard	277
SATYRIDAE: Elymniinae	156 *Enodia anthedon borealis* A.H. Clark	283
	157 *Satyrodes eurydice eurydice* (Linnaeus in Johansson)	284
Satyrinae	158 *Neominois ridingsii minimus* Austin	310
	159 *Coenonympha inornata benjamini* McDunnough	288
	160 *Coenonympha ochracea mackenziei* Davenport	290
	161 *Cercyonis pegala ino* Hall	287
	162 *Cercyonis oetus charon* (W.H. Edwards)	285
	163 *Erebia rossi* (Curtis)**	297
	164 *Erebia disa mancinus* Doubleday	291
	165 *Erebia magdalena saxicola* Hilchie	295
	166 *Erebia discoidalis mcdunnoughi* dos Passos	293

SATYRIDAE: Satyrinae	167 *Erebia epipsodea epipsodea* Butler *Erebia epipsodea freemani* P. Ehrlich	Page 294
	168 *Erebia theano* (Tauscher)**	298
	169 *Oeneis macounii* (W.H. Edwards)	305
	170 *Oeneis chryxus chryxus* (Doubleday) *Oeneis chryxus caryi* Dyar	301
	171 *Oeneis uhleri varuna* (W.H. Edwards)	309
	172 *Oeneis alberta alberta* Elwes	299
	173 *Oeneis taygete edwardsi* dos Passos	308
	174 *Oeneis jutta chermocki* Wyatt *Oeneis jutta ridingiana* Chermock & Chermock**	303
	175 *Oeneis melissa beanii* Elwes	306
	176 *Oeneis polixenes brucei* (W.H. Edwards)	307
DANAIDAE: Danainae	177 *Danaus plexippus* (Linnaeus)	312

** Species not currently recorded from Alberta but reported from localities just outside the province.

Key to Families of Skippers and Butterflies in Alberta

If you are an experienced butterfly watcher you can probably recognize most families of butterflies in the field. If not, the following key will assist in correctly assigning your specimens to family. You will require preserved specimens in most instances since many familial characteristics are difficult to observe in the field.

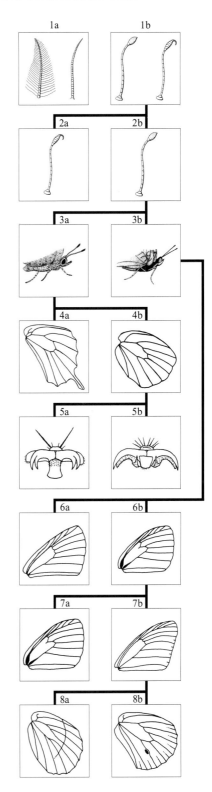

1a) Antennae threadlike or feathery, tapered at tip; typically dull coloured, nocturnal (night flying) insects although some are brightly coloured and diurnal (day flying) . . . . . . **Moths**
  b) Antennae knobbed at tip; typically bright coloured, although some are dull; diurnal . . . **Skippers and Butterflies** . . . 2

2a) Antennal knob with hook at tip; antennal bases further apart than diameter of eye; small, fast-flying insects that typically rest with fore wings and hind wings at different angles .
  . . . . **Skippers** . . . **HESPERIIDAE** p. 53
  b) Antennal knob without hook at tip; antennal bases closer together than diameter of eye; small to large insects that typically rest with fore wings and hind wings at similar angles . . .
  . . . . **Butterflies** . . . 3

3a) Fore legs of similar size to mid and hind legs, not reduced . . 4
  b) Fore legs reduced, as small as half size of hind legs 6

4a) Hind wing with one anal vein; medium species without tails or large species with hind wing tails . . . .
  . . . . **PAPILIONIDAE** p. 93
  b) Hind wing with two anal veins; medium species without tails or small species with or without tails 5

5a) Tarsal claws bifid (split in two); males or females . . . .
  . . . . **PIERIDAE** p. 111
  b) Tarsal claws normal, not bifid; females . . . .
  . . . . **LYCAENIDAE** p. 149

6a) Radius of fore wing 3 or 4 branched; males . . . .
  . . . . **LYCAENIDAE** p. 149
  b) Radius of fore wing 5 branched; males or females 7

7a) Fore wing with at least one vein swollen at base . . . .
  . . . . **SATYRIDAE** p. 279
  b) Fore wing veins normal, not swollen at base 8

8a) Hind wing discal cell open or closed by a vestigial vein; most species, if wings are red with black margins, then hind wing with median black line . . . .
  . . . . **NYMPHALIDAE** p. 205
  b) Hind wing discal cell closed by a vein; one species, wings red with black margins and hind wing without median black line . . . . **DANAIDAE** p. 311

2

Family **HESPERIIDAE**
SKIPPERS

Hesperiidae is the only family in the superfamily Hesperioidea in Alberta. Hesperiids are commonly called skippers because of their characteristic rapid, darting flight, which contrasts with the lazier flapping of true butterflies (superfamily Papilionoidea). Skippers also differ from true butterflies in having hooked tips to their antennae, antennal bases set further apart on their heads, and a resting posture in which fore wings and hind wings are held at different angles. Of the 3000 species of skippers, 26 occur in Alberta, most in the subfamily Hesperiinae. Hesperiine caterpillars feed mainly on grasses, while those of the other major subfamily, Pyrginae, usually eat leaves from trees or legumes.

Subfamily
HESPERIINAE
BRANDED SKIPPERS

Members of the skipper subfamily Hesperiinae are commonly called branded skippers because of the patch, or "brand," of specialized scented scales that males bear on their fore wings. Most hesperiines are brown or tawny yellow, and their larvae feed on grasses. There are 17 species known to occur in Alberta and four whose current ranges suggest that individuals may occasionally stray into our province.

Prairie region of Alberta, view across the Red Deer River with the Hand Hills in background.   F.A.H. Sperling.

Key to Species of Hesperiidae in Alberta

(** Species marked with a double asterisk are not recorded for Alberta, but have been found just outside the province.)

1a) Wings checkered, black and white 2

b) Wing colour variable, brown, orange gray; if black with a few white spots, then not checkered 5

2a) Pattern with more white than black, fore wing white spots elongate . . . . *Pyrgus communis* (Grote) p. 89

b) Pattern with more black than white, fore wing white spots squarish 3

3a) Dorsal hind wing with two rows of white spots, ventral hind wing reddish brown . . . *Pyrgus ruralis* (Boisduval) p. 90

b) Dorsal hind wing with few spots, ventral hind wing pale . . . 4

4a) Larger, wingspan 25 - 30 mm, ventral hind wing with two irregular dark bands . . . . *Pyrgus centaureae* (Rambur) p. 87

b) Smaller, wingspan 16 - 24 mm, bands on ventral hind wing more regular, not contrasting with ground colour, uncommon in Alberta . . . . *Pyrgus scriptura* (Boisduval) p. 91

5a) Ventral hind wing with large silver patch, fore wing with orange patch . . . . *Epargyreus clarus* (Cramer) p. 80

b) Hind wing lacking silver patch 6

6a) Wing colour dark gray, brown or black, not orange, often with pale or white markings 7

b) Wing colour yellow, orange, or silvery, variously marked . 15

7a) Ventral hind wing veins outlined in white markings . . . . *Polites rhesus* (W.H. Edwards) p. 75

b) Ventral hind wing veins not contrasting with background colour 8

8a) Ventral hind wing with two wavy dark brown bands . . . . *Thorybes pylades* (Scudder) p. 92

b) Ventral hind wing marked with dots, or uniform colour . . . 9

9a) Ventral hind wing with two or more rows of pale spots . . . 10

b) Ventral hind wing uniform colour 12

10a) Dorsal fore wing without or with one or two small indistinct subapical white spots . . . . *Erynnis icelus* (Scudder & Burgess) p. 83

b) Dorsal fore wing with several distinct subapical white spots 11

11a) Dorsally, wings brownish, uniform colour . . . .
. . . . *Erynnis afranius* (Lintner) p. 82

b) Dorsally, wings two-toned, fore wing dark gray-brown, hind wing
dark brown . . . . *Erynnis persius* (Scudder) p. 84

12a) Dorsal fore wing with white dots 13

b) Dorsal fore wing without white dots 14

13a) Fore wing white dots limited to a few small dots; checkered
fringes; ventral hind wing purplish gray; fore wing pointed
. . . . *Amblyscirtes vialis* (W.H. Edwards) p. 59

b) Fore wing white dots in rows; fringes uniformly coloured;
ventral hind wing dark brown; fore wing rounded . . . . .
. . . . *Pholisora catullus* (Fabricius)** p. 86

14a) Uniformly dark brown except apical fore wing of female with
few white spots, male fore wing stigma black . . . .
. . . . *Euphyes vestris* (Boisduval)** p. 62

b) Smaller; fore wings pointed, light brown; ventral hind wing
pale banded and grayish overscaling. . . . .
. . . . *Amblyscirtes oslari* (Skinner) p. 57

15a) Ventral hind wing with a light-coloured band or angular spots
. . . . 16

b) Ventral hind wing marked otherwise, without angular spots
(round spots, patches or no markings) 23

16a) Ventral hind wing with a light-coloured band, sometimes faint
. . . . 17

b) Ventral hind wing with a row of angular spots 18

17a) Dark border on dorsal fore wing with indistinct gradual transition
to orange area . . . . . *Polites mystic* (W.H. Edwards) p. 73

b) Dark border on dorsal fore wing with distinct abrupt, scalloped
boundary with orange area . . . .
. . . . *Ochlodes sylvanoides* (Boisduval) p. 70

18a) Ventral hind wing with elongate spot about three times longer
than other spots in the row . . . .
. . . . *Polites draco* (W.H. Edwards) p. 72

b) Ventral hind wing without elongate spot 19

19a) Ventral hind wing with white veins . . . .
. . . . *Hesperia uncas* W.H. Edwards p. 68

b) Ventral hind wing without white veins 20

20a) Ventral hind wing with the most anal spot offset inwards from
the rest. . . . . *Hesperia nevada* (Scudder) p. 66

b) Ventral hind wing with spot in line 21

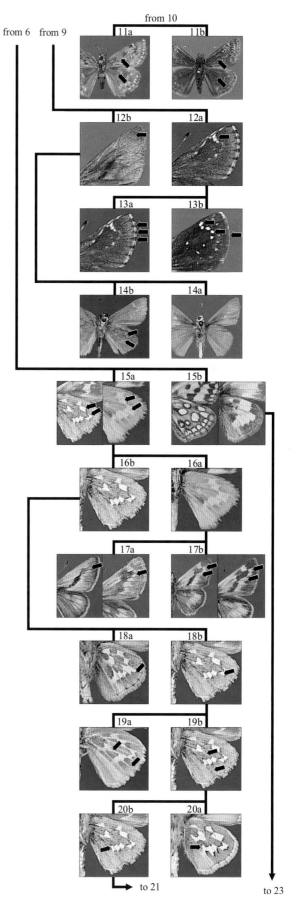

55

from 15   from 20

21a) Ventral hind wing yellowish or yellowish green . . . .
. . . . *Hesperia comma assiniboia* (Lyman) p. 63
   b) Ventral hind wing brown or greenish brown 22

22a) Ventral hind wing anal area green or greenish brown . . . .
. . . . *Hesperia comma manitoba* (Scudder) p. 63
   b) Ventral hind wing anal area yellowish orange . . . .
. . . . *Hesperia pahaska* (Leussler)** p. 67

23a) Ventral hind wing with markings (patches, lines) 24
   b) Ventral hind wing unmarked 28

24a) Ventral hind wing with a large yellow patch 25
   b) Ventral hind wing marked otherwise 26

25a) Ventral hind wing yellow patch single . . . .
. . . . *Poanes hobomok* (Harris) p. 71
   b) Ventral hind wing yellow patch double . . . .
. . . . *Polites peckius* (Kirby) p. 74

26a) Ventral hind wing with pale rounded spots . . . .
. . . . *Carterocephalus palaemon* (Pallas) p. 78
   b) Ventral hind wing brownish yellow with whitish veins or grayish
with faint to prominent white submarginal band 27

27a) Ventral hind wing brownish yellow with whitish veins . . . . . .
. . . . *Oarisma garita* (Reakirt) p. 69
   b) Ventral hind wing gray with faint orange to prominent white
submarginal band . . . .
. . . . *Amblyscirtes simius* W.H. Edwards** p. 58

28a) Dorsal fore wing at least one-half brown 29
   b) Dorsal fore wing orange, margins may be brown 31

29a) Ventral hind wing brown . . . .
. . . . *Polites themistocles* (Latreille) p. 76
   b) Ventral hind wing orange or yellowish orange 30

30a) Smaller; fore wing rounded; ventral hind wing orange . . . . . .
. . . . *Ancyloxypha numitor* (Fabricius) p. 60
   b) Larger; fore wing pointed; ventral hind wing yellowish orange
with indistinct pale submarginal spots sometimes present
. . . . *Hesperia leonardus* Dodge** p. 65

31a) Larger, wingspan 25-35 mm; dorsal fore wing with a dark line
along the distal margin of the discal cell . . . .
. . . . *Atrytone logan* (W.H. Edwards) p. 61
   b) Smaller, wingspan 23-27 mm; dorsal fore wing lacking the
darkened area along the distal margin of the discal cell .
. . . . *Thymelicus lineola* (Ochsenheimer) p. 77

Amblyscirtes Scudder, [1871]
ROADSIDE SKIPPERS

Etymology. The name is possibly from the Greek *amblysko* meaning "misbegotten," or from *ambl* = "blunt" + *skirtao* = "leap," perhaps referring to flight behaviour.

Amblyscirtes oslari (Skinner, 1899)
Oslar's Roadside Skipper

Etymology. The species is named after the collector of the type specimens, E.J. Oslar.

Identification. This is a plain, nondescript, brown skipper with a wingspan of 26-29 mm. Its general appearance is similar to the Dun Skipper, *Euphyes vestris* from which it can be separated by a smaller black spot on the dorsal fore wing, gray overscaling on the ventral surface, subtly checkered wing fringes and smaller size.

Life History. The eggs are white and laid on the underside (shaded) surface of grass leaves. The eggs are slightly oval in dorsal view and hemispherical in lateral view. There is one brood per year. First instar larvae are creamy yellow and turn greenish yellow after feeding. The head and collar are black. Mature larvae are light yellow-green and overwinter, with pupation occurring in the spring. It is suspected that the larvae feed on Blue Grama Grass (*Bouteloua gracilis*) in Alberta and they have been found on *B. curtipendula* in Colorado. Adults have been collected in Alberta from June 7 to 17. As more individuals are recorded, it is expected that the flight period will extend from late May to late June. Males perch on rocks at the bottoms of ravines and coulees. As with most perching species, males leave their perches to investigate passing objects for prospective mates. This skipper seldom visits flowers.

Range and Habitat. Oslar's Roadside Skipper is found in southern Alberta and Saskatchewan, south to Arizona and Texas. In Alberta, this skipper is known from the Pinhorn Grazing Reserve, near Writing-on-Stone Provincial Park, and Lethbridge, and is associated with ravines and narrow coulees.

Amblyscirtes oslari
Male dorsal

Amblyscirtes oslari
Male ventral

Apr May Jun Jul Aug Sep Oct

Edmonton

Calgary

Amblyscirtes simius W.H. Edwards, 1881a
Simius Roadside Skipper

Amblyscirtes simius
Male dorsal

Amblyscirtes simius
Male ventral

Etymology. *Simius* is from the Greek *simos* meaning "snub-nosed."

Identification. Both Burns (1990) and Scott (1992) have documented substantial genus-level differences between *simius* and other *Amblyscirtes*. It is clearly not an *Amblyscirtes* but a better generic home is not available, so it is left in this genus for the purposes of this book. Unlike other members of this genus known to occur in Alberta, *Amblyscirtes simius* has discal markings and slight, to extensive, dark yellow to yellow-orange overscaling. This contrasts markedly with the nearly black appearance of *Amblyscirtes vialis* and *Amblyscirtes oslari.*

Life History. Eggs are laid on the underside of Blue Grama Grass (*Bouteloua gracilis*) leaves, which are eatern by the larvae. Eggs are slightly yellowish cream when laid but develop two red rings after a few days . First instar larvae diapause and overwinter before feeding. They are yellow-cream while mature larvae are light blue-green. Adults are reported to fly from May to June (June in Saskatchewan). Mating occurs on high ground where the males tend to perch, usually early and late in the day.

Range and Habitat. *Amblyscirtes simius* occurs on short grass prairie, ranging from Mexico through the Great Plains to southern Saskatchewan (e.g., Rosefield, Frenchman River Valley). The probability of occurrence in Alberta is low. This skipper should be watched for in southeastern Alberta where Blue Grama Grass is abundant.

Amblyscirtes vialis (W.H. Edwards, 1862)
Roadside Skipper

Etymology. The species name is derived from the Latin *via* meaning "road."

Identification. This small species (wingspan 22-25 mm), with its diagnostic dark gray colour and small white spots at the fore wing apex, should not be confused with any other Alberta skipper.

Life History. The eggs are round and white, turning slightly cream after a few days. First instar larvae are yellow-cream; mature larvae are pale green with a dull white head. Mature, fully fed larvae overwinter. The pupae are mainly green with small red and yellow anterior patches. Larval hosts are reported to include many species of grasses, such as bluegrass (*Poa* spp.*)*, oats *(Avena* spp.*)* and bent grass *(Agrostis* spp.*)*. Adults have been found from May 22 through July 11, and are most abundant in early June. Compared to other skippers, Roadside Skippers fly low to the ground with a weaker flight pattern. Males perch on low vegetation and spend much time close to the ground.

Range and Habitat. This skipper is found from Florida and California north to southern Canada. In Alberta it occurs in most regions except the mountains north of the Crowsnest Pass. The Roadside Skipper is found in poplar forests and clearings, including the riparian forests along prairie rivers.

Amblyscirtes vialis
Male dorsal

Amblyscirtes vialis
Male ventral

Agrostis stolonifera
Bent Grass or Redtop

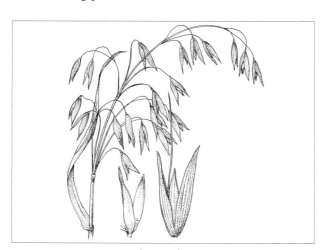

Avena sativa
Oats

Ancyloxypha Felder, 1862

Etymology. *Ancyloxypha* is derived from the Greek words *ankylos* meaning "curved" or "hooked" and *xiphos* meaning "sword."

Ancyloxypha numitor (Fabricius, 1793)
Least Skipper

Zea mays
Cultivated Corn

Ancyloxypha numitor
Male dorsal

Ancyloxypha numitor
Male ventral

Etymology. The specific epithet numitor is derived from Roman myth. Numitor was king of Alba, and grandfather of Romulus and Remus.

Identification. The Least Skipper is small (wingspan 19-25 mm) with distinctive two-toned wings. The dorsal wing surface is dark brown with an orange centre on the hind wings. There is often a small patch of orange on the fore wings. The ventral sides of the fore wings are black and the hind wings are orange.

Life History. Freshly laid eggs are bright yellow but soon develop an orange-red band around the middle. Mature caterpillars are grass-green with dark brown heads. The pupae are cream-coloured with brown lines and patches. Larvae feed on a variety of grasses, often aquatic to semi-aquatic species. Some of these are bluegrass *Poa* spp.), southern wild rice (*Zizaniopsis* spp.), cutgrass (*Leersia* spp.) and Corn (*Zea mays*). The major flight period is expected to be in July; the only Alberta record is July 3. Males are reported to patrol slowly near or above grassy areas. Adults nectar at low plants with small flowers.

Range and Habitat. The Least Skipper ranges from Nova Scotia west to southern Alberta and south to Florida and Texas. The sole Alberta record is from Lethbridge in 1909. This skipper should be watched for along wet grassy areas near standing or slowly moving water.

Atrytone Scudder, [1871]

Etymology. Atrytone is the Greek word for the Roman warrior-goddess, Minerva.

Atrytone logan (W.H. Edwards, 1863b)
Delaware Skipper

Etymology. The derivation of the species name is unknown.

Identification. The Delaware Skipper has a wingspan of 25-35 mm and is bright orange above with narrow black margins and dark veins. The underside is bright yellow except that the fore wing is black at the base and along the lower margin. Alberta specimens show characteristics of the eastern (nominate) subspecies and the southwestern subspecies (*lagus*) as well as intermediate characteristics (Thormin, Kondla and Bird 1980). Contemporary works place *logan* in the genus *Atrytone* but Burns (1994) suggests that it is properly placed in *Anatrytone*.

Life History. There is one brood per year. Eggs are hemispherical, with two red rings, and are laid on grass blades. Mature larvae have light bluish green bodies with minute black tubercles. A crescent-shaped band occurs on the posterior segments of the caterpillars. The head is white with a black marginal band and three vertical lines on the front. Pupae are black with greenish areas. A variety of grasses are utilized as food plants including panic grass (*Panicum* spp.) and *Schizachyrium*. In Alberta, adults have been found from May 5 to August 7, with most observations in early July. Half-grown larvae overwinter. Males perch, often on buckbrush (*Symphoricarpos* spp.). Adults nectar on milkweed (*Asclepias* spp.), thistles (*Cirsium* spp.) and Skeleton-weed or Prairie Pink (*Lygodesmia juncea*).

Range and Habitat. The Delaware Skipper occurs from Maine in the northeast and Florida in the southeast, west to northeastern New Mexico and southeastern Alberta. This skipper is known from the southeast corner of the province northwest to Drumheller and west to Lethbridge. It is found in shrubby ravines, coulees and along stream margins.

Atrytone logan
Male dorsal

Atrytone logan
Male ventral

Atrytone logan
Female dorsal

Atrytone logan
Female ventral

Apr May Jun Jul Aug Sep Oct

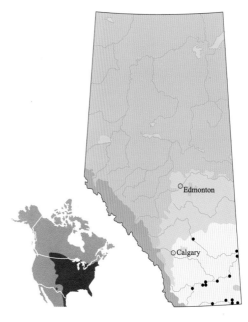

Edmonton

Calgary

61

Euphyes Scudder, [1871]

Etymology. The name is derived from Euphues or the anatomy of wit, a literary work by Jon Lyly, published around 1578 or 1579.

Euphyes vestris (Boisduval, 1852)
Dun Skipper

Euphyes vestris
Male dorsal

Euphyes vestris
Male ventral

Etymology. The species epithet appears to be derived from the Latin *vestis*, meaning "a covering."

Identification. This skipper has uniform brown wings and head.

Life History. Oviposition is reported on several species of sedge (*Carex* spp.). The eggs are pale green and hemispherical in shape. The mature larvae are pale whitish green with horizontal marks. The light brown head has a black spot in the centre and two light-coloured vertical bands. The pupae are pale with a whitish dusting. Pupation occurs in a silk-lined tube near the host plant. The mature larvae overwinter.

Range and Habitat. The Dun Skipper is found in moist areas and open woods of eastern North America from southern Saskatchewan and Montana to the Gulf of Mexico, and in the mountains from southern British Columbia to northern California.

Carex douglasii
Douglas sedge

Hesperia Fabricius, 1793

Etymology. The name refers to Hesperia , who, in Greek mythology, was the daughter of the river god Kebren.

Hesperia comma (Linnaeus, 1758)
Common Branded Skipper
subspecies: *Hesperia comma assiniboia* (Lyman, 1892)
Hesperia comma manitoba (Scudder, 1874)

Etymology. The species name may refer to the comma-shaped marking on the fore wing of the male. The subspecies names were derived from geographic districts of western Canada, with *assiniboia* recognizing the district of Assiniboia, formerly a part of the Northwest Territories, while *manitoba* refers to the province of Manitoba.

Identification. The Common Branded Skipper is medium-sized with a wingspan of 27-30 mm. Its wings are orange above with dark outer margins. Males have a prominent black stigma. There are fourteen named subspecies in the *Hesperia comma* complex in North America. This is unsatisfactory as clearly some or many of these subspecies are distinct species. They are treated as subspecies here for consistency with contemporary literature. *Assiniboia* and *manitoba* are likely distinct species on the basis of unequivocal differences in phenotype, phenology, distribution and habitat. In Alberta there are phenotypes of both subspecies represented. In *H. c. manitoba* the ventral hind wing is dark greenish brown. In contrast, *H. c. assiniboia* is more variable, with the ventral hind wing colour ranging from yellowish to grayish green. The band of spots on the ventral hind wing varies from a few spots to almost continuous. Populations in the Peace River area are yellowish orange on the ventral hind wing and lack silver patches.

Life History. There is one brood per year, the eggs overwinter. Eggs are hemispherical and whitish or pinkish. Early instar caterpillars are cream-coloured with dark heads, while later instars turn dull green. Larvae are reported to feed on a wide variety of grasses primarily spear grass, porcupine grass, needle grass (*Stipa* spp.), fescue (*Festuca* spp.), brome grass (*Bromus* spp.) and grama grass (*Bouteloua* spp.). The pupae are green or brown.

Hesperia comma assiniboia
Male dorsal

Hesperia comma assiniboia
Male ventral

Hesperia comma assiniboia
Female dorsal

Hesperia comma assiniboia
Female ventral

Hesperia comma manitoba
Male dorsal

Hesperia comma manitoba
Male ventral

Hesperia comma manitoba
Female dorsal

Hesperia comma manitoba
Female ventral

Bromus tectorum
Downy Chess

Adults nectar on a variety of flowers with Dotted Blazing-star (*Liatris punctata*) and *Aster canescens* serving as frequent nectar sources in prairie regions, while *Senecio* and *Aster* are visited in the mountains. Males mostly perch or fly between nectar sources. The flight period of *H. c. manitoba* is June 4 to September 19, but peaks in July and early August. *H. c. assiniboia* adults have been observed from July 29 through September 30, with peak flights during August and early September. Mountain populations fly only in even-numbered years.

Range and Habitat. The Common Branded Skipper is found from Labrador to Alaska and south to New England states, western Texas and Baja California. In Alberta, *H. c. manitoba* is essentially a mountain creature, with an isolated record from Fort Chipewyan, whereas *H. c. assiniboia* is found throughout the prairie grasslands and more locally in the aspen parklands north to the boreal forest near Redwater. Isolated populations occur in the Peace River region, mostly along the Peace River. Adults of *H. c. manitoba* are found in mountain meadows, along roads and other clearings at elevations below treeline. Adults of *H. c. assiniboia* occur in prairies, grassy valley sides, aspen parkland and sand dune areas in the boreal forest.

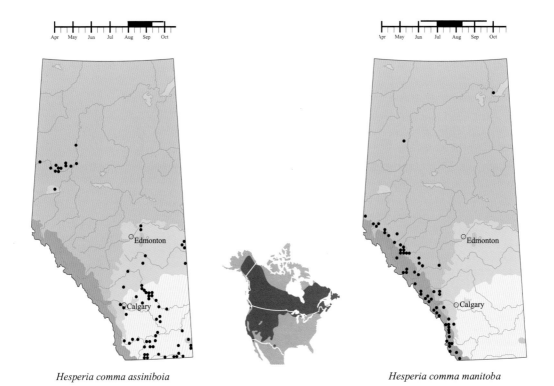

Hesperia comma assiniboia

Hesperia comma manitoba

Hesperia leonardus (Harris, 1862)
Leonard's Skipper
subspecies: *Hesperia leonardus pawnee* Dodge, 1874

Etymology. The species is named in honour of the Reverend L.W. Leonard of New Hampshire, a correspondent of the author. *Pawnee* may refer to an American Indian tribe.

Identification. Leonard's Skipper is slightly larger on the average than most Alberta *Hesperia* species. Males are tawny yellow with few spots or markings on the ventral hind wing. The stigma is large with yellow androconial scales in the centre. Females are darker with well developed ventral hind wing spots.

Life History. The larvae are grass feeders, readily using lawn grasses; it is expected that Blue Grama Grass (*Bouteloua gracilis*) is this skipper's natural host, as oviposition has been reported on this species. In Montana, it flies from mid-July to September.

Range and Habitat. Leonard's Skipper ranges from eastern Canada and the United States west into Saskatchewan and the Rocky Mountain States. The probability of occurrence in Alberta is moderate. It should be watched for in the grasslands of the southeastern corner of the province.

Hesperia leonardus
Male dorsal

Hesperia leonardus
Male ventral

Hesperia leonardus
Female dorsal

Hesperia leonardus
Female ventral

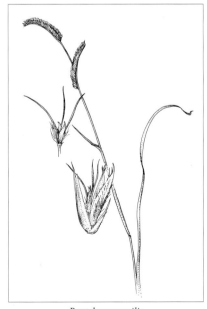

Bouteloua gracilis
Blue Grama Grass

Hesperia nevada (Scudder, 1874)
Nevada Skipper

Hesperia nevada
Male dorsal

Hesperia nevada
Male ventral

Hesperia nevada
Female dorsal

Hesperia nevada
Female ventral

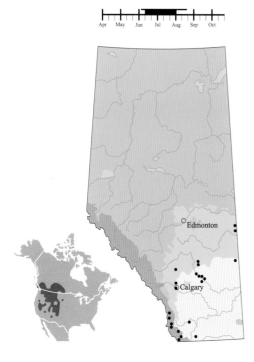

Etymology. The species was either named after the state of Nevada or the Spanish word *nevada* meaning "snow clad."

Identification. The Nevada Skipper has a wingspan of 25-34 mm and is bright tawny orange dorsally with a sharply defined dark border. The ventral hind wing is gray-green. A distinctive feature of the Nevada Skipper is the anterior silver spot which is displaced inwardly relative to the other spots on the ventral hind wing.

Life History. There is one brood per year. The eggs are dull white. Mature caterpillars are olive-coloured and have dark heads with cream marks. Several species of grasses are reported as larval hosts: needle grass, spear grass, porcupine grass (*Stipa* spp.), fescue (*Festuca* spp.) and june grass (*Koeleria* spp.). In Colorado, eggs have been found on *Festuca saximontana*, *Koeleria macrantha* and *Stipa comata*. Oviposition on has been observed on squirreltail (*Sitanion* spp.). Eggs are laid 2-4 cm above the ground on the underside of leaves. First stage larvae are yellowish cream. Adults have been found from June 4 to August 17, with most flight records occurring in the latter part of June and throughout July. Males perch, often on ridges and hilltops.

Range and Habitat. The Nevada Skipper occurs from southern British Columbia, Alberta and Saskatchewan south to Nevada, northern Arizona and New Mexico. Its distribution in Alberta coincides with the southern aspen parkland, mountains and foothills. This skipper is found in fescue grassland and in aspen parkland and foothills, often on ridge tops and hillsides. It can also be found in low elevation grasslands of the mountains.

Hesperia pahaska (Leussler, 1938)
Pahaska Skipper
subspecies: *Hesperia pahaska pahaska* (Leussler, 1938)

Etymology. *Pahaska* may be a word of American Indian origin.

Identification. The Pahaska Skipper is tawny orange dorsally with narrow brown borders on the wings. Markings are variable, but ventrally the ground colour is greenish to brown with well developed spots on the hind wing. Males have a long black stigma with yellow androconial scales in the centre. In females, the brown border margins on the fore wing are indistinct.

Life History. Oviposition has been observed on Blue Grama Grass (*Bouteloua gracilis*) in Colorado, and larvae are reported to feed on *Bouteloua gracilis* and *Tridens pulchella.* The flight period is from mid-June through early July in Montana, and late June in Saskatchewan. MacNeill (1964) refers to a single individual with "Banf" given as the collection locality. It is highly likely that the specimen was mislabelled or that the name refers to a place other than Banff, Alberta as *Bouteloua gracilis*, the reported larval host plant, does not occur in the Banff area.

Range and Habitat. The Pahaska Skipper is found through the Great Basin mountain areas and onto the Great Plains, ranging north into northern Montana (Hill County) and southern Saskatchewan (Rosefield, Frenchman River Valley.) The probability of occurrence in Alberta is moderate. This skipper should be watched for along sparsely vegetated slopes and valleys, especially in the Milk River Basin in southern Alberta.

Hesperia pahaska
Female dorsal

Hesperia pahaska
Female ventral

Milk River near Writing-on-Stone Provincial Park.

T.W. Thormin.

Hesperia uncas W.H. Edwards, 1863b
Uncas Skipper
subspecies: *Hesperia uncas uncas* W.H. Edwards, 1863b

Hesperia uncas
Male dorsal

Hesperia uncas
Male ventral

Hesperia uncas
Female dorsal

Hesperia uncas
Female ventral

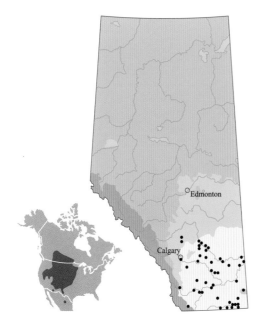

Etymology. The specific epithet appears derived from the Latin *uncas* which means "hooked" or "crooked."

Identification. The general appearance of the Uncas Skipper is similar to that of the other *Hesperia* in Alberta, but it is larger, with a wingspan of 25-41 mm. It has a different maculation pattern on the ventral hind wing with pronounced white spots, interconnected with white veins against a background of gray-green and dark areas.

Life History. There are two broods per year. The eggs are cream-coloured. First instar larvae are cream-coloured with a black head. Mature larvae are brownish gray on the thorax and dorsal body; ventrally they are grayish tan. Known food plants include species of grama grass (*Bouteloua* spp.) and spear, porcupine or needle grass (*Stipa* spp.). Other grasses are expected as host plants. In Alberta, adults have been found from May 22 to August 20, but are most common in the June and August.

Range and Habitat. The Uncas Skipper ranges from southern Alberta and Saskatchewan south through the western United States (except Washington). In Alberta it has been reported through the prairies north to Olds. It frequents mixed grass prairie and valleys and coulees in the drier regions. Hilltops and crests with very short grass appear to be favoured areas. This skipper sits on rocks and flies with *H. nevada* and *H. comma assiniboia*.

Stipa comata
Needle-and-thread or Spear Grass

68

Oarisma Scudder, [1871]

Etymology. The Greek word *oarisma* means "familiar discourse" or "loving conversation."

Oarisma garita (Reakirt, 1866)
Garita Skipper

Etymology. The species epithet *garita* may be derived from La Garita Mountains of southwestern Colorado, or from the Greek *garrio* meaning "to chatter or babble."

Identification. The Garita Skipper is small with a wing-span of 19-25 mm. Dorsally it is dark brown with a bronze sheen. The ventral fore wing is mostly bronze-orange and the hind wing bears a large greenish area with light-coloured veins.

Life History. There is a single brood per year. The eggs are green. Larvae do not make silk nests, which is unusual in the Hesperiidae. First instar larvae, after feeding, are green with white and whitish green lines and bands. Presumably these stripes help camouflage the larvae. They overwinter as half-grown larvae. The mature caterpillars are green with one white line on the back and three on each side. Many grasses are used as hosts, including Kentucky Bluegrass (*Poa pratensis*). Adults have been found from June 3 through July 28 with peak abundance occurring in late June and early July. Males patrol for females in grassland habitat and also perch and defend territories. We have no records of flower visitation.

Range and Habitat. The Garita Skipper ranges from southern British Columbia, central Alberta and southern Manitoba, south to northern Arizona and New Mexico. In Alberta, this skipper occurs throughout the prairies, southern mountains and aspen parklands. A northern population occurs in the Peace River District. The Garita Skipper inhabits a wide variety of grasslands and meadows including low elevation grasslands and mountain meadows, but is most abundant in fescue and mixed grass prairies. It is uncommon in the more arid grasslands.

Oarisma garita
Male dorsal

Oarisma garita
Male ventral

Poa pratensis
Kentucky Bluegrass

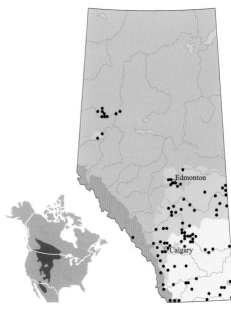

Ochlodes Scudder, [1871]

Etymology. From Greek *ochlodes*, meaning "turbulent, unruly."

Ochlodes sylvanoides (Boisduval, 1852)
Woodland Skipper
subspecies: *Ochlodes sylvanoides napa* (W.H. Edwards, 1865)

Ochlodes sylvanoides napa
Male dorsal

Ochlodes sylvanoides napa
Male ventral

Ochlodes sylvanoides napa
Female dorsal

Ochlodes sylvanoides napa
Female ventral

Etymology. The species name is perhaps derived from the Latin word *sylva* meaning "woods" or "forest." The subspecies may refer to the Greek *nape*, a "woody dell."

Identification. The Woodland Skipper is medium-sized with a wingspan of 20-28 mm. It is bright yellow-orange, especially on the ventral surface. Its appearance is similar to that of *Polites mystic*, but the dark border of the dorsal fore wings is sharply contrasting and toothed in *Ochlodes sylvanoides* but diffuse and not toothed in *Polites mystic*.

Life History. There is one brood per year. The pupae are yellow-tan with a light grayish hue. Unfed first instar larvae overwinter. First instar larvae are cream with a black head. Third instar larvae are green. Fourth instar are a dull grayish cream and mature larvae are dull yellow-tan with a greenish tinge and two dark bands. Larvae are reported to eat a variety of broad-leaved grasses. In Alberta, adults have been found from July 31 through September 7, with peak activity occurring about the second week of August. Adults nectar avidly. Males spend a good deal of time perching on vegetation in depressions.

Range and Habitat. *Ochlodes sylvanoides* is known from southern British Columbia south to Baja California and east into southern Alberta, South Dakota and Colorado. In Alberta it ranges from the extreme southern edge of the province north to Beaver Mines Lake. This butterfly has been found in riparian shrubbery, sagebrush slopes and prairie grassland along the Milk River. In the foothills and mountains, grassy areas appear to be its preferred habitat.

Poanes Scudder, [1871]

Etymology. Probably from the Greek *poa*, meaning "a grassy place."

Poanes hobomok (Harris, 1862)
Hobomok Skipper
subspecies: *Poanes hobomok hobomok* (Harris, 1862)

Etymology. The species is named in honour of Chief Hobomok, of the Wampanoag Indians, who helped the English when they landed at Plymouth in 1621.

Identification. A medium-sized skipper (wingspan 25-35 mm) with light orange, brown-bordered dorsal wing surfaces. Females have less orange above and a more extensive dark area at the base of the fore wing. The ventral surface of the wings has a purplish gray border that helps distinguish this species from the more wide-spread Peck's Skipper (*Polites peckius*).

Life History. There is one brood per year. The caterpillars are dark green or brown with short dark spines and a dark head. They are known to feed on several types of grasses including panic grass (*Panicum* spp.) and bluegrass (*Poa* spp.). Either the larvae or pupae overwinter. Adults have been found on the wing on June 5 and 13, although further research will probably show a flight period from late May to early July. Males are reported to perch on vegetation in clearings. Adults are known to nectar on various flowers including fleabane (*Erigeron* spp.) and can be seen flying along road margins and trails through the woods.

Range and Habitat. The Hobomok Skipper is known from Nova Scotia in the northeast and Arkansas in the southeast, west to east-central Alberta and New Mexico. In Alberta, it is known only from the vicinities of Elk Point and Cold Lake. This species is found in clearings and along edges of poplar forests.

Poanes hobomok
Male dorsal

Poanes hobomok
Male ventral

Poanes hobomok
Female dorsal

Poanes hobomok
Female ventral

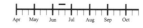

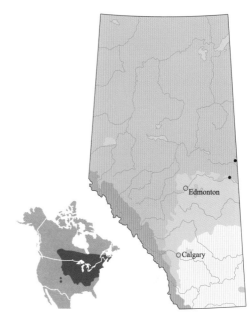

71

Polites Scudder, [1871]

Etymology. In Greek, *polites* means "citizen"; hence the species name may simply mean "native" or perhaps "common to the area."

Polites draco (W.H. Edwards, 1871)
Draco Skipper

Polites draco
Male dorsal

Polites draco
Male ventral

Polites draco
Female dorsal

Polites draco
Female ventral

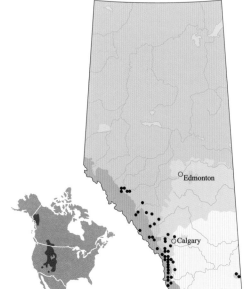

Etymology. The species name could be derived from the Latin *draco* which means dragon. Alternately, Draco was an Athenian lawgiver. The original description does not give any clues to the derivation of the name.

Identification. The Draco Skipper is medium-sized, with a wingspan of 22-26 mm, and is distinguished by an irregularly shaped band of cream patches on the predominately brownish ventral hind wing. The middle cream patch is about three times longer than the other patches. Dorsally, males are orange with a black spot by the stigma (scent patch). Females are mostly brown dorsally with only a trace of orange.

Life History. There is one brood per year. The eggs are pale green and have been found on fescue *(Festuca* spp.) and *Koeleria macrantha* in Colorado. Larvae have been reared on Kentucky Bluegrass *(Poa pratensis)*. First instar larvae are cream when newly hatched, but soon become covered with hundreds of tiny, brown spots imparting a tan appearance to the body. Second instar larvae are brown. Mature larvae are dark brown with a mid-dorsal blackish brown band. Males perch on the ground and on herbs, waiting for females. Adults have been found on the wing from June 5 to August 6.

Range and Habitat. The Draco Skipper occurs primarily in the Rocky Mountains but there is a disjunct population in southwestern Yukon Territory. In Alberta this skipper is known from the Cypress Hills and the mountain foothills region north to Prospect Mountain. The Draco Skipper is found in foothills grasslands and forest openings. It is most abundant in small pockets of grassland along valley floors.

Polites mystic (W.H. Edwards, 1863a)
Long Dash Skipper
subspecies: *Polites mystic mystic* (W.H. Edwards, 1863a)

Etymology. The name is derived from the Greek *mystikos* meaning "mysterious, mystical."

Identification. A medium-sized skipper with a wing-span of 22-30 mm. Females are substantially larger than males and are orange and brown dorsally. On the males' wing, the black stigma (scent patch) joins a black line near the wing tip resulting in the long dash that gives the species its common name. The ventral wing surface is yellow-orange with a faint yellow band across the middle of the hind wing.

Life History. There is one brood per year. The eggs are greenish white to pale yellow-green. Mature caterpillars are brown except for middorsal blackish brown line and black head. *Agrostis gigantea*, Kentucky Bluegrass (*Poa pratensis)* and *Poa agassizensis* are the only confirmed hosts. Half grown larvae overwinter. Males spend much of their time perching on low vegetation. Adults have been found from May 24 to August 21.

Range and Habitat. The Long Dash Skipper ranges from the Maritimes across southern Canada through to British Columbia and south to Colorado and Virginia. In Alberta it has been found through most of the province north to Fort Vermilion. The Long Dash Skipper is most frequently found in the aspen parkland and prairie areas, along road sides, weedy areas and in meadows.

Polites mystic
Male dorsal

Polites mystic
Male ventral

Polites mystic
Female dorsal

Polites mystic
Female ventral

Cordilleran region of Alberta, Waterton Lakes National Park.

F.A.H. Sperling.

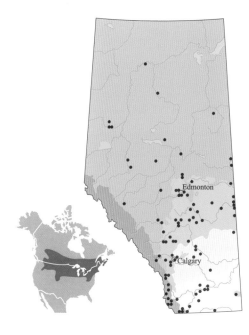

73

Polites peckius (W. Kirby, 1837)
Peck's Skipper

Polites peckius
Male dorsal

Polites peckius
Male ventral

Polites peckius
Female dorsal

Polites peckius
Female ventral

Etymology. The species name is probably an honorific.

Identification. This medium-sized skipper has a wing-span of 20-26 mm. The distinguishing feature is a large yellow patch on the ventral hind wing that is delineated by sharply contrasting edges. Males have a black scent patch (stigma) along the leading edge of the fore wing. Females are darker.

Life History. There is one brood per year. Females let eggs drop from the abdomen, as does *P. mystic*. The eggs are hemispherical in shape and light greenish white to cream. First instar larvae are cream after hatching. Mature caterpillars are maroon brown with a dark dorsal stripe and light brown mottling and have a black head. Many species of grasses serve as larval food plants, including common lawn grasses. The pupae are mostly reddish purple. The larvae or pupae overwinter. Males spend much of their time perching in wait for females and are seen frequently on city lawns and in parks. Adults have been found from June 5 to August 23.

Range and Habitat. This species has a widespread distribution from Labrador south to Georgia, west to Arizona and southern British Columbia, and north to northeastern Alberta. In Alberta Peck's Skipper has been found in most regions, but with only a few records north of Edmonton. It occurs in grassy and weedy areas, primarily in the aspen parklands and prairie regions.

Apr May Jun Jul Aug Sep Oct

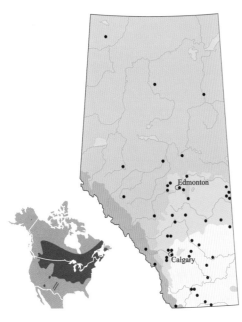

Red Deer River valley, Nacmine, Alberta.　　　F.A.H. Sperling.

Polites rhesus (W.H. Edwards, 1878)
Rhesus Skipper

Etymology. Rhesus was a Thracian king who fought as an ally of Troy.

Identification. The prominent white veins on the ventral hind wings distinguish this species from all other skippers except *Hesperia uncas. Polites rhesus* can be separated from *Hesperia uncas* by its smaller size (wingspan 26-30 mm), lack of orange-brown areas on the dorsal surface and the presence of a pronounced white fringe on the wing.

Life History. There is one brood per year. Eggs are pale green. First instar larvae are yellowish cream, turning greenish after feeding, and have a black head. Second instar larvae are greenish cream with a black head. Mature larvae are light gray-green, but some are brownish green. Mature larvae overwinter. Larvae feed on Blue Grama Grass (*Bouteloua gracilis*) in Colorado. The adult flight period is reported to be short and usually early in the season. The only Alberta flight record is May 22. In Colorado the Rhesus Skipper is reported to experience great fluctuations in abundance, presumably as a result of moisture conditions.

Range and Habitat. The Rhesus Skipper ranges from extreme southern Alberta and Saskatchewan south to New Mexico and Arizona. In Alberta it is known from a single specimen collected in 1977 in the Milk River Valley on the Pinhorn Grazing Reserve. This species is found in dry grasslands.

Polites rhesus
Male dorsal

Polites rhesus
Male ventral

Pinhorn Grazing Reserve.   J.O. Hrapko.

Polites themistocles (Latreille, [1824])
Tawny-edged Skipper

Polites themistocles
Male dorsal

Polites themistocles
Female dorsal

Polites themistocles
Female ventral

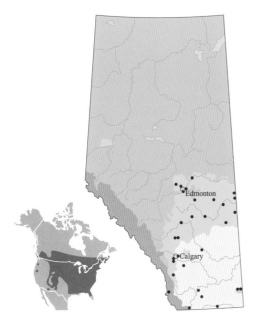

Etymology. Themistocles was an Athenian statesman.

Identification. This medium-sized skipper, with a wing-span of 20-26 mm, is mostly dark brown dorsally with a distinctive strip of orange along the front margin. Males have a dark stigma (scent patch) near the dorsal leading edge of the fore wing.

Life History. There is one brood per year. Eggs are cream with numerous small red spots. First instar larvae are tan with a black head. Mature caterpillars vary in colour from yellowish, greenish to purplish brown with a dark line on the side, and have a black head. The larvae or pupae overwinter. The pupae are dirty white to light mottled brown. Kentucky Bluegrass *(Poa pratensis)* is the major host and *Koeleria macrantha* has also been confirmed as a larval food plant. Most eggs are laid on leaves of dicotyledonous plants near the grasses. Males perch on low vegetation and wait for females. Adults have been found from June 10 to July 28.

Range and Habitat. The Tawny-edged Skipper occurs from Nova Scotia south to Florida, west to the Rocky Mountains and into parts of the Pacific Northwest. In Alberta this skipper has been found sporadically in the prairies, aspen parklands north to the Edmonton area and in the southern mountains. It is found in moist grasslands and along roads, creeks and streams in the prairies.

Koeleria macrantha
June Grass

Thymelicus Hübner, 1819

Etymology. Possibly from the Greek *thymelikos* meaning "theatrical musician."

Thymelicus lineola (Ochsenheimer, 1808)
European Skipper

Etymology. The name *lineola* is Latin for "small line."

Identification. This small skipper is burnt orange with a brassy sheen. The wings have a narrow black border and the distal portions of the veins have black scales. Males have a narrow black stigma on the fore wing. Wingspan is about 26 mm. Overall it is intermediate in size between the Garita Skipper and the Delaware Skipper. The Garita Skipper is dark brown on the upper surface; the Delaware Skipper differs in having a black line at the end of the fore wing both dorsally and ventrally.

Life History. There is one brood per year. The white, hemispherical eggs are laid in a vertical row on the medial surface of grass leaf sheaths next to the stems. Timothy (*Phleum pratense*) is a preferred host plant. First instar larvae overwinter in the egg attached to the grass stem and hatching occurs the following spring. The mature larvae have a dark dorsal stripe and white or yellow longitudinal stripes at the front. The head is light brown. The pupae are green to yellow green with a dark dorsal stripe and have down-curved horns on the front. In Alberta, adults have been found from July 1 to July 29. Males patrol grassy areas with a steady meandering flight for much of the day.

Range and Habitat. Introduced from Europe into eastern North America, the European Skipper has spread west, probably through movement of hay and livestock bedding. First discovered in 1910 near London, Ontario, this species did not spread significantly until the 1950s and early 1960s. It is now widespread, ranging from Newfoundland west to British Columbia and south to Colorado and North Carolina. In many parts of the range populations are still quite local in occurrence. In Alberta, a population has been found south of Edmonton. Other local populations are expected to be discovered in the future as the species continues to expand its range. The European Skipper can be found in relatively moist, grassy areas, notably hay fields and roadsides.

Thymelicus lineola
Male dorsal

Thymelicus lineola
Male ventral

Phleum pratense
Timothy

Subfamily
HETEROPTERINAE

This subfamily of skippers is poorly represented in Alberta, with only the Arctic Skipper (*Carterocephalus palaemon*) occurring in the province.

Carterocephalus Lederer, 1852

Etymology. From the Greek *karteros* meaning "strong" and *kephale* meaning "head."

Carterocephalus palaemon (Pallas, 1771)
Arctic Skipper
subspecies: *Carterocephalus palaemon mandan* (W.H. Edwards, 1863b)

Carterocephalus palaemon mandan
Male dorsal

Carterocephalus palaemon mandan
Male ventral

Etymology. The specific epithet is derived from Palaemon, god of the sea in Greek myth. The subspecific epithet *mandan* may refer to the Mandan Indians who once lived on the northeastern Great Plains.

Identification. The Arctic Skipper is distinctive on the dorsal side, with bold orange checks on a black background. Wingspan for this skipper is 20-30 mm. Populations from the aspen parkland and boreal forest are smaller on average and have a yellowish ventral hind wing with the pale or silvered spots typical of the subspecies *mandan*. Populations from the mountains are larger with a purplish brown colouring on the ventral hind wing and perhaps should be a distinct subspecies.

Life History. There is one brood per year. Eggs are greenish white. Mature caterpillars are greenish to ivory coloured with a dark dorsal stripe, a yellow lateral stripe and a dark line of spots below each lateral stripe. The larvae overwinter. The pupae resemble a fragment of faded grass. Larvae are known to feed on grasses from nine genera, including brome grass (*Bromus* spp.), bluegrass (*Poa* spp.) and reed grass (*Calamagrostis* spp.). Broad-leaf grasses seem to be preferred. Adults have been found in Alberta from May 1 to August 7. In the boreal forest and aspen parkland zones, peak flight appears to be during the first three weeks of June, while in the foothills and mountains, peak flight is late June and early July. Males perch on grass stalks and sometimes patrol small clearings or along trails.

Range and Habitat. The Arctic Skipper is a holarctic species, distributed across northern Europe and Asia as well as North America. On our continent, it ranges across northern Canada to Alaska in forested areas, south to southern Wyoming in the Rocky Mountains and central California in the Sierra Nevada Mountains. This skipper has been found throughout Alberta with the exception of the southern prairies and the Cypress Hills. The Arctic Skipper frequents meadows, clearings and open stands of pine, mixed and poplar forests. This species may also be found in riparian forests and thickets along northern prairie streams.

Bromus tectorum
Downy Chess

Calamagrostis canadensis
Marsh Reed Grass or Bluejoint

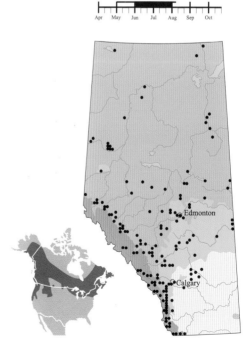

Carterocephalus palaemon at Livingstone River.   G.J. Hilchie.

79

Subfamily
PYRGINAE
BROAD-WINGED SKIPPERS

Members of the subfamily Pyrginae, commonly called broad-winged skippers, are usually larger than Hesperiine skippers. Adults are dark brown or checkered black-and-white, and males lack conspicuous patches of androconial scales (stigmas) on their fore wings. Pyrgine caterpillars feed mainly on leaves from trees (birch, poplar) or plants from the pea family (Leguminosae). Nine species are known to occur in Alberta with an additional species predicted to occur.

Epargyreus Hübner, 1819

Etymology. From Greek *epargyros* meaning "silver-plated."

Epargyreus clarus (Cramer, [1775])
Silverspotted Skipper
subspecies: *Epargyreus clarus clarus* (Cramer, [1775])

Epargyreus clarus
Male dorsal

Epargyreus clarus
Male ventral

Etymology. The species name clarus means "clear" in Latin, probably a reference to the silver spot.

Identification. The Silverspotted Skipper is the largest skipper in Alberta, with a wingspan of 44 to 60 mm. It is dark brown with large translucent gold patches on the ventral fore wings and a large silver spot on the ventral hind wing.

Life History. There is one brood per year. The caterpillars develop from greenish, globular eggs. First instar larvae are bright yellow, they fold the edge of the leaf; later instars weave webs. Mature caterpillars are light yellow-green with a reddish brown head. The brown pupae have light and dark markings and are protected by a loose cocoon in the ground litter where they overwinter. Numerous woody legumes have been reported as larval hosts; Wild Licorice (*Glycyrrhiza lepidota*) is the reported host in Alberta, North Dakota and Colorado. Peavine (*Lathyrus* spp.) and milk vetch (*Astragalus* spp.) are also used. Adults fly from May 6 to August 1. The peak flight period is late June and early July. Males are aggressive fliers and often have aerial encounters with other males.

Range and Habitat. This is one of the most widely distributed North American skippers. This species ranges from British Columbia to Quebec, south to Florida and Mexico. In Alberta, the Silverspotted Skipper is found from the southeast corner of the province north to Edmonton and west to Nanton. Virtually all records are from river valley and hill systems in the prairie and aspen parkland regions. Adults can be found in small clearings in aspen woods, edges of poplar groves, along prairie streams, in badlands and in ravines.

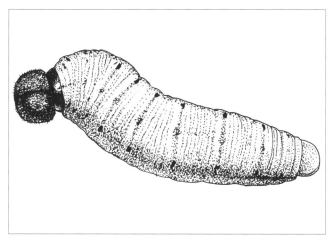

Epargyreus clarus larva

Glycyrrhiza lepidota
Wild Licorice

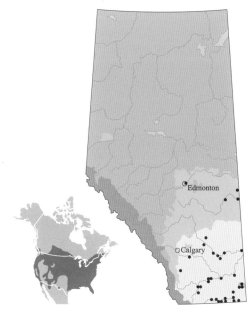

Arid grassland at Canadian Forces Base Suffield. Prickly Pear (*Opuntia polyacantha* Haw.; Cactaceae) blooming in foreground.

A.T. Finnamore.

Erynnis Schrank, 1801

Etymology. The name *Erynnis* is derived from Greek myth. The Erinnyes were infernal spirits who brought retribution for homicide.

Erynnis afranius (Lintner, [1878])
Afranius Duskywing

Thermopsis rhombifolia
Golden or Buffalo Bean

Erynnis afranius
Female dorsal

Erynnis afranius
Female ventral

Etymology. Perhaps from Afranius, the name of a Roman family.

Identification. With a wingspan of 25-35 mm, this species is similar to *Erynnis persius*. It can be distinguished by being generally paler with more distinct, light markings and has a brownish colour to the upper surface rather than the two-tone, gray-brown of *E. persius*. The table on page 85 lists the differences between these two similar species.

Life History. There are two broods per year. The eggs are cream, turning yellowish and then reddish orange. First stage larvae are pale yellow with a brownish orange head. The caterpillars are pale green with a dark stripe on the back and a black head. The larvae overwinter. The pupae are green. Silvery Lupine (*Lupinus argentus*) and Golden Bean (*Thermopsis rhombifolia*) are reported larval food plants. Oviposition has been observed at Grassy Lake, Alberta on Buffalo Bean (*Astragalus crassicarpus*). Adults take nectar from Golden Bean. The range of flight dates is from May 6 to August 31. It is double-brooded with most spring adults on the wing from mid-May to mid-June and the summer adults mostly flying from mid-July to mid-August. Males perch to await females.

Range and Habitat. This western species occurs from Mexico City northeast to southwestern Manitoba and northwest to southern Alberta. The Afranius Duskywing is essentially a prairie species in Alberta, having been found north to the Drumheller area and west to the foothills near Nanton. Its habitat is native grasslands, particularly along river valleys and prairie creeks as well as uplands such as the Cypress Hills.

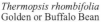

Apr May Jun Jul Aug Sep Oct

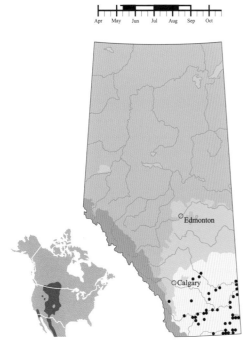

Edmonton

Calgary

Erynnis icelus (Scudder and Burgess, 1870)
Dreamy Duskywing

Etymology. The species name comes from Greek myth; Ikelos was the son of Hypnos, winged god of sleep.

Identification. The Dreamy Duskywing is a dark gray-brown skipper with a wingspan of 25-30 mm. The dorsal fore wings are dark gray crossed by two black lines. One or two small white dots may be present apically along the leading edge of the fore wing. The dorsal hind wing is dark brown. The ventral wing surface is generally brown with pale spots. *E. icelus* can be distinguished from other Alberta *Erynnis* by the more banded dorsal surface of the fore wing, pronounced gray area on the dorsal surface of the fore wing and rows of pale spots on the ventral surface.

Life History. There is one brood per year. The eggs are green but change to pink before hatching. The caterpillars are pale green with white dots and a reddish brown head. Larvae feed on a variety of trees including aspen and poplar (*Populus* spp.), willow (*Salix* spp.) and rarely birch (*Betula* spp.). The caterpillars make leaf shelters from which they feed. The larvae overwinter and pupate the following spring. The pupae are reddish to yellowish brown. Males use both perching and patrolling behaviours to locate females. Adults roost with their wings spread horizontally. Flight records range from May 1 to July 9 with most records in late May and early June.

Range and Habitat. This skipper is widespread in North America, ranging from Nova Scotia in the east to the Mackenzie River in the northwest, south to Georgia and New Mexico. Its range is patchy in western and coastal United States. The Dreamy Duskywing has been found throughout Alberta, but tends to be local on the prairies. It inhabits open forests, along their edges and in clearings, and along streams on the prairies.

Erynnis icelus
Male dorsal

Erynnis icelus
Male ventral

Populus balsamifera
Balsam Poplar

Apr May Jun Jul Aug Sep Oct

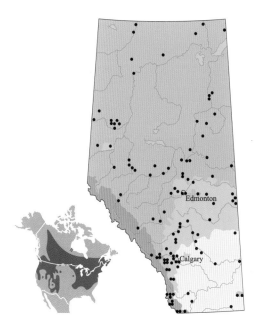

83

Erynnis persius (Scudder, 1863)
Persius Duskywing
subspecies: ***Erynnis persius borealis* (Cary, 1907)**
***Erynnis persius fredericki* H.A. Freeman, 1943**

Lupinus argenteus
Silvery Lupine

Erynnis persius
Male dorsal

Erynnis persius
Male ventral

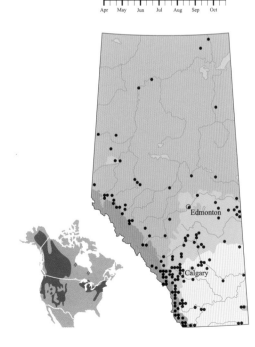

Etymology. The species is named after a Roman poet, Persius, of the third century A.D. The subspecies *borealis* is after the latin *boreus* meaning "northern." Freeman named *fredericki* after R. C. Fredericki, who, along with his wife, collected most of the type specimens.

Identification. A gray-brown skipper with a wingspan of 26 to 35 mm with the females larger than the males. It can be distinguished from *Erynnis icelus* by the presence of several distinct white spots near the apex of the fore wing above and by the less gray colouring on the fore wing below. It can be easily confused with the very similar *E. afranius* but has a generally darker appearance. The upper side has a more distinct two-tone colour with the fore wings dark gray and the hind wings dark brown.

Life History. There is one brood per year. Eggs are pale yellowish, turning orange with age. Caterpillars are pale green with a dark green line on the back and a brownish black head. The pupae are dull olive-green with pale dots. Caterpillars apparently feed on legumes with various species of lupine (*Lupinus*), golden bean (*Thermopsis*) and milk vetch (*Astragalus*) reported as food plants in the literature. Oviposition has been observed on *Astragalus* at Beaver Mines, Alberta. Mature larvae overwinter. Adults have been found from May 4 to August 8, mostly late May on the prairies and late June to early July in the mountains and boreal forest. Males display perching behaviour to locate females.

Range and Habitat. In eastern North America this species ranges through the New England and Great Lakes regions, south in the Appalachians to Virginia. It is more widely distributed in the west with a patchy distribution in the western states; northeast to central Manitoba and northwest to northern Alaska. The Persius Duskywing occurs in all parts of Alberta but is uncommon and local on the prairies. Habitats are open forests, forest clearings, meadows, forest edges and river valleys in the prairies. Southern Alberta populations are referred to the subspecies *fredericki* while northern populations may be placed in the subspecies *borealis*.

Differentiation Between *Erynnis persius* and *Erynnis afranius* in Alberta

	Erynnis persius	*Erynnis afranius*
Wing characters	two-tone dorsal colour; fore wing dark grey, hind wing dark brown	more uniform brown dorsal surface (especially summer brood)
	less distinct light markings	more distinct light markings
	thick coat of long, hair-like scales in basal area of dorsal fore wing of male	thick coat of long scales lacking
	dorsal hind wing pale spots less pronounced	dorsal hind wing pale spots more pronounced
	generally darker	generally paler (although the spring brood is darker and smaller than the summer brood, hence easier to confuse with *E. persius*)
Distribution and Phenology	throughout province but rare in prairies	largely a prairie species, filtering into the southern foothills and possibly southern edges of aspen parkland along river valleys and in sand dune areas
	single brooded; May and early June on the prairies; June, July and early August in the mountains and boreal forest	double brooded; spring generation in May-June, summer generation in July-August (possibly early September)
Male Genitalia	gnathos with dorsal tooth	gnathos without dorsal tooth
	massive upper lobe of right valva (more than 0.8 mm long and more than 0.6 mm wide)	smaller upper lobe of right valva
	left valva with middle lobe widened, separated from upper	left valva with middle lobe slender, separated from upper lobe by wide space
	heavy keel on inner face of middle lobe of left valva extending about halfway to the tip	weak inner keel that stops almost at the base

Pholisora Scudder, [1871]

Etymology. Possibly from the Greek *pholis*, "lurking in a hole," and *ora*, "season, especially spring."

Pholisora catullus (Fabricius, 1793)
Common Sootywing

Pholisora catullus
Male dorsal

Pholisora catullus
Male ventral

Etymology. Catullus was a Roman adversary of Pompeius.

Identification. This is a small black skipper with small white dots on both dorsal and ventral fore wings. Gray submarginal spots are present on the dorsal hind wing. Wing fringes are uniformly dark, differentiating the Common Sootywing from *Amblyscirtes* species in which the fringes are checkered or light-coloured.

Life History. Larvae feed on many species including Lamb's Quarters or Pigweed (*Chenopodium album*), Green Amaranth (*Amaranthus retroflexus*) and mallows (*Malva* spp.). In Montana, adults are known to fly from mid-May through mid-August.

Range and Habitat. The Common Sootywing is a wide-ranging species, from southern British Columbia, through Washington, Idaho, Montana into North Dakota and south to Mexico. This skipper may be abundant in lowlands where it frequents gullies, ditches and other weedy places. This species was reported from Alberta by Gregory (1975) but no verifiable collection records could be located. The probability of occurrence is high. It should be watched for in southern and eastern Alberta grasslands.

Milk River near the Alberta/Montana border.   A.T. Finnamore.

Pyrgus Hübner, 1819

Etymology. The genus name may be based on the Greek *pyrgos* meaning "tower," or more likely *pyrgites* meaning "sparrow."

Pyrgus centaureae (Rambur, 1840)
Grizzled Skipper
subspecies: ***Pyrgus centaureae freija*** (Warren, 1924)
Pyrgus centaureae loki Evans, 1953

Etymology. The origin of the species name *centaureae* is not certain. The name possibly refers to Centaurs, creatures of Greek myth that were half man and half horse. An alternate source is from *Centaurea*, an old world herb (knapweed). The subspecies name *freija* is derived from Freya, the Norse goddess of love and fertility and wife of Odin. The subspecies name *loki* is also derived from Norse myth and refers to Loki, a god who was noted for being a trouble-maker.

Identification. The Grizzled Skipper is black above with small white checks. It is larger (wingspan 25-30 mm) than the similar Two-banded Checkered Skipper and also lacks the banded appearance of that species. The boreal subspecies *P. c. freija* is darker than the montane subspecies *P. c. loki*.

Life History. There is one brood per year. The early stages and host plants are poorly known. Scott (1992) reported it on blueberry (*Vaccinium*) in Colorado. In Europe the larvae are reported to feed on Cloudberry or Baked-apple Berry (*Rubus chamaemorus*) and in Michigan on Wild Strawberry (Fragaria virginiana). Oviposition was reported on Cinquefoil (*Potentilla diversifolia*) in Colorado. In Alberta, adults have been found from May 7 through August 7. These skippers are most likely to be seen in late June at low elevations through to late July in alpine meadows. Males patrol in depressions and other low alpine habitats. At cooler temperatures males tend to perch. These skippers nectar on stonecrop (*Sedum* spp.), strawberry, cinquefoil (*Potentilla* spp.) and other flowers.

Pyrgus centaureae freija
Male dorsal

Pyrgus centaureae freija
Male ventral

Pyrgus centaureae loki
Male dorsal

Pyrgus centaureae loki
Male ventral

Pyrgus centaureae loki
Female dorsal

Pyrgus centaureae loki
Female ventral

Fragaria virginiana
Wild Strawberry

Range and Habitat. The Grizzled Skipper is a circumboreal species, occurring in northern areas of Europe, Asia and North America. On this continent, it ranges across the boreal forest, south in the Appalachian Mountains to North Carolina and south in the Rocky Mountains to New Mexico. In Alberta, *P. c. loki* has been found in the mountains south to the Crowsnest Pass, while *P. c. freija* is known from several localities in the boreal forest. In Alberta the northern subspecies occurs in small clearings of Black Spruce (*Picea mariana*) bogs. The mountain subspecies is most commonly encountered in alpine meadows, but it is seen occasionally in clearings in the subalpine and dry montane forests.

Pyrgus centaurae at Highwood River.   C.D. Bird.

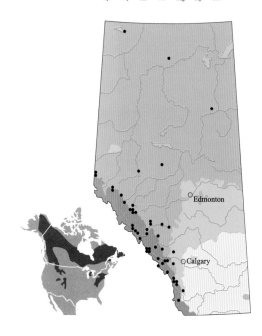

Rubus chamaemorus
Cloudberry or Baked-apple Berry

Pyrgus communis (Grote, 1872)
Checkered Skipper

Etymology. The species name is from the Latin *communis* which means "common."

Identification. *Pyrgus communis* is a white and black skipper with two pale olive-coloured bands on the ventral hind wings. Its wingspan is 25-30 mm.

Life History. There are two broods per year. The eggs are pale green. Mature caterpillars are tan with a darker median line, brown sides with a white line and a black head. The pupae are partly green and brown, with green more pronounced towards the head. Many species of mallow are reported as larval hosts including species of *Malva* and *Sphaeralcea*. Alberta populations occur in areas where neither plant occurs so other species must also serve as food plants. Adults have been found from May 17 to September 17, with most records occurring in June and August. The prolonged flight period suggests at least two broods, perhaps more in Alberta. Males perch and patrol small areas, usually low places. Adults nectar freely at *Aster* spp. and fleabane (*Erigeron* spp.).

Range and Habitat. The Checkered Skipper occurs across most of the United States, from the southern prairie provinces and extreme southern British Columbia in the north to Argentina in the south. This skipper is found in prairie grassland, the aspen parkland of southern Alberta and the Peace River valley grasslands. There are a few records from sand dune areas of the boreal forest.

Pyrgus communis
Male dorsal

Pyrgus communis
Male ventral

Pyrgus communis
Female dorsal

Pyrgus communis
Female ventral

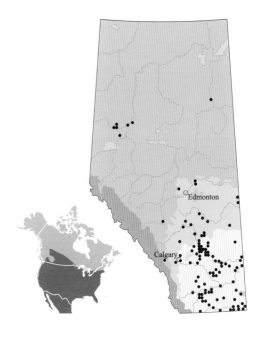

Sphaeralcea coccinea
Scarlet Mallow

Pyrgus ruralis (Boisduval, 1852)
Two-banded Checkered Skipper

Pyrgus ruralis
Female dorsal

Pyrgus ruralis
Female ventral

Potentilla diversifolia
Mountain Cinquefoil

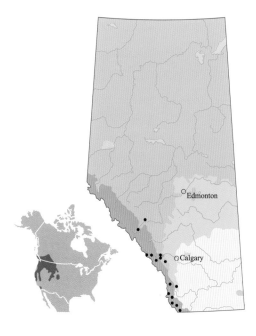

Etymology. The species name *ruralis* means "belonging to the countryside" in Latin.

Identification. *Pyrgus ruralis* is a small (wingspan 20-25 mm) blackish skipper with two bands of white spots. It is much darker than *Pyrgus centaureae* with which it may be confused. In addition, *P. ruralis* has reddish brown markings on the ventral hind wing.

Life History. There is one brood per year. The eggs are green to yellow. Larval stages have not been described, although they are reported to feed on several species of cinquefoil (*Potentilla* spp.). In Alberta, adults have been observed from May 1 to July 13, with population peaks during the last two weeks of May and first week of June. Males patrol close to the ground, usually in areas with depressions. Adults have not been observed nectaring.

Range and Habitat. *Pyrgus ruralis* is a western species, occurring from southern California and Colorado north to southern Alberta and British Columbia. In Alberta the distribution is spotty in the mountains north to Nordegg. We expect a population may be present in the Athabasca Valley near Jasper. The Two-banded Checkered Skipper is typically found on dry non-forested slopes and along stream-side clearings at low elevations in the mountains, and on *Dryas* beds along streams.

Potentilla fruticosa
Shrubby Cinquefoil

Pyrgus scriptura (Boisduval, 1852)
Small Checkered Skipper

Etymology. The name *scriptura* is a Latin word which means "written."

Identification. This skipper is distinguished from *Pyrgus communis* by its smaller size (wingspan 16-25 mm), glossy, dark gray and brown dorsal colouration and the lack of a costal fold in the fore wing of males.

Life History. There is one brood per year. The eggs are cream-coloured. Larval hosts are from the mallow family (Malvaceae) including Scarlet Mallow (*Sphaeralcea coccinea*) in Colorado and Cultivated Mallow (*Sida hederacea*) in California. Adults are known to fly from early spring to fall, with two to three broods. July 23 is the one recorded flight date for Alberta. Males are reported to patrol all day in low areas and shallow gullies, flying 10-20 cm above the ground.

Range and Habitat. The Small Checkered Skipper ranges from southern California across the southern Great Basin to Texas and north on the Great Plains to Alberta. In Alberta one specimen was found along the Lost River south of Manyberries in 1951. This skipper should be watched for in native grasslands, hillsides and along roads where mallows grow.

Pyrgus scriptura
Male dorsal

Pyrgus scriptura
Male ventral

Pyrgus scriptura
Female dorsal

Pyrgus scriptura
Female ventral

Soapweed (*Yucca glauca* Nutt.; Liliaceae) in Lost River, south of Onefour, southeastern Alberta.

G.J. Hilchie.

91

Thorybes Scudder, [1871]

Etymology. The generic name is derived from the Greek *thorybos,* meaning "noise of crowded assembly, applause, cheers, uproar."

Thorybes pylades (Scudder, 1870)
Northern Cloudywing

Trifolium hybridum
Alsike Clover

Thorybes pylades
Male dorsal

Thorybes pylades
Male ventral

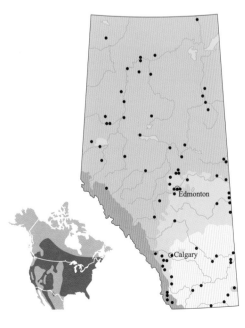

Etymology. The species name *pylades* means "faithful friend" in Greek and comes from Pylades who was a friend of Orestes.

Identification. *Thorybes pylades* is a large, dark brown skipper with a wingspan of 30-39 mm. Skippers from prairie populations are larger than those from northern areas. The upper fore wing has small white triangular spots near the margin and the ventral undersides of the wings have gray frosting along their edges.

Life History. There is one brood per year. The eggs are pale green. Mature caterpillars are dark green to purplish, with pink and purple stripes. A large variety of legumes are used as hosts; over ten genera are reported in the literature. Clovers (*Trifolium* spp.), vetch (*Vicia* spp.) , pea vine (*Lathyrus* spp.) and Alfalfa (*Medicago sativa*) appear to be most commonly used. The pupae overwinter. Adults have been found from May 14 to July 21, with populations peaking in mid-June. Males perch on low vegetation. Adults nectar at various flowers and visit seeps and puddles to obtain moisture.

Range and Habitat. The Northern Cloudywing ranges through most of North America from south-central Mexico north to the southern Northwest Territories. This skipper is found throughout Alberta, but is rare in prairie grasslands and the mountains north of the Bow River. *Thorybes pylades* adults may be found in and along the edges of poplar forests and pine forests, along prairie streams and even in badlands coulees. The prairie form is larger and lighter than those from the mountains and boreal forest.

3

Family **PAPILIONIDAE**
PARNASSIANS and SWALLOWTAILS

There are over 500 species known in the Papilionidae, but most are natives of the tropics. This family includes some of the largest and most striking butterflies in the world, such as the birdwings of Australasia, and arguably the most beautiful of our province's species as well. The species that occur in Alberta belong to two subfamilies, the Parnassiinae (parnassians) and the Papilioninae (swallowtails). Although adults from these two groups appear to be very different from each other, parnassians and swallowtails are grouped in the same family because of similarities in fore leg structure, wing venation and larval morphology.

Subfamily
PARNASSIINAE
PARNASSIANS
Parnassius Latreille, 1804

Etymology. *Parnassius* alludes to Mount Parnassus in Greece, a mountain sacred to the god Apollo; in fact, the type species for this genus is *Parnassius apollo* Linnaeus. Latreille undoubtably chose the generic name because *Parnassius* butterflies are found in montane habitats.

Identification. Parnassians are distinguished by wings that have a white ground colour with semi-transparent borders, and by their hairy bodies. The latter feature helps them retain heat in chilly mountain conditions. Like many mountain butterflies, parnassians often show intraspecific colour variation (variation between individuals of a species) associated with altitude; the higher up the mountainside, the darker the colour. Females have darker wings than the males, but males tend to have hairier bodies than females. Although parnassians appear superficially like whites (family Pieridae, subfamily Pierinae) they have a larger wingspan (50-65 mm). Mated female parnassians carry a waxy pouch at the end of the abdomen, the sphragis, that is attached by the male during copulation. The sphragis prevents the female from mating again but allows her to lay eggs; it also has a species-specific morphology. After mating the female scatters eggs on the ground near the larval food plant. Larvae are slightly dorsoventrally flattened and, like swallowtail larvae, possess eversible structures (osmeteria) near the head whose unpleasant scent may repel predators. There is one brood per year in Alberta.

1b

1a

2a

2b

3b

3a

4a

4b

5a

5b

6a

6b

7a

7b

Key to Species of Papilionidae in Alberta

(** Species marked with a double asterisk are not recorded for Alberta, but have been found just outside the province.)

1a) Hind wing without tails. 2
 b) Hind wing tails present 3

2a) Antenna all black; gray bar across dorsal front wing disc
. . . . *Parnassius clodius* Ménétriés p. 95
 b) Antenna white-ringed; black spot in dorsal front wing disc
. . . . *Parnassius smintheus* Doubleday p. 96

3a) Hind wing centre stripe present 4
 b) Hind wing centre black or yellow, without stripe 7

4a) Hind wing two-tailed . . . .
. . *Papilio (Pterourus) multicaudatus* W.F. Kirby p. 108
 b) Hind wing one-tailed 5

5a) Ground colour white; stripes wide . . . .
. . . . *Papilio (Pterourus) eurymedon* Lucas p. 107
 b) Ground colour yellow or cream; stripes narrow. 6

6a) Ventral hind wing marginal spots orange. Dorsal hind
wing first marginal spot orange. . . . .
Papilio (Pterourus) canadensis Rothschild & Jordan p. 105
 b) Ventral hind wing marginal spots yellow. Dorsal hind
wing first marginal spot yellow. . . . .
. . . . *Papilio (Pterourus) rutulus* Lucas ** p. 109

7a) Hind wing eye spot round and centred. . . . .
. . . . *Papilio (Papilio) zelicaon* Lucas p. 102
 b) Hind wing eye spot connected to margin or low and
oval. . . . . *Papilio (Papilio) machaon* Linnaeus p. 99

Papilo canadensis at Beaver Mines, Alberta.   G.J. Hilchie

Parnassius clodius Ménétriés, 1855
Clodius Parnassian

Etymology. Clodius was the name of a Roman family that had several famous members, both aristocratic and plebeian.

Identification. This species is unlikely to be encountered in Alberta except in Waterton Lakes National Park. It is distinguished from the more common Smintheus Parnassian by the completely black antennae, gray rather than black markings of the wings, especially on the dorsal fore wing disc, and a large white sphragis on the abdomen of the mated female.

Life History. Early stages are unknown in Alberta. In Oregon, larvae of the Clodius Parnassian feed on *Corydalis* and Bleeding-heart (*Dicentra* spp.) which occurs wild in Glacier National Park, Montana and as an ornamental in Alberta.

Range and Habitat. There are only two confirmed records for *Parnassius clodius* in Alberta; Bertha Lake (1770 m) and Goat Lake (1980 m) in Waterton Lakes National Park, collected in early August by D.G. Wales. In other parts of its range, the Clodius Parnassian is usually found in lush forest clearings.

Parnassius clodius
Male dorsal

Parnassius clodius
Female dorsal

Dicentra spectabilis
Bleeding-heart

95

Parnassius smintheus Doubleday, 1847
Smintheus Parnassian

Parnassius smintheus
Male dorsal

Etymology. Apollo was the Greek god of sunlight, prophecy, music and poetry. Apollo smintheus was the title given to this god in his role as protector of crops.

Identification. Shepard *et al.* (1994) showed that Rocky Mountain forms previously referred to as *Parnassius phoebus* (Fabricius) are *P. smintheus*. *Parnassius smintheus* is characterized by narrow white rings around each segment of the antennae, black wing markings, particularly on the dorsal fore wing disc, and a small, dark brown sphragis on the end of the abdomen of the mated female. Both sexes tend to be smaller and darker at higher latitudes; darker wing bases allow adults to warm up more quickly in the sun.

Life History. In Alberta, larvae have been found at Windsor Mountain, Plateau Mountain and Frank townsite on Common Stonecrop (*Sedum lanceolatum*). Larvae are black with dense short hairs and small yellow spots on each segment. There is one generation per year and adults have been reported from June 2 to October 10. The main flight period begins as early as mid-June in the southern Alberta Rocky Mountains, but not until August in the north.

Parnassius smintheus
Female dorsal

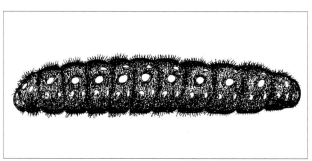

Parnassius spp. larva

Sedum lanceolatum
Common Stonecrop

Males patrol slowly over open areas where the larval food plants grow, flying a metre above the ground in search of females. Adults nectar on a variety of flowers in the daisy family (Compositae).

Range and Habitat. The Smintheus Parnassian is a strictly western North American species. In Alberta, it is found throughout the Rocky Mountains in subalpine meadows and dry, mostly south-facing mountain slopes. This butterfly is particularly common in mountain valley floors in the southern part of Alberta. One outlying population on the valley sides of the Milk River north of Del Bonita may be the only truly prairie-dwelling population in North America. It has been found on the Saskatchewan side of the Cypress Hills (Hooper 1986), but not yet on the Alberta side even though the larval food plant grows there. The Smintheus Parnassian is less frequently encountered in the northern Rocky Mountains, where it occurs on rocky slopes in alpine and subalpine areas.

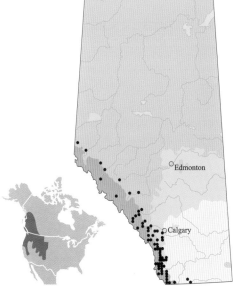

Parnassius smintheus at Windsor Mountain, North of Waterton Lakes National Park.

J.H. Acorn.

97

Subfamily
PAPILIONINAE
SWALLOWTAILS
Papilio Linnaeus, 1758

Etymology. The genus gets its name from the Latin *papilionis* meaning "butterfly" or "moth."

Identification. Swallowtail butterflies of the genus *Papilio* have a worldwide distribution. The more than 200 known species are divided into 42 species groups, two of which, the Old World swallowtails (*Papilio*) and the tiger swallowtails *(Pterourus)* occur in Alberta. Alberta swallowtails are distinguished from other butterflies by their large size (wingspan more than 7.5 cm), tails on the hind wings, and a bold black and (usually) yellow colour pattern. There is one brood per year. Swallowtail eggs are spherical and green or yellowish. Like parnassians, the larvae have osmeteria; eversible tubes located just behind the head capsule that may be used to repel predators. Early instar larvae are black with a white patch in the middle and have spines with fleshy bases, making them look like unappetizing bird droppings. The green or brown pupae are held upright against twigs by a silk girdle and resemble leaves or broken branches. The pupae are the overwintering stage for *Papilio*. Pupae are often parasitized by large black ichneumonid wasps (*Trogus* spp.).

PAPILIO (PAPILIO)
OLD WORLD SWALLOWTAILS

The Old World swallowtails form a species complex, the *Papilio machaon* group, that includes about six species ranging throughout most of the Northern Hemisphere. Late instar larvae have black and green bands on each segment interspersed by small yellow or orange spots. The ratio of yellow to orange spots varies geographically and can help to distinguish populations. Larvae feed on numerous species of the carrot family (Umbelliferae) as well as a few members of the daisy family (Compositae), both of which are unusual food plants for swallowtails as a whole.

The most common adult form of Old World swallowtails in Alberta is mainly yellow with black markings along the veins and outer borders of the wings. A dark form, which is also present in varying proportions, which is characterized by a predominantly black pattern on the wings and yellow spots rather than a yellow band on the abdomen. Males of the *Papilio machaon* species group usually patrol grassy or sparsely treed hilltops that combine good nectar sources with panoramic views. Encounters between patrolling males lead to short aggressive chases, while females are pursued until they land in a grassy spot. Mating lasts about half an hour. There is occasional hybridization between species in the Old World swallowtail group (Sperling 1987, 1990).

Papilio (Papilio) machaon Linnaeus, 1758
Old World and Artemisia Swallowtails

subspecies: *Papilio (Papilio) machaon dodi* McDunnough, 1939
Papilio (Papilio) machaon hudsonianus A.H. Clarke, 1932
Papilio (Papilio) machaon pikei Sperling, 1987

Etymology. Machaon was the physician son of Asclepius, the Greek god of health. *Papilio machaon hudsonianus* was described along the Hudson Bay Railway in northern Manitoba and the subspecific name is appropriately descriptive of its forest habitat. The subspecies *dodi* was named after F.H. Wolley-Dod, the first serious lepidopterist in Alberta. The last subspecies was recently discovered and named after one of the authors of this book, E.M. (Ted) Pike.

Identification. Old World and artemisia swallowtails are best distinguished by the shape of the eye spot on the inner margin of the dorsal side of the hind wing. This eye spot is club-shaped and connected to the wing's margin, or at least oval and located low in the area of red scales. Three similar-looking subspecies occur in Alberta and to reduce confusion we refer to them by their Latin names. Swallowtails identified as *Papilio bairdii brucei* W.H. Edwards and as Badlands Old World swallowtails (*Papilio machaon* ssp.) in the *Butterflies of Saskatchewan* (Hooper 1973) are the summer and spring generations, respectively, of *Papilio machaon dodi* (Hooper 1986). Butterflies that Hooper (1973) referred to as Cypress Hills Old World swallowtails ("*P. m. dodi*") appear to be a hybrid population between *Papilio zelicaon* and one or more subspecies of *P. machaon* (see Hybrid Swallowtails, p. 104). Clearly, this is a confusing group of butterflies. *Papilio machaon* has two generations per year. Spring generation adults of *P. m. dodi* look much like *P. zelicaon*. Summer generation adults generally have more yellow scales and hairs. Dark form adults comprise less than 2% of any population in Alberta. *P. m. dodi* also tends to have more pointed fore wings and narrower hind wing tails than *P. zelicaon*. Both *P. m. pikei* and *P. m. hudsonianus* are distinguished from *P. m. dodi* by yellow hair extending around the underside of the thorax and by yellow scales at the base of the underside of the fore wing. The latter two subspecies are separated by habitat and locality.

Papilio machaon dodi
Male dorsal

Papilio machaon dodi
Male ventral

99

Papilio machaon hudsonianus
Male ventral

Papilio machaon pikei
Male ventral

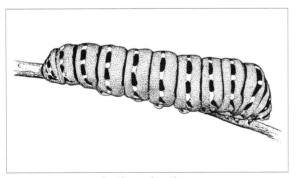

Papilio machaon larva

Life History. Larvae of *P. m. dodi* and *P. m. pikei* feed exclusively on Dragonwort (*Artemisia dracunculus*), as do other subspecies of *P. machaon* found in the western United States. Not all pupae of *P. m. dodi* or *P. m. pikei* that are produced in late summer will emerge as adults during the following year. A small proportion will wait an additional year or more to emerge, perhaps as a strategy to avoid drought such as occurred in southern Alberta in 1985. The larval food plant of *P. m. hudsonianus* has not been established. Judging from a photo of a late instar larva taken by Gary Anweiler in Saskatchewan, the food plant may be a Palmate-leaved Coltsfoot (*Petasites palmatus*). It is also possible that *P. m. hudsonianus* larvae feed on members of the carrot family (Umbelliferae). *Papilio machaon dodi* has been collected from May 3 to August 23. The peak for the first generation is the second half of May and the first half of June, while for the second generation it is late July and early August. *Papilio machaon pikei* has been recorded from June 9 to July 9, while *P. m. hudsonianus* has been found from May 31 to July 28 and most were collected in the second half of June. Nectar sources include groundsel (*Senecio* spp.), sweet broom (*Hedysarum* spp.) and Alfalfa (*Medicago sativa*).

Artemisia dracunculus
Dragonwort

Petasites palmatus
Palmate-leaved Coltsfoot

Range and Habitat. *Papilio machaon dodi* is found in southern Alberta, while *P. m. pikei* is restricted to the Peace River region. *P. m. pikei* and *P. m. dodi* occur in dry grassland habitats along eroding river banks, badlands and roadcuts near the larval food plant. Populations are patchily distributed along major river valleys and badlands. Males of *P. m. dodi* and *P. m. pikei* tend to fly along the upper edge of deep river valleys and accumulate at prominences. Males also patrol slopes well below valley edges, looking for females near patches of larval food plants. In contrast, *P. m. hudsonianus* is found in the boreal forest region, especially near openings along roads, bogs or sparsely treed hilltops. It is rarely collected in Alberta, but is distributed over a broad region within the province.

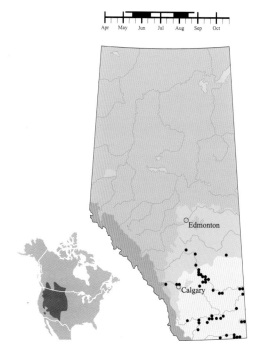

Papilio machaon dodi

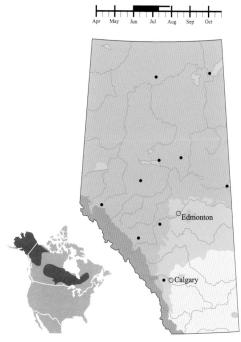

Papilio machaon hudsonianus

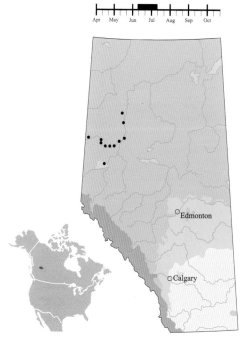

Papilio machaon pikei

101

Papilio (Papilio) zelicaon Lucas, 1852
Anise Swallowtail

Papilio zelicaon
Male dorsal

Papilio zelicaon
Male ventral

Etymology. *Zelos* is Greek for "emulation, zeal." The suffix "caon" may refer to Chaonia, a district in the northwest of Greece. However, since Lucas drew several comparisons between *Papilio zelicaon* and *Papilio machaon*, the suffix may have been an attempt to make the names of the two species sound similar.

Identification. Adults of *Papilio zelicaon* are best identified by the round, centred, anal eye spot on the upper side of the hind wing. *P. zelicaon* usually has more black colouration than *P. machaon*, especially at the base of the ventral fore wing and on the thorax and abdomen. The black "*nitra*" form comprises up to 10% of some *P. zelicaon* populations in southern Alberta.

Life History. Larvae feed entirely on members of the carrot family (Umbelliferae) and, unlike *P. machaon* larvae, will not feed on Dragonwort (*Artemisia dracunculus*). Eggs are laid on flowerheads or leaves. In the Waterton area, larvae frequently occur on White Angelica (*Angelica arguta*), while in northern Alberta they are common on Cow Parsnip (*Heracleum lanatum*). Larvae have also been found in Alberta on Mountain Parsnip (*Angelica dawsoni*), Kneeling Angelica (*A. genuflexa*), Mountain Wild Parsnip (*Lomatium dissectum*), Western Wild Parsley (*L. triternatum*), Water Parsnip (*Sium suave*), and Heart-leaved Alexanders (*Zizia cordata*), as well as two cultivated umbellifers, Garden Celery (*Apium graveolens*) and Garden Parsnip (*Pastinaca sativa*). The main larval food plant on the prairies of southern Alberta is unknown, though it seems likely to be a prairie parsley (*Lomatium* spp.). There is usually only a single generation per year for *P. zelicaon*. The main flight period is variable, with adults generally emerging later in cooler habitats, especially in the mountains. Adults have been collected in Alberta from April 23 to August 19, though the main flight period varies from the second half of May in the Wintering Hills south of Drumheller, to the first half of July in Waterton National Park. A few fresh adults have been collected near Drumheller in early August. A typical nectar source for hilltopping male *P. zelicaon* is the Common Dandelion (*Taraxacum officinale*).

Whenever males of both colour forms occupy the same hilltop, it seems that the black form males obtain the choice spots on the very peak of the hill. Little data have been collected on the mating behaviour of *P. zelicaon*, however, and explanation of this interesting phenomenon awaits someone with a little time and patience to study it.

Range and Habitat. *Papilio zelicaon* is generally found in moist meadows in forested areas, but in Alberta it can also be found in habitats ranging from parkland or prairie hilltops to subalpine meadows. Adults have even been seen hilltopping on alpine peaks.

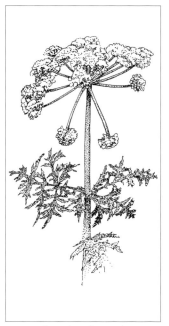

Lomatium dissectum
Mountain Wild Parsnip

Lomatium triternatum
Western Wild Parsley

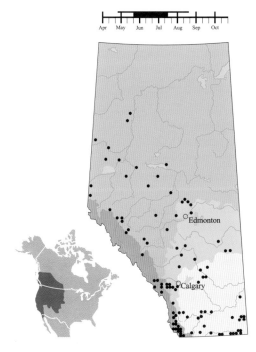

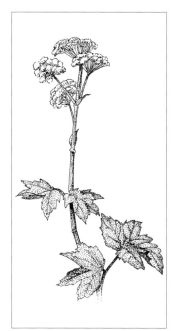

Heracleum lanatum
Cow Parsnip

Angelica arguta
White Angelica

HYBRID SWALLOWTAILS

Identification. Hybrids between *Papilio zelicaon* and *Papilio machaon* are rare and difficult to recognize. If backcrosses occur between a hybrid and either of the parent species, the resultant offspring can exhibit the full range of characteristics of both species. Hybrid populations occur in west-central Alberta and the Cypress Hills (Sperling 1987); Hooper's (1973) "Old World Swallowtails" refers to butterflies from the latter population. Hybrid adults look much like *Papilio machaon dodi* and are best distinguished by habitat, locality and molecular characters. Most individuals from hybrid populations have a club-shaped eye spot with a rounded wing shape like that of *P. zelicaon*.

Life History. Larvae of hybrid populations are found on Heart-leaved Alexanders (*Zizia cordata*) in the area west of Calgary and on Cow Parsnip (*Heracleum lanatum*) in the moister areas north and west of Red Deer. At Bragg Creek, immediately west of Calgary, most larvae have yellow spots that distinguish them from the orange-spotted larvae of *P. m. dodi* at Calgary and eastward. Adult *Papilio zelicaon* x *machaon* hybrids have been collected in the Alberta foothills from May 22 to August 2, with the main flight period in the first half of June. Sometimes pure *P. zelicaon* adults are collected at the same localities later in the summer; these may have dispersed from homogeneous *P. zelicaon* populations in the mountains. Hybrid swallowtails in the Cypress Hills have been collected mostly in late June and early July. Where hybrids are rare, most specimens are collected together with apparently pure *P. zelicaon* or *P. machaon*. Hybrid swallowtails have been collected latest in the season, both for the southern prairies (September 28) and the Peace River region (July 22).

Range and Habitat. Most hybrid populations occur in mixed forests in central Alberta, between 1000 and 2000 m in elevation. The parental species seem to hybridize much less frequently in the southern Alberta prairies and in the Peace River region, as well as where their ranges overlap in the rest of western North America.

Observations of natural matings are rare, however, the mating behaviour of *P. zelicaon* and *P. machaon* is similar, and it is easy to see how hybrids could occur. It is more difficult to understand why the species do not merge wherever they contact each other. One possible explanation is that the frequency of hybrids is higher in areas, such as the boreal forest, where contacting populations of the parental species have similar habitat preferences. In dry-land regions, in addition to distinct habitat preferences, the two species may have behavioural differences which inhibit hybridization.

PAPILIO (PTEROURUS) Scopoli, 1977
TIGER SWALLOWTAILS

The subgenus *Pterourus*, represented in Alberta by the *Papilio glaucus* group, is the only subgenus of swallowtails that is restricted to North America and adjacent Central America. Like the *Papilio machaon* group, the *P. glaucus* group is most diverse in western North America. Six species are currently recognized in this group, three of which occur commonly in Alberta. Most species form hybrids occasionally in zones where their ranges meet or overlap. Late instar larvae have a distinctive pattern, with large eye spots on the thoracic segments followed by a single band and a smooth green background. They feed on the foliage of a wide variety of trees and shrubs. Pupae are similar to those of the *P. machaon* group, but are slightly narrower and less bent. The distinctive pattern of black stripes on a yellow or white background of the adults gives them their common name of tiger swallowtails.

Papilio (Pterourus) canadensis Rothschild and Jordan, 1906
Canadian Tiger Swallowtail

Etymology. The name *canadensis* accurately describes the range of this species, which extends across most of Canada.

Identification. Previously considered a subspecies of the Eastern Tiger Swallowtail (*Papilio glaucus*), the Canadian Tiger Swallowtail has recently been given species status on the basis of a number of genetic differences and the relatively narrow hybrid zone it forms with *P. glaucus* (Hagen *et al*. 1991). It is the only member of the species group that occurs in central and northern Alberta. The ground colour of males is always yellow when specimens are fresh, but females may be either a lighter, creamy yellow or more orange-yellow than the males. There is only one tail per wing, and Alberta specimens have wingspans from 8.5 to 10 cm. The Western Tiger Swallowtail (*Papilio rutulus*) sometimes hybridizes with the Canadian Tiger Swallowtail in southern British Columbia, near Nelson.

Papilio canadensis
Male dorsal

Papilio canadensis
Male ventral

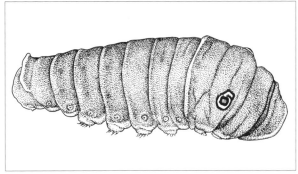

Papilio canadensis late instar larva

Life History. Larvae of *Papilio canadensis* have been collected on Trembling Aspen (*Populus tremuloides*), willows (*Salix* spp.) and domestic crabapple (*Malus* spp.). Eggs are laid on the middle of the upper side of small leaves of the host plant, about one millimetre from the central vein. The eggs are bright green when first laid and have a deep yellow ring of cement at the base that dries and clears in about five minutes. Larvae spin a silk mat on which to rest when not feeding. First and second instar larvae, which resemble bird droppings, rest in the central area of leaves and feed at the leaf edge. Third and later instar larvae cut leaves off when they finish feeding. Adults have been collected from May 12 to August 12, with the main flight period in June. Males tend to patrol along streams, forest edges and trails, but also gather on hilltops or congregate at wet soil where they drink mineral-rich water. Females fly in the same habitats but move more rapidly and circuitously than males in their search for leaves on which to lay eggs. Both sexes nectar at a variety of flowers, especially Common Dandelion (*Taraxacum officinale*).

Range and Habitat. Adults are common along trails through mixed forest or along the edges of aspen parkland. The Canadian Tiger Swallowtail is common throughout most of Alberta except in the southern grasslands, where it exists as rare and localized populations.

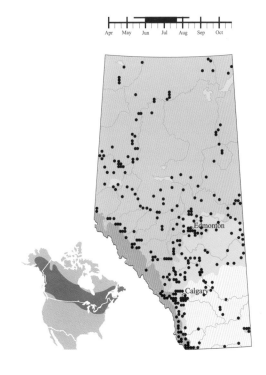

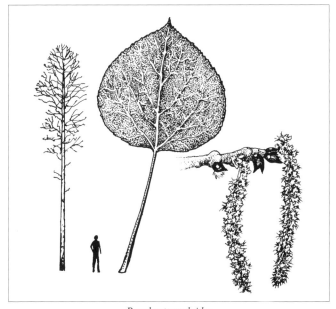

Populus tremuloides
Trembling Aspen

Papilio (Pterourus) eurymedon Lucas, 1852
Pale Swallowtail

Etymology. From the Greek *eurys* meaning "broad" and *medon* meaning "guardian." The Eurymedon was a river in ancient Greece, and also the name of a mytho-logical king of giants.

Identification. This species has the black wing stripes shared by other species in the tiger swallowtail group, but its background colour is pale white without any yellow. The black wing bands are wider than those of the other species and are usually wider than the white areas between the bands. There is only one tail on each hind wing, and the wingspan is 9 to 10 cm in Alberta specimens.

Life History. Larvae of the Pale Swallowtail have not yet been recorded in Alberta. Elsewhere, larvae are reported to feed on *Ceanothus* spp., cherry (*Prunus* spp.) and domestic crabapple (*Malus* spp.). Adults have been collected from June 23 to August 1.

Range and Habitat. This species is the rarest swal-lowtail in Alberta. It is found in the southwestern corner of Alberta, north to the Crowsnest Pass and east to Police Outpost Provincial Park. Many records from Waterton Lakes National Park may represent butterflies that strayed in from British Columbia. *Papilio euryme-don* inhabits dry montane forest.

Papilio eurymedon
Male dorsal

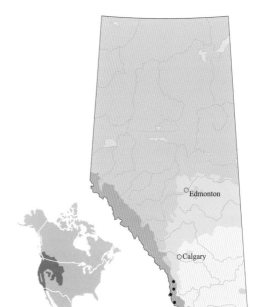

Malus sp.
domestic crabapple

Papilio (Pterourus) multicaudatus W.F. Kirby, 1884
Two-tailed Swallowtail

Papilio multicaudatus
Male dorsal

Etymology. The Latin name translates to "many-tailed," a good description of the only swallowtail in Alberta that has more than one tail per wing.

Identification. *Papilio multicaudatus* looks much like the Canadian Tiger Swallowtail (*Papilio canadensis*), but has a second, smaller tail on each hind wing. Its wing stripes are also a bit narrower than those of *P. canadensis* and its wingspan is usually more than 10 cm. Its background colour is the same shade of yellow found in male Canadian Tiger Swallowtails.

Life History. There are no larval records for Alberta, but elsewhere, hosts include cherry (*Prunus* spp.) and Saskatoon (*Amelanchier alnifolia*). Oviposition has been observed on Chokecherry (*Prunus virginiana*) at Milk River, Alberta. Adults have been collected from June 7 to September 2, but most are from late June.

Range and Habitat. The Two-tailed Swallowtail is found along the southern border of Alberta, at Waterton, along the Milk River (especially at Police Coulee) and rarely north to Lethbridge and Taber. It flies along coulees and the edges of riparian forest. The large wing span of this butterfly makes it a fast flier well suited to soaring. Adults commonly nectar on thistles (*Cirsium* spp.).

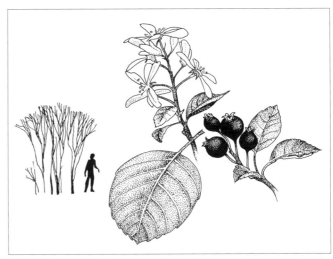

Amelanchier alnifolia
Saskatoon

Papilio (Pterourus) rutulus Lucas, 1852
Western Tiger Swallowtail

Etymology. The species name may be derived from the Latin *rutilus*, meaning "ruddy in colour," or more likely the name of a Roman tribe.

Identification. The Western Tiger Swallowtail is very similar in appearance to the Canadian Tiger Swallowtail (*Papilio canadensis*) but differs in having the first spot of the submarginal spots of the hind wing yellow rather than orange and the ventral hind wing marginal spots yellow.

Papilio rutulus
Male dorsal

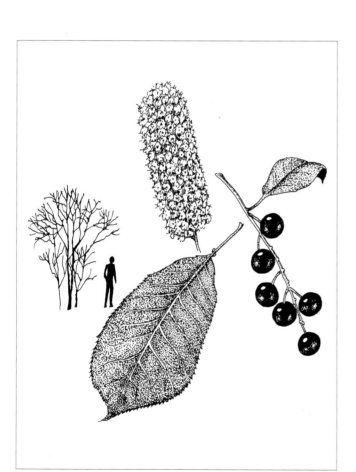

Prunus virginiana
Choke Cherry

Papilio rutulus
Male ventral

Salix exigua
Sandbar Willow

Life History. Larvae are similar to the Canadian Tiger Swallowtail and are reported to feed on similar plants, including poplars (*Populus* spp.), willows (*Salix* spp.) as well as cherry (*Prunus* spp.). Adults fly from the middle of May through July and occasionally to August.

Range and Habitat. The Western Tiger Swallowtail is found mainly west of the Rocky Mountains, with populations extending onto the eastern slopes where they overlap with the range of the Canadian Tiger Swallowtail. *Papilio rutulus* was reported in Alberta by Ferris and Brown (1981) but no authenticated records have been made to date. There is a high probability that this species occurs in the mountains of the Waterton Lakes National Park to Crowsnest Pass area of Alberta, as there are records to the west (Kootenay River, British Columbia) and just to the south (Glacier and Toole Counties, Montana).

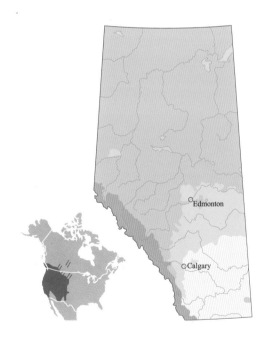

West Castle River area, north of Waterton Lakes National Park.   A.T. Finnamore.

4

Family **PIERIDAE**
WHITES, MARBLES and SULPHURS

There are 23 species of Pieridae in Alberta. The family can be divided into three subfamilies whose common names are based on wing patterns: Pierinae, the whites; Anthocharinae, the marbles; and Coliadinae, the sulphurs. Wing colours in pierids are derived from waste products stored in the caterpillar stage. The appearance of certain colours is produced by admixtures of two other colours of scales. For example, "green" is composed of interspersed yellow and black scales. Although butterflies are seldom considered agricultural pests, there are several pierid species whose caterpillars sometimes infest vegetable crops (*Pieris rapae*), Alfalfa (*Colias eurytheme, C. philodice*) and even evergreen stands (*Neophasia menapia*).

Subfamily
PIERINAE
WHITES

Pierines are commonly called whites because of their predominantly black-and-white appearance. These markings help the butterflies use the rays of the sun to warm up on a cool day. Dark markings near the body absorb light. The heat diffuses to the flight muscles, which cannot function if they are cold. As butterfly wings do not conduct heat well, only the most basal parts of the wings can help heat the body. The middle of the upper side of the wings of pierines is largely white, and these butterflies hold them apart at just the right angle so that the light is bounced back and forth between the wings until it reaches the dark basal part near the body, where heat can be transferred to the flight muscles. Alberta has seven species of whites. Larvae of most species feed on plants in the mustard family (Cruciferae), which includes common garden vegetables like cabbage and broccoli. The Cabbage Butterfly (*Pieris rapae*) is one of the most common species of butterflies in urban and agricultural areas because of its preference for cultivated crucifers as larval hosts. On the other hand, larvae of the Pine White (*Neophasia menapia*) are unique among our pierids in feeding on evergreen needles.

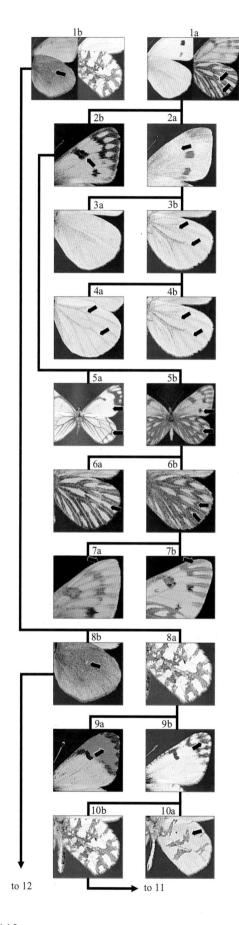

to 12   to 11

Key to Species of Pieridae in Alberta

1a) Ventral hind wing uniformly coloured and without markings, or with veins outlined by dark scales 2

b) Ventral hind wing with markings marbled, or a spot at end of disc 8

2a) Dorsal fore wing without markings in disc 3

b) Dorsal fore wing with bar across end of disc 5

3a) Ventral hind wing without markings along veins . . . .
. . . . *Pieris rapae* (Linnaeus) p. 121

b) Ventral hind wing veins outlined by dark scales, at least at base of wing 4

4a) Ventral hind wing markings dark and sharply defined or absent; dorsal fore wing of female white; found in moist boreal forest . . . . *Pieris oleracea* Harris p. 119

b) Ventral hind wing markings light and suffused; dorsal fore wing of female with submarginal spots; found in mountainous regions . . . . *Pieris marginalis* Scudder p. 117

5a) Fore wings without spots on posterior margin; ventral hind wing submarginal band is perpendicular to veins . . . .
. . . . *Neophasia menapia* (Felder & Felder) p. 115

b) Dorsal or ventral fore wings usually with spot in cell Cu2; ventral hind wing with submarginal band of chevrons or angled markings 6

6a) Ventral hind wing markings brownish green and distinct; submarginal markings are generally not connected laterally between veins . . . . . *Pontia sisymbrii* (Boisduval) p. 126

b) Ventral hind wing markings dark green or indistinct and yellow; submarginal markings are connected between veins . . . 7

7a) Submarginal band on ventral fore wing apex not connected along veins to fore wing margin; markings reduced in males, brownish in females . . . .
. . . . . . *Pontia protodice* (Boisduval & Le Conte) p. 125

b) Submarginal band on ventral fore wing apex connected along veins to fore wing margin; markings black in both males and females . . . . *Pontia occidentalis* (Reakirt) p. 123

8a) Ventral hind wing with marbled green pattern 9

b) Ventral hind wing with spot at end of disc, which may be silver, pink or cream 12

9a) Dorsal fore wing apex with orange patch . . . .
. . . . *Anthocharis sara* Lucas p. 128

b) Dorsal fore wing apex black and white 10

10a) Ventral hind wing marbling condensed to a few diagonal bands
. . . . *Euchloe olympia* (W.H. Edwards) p. 132

b) Ventral hind wing marbling as extensive as, or more than, pale areas 11

11a) Ventral hind wing marbling diffuse, not in distinct bands, occupying most of wing; ventral fore wing apical markings yellowish green; smaller. . . . . *Euchloe creusa* (Doubleday) p. 131

b) Ventral hind wing marbling indistinct, interrupted by large white patches; ventral fore wing apical markings yellowish; larger . . . . . *Euchloe ausonides* (Lucas) p. 129

12a) Fore wing apex pointed; dorsal fore wing black border outlines a "dogface" . . . . *Zerene cesonia* (Stoll) p. 148

b) Fore wing apex blunt; dorsal fore wing black border uniform in width (most males) or broken, reduced, or absent (most females). 13

13a) Dorsal fore wing surface predominantly green and/or black; occurs in alpine habitats only . . . . *Colias nastes* Boisduval p. 143

b) Dorsal fore wing surface predominantly white, cream, yellow or orange; varied habitats 14

14a) Dorsal wing surface with orange scales restricted to discal spot or absent 15

b) Dorsal wing surface with orange areas (may be only a flush) 21

15a) Dorsal hind wing discal spot absent; ventral hind wing discal spot unringed 16

b) Dorsal hind wing discal spot orange (may be light); ventral hind wing discal spot with pink or brown ring 17

16a) Dorsal fore wing border wide (more than 5 mm at apex); in boreal forest only . . . . *Colias palaeno* (Linnaeus) p. 144

b) Dorsal fore wing border narrow (less than 5 mm at apex in males and vestigial in females); in prairies only . . . . *Colias alexandra* W.H. Edwards p. 134

17a) Ventral hind wing and/or ventral fore wing with submarginal spots; most females with border extending down outer margin of dorsal hind wing . . . . *Colias philodice* Godart p. 146

b) Ventral hind wing and ventral fore wing without submarginal spots; most females with trace or no border on dorsal hind wing 18

18a) Female; medial area of dorsal fore wing white and/or with light orange tinge . . . . *Colias christina* W.H. Edwards p. 136

b) Male or female; medial area of dorsal fore wing yellow only 19

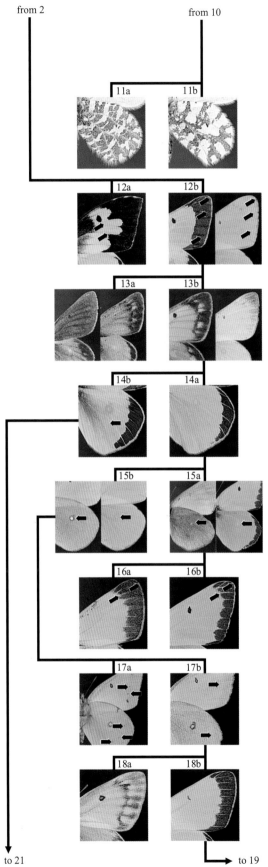

from 14   from 18

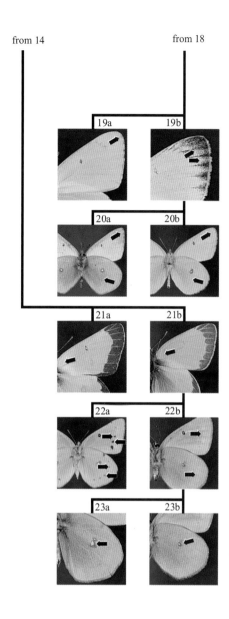

19a) Large to medium size (fore wing length 26-32 mm, mean=28.5 mm, n=26); pointed fore wing; females with border of dorsal fore wing absent at apex, or weaker marginally than submarginally . . . . *Colias gigantea* Strecker p. 139

b) Medium to small size (fore wing 22-27 mm, mean=25 mm, n=30) rounded fore wing; females with border of dorsal fore wing reduced to margin and most extensive at apex 20

20a) Ventral hind wing and ventral fore wing with extensive dark scaling; ventral hind wing is generally greenish; females with partial border on dorsal hind wing; females white or yellow; in mountains . . . . *Colias pelidne* Boisduval & Le Conte p. 145

b) Ventral hind wing and ventral fore wing with little dark scaling; ventral hind wing is yellowish; females without border on dorsal hind wing; females yellow; any mixed forest areas . . . . *Colias interior* Scudder p. 141

21a) Dorsal fore wing orange not continuous to wing base . . . . *Colias christina* W.H. Edwards p. 136

b) Dorsal fore wing orange continuous to wing base 22

22a) Ventral hind wing and/or ventral fore wing with submarginal spots . . . . *Colias eurytheme* Boisduval p. 138

b) Ventral hind wing and ventral fore wing without submarginal spots 23

23a) Ventral hind wing discal spot large (more than 1 mm diameter), with wide, distally smeared ring; males without sex patch at base of dorsal fore wing and with medium or pale orange dorsal wing colour; boreal areas. . . . . *Colias canadensis* Ferris p. 135

b) Ventral hind wing discal spot small (1 mm diameter), with narrow ring; males with sex patch at base of dorsal fore wing and with deep orange dorsal wing colour; subalpine areas . . . . *Colias meadii* W.H. Edwards p. 142

Neophasia Behr, 1869

Etymology. *Neo* means "new," and *phasis* is a phase or appearance. In Behr's description, he compared his new genus to one called *Leucophasia*. Perhaps Behr's name refers to the New World distribution of *Neophasia*, or indicates its different colour pattern.

Neophasia menapia (Felder and Felder, 1859)
Pine White
subspecies: *Neophasia menapia menapia* (Felder and Felder, 1859)

Etymology. In Latin, Menapia refers to a people of northern Gaul, or their territory.

Identification. This species is easily recognized by the heavy black markings on the fore wing apex, which contrast with the more delicately patterned and largely white remainder of the wing surface. Females have a creamier ground colour, with darker markings, and may have orange scales on the hind wing margin. This is also our only species of pierid in which there is a sub-marginal line on the hind wing that is clearly perpendicular to the slightly darkened wing veins, rather than a band composed of a series of chevrons in each cell.

Life History. This primitive genus of whites is unusual among the Pieridae, in that the larvae of its two species feed on conifers, rather than the mustards (Cruciferae) on which most of its relatives feed. Larvae of the Pine White may feed on a number of members of the pine family (Pinaceae), including pines (*Pinus* spp.), Douglas Fir (*Pseudotsuga menziesii*), firs (*Abies* spp.), hemlocks (*Tsuga* spp.) and even spruces (*Picea* spp.). Ponderosa Pine (*Pinus ponderosa*) is the primary host, though they may be common on other pines, such as Lodgepole Pine (*Pinus contorta* var. *latifolia*). Occasional large outbreaks of the Pine White have been recorded in the Pacific Northwest since the late 1800s. Some of these outbreaks caused up to 25% mortality of pines (in Idaho), largely because the weakened trees were then attacked by bark beetles. Other outbreaks have been considered a sufficient threat to warrant large scale spraying operations (e.g., on Vancouver Island in 1961). Outbreaks subside within three years, however, due to a build up of natural enemies, such as parasitic wasps and predacious bugs. Spraying only interferes with this process.

Neophasia menapia menapia
Male dorsal

Neophasia menapia menapia
Female dorsal

Pinus ponderosa
Ponderosa Pine

115

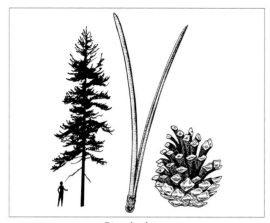

Pinus banksiana
Jack Pine

Pseudotsuga menziesii
Douglas Fir

Apr May Jun Jul Aug Sep Oct

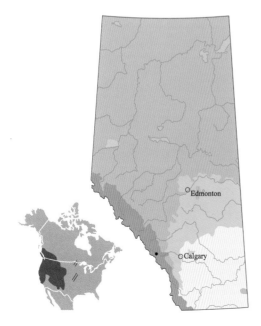

Eggs of the Pine White are light green, with sculptured ridges and white edges. Females lay from five to twenty eggs on a needle, high in the tree, and young larvae feed in groups encircling the needle. This gregarious larval feeding is unique among the pierids. Older Pine White larvae feed singly, and are dark green with white stripes and have a light green head. Mature larvae descend from the tree on long silk threads and pupate against tree trunks, shrubs and grasses. Pupae also have light stripes on a green background, though some are substantially darker than others. There is a single generation of adults that emerges in late summer (August 2 to September 5 in Alberta). Adults swarm around the tops of the larval host trees, coming down mainly in the morning to nectar on flowers. Eggs overwinter and hatch about the time new needles appear in the spring. Larvae grow very slowly for the first few weeks, but very rapidly during the last instars in July. No immature stages of the Pine White have been found in Alberta and adult specimens have been collected here only occasionally.

Range and Habitat. *Neophasia* is one of the few genera of butterflies in Alberta that originated in southern North America. One of its two species occurs north of the American southwest, the other is found mainly in Mexico. The most closely related genus is found throughout Latin America. The Pine White is found through all of the western United States, west of South Dakota and Nebraska, and north to central British Columbia. Only a few records are known for Alberta, all are from 1922 or earlier and are from the vicinity of Banff. During outbreaks, females may fly far from where they originated. Migrants from British Columbia may account for our Alberta records. These specimens may be referred to the subspecies *Neophasia menapia menapia*. Preferred habitat is montane forest, particularly stands of Ponderosa Pine (*Pinus ponderosa*), which is a rare species in Alberta.

Pieris Schrank, 1801

Etymology. Pieris was a daughter of Pierus, a Muse in ancient Greek mythology.

Identification. Members of both *Pieris* and *Pontia* are approximately the same size, and adults are mainly white (especially on the upper side), with varying amounts of yellow and black or dark brown scales. The green areas on the ventral hind wing are actually made up of mixtures of yellow and black scales. For the species that occur in Alberta, these green areas either line the veins or are uniformly spread over the ventral hind wing. Caterpillars of all species feed on members of the mustard family (Cruciferae). *Pieris* is separated from *Pontia* by the absence of a dark bar at the end of the fore wing disc, and the relatively small number of distinct dark markings, particularly on the fore wing. There are three species of this genus in Alberta.

Pieris marginalis Scudder, 1861
Margined White

Etymology. The species epithet of the Margined White probably refers to the darker markings on the fore wing margins of some populations of this species.

Identification. *Pieris marginalis* has only recently been separated from the other species in the complex. Geiger and Shapiro (1992) have shown that *Pieris marginalis* shows a large genetic distance (based on 21 allozyme loci) from *Pieris oleracea*. The Eurasian species in the complex are even more distinct; these species also occur in Alaska and the Yukon Territory and potentially range into northern Alberta. Unfortunately, the wing patterns of the species in the *Pieris napi* (Linnaeus) complex are not always adequate for identifying single specimens, and there was very little indication that so much genetic diversity is hidden away within the butterflies. Most specimens of *P. marginalis* can be distinguished from *P. oleracea* by the dark, suffused scaling along the veins of the ventral hind wing. Females of *P. marginalis* also have darker markings on the dorsal fore wing.

Pieris marginalis
Male dorsal

Pieris marginalis
Male ventral

Sisymbrium altissimum
Tumbling Mustard

117

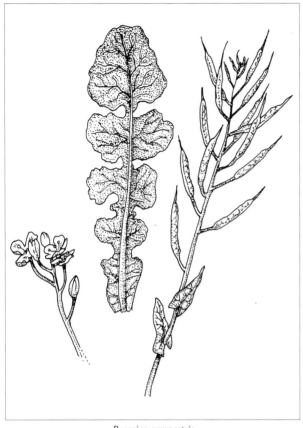

Brassica campestris
Rape

Life History. The larvae of *Pieris marginalis* have not been reared in Alberta, though they undoubtedly feed on various mustards (Cruciferae) in forested areas. The adults fly at least from May 22 to August 25, with most records from June to early August. This species probably has only a single generation in Alberta, with the pupae overwintering.

Range and Habitat. This species is restricted to moist forests in mountainous areas of western North America from New Mexico and California to at least the Alaskan panhandle. It is currently difficult to give a more precise picture of the range of this species, as it is so difficult to distinguish from related species in the field. In general, *Pieris marginalis* will be found in the mountains, while *Pieris oleracea* will be found in boreal forest. Both species are widespread but locally uncommon. Specimens from the far northern parts of Alberta, such as the Caribou Mountains, may also be referable to *P. marginalis*.

Scree slope near Cataract Creek, Alberta.

A.T. Finnamore

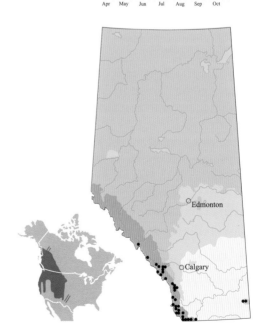

Pieris oleracea Harris, 1929
Mustard White

Etymology. The species name is from *oleraceous*, which is a descriptive term for herbs used in cooking and refers to the cruciferous (mustard family) host plants of the larvae. Interestingly, Harris' initial description of the butterfly was published in a horticultural journal, *The New England Farmer*.

Identification. The Mustard White has long been considered a subspecies of *Pieris napi*, which was believed to have a broad holarctic distribution. Extensive morphological investigation by Warren (1968) and Eitschberger (1981, 1983) and particularly enzyme analysis by Geiger (Geiger and Scholl 1985, Geiger and Shapiro 1992) have led to the conclusion that the North American populations represent several additional species. At least two of these, *Pieris oleracea* and *Pieris marginalis*, occur in Alberta. *Pieris oleracea* usually is almost completely white on the upper side of the wings, while veins on the underside of the hind wing are outlined with sharply defined dark scaling. In the summer form, the dark markings on the ventral hind wing may be greatly reduced or absent. On some females there are faint submarginal spots on the dorsal fore wing, but not dark spots and markings along the ends of the veins and lower fore wing margins as in *P. marginalis*. There is never a distinct black fore wing tip as in the Cabbage Butterfly, *Pieris rapae*.

Life History. Caterpillars of the Mustard White are reported to feed on a variety of woodland crucifers (Cruciferae), especially whitlow-grasses (*Draba* spp.) and cresses (*Arabis* spp.). Larval host plants are still unknown for Alberta. The caterpillars are green with narrow yellow lines running down the sides and back. Adults are out early in the spring and there is a second generation later in the summer. The pupae overwinter. The flight period is from April 18 to August 27. There is only one generation in cooler habitats, with the main flight in mid-June.

Pieris oleracea
Male dorsal

Pieris oleracea
Male dorsal

Pieris oleracea
Summer form ventral

Draba cana
Whitlow-grass

119

Arabis drummondii
Drummond's Rock Cress

Range and Habitat. *Pieris oleracea* occurs across the boreal region of Canada, particularly in open woods and small clearings in moist coniferous forest. The species is widespread but locally uncommon in Alberta. *Pieris oleracea* appears to be replaced by *Pieris rapae* (the Cabbage Butterfly) in areas where the forest has been opened for agriculture. It is known that *Pieris oleracea* overlaps with, but remains separate from, an almost indistinguishable species, *Pieris virginiensis* (the Virginia White) in the eastern United States. In contrast, the interaction between *P. oleracea* and *P. marginalis* in Alberta is not well understood. Most of the Alberta populations are likely to be *Pieris oleracea*, while populations in the mountains are *Pieris marginalis*. The two species appear to interact, and perhaps intergrade, on both sides of the Bow River. It will be highly informative to study the interaction between *P. oleracea* and *P. marginalis* to see if they remain distinct genetically where they encounter each other in western Canada.

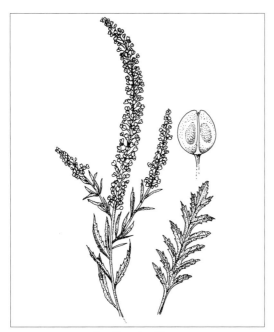

Lepidium densiflorum
Common Peppergrass

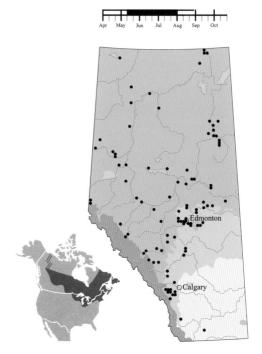

Pieris rapae (Linnaeus, 1758)
Cabbage Butterfly

Etymology. *Rapa* is a Latin word for "turnip" and so it is clear that Linnaeus named this butterfly after its larval food plants, which include cabbages, turnips and many other members of the mustard family (Cruciferae).

Identification. Almost everyone is familiar with this common white butterfly. It is best distinguished from other whites by the distinct black tips on the dorsal fore wing and the relatively uniform distribution of black and yellow scales on the ventral hind wing. Individuals from the summer generations are large and almost entirely white above, and mostly yellow below. Spring adults are smaller and have much more black scaling, which allows them to warm up faster on cool spring days. Females have two black submarginal spots on the dorsal fore wing, while males have only one.

Life History. Larvae of the Cabbage Butterfly are a serious pest on cabbage, cauliflower, broccoli (*Brassica oleracea*) and some other cultivated members of the mustard family. They also feed on weedy mustard species. The larvae are green with narrow yellow lines running down the sides and back. Cabbage Butterflies overwinter as pupae which may be green or brown to match substrate colour and light conditions. Eggs are light green or yellow and are conically elongated with longitudinal furrows. There can be three generations per year, especially in the warmer southern parts of the province. Adults have been collected from April 3 to November 16 and are especially common in late summer.

Pieris rapae
Male dorsal

Pieris rapae
Male ventral

Pieris rapae
Female dorsal

Pieris rapae
Summer form dorsal

Brassica oleracea var. *capitata*
Cabbage

121

Brassica oleracea var. *botrytis*
Broccoli

Brassica oleracea var. *botyrytis*
Cauliflower

Range and Habitat. The Cabbage Butterfly is found throughout Alberta where there are vegetable gardens or weedy areas. The Cabbage Butterfly was introduced to Quebec from Europe in about 1860 and has since spread over virtually the entire continent. The first specimen collected in Alberta was taken near Calgary on July 20, 1899, by Wolley-Dod. Cabbage Butterflies are numerous in agricultural areas, but are virtually absent from undisturbed habitats except as straying migrants.

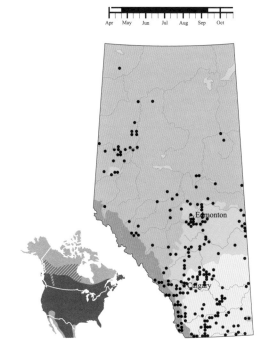

Pontia Fabricius, 1807

Etymology. Pontia refers to the Black Sea region, or to an area along its western edge.

Identification. The species in this genus are similar to those in *Pieris*, but can be distinguished by the dark bar across the end of the fore wing disc. In addition, the ventral hind wing has more extensive green areas along the veins that usually form a submarginal band of chevrons. *Pontia* larvae feed on a variety of mustards (Cruciferae). They have spiny bumps and a pattern of alternating light and dark bands across each segment. Pupae are the overwintering stage. Immatures have not been reared for Alberta populations of our three species.

Pontia occidentalis (Reakirt, 1866)
Western White
subspecies: *Pontia occidentalis occidentalis* (Reakirt, 1866)

Etymology. *Occidentalis* means "coming from the west," an appropriate name for a white which is found primarily in the western part of the continent.

Identification. *Pontia occidentalis* is by far our most common *Pontia*. The summer generation of adults is very similar to the Checkered White but is distinguished by the more continuous submarginal band on the fore wing. Also, the markings are more black than brown (though the females are more brown and have more extensive dark markings in both species). Markings on the ventral hind wing are more distinct, while the dark spot on the lower margin of the ventral fore wing is smaller. Adults of the spring are darker and more similar to those of the California White (for differences, see *Pontia sisymbrii*). A dark spring generation does not seem to be present in the Checkered White. More study is needed, however, as it is possible that we cannot distinguish between spring generation specimens of Checkered and Western Whites.

Pontia occidentalis occidentalis
Male dorsal

Pontia occidentalis occidentalis
Male ventral

Pontia occidentalis occidentalis
Female dorsal

Pontia occidentalis occidentalis
Female ventral

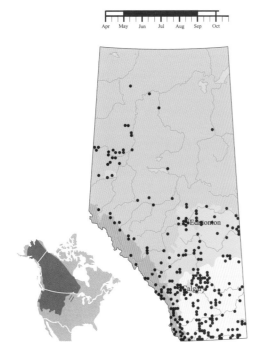

Life History. Like the Checkered White, the Western White has been recorded on numerous mustard species throughout its range. In the mountains, it has only one brood and adults emerge in late spring. In warmer areas there are two broods and late specimens may represent a partial third brood. Specimens have been collected in Alberta from April 1 to October 5. The summer brood is more abundant in the southern agricultural areas and can be found swarming on alfalfa flowers in August. As the flight period, range and habitat of this species overlap with those of our other two *Pontia* species, it would be interesting to determine the extent to which their larvae compete for food plants. Adults of the Western White are hilltoppers; that is, males congregate on high peaks and wait for females to arrive to mate. Thus the best place to find this species is on hilltops or prominent river banks, together with swallowtails *(Papilio machaon* group species). The females of *P. occidentalis* are more difficult to find, as they usually fly along valley floors and can be widely scattered.

Range and Habitat. The Western White occurs from Alaska south to central California and northern New Mexico, and east to Manitoba. In Alberta, it ranges across most of the province, although in the northeastern corner of the province it is known only from Mildred Lake. Populations in Alberta are referred to *Pontia occidentalis occidentalis*. Preferred habitats are prairies, parkland meadows or grassy roadsides, as well as openings in montane forest on the western edge of the province.

Pontia occidentalis at Plateau Mountain, Alberta.

G.J. Hilchie.

Pontia protodice (Boisduval and Le Conte, 1829)
Checkered White

Etymology. The derivation of *protodice* is uncertain. *Proto* refers to something which comes first, while *dice* may be related to *dico*, which is to indicate or to dedicate, or to *dicis*, which means for the sake of appearances or form. Perhaps Boisduval and LeConte thought this species showed an especially primitive wing pattern.

Identification. The Checkered White is especially difficult to distinguish from the Western White. Until recently, their status as separate species was uncertain, as many intermediate specimens had been found. Careful study of genetic markers and several structural characters has shown that there is very little, if any, interbreeding between them in most areas. Forms like these, which are superficially identical but nevertheless maintain a separate genetic identity, are referred to as "sibling species." In general, the dark wing markings are more brown than black in the Checkered White and the ventral hind wing markings may be almost completely absent. The submarginal band on the apex of the dorsal fore wing is discontinuous, while the dark spot on the lower edge of the ventral fore wing is large. The dark wing markings are more extensive in females than in males.

Life History. The larvae likely feed on several crucifer species in Alberta, including mustard (*Brassica* spp.) and peppergrass (*Lepidium* spp.). In Alberta, there seems to be a single adult generation which emerges in the summer (June 24 to September 3).

Range and Habitat. The Checkered White is found in southern Canada, across the continental United States and into Mexico. It is uncommon or absent in the American northwest and British Columbia. In Alberta, only a few scattered records are known, from the southern half of the province north to Primrose Lake. Preferred habitats are parkland meadows and prairies.

Pontia protodice
Male dorsal

Pontia protodice
Male ventral

Pontia protodice
Female dorsal

Pontia protodice
Female ventral

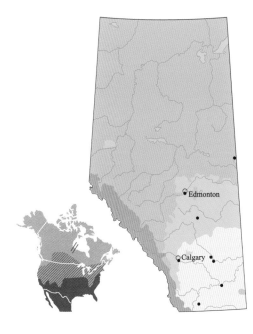

Pontia sisymbrii (Boisduval, 1852)
California White
subspecies: *Pontia sisymbrii flavitincta* (J.A. Comstock, 1924)

Pontia sisymbrii flavitincta
Male dorsal

Pontia sisymbrii flavitincta
Male ventral

Pontia sisymbrii flavitincta
Female dorsal

Pontia sisymbrii flavitincta
Female ventral

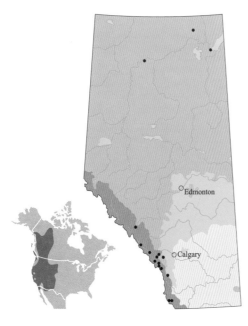

Etymology. *Sisymbrium* refers to a watercress or moisture-loving garden plant. In botanical nomenclature it is a genus of weedy mustards, which includes some of the larval food plants of the California White. The subspecies name *flavitincta* is derived from the Latin *flavus* and *tincta* meaning "yellowish" and "tinged," respectively.

Identification. The California White is similar to the spring form of the Western White. Both have dark markings on the ventral hind wing, but they can be distinguished by their colour and pattern. In the California White the markings appear more brownish green and are more distinct from the white background. The chevrons in the submarginal band have a characteristic arrow-like shape, as they do not merge. The markings on the top of the fore wing tend to be narrow.

Life History. Specimens have been collected from May 7 to July 1 in Alberta. Larvae probably feed on rock cress (*Arabis* spp.) or weedy mustards (*Sisymbrium* spp.).

Range and Habitat. This species ranges from central Yukon Territory and western Northwest Territories, south to Baja California and New Mexico. In Alberta it is uncommon and has a patchy distribution. It is found mainly at the base of the Rocky Mountains, from the Kootenay Plains to the West Castle River. There are also several records from the northeast corner of the province, from Fort Vermilion to Fort Chipewyan. Populations from the mountains are referable to *Pontia sisymbrii flavitincta*, while those in the northern boreal forest await critical examination for placement at the subspecies level. Preferred habitats are dry slopes or rocky exposures in coniferous forests. *Pontia sisymbrii* has a much narrower habitat range than our two other *Pontia* species.

126

Subfamily
ANTHOCHARINAE
MARBLES and ORANGE TIPS

There are four species of anthocharines in Alberta, commonly called marbles and orange tips. Marbles have a greenish yellow marbled pattern on their ventral hind wings, as do orange tips, but the latter species also have a bright orange patch on the tip of the dorsal fore wing. Anthocharine caterpillars, like those of most pierines, feed mainly on plants of the mustard family (Cruciferae).

Euchloe olympia at Sandy Point, Alberta.   J.H. Acorn.

Anthocharis Boisduval, Rambur and Graslin, 1833
ORANGE TIPS

Etymology. *Antho* refers to flowers and *charis* means "favour"; so the name means "flower-loving."

Identification. Most species in this genus can be easily distinguished by the orange patch on the tip of the fore wing of males. *Anthocharis* is related to *Euchloe* and both genera have a green pattern resembling marble on the ventral hind wing.

Anthocharis sara Lucas, 1852
Sara Orange Tip
subspecies: *Anthocharis sara stella* W.H. Edwards, 1879

Anthocharis sara stella
Male dorsal

Anthocharis sara stella
Male ventral

Anthocharis sara stella
Female dorsal

Anthocharis sara stella
Female ventral

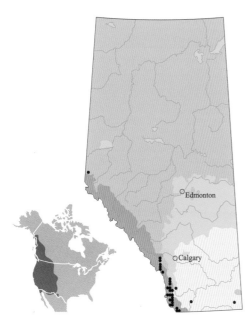

Etymology. Lucas gave no derivation for *sara* in his original description, and neither did Edwards in his description of Stella; possibly they were referring to particular women.

Identification. The Sara Orange Tip is our only species with orange wing tips. On males, the ground colour is white and the orange patch extends right to the black margin of the wing. In females the ground colour is bright yellow and the orange patch is smaller. The green markings on the underside of the hind wings and tip of the fore wing are divided by fine lines into a granular pattern. Alberta populations of this species are generally referred to *Anthocharis sara stella*. Using electrophoretic data Geiger and Shapiro (1986) demonstrated that *A. sara* and *A.s. stella* may be differentiated at the species level. *Anthocharis sara* has been increasingly recognized as a species complex, the taxonomy of which needs more research.

Life History. Larval hosts for the Sara Orange Tip are a variety of crucifers (Cruciferae), though there are no records yet for Alberta. Larvae are dark green with small black dots and a wide, white lateral stripe. The pupae overwinter and there is only one generation per year. The flight period extends from May 7 to August 1.

Range and Habitat. The Sara Orange Tip is found from the southern Yukon Territory to northern Mexico. Most Alberta records are from the mountains between Banff and Waterton. It has also been taken north to the Torrens River and east to St. Mary's Dam and Manyberries. This species can be seen in meadows in coniferous forest.

Euchloe Hübner, 1819
MARBLES

Etymology. The name *Euchloe* is probably composed of the Greek *eu*, meaning "true or good," and *chlor*, meaning "yellowish green," and may refer to the green marbling on the dorsal hind wing of species of this group. Chloe was also a lover of Daphnis in a Greek pastoral romance, and so perhaps *Euchloe* is simply another ancient name.

Identification. Species of *Euchloe* have a variety of beautiful green marbled patterns on the underside of the hind wing, but differ from *Anthocharis* in lacking bright orange patches on the fore wings. In our three species, the ventral hind wing markings are coarser than in *Anthocharis*. The dorsal hind wing of *Euchloe* females is frequently dull yellow.

Marbles rest with the fore wings tucked between the hind wings, with only the tops showing. The marbled pattern on the ventral hind wing and the tip of the ventral fore wing help the butterflies to blend into the vegetation. The Olympia Marble is found in grasslands and has relatively sparse marbling, while the other two marbles live in more lush habitats and have more extensive marbling.

The larvae of our three species are green to blue-green with scattered small black dots and two yellow or orange lines down each side. There is one brood per year. The pupae have long, pointed heads and over-winter. As with most other members of the Anthocharinae and Pierinae, the host plants are members of the crucifer family (Cruciferae).

Euchloe ausonides (Lucas, 1852)
Large Marble
subspecies: *Euchloe ausonides mayi* Chermock and Chermock, 1940

Etymology. Ausonia refers to Italy and *ides* means "to resemble." Lucas' choice of name refers to the similarity between this species and *Euchloe ausonia*, a species originally described from northern Italy. The subspecies *mayi* was named after J.F. May, a friend of the Chermocks.

Euchloe ausonides mayi
Male dorsal

Identification. The Large Marble is the most common *Euchloe* in Alberta. As its name implies, it is partly distinguished by its larger size (fore wing 19.0-23.5 mm) . Its ventral hind wing marbling is more extensive than in the Olympia Marble, but less than that on the Northern Marble. Most Alberta populations belong to *Euchloe ausonides mayi*, while populations along the 49th parallel resemble *E. a. coloradensis* (Hy. Edwards).

Euchloe ausonides mayi
Male ventral

Life History. The host plants used by *Euchloe ausonides* include several genera in the mustard family (Cruciferae). In Alberta, it has been found ovipositing on Drummond's Rock Cress (*Arabis drummondii*) in the Peace River area. The flight period is May 4 to August 6, with a single record reported from October 12. The peak flight is in late May to early July.

Range and Habitat. The Large Marble ranges from Alaska to northern Ontario and south to New Mexico and central California. It can be found throughout much of Alberta, but not always at the same localities as the other two species. Preferred habitats are aspen parkland, dry meadows in mixed forest and open pine forest.

Arabis drummondii
Drummond's Rock Cress

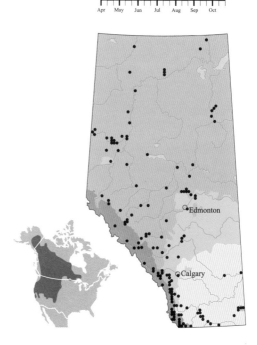

Bog, Caribou Mountains, boreal region of Alberta.   G.J. Hilchie.

Euchloe creusa (Doubleday, [1847])
Northern Marble

Etymology. Creusa was a name given to several mythological princesses in ancient Greece.

Identification. The Northern Marble is a small butterfly (16.0-20.5 mm). The marbling on the ventral hind wing is the most extensive of our three species of Euchloe and does not form distinct bands. Ventral fore wing apical markings in *E. creusa* are yellowish green whereas those in *E. ausonides* are yellow.

Life History. Host plants known for the species are draba or whitlow-grass (*Draba* spp.) and rock cress (*Arabis* spp.) including Whitlow-grass (*Draba cana*) at Moraine Lake, Alberta. There is a single generation of adults with a flight period from May 15 to August 9. One individual has been reported from September 25. Most records are from June and July.

Range and Habitat. The Northern Marble ranges from Alaska to northern Saskatchewan and south to Glacier County, Montana including the Rocky Mountains of Alberta, and with scattered records from Fort Vermilion, Pine Lake and north of Fort McKay. Preferred habitats are subalpine forest and other coniferous forest openings.

Euchloe creusa
Male dorsal

Euchloe creusa
Male ventral

Euchloe creusa
Female dorsal

Euchloe creusa
Female ventral

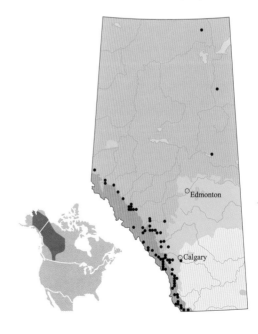

Draba cana
Whitlow-grass

Euchloe olympia (W.H. Edwards, 1871)
Olympia Marble

Euchloe olympia
Male dorsal

Euchloe olympia
Male ventral

Euchloe olympia
Female ventral

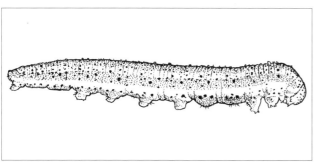

Euchloe olympia larva

Etymology. Olympia refers to the home of the Greek gods.

Identification. The Olympia Marble has the ventral hind wing marbling condensed into just three main diagonal bands. The apex of the ventral fore wing and the lower angle of the ventral hind wing are only lightly marked with green. Many specimens have a light pink tinge on the wings.

Life History. The host plants for this species include several rock cresses (*Arabis* spp.), but hosts are as yet unknown for Alberta. There is a single generation, with a flight period from May 2 to July 17. The peak is from mid-May to mid-June. Males patrol actively for females on prairie hillsides.

Range and Habitat. The Olympia Marble is distributed from southeastern Alberta and southern Ontario to Maryland and Texas. In Alberta, it is found from the southeastern corner west to the base of the Rocky Mountains north of Waterton Park and north to Drumheller and Veteran. Preferred habitats are native prairie grassland and badlands.

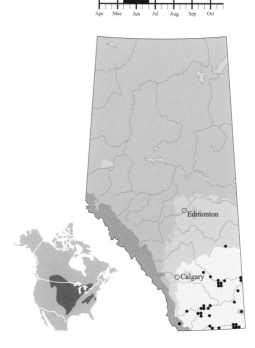

Subfamily
COLIADINAE
SULPHURS

Pierids in this subfamily are commonly called sulphurs because of their yellow and orange wing colouration. The wings are often edged with different colours, and males and females are usually sexually dimorphic in wing pattern. Their caterpillars feed mainly on plants from the pea family (Leguminosae). There are 12 species of sulphurs in Alberta, all but one in the genus *Colias*.

Colias Fabricius, 1807

Etymology. Kolias was another name for Aphrodite, the Greek goddess of love.

Identification. As a group, butterflies of the genus *Colias* are easy to recognize. They are medium-sized (most have a fore wing length of 20-30 mm) and have a small spot at the distal end of the disc on the underside of the hind wing. In most species the ground colour is yellow, though there are also orange, white or green "sulphurs." Males of all our species except *Colias nastes* have an uninterrupted dark band along the outer margin of the wings, while in females this band is partially broken, reduced or even absent. Some species have wing patterns that are similar under visible light, but differ considerably under ultraviolet light. As these butterflies can see ultraviolet wavelengths, they inhabit a world of colour that is hidden to us unless we use special equipment. The species within *Colias* are frequently difficult to distinguish. Structural characters that are usually useful in distinguishing butterflies, such as the male genitalia, vary little between *Colias* species. Even the wing patterns are relatively similar among species. There may be considerable polymorphism in ground colour within some species, but this variation is often paralleled in other species. Thus correct identification may require a series of specimens from single localities. A final identification may not be possible for single specimens. The immature stages are also reasonably uniform within the genus and have a form basic to pierids. The eggs are spindle-shaped, with fine ridges. Mature larvae are long and cylindrical and have a covering of fine, short hair or small spiny bumps. They are generally green, with a sprinkling of small black dots and one or two light bands running down each side. Pupae are green or blueish and are held upright against the substrate by a silk girdle. Larvae are usually the overwintering stage and some tundra species may take two years to become adults. Most of our species feed on members of the pea family (Leguminosae). *Colias philodice* and *Colias eurytheme* occasionally become agricultural pests on alfalfa and clover. A few closely related species feed on members of the heather family (Ericaceae), and one Alberta species feeds on members of the willow family (Salicaceae). There are eleven species of *Colias* in Alberta and one additional sulphur, *Zerene cesonia* (the Dog Face), has been reported for the province on the basis of a single specimen.

Colias alexandra W.H. Edwards, 1863b
Alexandra Sulphur

Colias alexandra
Male dorsal

Colias alexandra
Male ventral

Apr May Jun Jul Aug Sep Oct

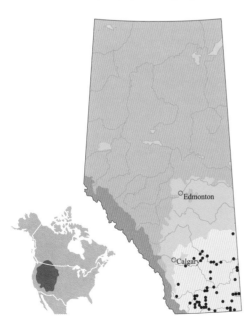

Edmonton

Calgary

Etymology. Edwards did not give the derivation of the name *alexandra* in his original description. According to Pyle (1981), it was named after Alexandra, who in 1863 married Edward VII, the son and heir of Queen Victoria. Alexandra became Queen only in 1901, after the butterfly was named, so the common name "Queen Alexandra's Sulphur" is inappropriate.

Identification. Males of *Colias alexandra* are yellow with no orange areas dorsally, and have a narrower dorsal wing border (2 mm) than *Colias christina* (3.5 mm) and the wing fringes are yellow. Males are smaller than *C. christina* (fore wing 25-27 mm) with a wing length of 22-23 mm. Females are white (99%) or, rarely, yellow, with greatly reduced wing borders. Submarginal spots are absent on the ventral surface. Both sexes have an unringed white discal spot on the ventral hind wing which distinguishes them from all other *Colias* species in Alberta except *Colias palaeno*. Specimens of *C. alexandra* are readily separated from those of *C. palaeno* by their habitat preferences and narrower wing border. Antennae are pale buff in colour. Assignment to a subspecies is difficult as the appearance of *C. alexandra* is remarkably consistent in Alberta. They differ from the nominate subspecies by virtue of their smaller size, narrower fore wing black borders, darker grayish green ventral hind wing, and white females. These differences are more substantial than the differences between the nominate subspecies and the subspecies *C. alexandra apache* Ferris (Kondla 1993). Until further studies are available, no subspecies name can be assigned to the Alberta populations.

Life History. Larvae of *C. alexandra* feed on various members of the pea family (Leguminosae) and are light green with a white and pink lateral band. No host records are known for Alberta. *C. alexandra* has two generations and specimens have been collected from May 13 to July 3, and from July 23 to September 1. The larvae overwinter.

Range and Habitat. The Alexandra Sulphur ranges from southern Alberta and Saskatchewan to Colorado, and west of the Great Basin, in grasslands of both the prairies and foothills.

134

Colias canadensis Ferris, 1982
Canada Sulphur

Etymology. The species epithet is descriptive of its distribution in northwestern Canada.

Identification. Adults of *Colias canadensis* have a wide, distally smeared, ventral hind wing spot, which distinguishes them from all other orange *Colias* in Alberta. The dorsal surface of the wings is orange to the wing base, as in *Colias meadii*, but the orange is a lighter shade. Also the fore wing of *C. canadensis* has a more rounded outer margin than *C. meadii*, and there is no scent patch (stigma) in males. Females generally have a white ground colour, but can also be orange or yellow, and are distinguished from other white *Colias* by the more pink, distally smeared discal spot, and the more complete banding on the dorsal fore wing surface. Originally described as a subspecies of *Colias hecla* Lefèbvre (the Hecla Sulphur), the Canada Sulphur was elevated to species status because it coexists with the Hecla Sulphur in eastern Alaska (Ferris 1988a). Previous literature references to *Colias hecla* in Alberta are now known to be references to *Colias canadensis*.

Life History. The larvae of this species are unknown, although Ferris (1988a) speculates that they feed on members of the pea family (Leguminosae). Adults have been collected in Alberta from May 5 to August 3, and the peak flight at low elevations is late May to June, while the peak is July at high elevations. There is one generation per year; the larvae overwinter.

Range and Habitat. The Canada Sulphur is found sporadically in the boreal forest and Rocky Mountains of Alberta south to the upper Red Deer River. It ranges across northwestern British Columbia through Yukon Territory to eastern Alaska. In Alberta this species occurs in the mixed forest of the boreal region, birch, willow patches on mountain valley floors and some alpine areas above treeline.

Colias canadensis
Male dorsal

Colias canadensis
Female dorsal

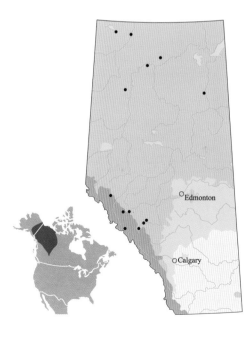

135

Colias christina W.H. Edwards, 1863b
Christina Sulphur
subspecies: *Colias christina christina* W.H. Edwards, 1863b

Colias christina christina
Male dorsal

Colias christina christina
Male ventral

Colias christina christina
Female dorsal

Colias christina christina
Female ventral

Etymology. Edwards named many species after people he knew, especially if they collected for him. *Colias christina* was named after Christina Ross, who was the wife of the chief factor of Fort Simpson. She collected the type specimens for this species from near Fort Smith.

Identification. Males of *Colias christina* are variable but usually have extensive orange ground colour on the dorsal wing surface, which is replaced by yellow near the base of the wings. The wing fringes are pink and, in the northern populations, there are often ventral submarginal spots. The ventral discal spot is ringed and may also have a satellite spot (especially in northern regions), and an orange dorsal hind wing spot is present. Females may be white, yellow, orange or combinations of these colours, though like the males, the orange area does not include the wing base. The dorsal wing border of females is usually absent on the hind wing and varies from slightly reduced to absent on the fore wing. Almost all females are white at Bragg Creek and in the southern Alberta foothills, where females of a similar species, *Colias philodice*, are usually yellow. Conversely, females of *Colias christina* are mainly orange in the Peace River region, where *C. philodice* females are usually white. The antennae are pinkish.

For about 100 years, the species *C. christina* was treated in the literature as a full species. In the early 1960s it was placed as a subspecies of *Colias alexandra* in a published list without supporting research. For the next 30 years, this species was placed in *C. alexandra* by other writers but Ferris (1993) and Kondla (1993) show clearly that these two taxa are separate species. The great variability of this species over the province provides a challenge to assignment of a subspecies name. Phenotypes of many of the currently recognized subspecies are sometimes found mixed within the specimens examined. No one subspecies or combination of names can be satisfactorily assigned to the southern and mountain populations in Alberta, although northern boreal forest populations are clearly referable to *Colias christina christina*.

Life History. In Alberta, oviposition by *Colias christina* has been observed northwest of Cochrane on Buffalo Bean (*Thermopsis rhombifolia*) and on *Hedysarum sulphurescens* in the Prospect Mountain area. In Manitoba, larvae of *Colias christina* have been collected and reared to adults on sweet vetch (*Hedysarum* sp.) by W. Krivda (Klassen *et al.* 1989). *Colias christina* has only one generation in Alberta. Adults have been collected from May 10 to September 26, with a main flight in late June to mid-August. It is likely that the larvae overwinter.

Range and Habitat. *Colias christina* ranges across forested northern Canada from Alaska to Manitoba. It is found south in the Rocky Mountains to Wyoming. The Christina Sulphur occurs mainly in forested areas, especially near pines and in some fescue grasslands.

Hedysarum sp.
Sweet Vetch

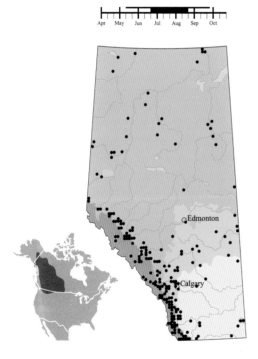

Thermopsis rhombifolia
Golden or Buffalo Bean

Colias eurytheme Boisduval, 1852
Alfalfa Butterfly

Colias eurytheme
Male dorsal

Colias eurytheme
Female ventral

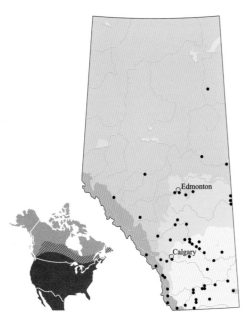

Etymology. Many of Boisduval's names were created by using the same ending as the name of a similar species. For example, he compared *Colias eurytheme* (*eury* = broad) to *Colias chrysotheme* (*chrys* = gold) in his original description. The suffix *-theme* relates to the presentation or composition (literally, a theme).

Identification. Specimens of *C. eurytheme* are often quite large, but otherwise resemble *C. philodice*. Like *C. philodice*, they consistently have a submarginal row of spots on the ventral wing surface, but they are separated from *C. philodice* by the orange colouration on the dorsal wing surface of males and most females. Unlike males of *C. christina*, the orange colouration of *C. eurytheme* extends to the base of the wing and, unlike *Colias meadii* and *Colias hecla*, there is a ring that uniformly surrounds the ventral hind wing discal spot, often with a satellite spot. White females may be confused with those of *C. philodice*.

Life History. Larvae of the Alfalfa Butterfly feed on numerous legumes, including Alfalfa (*Medicago sativa*), but have not yet been reported for Alberta. Adults have been collected from June 1 to September 20 in Alberta, mainly in late summer. Their abundance varies greatly from year to year, but they are usually sparse. There are two overlapping broods per year. The species is not believed to overwinter in Alberta. Most Alberta specimens probably dispersed from more southerly parts of the species' range. Hybridization with *C. philodice* has been documented outside Alberta and for many years this species was treated as conspecific with *C. philodice*.

Range and Habitat. The Alfalfa Butterfly ranges throughout North America from the southern edge of Canada to Mexico. It is found less frequently in boreal regions north to Newfoundland and north-central Alberta. Alberta records are mainly from the southern agricultural regions. Specimens that may belong to this species have been collected from Shell Pit, north of Fort McMurray. Bowman's *Colias eurytheme alberta* was described from Wembley, in the Peace River region, but is presently recognized as a synonym of *C. christina*. Preferred habitat is open areas, especially alfalfa and clover fields.

Colias gigantea Strecker, 1900
Giant Sulphur
subspecies: *Colias gigantea gigantea* Strecker, 1900
Colias gigantea harroweri Klots, 1940

Etymology. The name *gigantea* suits our largest *Colias* species well. The subspecies *harroweri* was named after James K. Harrower, an employee of the U. S. Forest Service at the time the species was described.

Identification. Both sexes of *Colias gigantea* are large and have a yellow ground colour. The ventral hind wing has a pink-edged discal spot, which may have a small satellite spot, and there are no submarginal spots or extensive dark scaling. Males may be similar to *Colias interior*, but are distinguished by their larger size and sharper fore wing apical angle. The inner margin of the dorsal fore wing black band in distal area is straight; it is curved in *C. interior*. The dorsal fore wing black spot is larger and darker; it is smaller and paler in *C. interior*. The dark outer band of the dorsal fore wing of females is greatly reduced or absent and, unlike that of *C. interior*, is reduced more in the marginal portion of the band than in the submarginal part.

Life History. Giant Sulphur caterpillars have not been found in Alberta, but are elsewhere reported to feed on willow (*Salix* spp.) and females have been observed to oviposit on *Salix*. Adults have been seen from June 8 to August 6 in Alberta, and the main flight is in late June. There is believed to be a single generation per year in Alberta with the larvae overwintering. Males are often seen while patrolling over and through willow fens while females are more sedentary and generally fly lower to the ground.

Colias gigantea harroweri
Male dorsal

Colias gigantea harroweri
Female dorsal

Colias gigantea harroweri
Female ventral

Salix exigua
Sandbar Willow

139

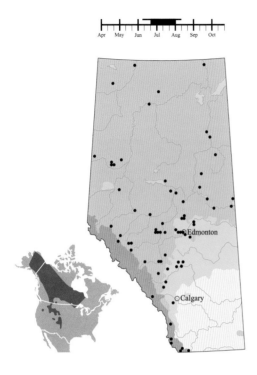

Range and Habitat. The Giant Sulphur is found in forested regions from Alaska to northern Ontario, and south in the mountains to Wyoming. Although flight times overlap where it occurs sympatrically with *Colias interior*, *Colias gigantea* is on the wing earlier than *C. interior* with about three weeks difference in peak flight periods. *Colias scudderii* Reakirt is a closely related species found in Colorado. There are numerous Alberta records for the Giant Sulphur, but it is only common in willow fens in boreal and mixed forest. Specimens from the Crowsnest Pass and Waterton areas are smaller and are assigned to the subspecies *Colias gigantea harroweri*.

Colias interior at Opal, Alberta.   J.H. Acorn.

140

Colias interior Scudder, 1862
Pink-edged Sulphur

Etymology. The name *interior* refers to the fact that this species is found in the interior of North America. In his original paper Scudder also described *Colias labradorensis* from the east coast, and *C. occidentalis* from the west.

Identification. Both sexes of *Colias interior* have a yellow ground colour and pink-edged ventral hind wing discal spots that only rarely have satellite spots. There are no ventral submarginal spots. The black border on the dorsal wing surface of females is restricted to the fore wing apex. White females are rare. Specimens of *Colias interior* are best distinguished from those of *Colias gigantea* by their smaller size, more rounded fore wing apex, curved inner margin of the black band in the distal area of dorsal fore wing and smaller and paler dorsal fore wing black spot. The species may also be confused with *Colias pelidne*, however, *interior* can be distinguished by the lesser amount of dark scaling on the ventral wing surfaces, the orange discal spot on the dorsal hind wing and the absence of extended black scaling on the dorsal hind wing.

Life History. Larvae of *Colias interior* have white and red lines down the side, and a dark dorsal stripe. They feed on the leaves of blueberry (*Vaccinium* spp.). Caterpillars of the Pink-edged Sulphur have not yet been reared from Alberta. Adults have been collected in Alberta from May 22 to September 13. There is only a single generation per year, with the peak flight period in July and early August. The larvae are believed to over-winter in Alberta.

Range and Habitat. The Pink-edged Sulphur ranges from northern British Columbia east to Labrador, and south to the northwest United States and parts of the Appalachian Mountains. In Alberta, *Colias interior* is common in the mountains and the central part of the province, and can be found north of Hay Lakes. It is found in the Cypress Hills but not the prairies. Preferred habitat for the species is dry pine forest with blueberry (*Vaccinium* spp.) in the understory.

Colias interior
Male dorsal

Colias interior
Male ventral

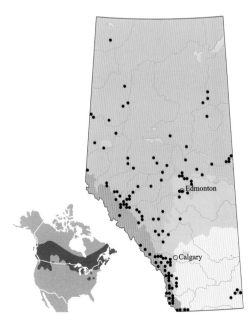

141

Colias meadii W.H. Edwards, 1871
Mead's Sulphur
subspecies: *Colias meadii elis* Strecker, 1885

Colias meadii elis
Male dorsal

Colias meadii elis
Female dorsal

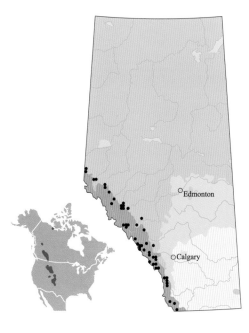

Etymology. Edwards named this species after Theodore L. Mead, who collected butterflies for him in central Colorado. Mead, who later married Edward's daughter, founded the New York Entomological Society. Elis is a district and town on the west coast of the Peloponnesus.

Identification. Both sexes have a deep orange ground colour extending to the base of the wings. In bright light, a light purplish sheen is sometimes visible on the wings, a trace of the extensive ultraviolet reflectance in this species. The ventral hind wing discal spot is small and rounded, with a narrow pink ring. Males have a distinct scent patch on the upper margin of the dorsal hind wing, which distinguishes them from all our other *Colias* species. Females have a marginal wing band broken by yellow spots, rather than the usual orange ones.

Life History. Larvae feed on various members of the pea family (Leguminosae) and have a yellow and a white line running down each side. In Alberta, they may take two years to complete development although there is usually one generation per year. The larvae overwinter. Adults have been collected from June 23 to September 12, and the main flight is in early August near Plateau Mountain. Farther north in the Alberta Rocky Mountains the main flight is in July. A study in the Kananaskis Valley has shown that darker individuals of *C. meadii and C. nastes* can fly in lower temperatures and darker conditions, as they absorb more heat from sunlight when they bask. The lighter individuals are more active under very bright and warm conditions, probably because they do not overheat as easily. Thus the extent of dark scaling on *Colias* wings is a function of different thermal habitats. In general, populations tend to be darker at higher elevations and more northerly latitudes.

Range and Habitat. Mead's Sulphur is distributed in the Rocky Mountains from northern British Columbia to northern New Mexico. Some populations in Siberia may also belong to *C. meadii*. All our Alberta populations are *C. m. elis*. Mead's Sulphur is most common in openings in lush subalpine valleys in Alberta, but is also found in low alpine meadows. The species is less common in the more northerly Alberta Rocky Mountains.

Colias nastes Boisduval, [1834]
Nastes Sulphur

subspecies: *Colias nastes streckeri* Grum-Grschimailo, 1895

Etymology. *Nastes* means "occupant, inhabitant" in Greek. The subspecies was named after Herman Strecker.

Identification. This species is easily identified as our only *Colias* that is predominantly green and/or black on the dorsal wing surfaces. Males are substantially darker than females, but both sexes have a partially broken dorsal wing border. Fresh specimens have a bright pink fringe on the wings and a distally smeared discal spot on the ventral hind wing.

Life History. Larvae of the Nastes Sulphur have been collected from Redcap Mountain, Alberta, on the Showy Locoweed (*Oxytropis splendens*); elsewhere they have been reported on a variety of alpine legumes. They are dark green with a pair of pink-edged stripes down each side. There is one brood per year; the larvae overwinter. Adults have been collected in Alberta from June 17 to September 21, and the main flight period is in July and early August. This "nasty" little sulphur can be very difficult to observe and collect. Adults fly rapidly over dry alpine slopes and fields, dropping down suddenly between rocks to hide. Like all other *Colias*, they are lateral baskers, which means that they perch with their wings tightly closed and the underside oriented at right angles to the incoming rays of sunlight.

Range and Habitat. This circumpolar species ranges in North America from Alaska to Labrador, and south in the mountains to the northern borders of Montana and Washington. In Alberta it is restricted to the Rocky Mountains. Preferred habitat is dry alpine slopes, generally well above treeline, although on hot, sunny days it can be found in the upper subalpine zone puddling with *Colias meadii*.

Colias nastes
Male dorsal

Colias nastes
Male ventral

Colias nastes
Female dorsal

Colias nastes
Female ventral

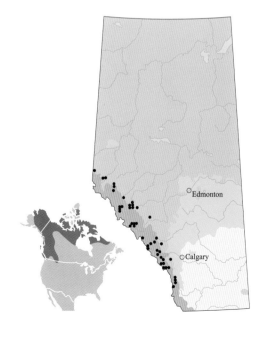

143

Colias palaeno (Linnaeus, 1761)
Palaeno Sulphur
subspecies: *Colias palaeno chippewa* W.H. Edwards, 1872b

Colias palaeno chippewa
Male dorsal

Colias palaeno chippewa
Male ventral

Colias palaeno chippewa
Female dorsal

Colias palaeno chippewa
Female ventral

Etymology. The name *palaeno* may be a form of Palaemon, a sea god originally called Melicertes. The subspecies name refers to the Chippewa Indians.

Identification. The Palaeno Sulphur is best identified by the small, unbordered discal spot on the ventral hind wing. It shares this characteristic with *Colias alexandra*, but *Colias palaeno* has a substantially wider black border on the dorsal wing surfaces. Males are yellow, while females are white or cream.

Life History. The larvae of *Colias palaeno* feed on bilberry (*Vaccinium* spp.) in Europe and are green with a yellow band down the side. Immatures have not yet been described from North America. Only two records are known from Alberta with flight dates of June 10 and 18. There is one brood per year; the larvae are believed to overwinter in Alberta.

Range and Habitat. *Colias palaeno* is found across much of Eurasia and northern North America. The only records from Alberta are from Fort Vermilion and near the British Columbia border west of Grande Prairie. Preferred habitats are boggy taiga and low arctic or alpine tundra.

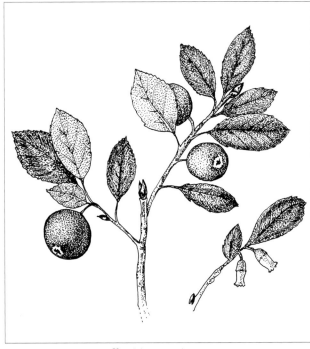

Vaccinium caespitosum
Dwarf Bilberry

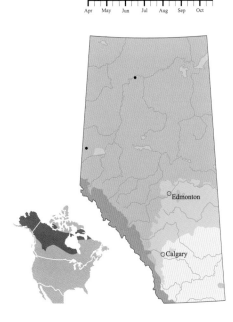

144

Colias pelidne Boisduval and Le Conte, 1829
Pelidne Sulphur
subspecies: *Colias pelidne skinneri* Barnes, 1894

Etymology. The name of this species may be based on: Pelides, the son of Peleus (Achilles); Peligni, a region and people of Italy; or the Greek word *pelidnos* meaning "livid." The subspecies was named after Henry Skinner, an American medical doctor who studied butterflies.

Identification. Males of *Colias pelidne* are mostly white, while females are light yellow or white. The species is similar to *Colias interior*. Both sexes are distinguished from *Colias interior* by the medial patch of dark scaling on the ventral fore wing surface, the pronounced linear smudge of black scales on the dorsal hind wing, and a pale, concolourous dorsal hind wing spot (light orange in females); in *C. interior* the dorsal hind wing spot is bright orange. Females may also be distinguished by the fact that their ground colour is usually lighter than in *Colias interior*.

Life History. Larval host plants are unknown in Alberta, but blueberry (*Vaccinium* spp.) and other members of the heather family (Ericaceae) are reported from the western United States. This species has one generation per year and adults have been collected from June 27 to September 6 in Alberta. The larvae overwinter.

Range and Habitat. The Pelidne Sulphur has three major disjunct populations in North America: one in the eastern arctic, one in the north central Yukon, and one in the north central Rocky Mountains. The last of these extends north to the most northerly Rocky Mountains in Alberta. In this province, the Pelidne Sulphur is restricted to high subalpine forests and shrubby areas.

Colias pelidne
Male dorsal

Colias pelidne
Male ventral

Colias pelidne
Female dorsal

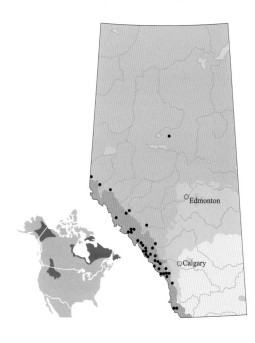

Vaccinium myrtilloides
Blueberry

145

Colias philodice Godart, [1819]
Clouded Sulphur

Etymology. *Philodice* may come from Phyllodoce, a sea nymph who was daughter of Nireus and Doris. Literally, *philodice* means "lover of justice or law-suits"!

Identification. This species is generally distinguished by the yellow ground colour, combined with the pointed fore wing apex and the submarginal row of spots on the ventral wing surface of most specimens. White females of *Colias philodice* may be separated from those of *Colias alexandra* by the presence of a black border on the dorsal surface of the hind wing. There appears to be no consistent way to distinguish them easily from white females of the normally orange *Colias eurytheme*, except by their association with other yellow, rather than orange, individuals. The proportion of white females varies considerably between populations in Alberta. They are uncommon (15%) at Bragg Creek, but make up more the 50% of the total number of females in the area around Empress and in the northern Peace River region.

Colias philodice
Male dorsal

Colias philodice
Male ventral

Colias philodice
Female dorsal

Colias philodice
Female dorsal

Colias philodice
Female dorsal

Colias philodice
Female ventral

Life History. Our most common *Colias*, this species may have at least two generations per year, possibly three in Alberta. Larvae feed on various herbaceous legumes and have been found in southern Alberta on cultivated clover (*Trifolium* spp.) and Alfalfa (*Medicago sativa*). The caterpillars of the Yellow Sulphur are grass-green with small raised black dots, a whitish lateral band and an indistinct dorsal band. The pupae overwinter. Adults have been collected from March 9 to November 22. Adults emerging early in the spring are usually smaller and darker than later individuals and normally lack the ventral hind wing submarginal spots.

Range and Habitat. The Clouded Sulphur is found in Alaska, across southern Canada and south to central America. It ranges throughout Alberta. Its preferred habitat is open areas from subalpine valleys to prairies, especially along roadsides.

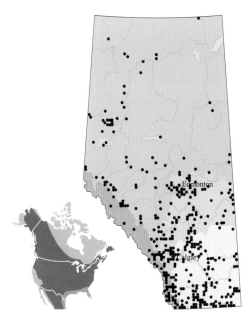

Colias philodice nectaring on Red Clover (*Trifolium pratense* L.; Leguminosae)

T.W. Thormin.

147

Zerene Hübner, 1819
DOG FACE

Etymology. The origin of *zerene* is unclear. Perhaps it is related to " xeric," meaning arid, and is a reference to the dryland associations of the genus.

Identification. The species in the primarily tropical genus *Zerene* are identified by the outline of a dog's head on the fore wing.

Zerene cesonia (Stoll, 1790)
Dog Face

Zerene cesonia
Female dorsal view

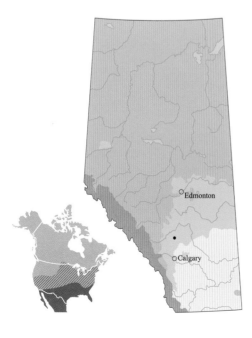

Etymology. It is speculated that the species name is derived from Cesson, the name of at least three cities in France.

Identification. This yellow Sulphur can be identified easily by its slightly pointed fore wing tip. More interestingly, the dorsal fore wing markings are in the shape of a poodle's head, with the outline formed by the wide black border. The female has more blurred marginal bands.

Life History. Larvae of the Dog Face are reported to feed on members of the pea family (Leguminosae), including clovers (*Trifolium* spp.), prairie clover (*Petalostemon* spp.) and Alfalfa (*Medicago sativa*). A single adult was collected in Alberta by Art Rupp, sometime in 1944. This species can only survive the winter in the southern United States and must recolonize most of its range each year.

Range and Habitat. The permanent range of the Dog Face extends from the southern United States to Argentina, but as the adult flies rapidly, it commonly wanders northward into many of the temperate areas of the United States. Two specimens were collected in Manitoba, both prior to 1942. Our single record from Alberta was collected at Didsbury and represents a major range extension for this species. The Dog Face is found in open, dry prairie habitats and should be watched for in late summer.

5

Family **LYCAENIDAE**
GOSSAMER WINGS

Members of the family Lycaenidae are collectively known as gossamer wings. In Alberta there are 34 species in three subfamilies that can be differentiated by their shapes and colours: Lycaeninae (coppers), Theclinae (hairstreaks) and Polyommatinae (blues). Lycaenid males have clawless, somewhat reduced fore legs while those of the females are fully functional. Caterpillars feed on host plants from at least 15 families in Alberta, often eating fruits and flowers rather than leaves. Instead of the usual cylindrical shape, lycaenid caterpillars are flattened and slug-like. Larvae of many species in the subfamily Polyommatinae (blues) have glands that produce a sugary exudate that is attractive to ants. In its most innocuous form, the relationship between blue larvae and ants is simply an exchange of food for protection from predators and parasites. In its most sinister incarnation, blue caterpillars feast on the ants' brood while the adult ants appear to be intoxicated by the caterpillars' exudate. Larvae of the European Large Blue (*Maculinea arion* Linnaeus) apparently produce such an addictive fluid that ants sometimes bring so many caterpillars into their nests that the colony is exterminated.

Subfamily
LYCAENINAE
COPPERS

Lycaenine butterflies are called coppers because their dorsal wing colouration is usually coppery or brownish gray. Confusingly, there is also a bright blue copper among Alberta's species [*Lycaena (Chalceria) heteronea*]. Coppers have black spots on the ventral surface of both wings, and the sexes are often dimorphic in wing pattern with the males showing much brighter dorsal wing colours. Another distinguishing feature of coppers is the radial vein of the fore wing which has four branches that originate from the end of the discal cell. Most male coppers use a perching strategy to find mates, darting out from their perch to investigate any passing insect. Nine species of lycaenines occur in Alberta and there are two other species that are likely to wander into our province.

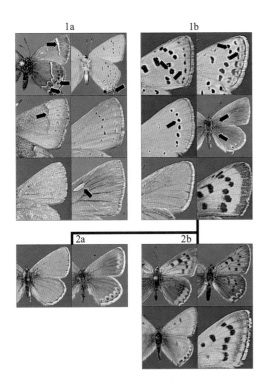

Key to Subfamilies of Lycaenidae in Alberta

1a) Ventral fore wing with postmedian band, row of spots or no line or markings, 0 to 1 discal spot present; dorsal wings gray, brown or rust; males have a mid-costa scent pad; tails and thecla spot present in many species; ventral wings gray, brown or green. . . . . **Theclinae** p. 151

b) Ventral fore wing with one or more rows of dark spots, 1,2 or 3 discal spots present **and** dorsal wing surface blue, copper, orange or brown with blue scales at wing base; dorsal scent patch absent in males; no tails (except for one species of blue); ventral wings orange, brown or silver/gray. 2

2a) Ventral fore wing with 1 or 2 discal spots; dorsal surface of males bright blue, females brown with at least some blue scales at wing base. . . . . **one species of Lycaeninae; Polyommatinae** p. 152

b) Ventral fore wing with 3 discal spots (rarely 2); dorsal surface of males bright copper, purple or brown/gray most with orange borders on hind wing, females dull brown and orange never with blue scales at wing bases (in one species male dorsal surface is blue and ventral fore wing with 2 or 3 discal spots). . . . . **Lycaeninae** p. 154

Plebejus saepiolus near Buffalo Lake, Alberta   C.D. Bird.

Key to Species of Theclinae in Alberta

(** Species marked with a double asterisk are not recorded for Alberta, but have been found just outside the province.)

1a) Ventral fore wing with no markings; green or gray 2
 b) Ventral fore wing with distinct line of spots or bands; brown, rust or gray. 4

2a) Ventral surface gray . . . .
 . . . . *Satyrium fuliginosum* (W.H. Edwards) p. 180
 b) Ventral surface green. 3

3a) Ventral hind wing post median line reduced to a band of white spots . *Callophrys sheridanii* (W.H. Edwards) p. 169
 b) Ventral hind wing post median line of one or two white spots. . .
 . . . . *Callophrys affinis* (W.H. Edwards)** p. 168

4a) Tails present on hind wings; thecla spot usually present 5
 b) Tails absent 11

5a) Ventral fore wing post median line well developed, contrasting dark and light 6
 b) Ventral fore wing post median line poorly defined, a row of spots or diffuse bands. 9

6a) Ventral hind wing without orange near tail or basal blue spot; dorsal rusty brown . . . .
 . . . . *Satyrium saepium* (Boisduval)** p. 183
 b) Ventral hind wing bordered with orange, orange near base of tail. 7

7a) Dorsal hind wing with orange spot; ventral gray; post median line with white portion of the band narrower than width of the dark inner margin. . . . .
 . . . . *Strymon melinus* Hübner p. 185
 b) Dorsal hind wing without spot; ventral ground colour brown or green; post median line with white portion of equal or greater width than the dark inner margin 8

8a) Ventral hind wing brown, dorsal hind wing steely blue . . . . . .
 . . . . *Mitoura spinetorum* (Hewitson) p. 178
 b) Ventral hind wing green; dorsal rust brown . . . .
 . . . . *Mitoura siva* (W.H. Edwards) **p. 177

9a) Ventral fore wing post median line diffuse, several bands; thecla spot near tail . . . . . . *Satyrium liparops* (Le Conte) p. 181
 b) Ventral fore wing post median line as row of spots, hind wing with blue basal spot near the tail; thecla spot absent . . 10

10a) Ventral hind wing blue patch capped with orange; orange submarginal band. . . . .
 . . . . *Satyrium acadicum* (W.H. Edwards) p. 179
 b) Ventral hind wing blue patch not capped with orange; thecla spot absent . . . . *Satyrium sylvinum* (Boisduval) p. 184

to 11

151

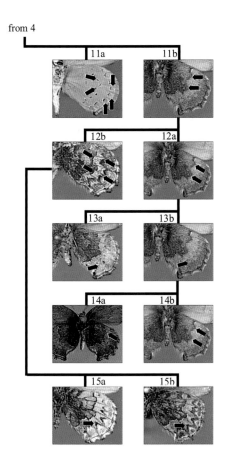

from 4

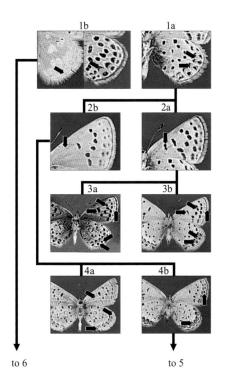

to 6   to 5

11a) Ventral hind wing with row of marginal orange spots; with post median row of spots. *Harkenclenus titus* (Fabricius) p. 170

b) Ventral hind wing without orange spots; with post median line or band. 12

12a) Ventral hind wing with a single irregular or broken band near middle of wing 13

b) Ventral hind wing with 2 or 3 irregular or broken bands near middle of wing 15

13a) Ventral hind wing marginal half grayish . . . . *Incisalia (Deciduphagus) polia* Cook & Watson p. 174

b) Ventral hing wing marginal half brown or reddish. 14

14a) Ventral hind wing band with a white outer margin; outer margin of wing reddish . . . . *Incisalia (Deciduphagus) mossii* (Hy. Edwards) p. 173

b) Ventral hind wing band without white outer margin; outer margin of wing brown . . . . *Incisalia (Deciduphagus) augustinus* (Westwood) p.172

15a) Ventral hind wing marginal chevrons sharply pointed and elongated; found in Lodgepole Pine forests. . . . . *Incisalia (Incisalia) eryphon* (Boisduval) p. 175

b) Ventral hind wing marginal chevrons blunt and short; found in Jack Pine forests . *Incisalia (Incisalia) niphon* (Hübner) p. 176

Key to Species of Polyommatinae in Alberta
(One Lycaeninae also keys here)

1a) Ventral hind wing with a submarginal orange-brown band or row of spots, sometimes with metallic flecking, sometimes without. 2

b) Ventral hind wing without a submarginal row of spots or with one or two orange spots near the posterior margin of the wing . 6

2a) Ventral fore wing with mid-discal black spot. 3

b) Ventral fore wing without mid-discal black spot 4

3a) Ventral wing black spots very heavy; wing fringe checkered black and white; ventral hind wing without metallic scaling on marginal spots. . *Euphilotes enoptes* (Boisduval) p. 188

b) Ventral wing black spots fine in prairie forms, heavier in mountain forms; wing fringe monotone; ventral hind wing with metallic scales on marginal spots. . . . . *Plebejus (Icaricia) acmon* (Westwood & Hewitson) p. 199

4a) Ventral wing orange band/spots on hind wing only; dark spots fade to brown; ventral fore wing veins lighter, contrasting against background . . . . *Plebejus (Icaricia) shasta* (W.H. Edwards) p. 202

b) Ventral wing orange band complete, extending from hind to . fore wing, more strongly developed in females. 5

5a) Ventral submarginal metallic spots narrower than orange
band. . . . . *Lycaeides melissa* (W.H. Edwards) p. 196
 b) Ventral submarginal metallic spots wider than orange band . .
. . . . *Lycaeides idas* (Linnaeus) p. 194

6a) Ventral hind wing with a large orange spot near the posterior
margin, sometimes a second weaker spot present; dorsal
surface blue. . . . .
. . . . *Plebejus (Vacciniina) optilete* (Knoch) p. 204
 b) Ventral hind wing with a small orange spot or none; dorsal
surface blue, brown or black, or some combination of
the three 7

7a) Ventral surface of fore wing with mid-discal spot 8
 b) Ventral surface of fore wing without mid-discal spot 10

8a) Ventral hind wing with uniform ground colour; males. . . . . . .
. . . . . . *Lycaena (Chalceria) heteronea* Boisduval p. 156
 b) Ventral hind wing with distinct light and dark areas 9

9a) Ventral hind wing with postmedian white band consisting of
sharply pointed triangular chevrons. . . . .
. . . . *Glaucopsyche piasus* (Boisduval) p. 193
 b) Ventral hind wing postmedian band not as above . . . .
. . . *Plebejus (Agriades) rusticus* (W.H. Edwards) p. 197

10a) Ventral surface submarginal band lacking . . . .
. . . . *Glaucopsyche lygdamus* (Doubleday) p. 191
 b) Ventral surface with submarginal band present as brown or
black spots, may be reduced to a few spots 11

11a) Ventral fore wing with postmedian band sinuate 12
 b) Ventral fore wing with postmedian band curved, or nearly
straight, but not sinuate. 13

12a) Ventral surface spots surrounded by large white circles . . . . .
. . . . . . *Plebejus (Icaricia) icarioides* (Boisduval) p. 201
 b) Ventral surface spots surrounded by small white circles; ventral
hind wing with small, marginal, orange spots . . . .
. . . . . . *Plebejus (Plebejus) saepiolus* (Boisduval) p. 203

13a) Ventral hind wing with orange spot on posterior margin, and
tail usually present . *Everes amyntula* (Boisduval) p. 189
 b) Ventral hind wing without orange spot. . . . .
. . . . *Celastrina ladon* (W. Kirby) p. 186

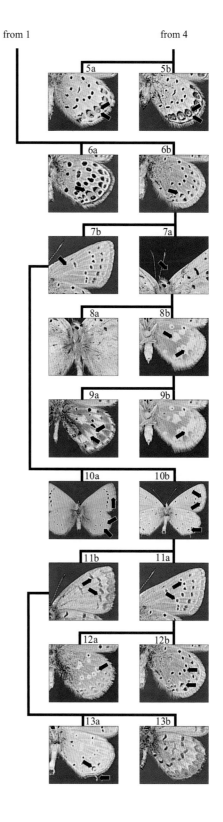

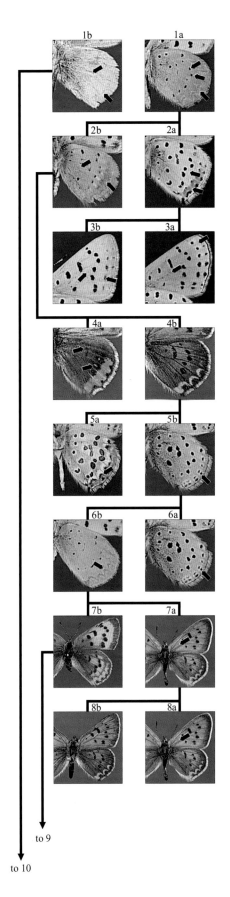

to 9

to 10

Key to Species of Lycaeninae in Alberta

1a) Ventral hind wing with discal spots and orange submarginal
    band or spots. 2
  b) Ventral hind wing discal spots absent and submarginal markings
    faint or absent; or with discal bands or faint spots and no
    orange submarginal markings 10

2a) Ventral hind wing gray with broad orange band. 3
  b) Ventral hind wing rust, brown or brown gray with submarginal
    orange band reduced to a line or row of spots 4

3a) Ventral fore wing orange with gray outer margin . . . .
    . . . . *Lycaena (Hyllolycaena) hyllus* (Cramer) p. 164
  b) Ventral fore wing gray with orange submarginal spots . . . . . .
    . . . . *Lycaena (Gaeides) dione* (Scudder) p. 163

4a) Dorsal hind wing discal area rust/brown with patches of blue
    scales basal to the orange submarginal band . . . .
    . . . . *Lycaena (Lycaena) phlaeas* (Linnaeus) p. 166
  b) Dorsal hind wing discal area orange, gray, purple or brown and
    variously marked, the submarginal orange band reduced to
    spots, or the same colour as the discal area, no blue
    scales. 5

5a) Ventral hind wing submarginal orange band reduced with a
    dark cap inward which in turn is capped with white;
    dorsal surface gray . . . .
    . . . . *Lycaena (Gaeides) editha* (Mead)** p. 162
  b) Ventral hind wing submarginal orange band/line variable, never
    capped inwardly with a dark spot. 6

6a) Ventral hind wing submarginal orange band reduced to a string
    of spots; ventral surface bright copper. . . . .
    . . . . *Lycaena (Lycaena) cuprea* (W.H. Edwards) p. 165
  b) Ventral hind wing submarginal orange band jagged, scalloped
    or may be reduced 7

7a) Dorsal surface with a purple sheen at least basally . . . . . males 8
  b) Dorsal surface orange and brown . . . . females 9

8a) Purple sheen at base of wing, marginal regions orange and
    brown . . . .
    . . . . . *Lycaena (Epidemia) helloides* (Boisduval) p. 159
  b) Purple sheen over whole wing . . . .
    . . . . *Lycaena (Epidemia) dorcas* W. Kirby p. 158

9a) Dorsal hind wing submarginal orange band reduced; discal
    area mostly brown . . . .
    . . . . *Lycaena (Epidemia) dorcas* W. Kirby p. 158

9a) Dorsal hind wing submarginal orange band reduced; discal
      area mostly brown . . . .
      . . . . *Lycaena (Epidemia) dorcas* W. Kirby p. 158
  b) Dorsal hind wing submarginal orange band complete; discal
      area orange and brown . . . .
      . . . . . *Lycaena (Epidemia) helloides* (Boisduval) p. 159

10a) Ventral hind wing gray, mottled discal bands. . . . .
       . . . . *Lycaena (Epidemia) mariposa* (Reakirt) p. 160
   b) Ventral hind wing spots faint or absent. 11

11a) Ventral hind wing two-tone with yellow basally and brown
      marginally. . . . .
      female *Lycaena (Epidemia) nivalis* (Boisduval)** p. 161
   b) Ventral hind wing monotone gray or silver 12

12a) Ventral hind wing with faint traces of submarginal orange
      banding; dorsal surface bright copper . . . .
      . male *Lycaena (Epidemia) nivalis* (Boisduval)** p. 161
   b) Ventral hind wing with no trace of orange spots 13

13a) Male dorsal surface bright blue, female dorsal surface brown.
      . . . . . . *Lycaena (Chalceria) heteronea* Boisduval p. 156
   b) Male dorsal surface bright copper, female dorsal surface orange
      and brown with distinct submarginal band on hind wing
      . . . . *Lycaena (Chalceria) rubida* (Behr) p. 157

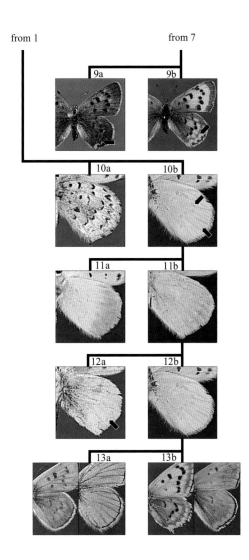

Lycaena Fabricius, 1807

Etymology. This may be another in a series of butterfly names that refer to mountains sacred to the Greek god Zeus, in this case Mt. Lycaeus. Other such mountains include Mt. Parnassus (= *Parnassius*), Mt. Helicon (= *Heliconius*, a tropical genus) and Mt. Olympus (*Euchloe olympia*).

Lycaena (Chalceria) Scudder, 1876a

Etymology. Chalcis was a city in ancient Greece that was located near copper mines, making it an appropriate namesake for this genus of coppers.

Lycaena (Chalceria) heteronea Boisduval, 1852
Blue Copper
subspecies: *Lycaena (Chalceria) heteronea heteronea* Boisduval, 1852

Lycaena heteronea heteronea
Male dorsal

Lycaena heteronea heteronea
Male ventral

Lycaena heteronea heteronea
Female dorsal

Lycaena heteronea heteronea
Female ventral

Etymology. From the Greek word *heteros*, meaning "different." This probably refers to this butterfly's blue rather than copper colour.

Identification. Males are bright blue dorsally while the females are less striking, ranging from a dull blue through gray-brown. The ventral surface of the fore wing has obvious spots, while on the hind wing these spots are small and inconspicuous.

Life History. There is one brood per year. Larvae of the Blue Copper are reported to feed on many of the umbrella plants (*Eriogonum* spp.). In Alberta, Subalpine or Sulphur Umbrella Plant (*Eriogonum umbellatum*) grows in the southern mountains. Eggs are reported to be the overwintering stage. The caterpillars are pale green with silvery white body hairs, while the chrysalids are green flecked with brown. In Alberta, the flight period is from June 28 to August 25. Adults nectar on yellow composites and Yarrow (*Achillea millefolium*). In contrast to other coppers, males patrol rather than perch and they also puddle. Thus the Blue Copper is aberrant in both colour and behaviour!

Range and Habitat. This species is found from southwestern Alberta and southern British Columbia south to New Mexico and California. Alberta specimens are placed in *Lycaena (Chalceria) heteronea heteronea*. In Alberta, the Blue Copper is found in the southwestern mountain region and is most common south of the Crowsnest Pass. This species prefers meadows and other forest openings on semi-arid hillsides, from middle to lower elevations. In British Columbia it appears to be fond of mock orange (*Philadelphus* spp.) and composite flowers.

Lycaena (Chalceria) rubida (Behr, 1866)
Ruddy Copper
subspecies: *Lycaena (Chalceria) rubida siria* (W.H. Edwards, 1871)

Etymology. From Latin *rubidus* meaning "deep-red" and *sirius*, Greek for the dog star.

Identification. The Ruddy Copper may be recognized by its metallic red dorsal surface, that is much brighter in males than females. The ventral sides of the wings are grayish or silvery, with faint black spots.

Life History. In Alberta this butterfly is associated with Wild Begonia (*Rumex venosus*). In more southern regions the larvae have been reared on many species of dock and sorrel (*Rumex* spp.). The Ruddy Copper over-winters in the egg stage. There is one brood per year. Males perch on prominent grass stems and flowers and investigate all passing butterflies vigorously. Both sexes are strong fliers and nectar readily. The flight period in Alberta is from June 12 to August 17 with a peak in July.

Range and Habitat. The Ruddy Copper is found through southern Saskatchewan and Alberta, south through Nebraska to Arizona and California, extending west into Oregon. The subspecies *Lycaena (Chalceria) rubida siria* ranges from southern Alberta to Colorado. These butterflies are seen in close association with their larval host plants on coulees, bluffs, sand dunes and river banks. The adults are avid flower visitors, preferring sunflowers (*Helianthus* spp.) along the edges of sand dunes.

Lycaena rubida siria
Male dorsal

Lycaena rubida siria
Male ventral

Lycaena rubida siria
Female dorsal

Lycaena rubida siria
Female ventral

Rumex venosus
Wild Begonia

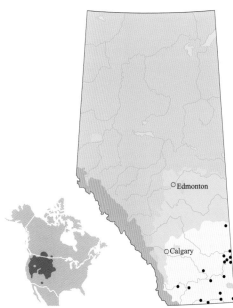

157

Lycaena (Epidemia) Scudder, 1876a

Etymology. From the Greek *epidemeo* meaning "to be prevalent."

Lycaena (Epidemia) dorcas W. Kirby, 1837
Dorcas Copper
subspecies: *Lycaena (Epidemia) dorcas dorcas* W. Kirby, 1837
Lycaena (Epidemia) dorcas florus (W.H. Edwards, 1883)

Lycaena dorcas florus
Male dorsal

Lycaena dorcas florus
Male ventral

Lycaena dorcas florus
Female dorsal

Lycaena dorcas florus
Female ventral

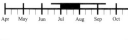

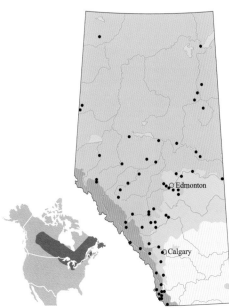

Etymology. From *dorkas*, Greek meaning "gazelle" or "antelope" and *floris* meaning "flower" in Latin.

Identification. This species is similar to the Purplish Copper, *Lycaena (Epidemia) helloides*, but is smaller, with a reduced orange submarginal band on the dorsal hind wing and wide dorsal dark borders (narrow in *L. helloides*). Males have purplish dorsal wing surfaces while females are variably orange and brown.

Life History. Larvae of the Dorcas Copper are reported to feed on a variety of cinquefoil (*Potentilla* spp.). Other host plants include species of dock and sorrel, (*Rumex* spp.) and species of knotweed and smartweed, (*Polygonum* spp.). *E. dorcas* is large and lives in habitats more associated with *E. helloides*. There is one brood per year; the eggs overwinter. Adults nectar freely at cinquefoil (*Potentilla spp.*) and goldenrod (*Solidago* spp.). They perch on bushes in meadows and clearings, and males use a perching strategy for finding mates. The flight period in Alberta is from June 15 to September 13.

Range and Habitat. The Dorcas Copper is found across boreal North America, ranging south to Maine in the east, possibly New Mexico in the west and north to the Yukon Territory and Alaska. Most Alberta specimens can be placed as *Lycaena (Epidemia) dorcas dorcas*. Kondla has compared our boreal specimens with *L. dorcas dorcas* collected from Manitoba (the province of the type locality) and found them to be the same. Only populations from the mountains and foothills south of the Bow Valley are *L. dorcas florus*. The Dorcas Copper ranges throughout most of the province. It is found in moist places, such as bogs and fens in northern and central areas of Alberta and in moist meadows and along streams in the southern part of the province.

Lycaena (Epidemia) helloides (Boisduval, 1852)
Purplish Copper

Etymology. Perhaps from the Greek word *helodes* which means "frequenting marshes," an attribute of the butterfly. It may also be derived from *hellos* meaning "young deer, fawn," thus paralleling the name of the Dorcas ("gazelle") Copper.

Identification. A small species with the ventral wing surface orange and with reduced black spots on the hind wing. The ventral hind wing has a large orange submarginal band that is usually crooked. The dorsal wing surface of males is purplish with a large irregular orange band. Females are orange above with large black markings. The Purplish Copper is similar to the Dorcas Copper, *Lycaena* (*Epidemia*) *dorcas*, in appearance but is larger and has more complete submarginal bands both dorsally and ventrally.

Life History. The greenish white eggs are slightly flattened and ridged. Larvae are covered with small bumps that bear spines and hairs. They are grass-green with yellow stripes on the back and sides that have slanted lines between them. The Purplish Copper overwinters as a pupa. Several generations may occur over the summer. Larvae feed on dock (*Rumex* spp.), knotweed (*Polygonum* spp.), *Oxytheca* spp. and Low Willowherb (*Gayophytum racemosum*). They are rare on cinquefoil (*Potentilla* spp.). Adults are swift fliers, and nectar readily. Males perch on flowers and prominent stems and investigate passing butterflies. Asters and yellow composites are often chosen for perches. The flight period in Alberta is from May 17 to October 5 with the butterflies most abundant in June and again in late August.

Range and Habitat. The Purplish Copper ranges from Ontario west to British Columbia and south to Baja California and New Mexico. In Alberta, it occurs as far north as the Peace River region. The Purplish Copper is found in prairies and aspen parklands, often along water courses and around pond margins.

Lycaena helloides
Male dorsal

Lycaena helloides
Male ventral

Lycaena helloides
Female dorsal

Lycaena helloides
Female ventral

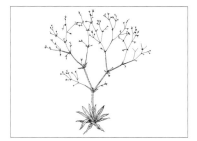
Oxytheca dendroides

Apr May Jun Jul Aug Sep Oct

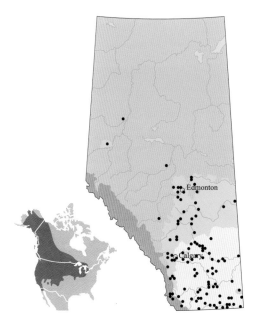

159

Lycaena (Epidemia) mariposa (Reakirt, 1866)
Mariposa Copper
subspecies: *Lycaena (Epidemia) mariposa penroseae* Field, 1938a

Lycaena mariposa penroseae
Male dorsal

Lycaena mariposa penroseae
Male ventral

Lycaena mariposa penroseae
Female dorsal

Lycaena mariposa penroseae
Female ventral

Etymology. From Spanish *mariposa* for butterfly. Field named the subspecies after Mrs. Spencer Penrose of Colorado Springs in acknowledgment of her interest in Lepidoptera.

Identification. The Mariposa Copper is a small butterfly that lacks the typical "copper" butterfly markings. In males, the dorsal wing surface has a purple sheen, but in females it is brown with black spots. The ventral wing surface of both sexes is mottled gray and black.

Life History. Larvae are reported to feed on Douglas Knotweed (*Polygonum douglasii*) in the field and on dock and sorrel (*Rumex* spp.) in captivity. Both sexes nectar and puddle readily. They sometimes occur in great numbers along streams and in flowery meadows. The flight period in Alberta is from June 13 to September 25, perhaps indicating two broods. The eggs overwinter.

Range and Habitat. The Mariposa Copper ranges from the Yukon Territory and Alaska in the north to California in the south and east into Alberta and Wyoming. The subspecies *Lycaena (Epidemia) mariposa penroseae* occurs from Alberta south to Wyoming. This butterfly is found in meadows and along trails in coniferous forests in the mountains, foothills, boreal forest and Peace River parkland. The correct taxonomic placement of northern Alberta populations requires additional research.

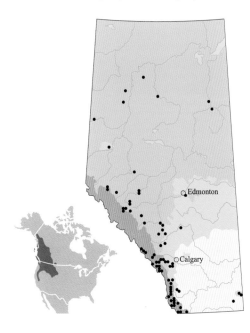

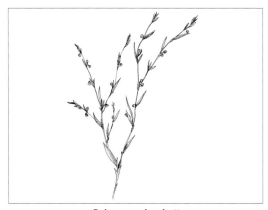

Polygonum douglasii
Douglas Knotweed

Lycaena (Epidemia) nivalis (Boisduval, 1869)
Lilac-bordered Copper

Etymology. *Nivis* is Latin for "snow."

Identification. Dorsally this species is similar to *Lycaena (Epidemia) dorcas* and *L. (E.) helloides*. Ventrally it may be distinguished by the yellow to white hind wing, with a distal lilac-coloured area.

Life History. In Montana, the flight period is from July through mid-August. Larvae are pale green with white and reddish purple dorsal stripes. They are suspected to feed on knotweed and smartweed (*Polygonum* spp.).

Range and Habitat. *Lycaena (Epidemia) nivalis* occurs from California north to British Columbia and Montana in the Canadian zone. The probability of occurrence is rated high for the Waterton Lakes National Park to Crowsnest Pass region of southwestern Alberta. The Lilac-bordered Copper is known from the adjacent Glacier County, Montana. Adults are found usually in meadows and along streams in sagebrush flats.

Lycaena nivalis
Male dorsal

Lycaena nivalis
Male ventral

Lycaena nivalis
Female dorsal

Lycaena nivalis
Female ventral

Polygonum coccineum
Water Smartweed

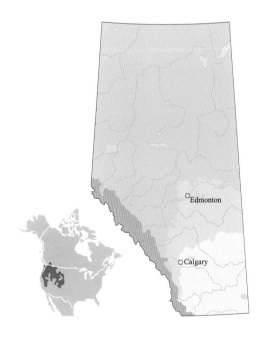

161

Lycaena (Gaeides) Scudder, 1876a

Etymology. Possibly from the Greek *gaia*, "the earth."

Lycaena (Gaeides) editha (Mead, 1878)
Edith's Copper

Lycaena editha
Male dorsal

Lycaena editha
Male ventral

Etymology. The species name is probably a patronym based on a woman's name.

Identification. Dorsally this species resembles *Lycaena (Gaeides) dione* in that the wings are gray with an orange submarginal band on the hind wing. Ventrally, characteristic splotches distinguish this species from all other *Gaeides*.

Life **History**. Larvae are suspected to feed on a variety of plants, including cinquefoil (*Potentilla* spp.), *Ivesia* spp., dock and sorrel (*Rumex* spp.) and *Horkelia* spp. Of these plants, *Potentilla* and *Rumex* spp. are known from Alberta. In Montana, the flight period is from late June through August.

Range and **Habitat**. Edith's Copper is widespread in the mountain regions of Montana, Washington and Idaho, south to Wyoming and Colorado. The probability of finding this species in Alberta is high. It should be watched for in the Waterton Park to Crowsnest Pass area and in the Milk River drainage of southern Alberta. Edith's Copper has been reported from High River, Alberta (Bowman 1934) but the authors were unable to authenticate this record. Adults prefer moist upland meadows.

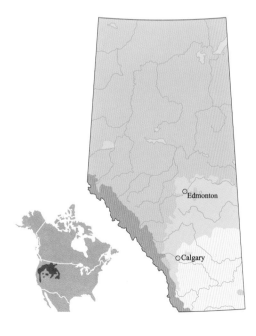

Potentilla diversifolia
Mountain Cinquefoil

Potentilla fruticosa
Shrubby Cinquefoil

Lycaena (Gaeides) dione (Scudder, 1879)
Great Gray Copper

Etymology. Dione was the mother of Aphrodite in Greek myth.

Identification. Our largest Copper, this species has a gray ventral surface with black spots and an orange submarginal band on the hind wing. The dorsal surface is gray, also with a submarginal orange band on the hind wing. The sexes are similar. Scott (1979) noted that *Lycaena (Gaeides) editha* and *Lycaena (Gaeides) xanthoides* differ by only two characters while *L.(G.) dione* differs from both by eight characters. Pratt, Wright and Ballmer (1991), using different characters and methods, showed that there is no real evidence for gene flow and clinal variation in the *editha/xanthoides/dione* group. Given the substantial phenotypic and biological differences it makes sense to treat *dione* as a separate species as per Opler (1992).

Life History. Larvae of the Great Gray Copper feed on a number of native and introduced plants, particularly dock and sorrel (*Rumex* spp.). Eggs are laid singly underneath leaves. Larvae are either green with a dark dorsal stripe or green with yellow green marginal areas and a reddish stripe. The chrysalids are pinkish brown with black marks. Pupation often takes place in the litter at the base of the host plant. There is one brood per year; the eggs overwinter. Adults nectar readily and perch on grasses, reeds and flowers, especially thistles (*Cirsium* spp.) and yellow composites. Males pursue passing butterflies vigorously. To observe these butterflies, disturb grasses and reeds in suitable habitats and watch flower heads, especially thistles. The Great Gray Copper has a peak flight activity in July, with a flight period from June 11 to September 17.

Range and Habitat. This species ranges from Illinois, west to central Alberta and south to Colorado. In Alberta, *Lycaena (Gaeides) dione* occurs in prairies, parkland areas and the southern foothills. The Great Gray Copper is found close to its larval host plant in moist areas around ponds, sloughs, streams and river banks.

Lycaena dione
Male dorsal

Lycaena dione
Male ventral

Apr May Jun Jul Aug Sep Oct

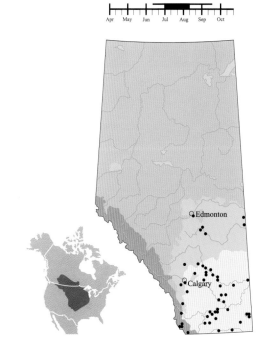

Lycaena (Hyllolycaena) Miller and Brown, 1979

Etymology. The first part of the name may refer to Hyllus, the son of Hercules and Deianira in Greek mythology. The second part, *lycaena*, refers to a closely related genus of butterflies.

Lycaena (Hyllolycaena) hyllus (Cramer, [1775])
Bronze Copper

Lycaena hyllus
Male dorsal

Lycaena hyllus
Male dorsal

Lycaena hyllus
Female dorsal

Lycaena hyllus
Female ventral

Apr May Jun Jul Aug Sep Oct

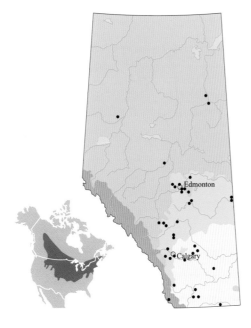

Etymology. Again, the species name may refer to the son of Hercules and Deianira.

Identification. The Bronze Copper has bright orange dorsal fore wings with brown spots. The ventral hind wing is gray with black spots, and has a bright orange submarginal band. Females have brown dorsal wing surfaces with orange patches and bright submarginal bands on the dorsal and ventral hind wings.

Life History. Caterpillars of the Bronze Copper are bright green with a dark dorsal line. Chrysalids are orange-brown with dark markings. Larval host plants are dock (*Rumex* spp.) and knotweed (*Polygonum* spp.). In Alberta the probable host is Water Smartweed, (*Polygonum coccineum*). The Bronze Copper flies only where dock is available.There is one brood per year; the eggs overwinter. Adults have a rapid jerky flight and may be seen along margins of streams and sloughs in tall grasses or visiting flowers. The flight period in Alberta is from July 2 through September 7.

Range and Habitat. This butterfly is found from Quebec west to Alberta and south into Colorado. In Alberta, this species is infrequently collected. It is common if its habitat is sampled at the right time. Most specimens have been collected in the southern half of the province. A few other specimens have been collected farther north, from Fort McMurray, Peace River and up to Fort Smith, in the Northwest Territories. The Bronze Copper is found along margins of sloughs, streams and rivers in prairie regions, usually close to its larval host plants. Kondla (1992) reports that boreal forest populations also occur in sedge fens.

Lycaena (Lycaena) cuprea (W.H. Edwards, 1870)
Lustrous Copper
subspecies: *Lycaena (Lycaena) cuprea snowi* (W.H. Edwards, [1881b])
Snow's Copper

Etymology. *Cuprea* from Latin meaning "copper." The subspecies name is an honorific of Snow, president of the University of Kansas in the late 1800s.

Identification. The Lustrous Copper is a small species, with gray ventral hind wings that have a distinctly darker marginal area. The dorsal wing surface of males is a bright metallic reddish orange while that of females is yellowish orange.

Life History. Little is known about the immature stages. In Colorado, larvae have been associated with Mountain Sorrel (*Oxyria digyna*) and the Pacific subspecies, *L. cupreus cupreus*, has been reported on dock and sorrel (*Rumex* spp.). The peak flight period is late July through early August, with a range of July 2 to September 2. There is one brood per year; the larvae overwinter.

Range and Habitat. This species is found from northern British Columbia south in the mountains to California. There are three subspecies, two of which are sometimes considered separate species. In Alberta, specimens can be placed as *Lycaena cuprea snowi*. Scott (1981) reported that Alberta populations most resemble *L .c. snowi* although the ventral hind wing submarginal and marginal black spots are characteristic of *L. c. artemisia* Scott. Material north of the Athabasca River may represent intergrades with *Lycaena cuprea henryae* (Cadbury), which was described from northern British Columbia. Lustrous Coppers are usually found above treeline, but may stray to meadows at lower elevations.

Lycaena cuprea snowi
Female dorsal

Lycaena cuprea snowi
Female ventral

Oxyria digyna
Mountain Sorrel

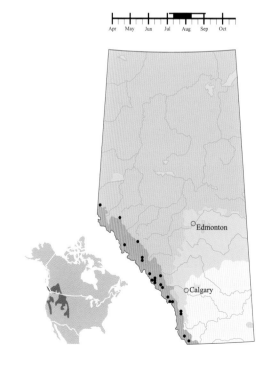

165

Lycaena (Lycaena) phlaeas (Linnaeus, 1761)
Little Copper
subspecies: *Lycaena (Lycaena) phlaeas arethusa* (Wolley-Dod, 1907)

Lycaena phlaeas arethusa
Male dorsal

Lycaena phlaeas arethusa
Male ventral

Rumex pauciflorus
Mountain Sheep Sorrel

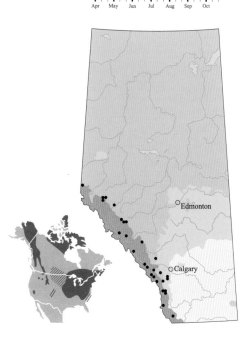

Etymology. *Phlegon* (Greek) means burning, and was one of the four horses of the sun; *phlogites* (also Greek) is a flame-coloured gem. Perhaps the species name was to mean flame, fire or something similar, in reference to its bright colours. Arethusa is the name of a wood nymph of the Greek goddess Artemis.

Identification. The Little Copper is a small butterfly with bright golden-orange bands on the dorsal surface of the hind wings, especially in males. The ventral wing surface is a light orange-brown. The dorsal surface of the fore wing has bright metallic golden patches.

Life History. Only immatures of the eastern subspecies of *Lycaena phlaeas* have been described. The eggs are pale green with vertical ribbing. Larvae are downy and either green with a rosy dorsal stripe or rose with pale yellow lateral markings. The pupae are brown with some green and are often near or attached to the host plant. The pupae are reported to overwinter. It is likely that the mountain subspecies of *Lycaena phlaeas* will have a similar life history. The eastern subspecies uses many species of dock and sorrel (*Rumex* spp.) and knotweed and smartweed (*Polygonum* spp.) as host plants. In Colorado, Mountain Sorrel (*Oxyria digyna*) is the reported host. In Alberta, *Oxyria* is the suspected host for the northern alpine populations, while *Rumex pauciflorus* is the suspected host for the northern subalpine meadow populations. Little Coppers perch on shrubs and flowers near larval host plants. They freely imbibe nectar and may chase other coppers. Peak flight period is mid-July to early August depending on locality and ranges from July 2 to September 12. There is one brood per year.

Range and Habitat. This species is circumpolar. In North America it ranges from the arctic islands and Alaska south to Wyoming with isolated populations in Oregon and California and east to Nova Scotia. *Lycaena phlaeas arethusa* occurs in the mountains and foothills of Alberta. In the southern mountains the Little Copper appears to be restricted to areas above treeline. In the northern mountains, these butterflies can be found on valley floors, near patches of sorrel along trails and in meadows, as well as on mountain tops.

Subfamily
THECLINAE
HAIRSTREAKS and ELFINS

Members of the subfamily Theclinae are collectively known as hairstreaks, although some species are also commonly called elfins (e.g., *Incisalia* spp., and some *Callophrys* and *Mitoura*). The radial vein in the fore wing has only three branches, in contrast with the four-branched radial vein of coppers. The hind wings often bear delicate hairlike tails and a black-and-red spot at the anal margin (the "thecla spot"). Males usually have a patch of scented androconial scales on the fore wing and, like male coppers, tend to use a perching strategy to find mates. There are 12 species of hairstreaks in Alberta, and four others whose ranges come close to our provincial borders.

Callophrys Billberg, 1820

Etymology. *Callophrys* appears to be a compound word originating from the Greek words, *kalos* meaning "beautiful" and *ophrys* meaning "eyebrow," perhaps in reference to the delicate banding on the ventral wing surface and, therefore, beautiful brow (line).

The classification of the butterflies associated with this genus is poorly understood. Some authorities split them into *Callophrys*, *Incisalia*, *Sandia*, *Mitoura* and *Xamia*. This classification is based primarily upon wing characters. All, however, display similar male genitalia. This latter fact is responsible for the lumping of these genera into a single genus by a second group of experts. We are following the first group, and have arranged the genera alphabetically within the Theclinae section.

Callophrys sheridanii at Beaver Mines, Alberta.   G.J. Hilchie.

Callophrys affinis (W.H. Edwards, 1862)
Immaculate Hairstreak

Callophrys affinis
Female dorsal

Callophrys affinis
Female ventral

Etymology. The species name means "related to" or "adjacent to" in Latin.

Identification. This green hairstreak has few markings on its wings; ventrally, it is yellow-green and dorsally, gray to brown. Females are occasionally somewhat tawny. In Alberta, *Callophrys sheridanii* comes closest in appearance, but differs in having a well-marked band of white on the ventral hind wing.

Life History. Larvae are reported to feed on Subalpine or Sulphur Umbrella Plant (*Eriogonum umbellatum*) which is found throughout southern Alberta. In Montana the butterfly flies from June through mid-August.

Range and Habitat. *Callophrys affinis* is most common in the Great Basin with populations occurring east of the Rocky Mountains on the Great Plains from Montana through to Colorado. *Callophrys affinis* is expected through much of central Montana up to the Canadian border. This butterfly has been recorded from Hill County and Toole County, Montana, which are in the Milk River watershed about five kilometres south of the Alberta border. The probability of occurrence of this species in Alberta is high. It should be watched for along the Milk River drainage and in the Waterton to Crowsnest Pass region where there are abundant populations of *Eriogonum umbellatum*, the reported host plant.

Callophrys sheridanii (W.H. Edwards, 1877)
Sheridan's Hairstreak
subspecies: *Callophrys sheridanii sheridanii* (W.H. Edwards, 1877)

Etymology. The species is named after Sheridan, Wyoming, which in turn was named in honour of Philip Henry Sheridan, a general of the U.S. Army in the 1800s.

Identification. Sheridan's Hairstreak is easily recognized as our only species that is green on the ventral surface of the wings. It also has a white line from the leading edge to the trailing edge of the ventral hind wing.

Life History. The larval host is Subalpine or Sulphur Umbrella Plant (*Eriogonum umbellatum*) in Washington and Colorado, and other species elsewhere. The butterfly has been seen perching on Sagebrush (*Artemisia tridentata*). The flight period in Alberta is from May 7 to June 20. There is one generation per year; the pupae overwinter.

Range and Habitat. Sheridan's Hairstreak ranges from southern Alberta and North Dakota, west into Washington. Alberta specimens are identified as *Callophrys sheridanii sheridanii* and are found in the mountains south of the Bow River valley. This species occurs on dry grassy slopes at moderate elevations.

Callophrys sheridanii sheridanii
Female dorsal

Callophrys sheridanii sheridanii
Female ventral

View eastward from Hailstone Butte, Alberta.   A.T. Finnamore.

169

Harkenclenus dos Passos, 1970

Etymology. *Harkenclenus* is a condensation of Harry Kendon Clench (1925 - 1980), an eminent American lepidopterist and lycaenid specialist.

Harkenclenus titus (Fabricius, 1793)
Coral Hairstreak
subspecies: *Harkenclenus titus immaculosus* (W.P. Comstock, 1913)

Harkenclenus titus immaculosus
Male dorsal

Harkenclenus titus immaculosus
Male ventral

Harkenclenus titus immaculosus
Female dorsal

Harkenclenus titus immaculosus
Female ventral

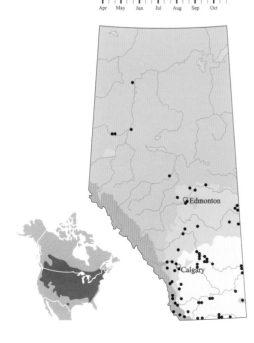

Etymology. Titus is a Latin proper name and could refer to: an orator in Rome in the second century B.C., a consul of Rome in 31 B.C., or even a fictitious name used in legal examples. The subspecies name is from *in* which means "not" and *maculosus* which means "spots" or "speckled" in Latin; hence, "spotless," possibly referring to the relatively unmarked dorsal wing surfaces.

Identification. The Coral Hairstreak is a small butterfly (wingspan 25-32 mm) that is brown on the ventral surface with weak spotting and a bright orange or coral-coloured submarginal band. Dorsal wing colour is brown, occasionally with a light orange or brown submarginal band or spot in the anal angle of each wing. Females are larger than males and have larger light spots on the dorsal surface. There is also sexual dimorphism in wing shape.

Life History. The green eggs are laid on the host plant in the fall, and hatch the following spring. Larvae feed on the flowers, leaves and fruit of several species of cherry (*Prunus* spp.), including Choke Cherry (*Prunus virginiana*) and the Saskatoon (*Amelanchier alnifolia*). Caterpillars secrete a sweet substance and are often tended by ants. The mature larvae have a dark head with a dull streak and a dull green body with a hint of yellow on the anterior. There are dull pink patches on the thorax. The pupae are brown with darker speckles and are covered with short hairs. Adults are rapid fliers and are difficult to catch in flight. Adults may be observed perching on flowers, shrubs and larval host plants; males fly up to investigate passing butterflies. The peak flight period is in July and early August and ranges from June 6 to August 31. There is one brood per year.

Range and Habitat. The Coral Hairstreak is found throughout Canada, from the Atlantic west to British Columbia, and south to Texas. *Harkenclenus titus immaculosus* is widespread in south and central Alberta north to Redwater. A disjunct population, that is darker than southern populations, is found in the Peace River district. It is widespread in Choke Cherry and Saskatoon thickets, along river valleys, bluffs, coulees, ravines and southern mountain valleys below 1500 m.

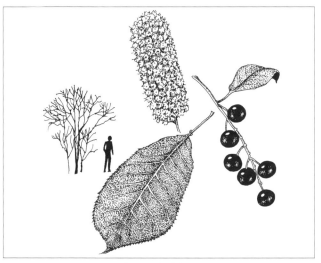

Prunus virginiana
Choke Cherry

Amelanchier alnifolia
Saskatoon

West Castle River valley, Alberta.

A.T. Finnamore.

171

Incisalia Scudder, [1871]

Incisalia (Deciduphagus) Johnson, 1992

Etymology. Deciduphagus is an arbitrary, euphonious, latinized combination referring to the use of deciduous plant species by the larvae of species in this subgenus (Johnson 1992).

Incisalia (Deciduphagus) augustinus (Westwood, 1852)
Brown Elfin
subspecies: *Incisalia (Deciduphagus) augustinus augustinus* (Westwood, 1852)

Ledum groenlandicum
Labrador Tea

Incisalia augustinus augustinus
Male dorsal

Incisalia augustinus augustinus
Male ventral

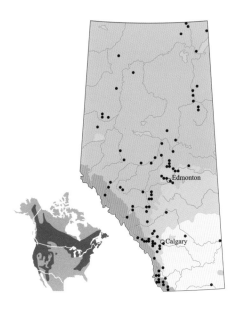

Etymology. The species name is derived from a Latin masculine proper name, Augustus.

Identification. The Brown Elfin is very similar to *Incisalia polia*, the Hoary Elfin, but lacks the gray on the ventral wing surface, and has faint, obscure postmedian and submarginal spots. The dorsal wing surface often has light brown patches.

Life History. Brown Elfin larvae are reported to feed on a variety of plants of the heather family (Ericaceae), including Bearberry or Kinnikinnick (*Arctostaphylos uva-ursi*), Labrador Tea (*Ledum groenlandicum*) and bilberry, blueberry and huckleberry (*Vaccinium* spp.). Eggs are laid usually on the flower bud of the host. Upon hatching, the caterpillars usually bore into and feed on the flower, later consuming the young fruits. Pupae overwinter in the ground near the host, with adults emerging the following spring. The caterpillars are bright green with dorsal stripes and oblique lateral lines and dashes. The chrysalids are light brown and covered with short hairs. This species is one of the earliest fliers in the spring and adults are active from April 16 to July 5. There is one brood per year.

Range and Habitat. The Brown Elfin ranges from Alaska to Newfoundland, south to Pennsylvania in the east, and to New Mexico and California in the west. Alberta populations are placed in the nominate subspecies *Incisalia augustinus augustinus*. In Alberta, the Brown Elfin is found through the boreal and montane forest regions in pine and spruce forests, also locally in Bearberry or Kinnikinnick patches in the prairie and aspen parkland.

172

Incisalia (Deciduphagus) mossii (Hy. Edwards, 1881)
Moss' Elfin
subspecies: *Incisalia (Deciduphagus) mossii schryveri* Cross, 1937

Etymology. The species and subspecies names are patronyms.

Identification. *Incisalia mossii* is similar to the Hoary Elfin, *Incisalia polia*, but the ventral hind wing is reddish brown instead of gray, and has a lighter gray distal area.

Life History. The eggs are pale bluish green. Larvae are variously coloured and have two red dorsal bands and a whitish lateral band. Pupae are chocolate brown with a dark line and dark spots. The pupae overwinter. The larval host is reported to be Common Stonecrop (*Sedum lanceolatum*). The flight period in Alberta is from May 7 to June 12. There is one brood per year.

Range and Habitat. Moss' Elfin occurs from New Mexico and California in the south to Alberta and British Columbia in the north. The only confirmed Alberta population is on the lower slopes of Windsor Mountain near the South Castle River. There is an unconfirmed sight record from Waterton Lakes National Park. Moss' Elfin has been found on the steep west-facing slopes dominated by Sagebrush (*Artemisia tridentata*). It is seen frequently in and near small ravines that are fed by snow melt.

Incisalia mossii schryveri
Male dorsal

Incisalia mossii schryveri
Male ventral

Incisalia mossii schryveri
Female dorsal

Incisalia mossii schryveri
Female ventral

Sedum lanceolatum
Common Stonecrop

Incisalia (Deciduphagus) polia Cook and Watson, 1907
Hoary Elfin
subspecies: *Incisalia (Deciduphagus) polia obscura* Ferris and Fisher, 1973

Incisalia polia obscura
Male dorsal

Incisalia polia obscura
Male ventral

Incisalia polia obscura
Female dorsal

Incisalia polia obscura
Female ventral

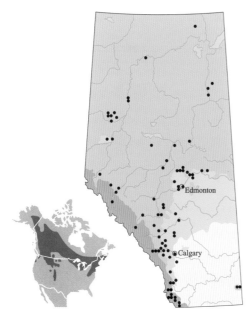

Etymology. The name comes from *polios*, which means "gray" in Greek. The subspecies name comes from the Latin *obscurus*, meaning "unclear" or "dusky."

Identification. The Hoary Elfin is a small, tailless species, with wings that are brown on both the dorsal and ventral surfaces. There is an irregular break in colour down the centre of the wing. The basal area of the ventral hind wing is dark brown and the distal half is flooded with gray. Some individuals have a partial white line on the ventral hind wing. Males have gray androconial patches on the fore wings.

Life History. Females deposit their small, circular eggs on the dorsal leaf surface of host plants. Bearberry or Kinnikinnick (*Arctostaphylos uva-ursi*) is a confirmed host; however, other plants are suspected. First instar larvae are pale green, while second and third instars are yellow-green with dorsal and lateral rosy stripes and shading. Fourth instar larvae are green and the chrysalids are dark brown. Adults perch on prominent twigs and stems. Males use a perching strategy to find females. Both sexes are rapid fliers, but flights are short in duration. The flight period in Alberta is from April 15 to June 29. There is one brood per year; the pupae overwinter.

Range and Habitat. Hoary Elfins are found from Alberta to Newfoundland in the northern coniferous forests, south to the New England states in the east and New Mexico in the west. *Incisalia polia obscura* is found in Alberta wherever coniferous forests are common, but has not been recorded on the prairies nor in most of the aspen parkland. It inhabits spruce and pine woods and occasionally poplar stands in areas where its food plants grow.

Incisalia (Incisalia) Scudder, [1871]

Etymology. Possibly from the Latin *incisus*, meaning "cut" or "carved."

Incisalia (Incisalia) eryphon (Boisduval, 1852)
Western Pine Elfin
subspecies: *Incisalia (Incisalia) eryphon eryphon* (Boisduval, 1852)

Etymology. The origin of the name is uncertain; it may be a mix of the Greek words *ery* meaning "drawing out" and *phon* "sound" or "voice"; alternatively, Eryphon may have been a classical personage.

Identification. The Western Pine Elfin is a small brown butterfly with distinct jagged lines on the ventral wing surface. Wing margins are checkered. Males have a dark androconial spot on the dorsal fore wing and are usually dark grayish brown on the dorsal surface. Females are light brown. In Alberta this species is easily confused with *Incisalia niphon*, the Eastern Pine Elfin. Most specimens can be distinguished by the lack of a spot in the discal cell of the ventral fore wing, and by crisp, sharply-defined markings. Eastern Pine Elfin markings are often more washed out than those of the Western Pine Elfin, and there is a reddish orange tinge on the ventral wing surface of the former species.

Life History. Larvae are reported to feed on several species of pine; of these, Lodgepole Pine (*Pinus contorta* var. *latifolia*) appears to be the host in Alberta. Caterpillars are velvety green with creamy white subdorsal and spiracle markings, and are covered by light brown hairs. Adults perch on pine boughs and have been observed on Kinnikinnick or Bearberry on the ground. Males pursue any moving object vigorously, including collectors. The flight period in Alberta is from April 17 to July 8. There is one brood per year; the pupae overwinter.

Range and Habitat. Isolated populations are found in the southwestern states, with the species' range extending north to central Alberta and northeastern British Columbia and east to Ontario. The two pine elfins, *Incisalia eryphon* and *Incisalia niphon*, may form a hybrid zone in north-central Alberta (Reist 1979).

Incisalia eryphon eryphon
Male dorsal

Incisalia eryphon eryphon
Male ventral view

Incisalia eryphon eryphon
Female dorsal

Incisalia eryphon eryphon
Female ventral

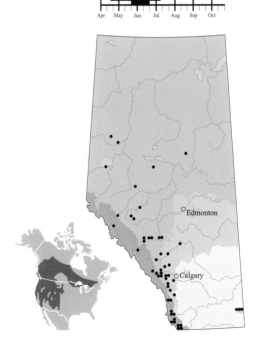

Incisalia (Incisalia) niphon (Hübner, [1823])
Eastern Pine Elfin
subspecies: *Incisalia (Incisalia) niphon clarki* T.N. Freeman, 1938

Incisalia niphon clarki
Male dorsal

Incisalia niphon clarki
Male ventral

Incisalia niphon clarki
Female dorsal

Incisalia niphon clarki
Female ventral

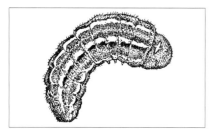

Incisalia niphon clarki larva

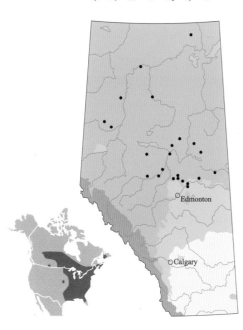

Etymology. The name of the species is derived from the Greek word *nipha* for "snow," perhaps referring to its early appearance in the spring. The subspecies name is a patronym.

Identification. The Eastern Pine Elfin is small, brown and similar to *Incisalia eryphon*. The dorsal wing surface is light brown with bright basal patches. Occasionally these patches may dominate the dorsal surface. There is usually a dark bar on the ventral fore wing in the discal cell, as well as the normal one at the end of the cell. In contrast, *Incisalia eryphon* usually lacks this extra bar. The submarginal band on the ventral hind wing is composed of short blunt triangles. The same band in *Incisalia eryphon* is usually composed of more elongated and sharply pointed triangles.

Life History. The larvae feed on a wide variety of pines including Jack Pine (*Pinus banksiana*). Larvae usually feed on young needles of the smaller pines. The caterpillars are pale green with a pair of cream stripes on each side and a white patch on the prothorax. The pupae are brownish black tinged with yellow. Unlike most hairstreaks, males patrol looking for females rather than perching, and often sun themselves on patches of sand or in clearings. Females perch on pine trees and rarely fly unless disturbed. To observe the butterflies, walk up and down cut lines and roads, banging the young trees; disturbed adults may fly to a nearby tree and alight. The flight period in Alberta is from May 6 to June 30. There is one brood per year; the pupae overwinter.

Range and Habitat. The Eastern Pine Elfin ranges from Alberta and the Northwest Territories in the west to the Maritimes and south to Florida in the east. Alberta material is placed in the subspecies *Incisalia niphon clarki*, but is usually not representative of typical populations. This is possibly due to hybridization with *Incisalia eryphon* along the hybrid zone of Jack Pine and Lodgepole Pine (*Pinus contorta.*). This species occurs in Jack Pine stands where there are young trees.

Mitoura Scudder, 1871

Etymology. From the Greek *mitos* meaning "thread" and *oura* meaning "tail."

Mitoura siva (W.H. Edwards, 1874)
Juniper Hairstreak

Etymology. Possibly from Siva, the Hindu god of restoration and destruction.

Identification. This small, pretty hairstreak is green ventrally with a boldly marked postmedial white line on both fore and hind wings. The upper side of the wings is grayish brown with a slight flush of dull orange. There is a delicate tail on the hind wing.

Life History. Larvae feed on junipers with a preference for Rocky Mountain Juniper (*Juniperus scopulorum*). In Montana, adults fly from late April through mid-July.

Range and Habitat. The Juniper Hairstreak is widely distributed in western North America and is found throughout Montana with more northerly populations reported in British Columbia and Saskatchewan. The probability of occurrence in Alberta is high, but due to its preference for the vicinity of its host plant, discovery of this butterfly will prove difficult. It is expected to occur in southern Alberta south of the Oldman and South Saskatchewan rivers with the highest probability in the Waterton Lakes National Park to Crowsnest Pass area where *Juniperus scopulorum* is common.

Mitoura siva
Male dorsal

Mitoura siva
Male ventral

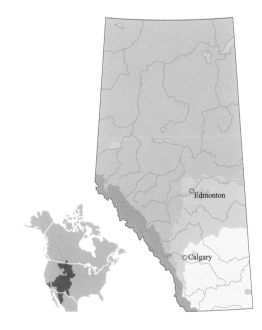

Mitoura spinetorum (Hewitson, 1867)
Thicket Hairstreak

Mitoura spinetorum
Male dorsal

Mitoura spinetorum
Male ventral

Mitoura spinetorum
Female dorsal

Mitoura spinetorum
Female ventral

Etymology. The name is derived from the Latin word *spinetum*, meaning "thicket," hence "from a thicket."

Identification. The dorsal wing surface of the Thicket Hairstreak is gray overshadowed by dark blue. The ventral surface is a rich chestnut brown, with a bright white line from the leading edge to the trailing edge of fore and hind wings. There is a submarginal row of dark spots and a tail on the hind wing.

Life History. Larvae feed on mistletoe (*Arceuthobium* spp.), a parasitic plant of pines. This hairstreak has been found only a few times in Alberta. The few observations we have indicate that adults are avid flower visitors and gather frequently on roads to puddle. The flight period in Alberta is from May 22 to July 2. There is one brood per year; the pupae overwinter.

Range and Habitat. The Thicket Hairstreak ranges from Mexico north to southern Alberta and central British Columbia. In Alberta, this species is found in the mountains from the Bow River Valley southward. It occurs on valley floors, in meadows, close to parasitized pine trees.

Arceuthobium americanum
Dwarf Mistletoe

Satyrium Scudder, 1876a

Etymology. Satyrium is from the Greek *satyrus*, a goat-like woodland deity typifying lasciviousness.

Satyrium acadicum (W.H. Edwards, 1862)
Acadian Hairstreak
subspecies: *Satyrium acadicum watrini* (Dufrane, 1939)
Satyrium acadicum montanensis (Watson and W.P. Comstock, 1920)

Etymology. Acadica comes from the name of the early French settlement in Nova Scotia. The subspecies name *montanensis* means "of the mountains" in Latin, while *watrini* may be an honorific.

Satyrium acadicum watrini
Male dorsal

Satyrium acadicum watrini
Male ventral

Identification. The Acadian Hairstreak is small with a single tail on the hind wing (a reduced second tail is barely visible). The dorsal surface is dark gray to brown, and males have an androconial (scent) patch on the fore wing. The ventral surface is light gray with well defined spots on the outer half of the wing. The orange thecla spot on the hind wing is distinct.

Life History. The eggs are laid on the host plants in the fall and overwinter. Larvae are green with two yellow stripes on each side of the body, oblique yellow to white bars also mark the sides. The pupae are dull yellow brown with dark spots. The reported host is the Sandbar Willow (*Salix exigua*), which is found in southern Alberta in damp areas around sloughs and riverbanks. Adults are strong fliers, and tend to perch on prominent flowers and shrubs. Nectaring has been observed on Buckbrush (*Symphoricarpos occidentalis*). When perching, the butterflies tend to face head down. The peak flight period is mid-to-late July ranging from July 8 to August 25. There is one brood per year.

Range and Habitat. This species ranges from eastern Canada and the United States, west to the Rocky Mountains. In Alberta it is found south of the Red Deer River. *Satyrium acadicum montanensis* is represented by populations in the Waterton Lakes National Park to Crowsnest Pass area and south into Montana. *Satyrium acadicum watrini* occurs to the east onto the prairies into Saskatchewan. Adults are found near moist areas and willow thickets around prairie sloughs, stream channels and other wetlands.

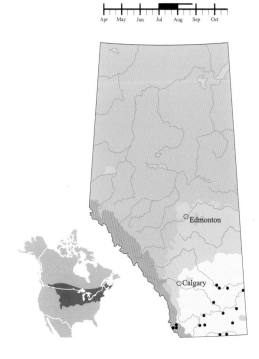

Apr May Jun Jul Aug Sep Oct

179

Satyrium fuliginosum (W.H. Edwards, 1861)
Sooty Gossamer Wing
subspecies: *Satyrium fuliginosum semiluna* Klots, 1930

Satyrium fuliginosum semiluna
Male dorsal

Satyrium fuliginosum semiluna
Male ventral

Lupinus argenteus
Silvery Lupine

Etymology. The species name is from the Latin *fuliginosus* for "sooty," "painted black," and the subspecies is from the Latin *semi* meaning "partial" and *luna* meaning "moon"; this refers to the type locality of the subspecies, Halfmoon Ranch, Wyoming.

Identification. The dorsal surface of the Sooty Gossamer Wing is a uniform gray. Males have an androconial patch on the fore wing. The ventral wing surface is lighter gray with small white-ringed dark spots. Tails and thecla spots are absent on the hind wings. This butterfly is similar to *Plebejus icarioides*, the Icarioides Blue.

Life History. The life history of this species is undescribed. The close association of adults with lupines (*Lupinus* spp.) and oviposition under lupines in other regions suggest that this may be the larval host. In British Columbia this butterfly was observed to nectar at mock orange (*Philadelphus* spp.). The flight period is expected to be from mid-July to early August. In Alberta the Sooty Gossamer Wing is known from a single date, June 25, 1925. There is believed to be one brood per year with the eggs overwintering.

Range and Habitat. The Sooty Gossamer Wing ranges from California and Colorado in the south to Washington and Alberta in the north. Two subspecies are recognized, *Satyrium fuliginosum fuliginosum* in California and *Satyrium fuliginosum semiluna* in the eastern portion of the range. In Alberta, a single specimen of *S. f. semiluna* was collected at Waterton Lake. It occurs in the sagebrush country of the mountains and foothills.

Satyrium liparops (Le Conte, 1833)
Striped Hairstreak

subspecies: *Satyrium liparops aliparops* (Michener and dos Passos, 1942)
Satyrium liparops fletcheri (Michener and dos Passos, 1942)

Etymology. *Liparops* is from the Greek *liparos* for "oily," "sleek," "shiny." *Aliparops* is from the Greek *an* for "without" and *liparops*, hence "not oily" or "not shiny." *Fletcheri* is named in honour of James Fletcher, an eminent Canadian entomologist.

Identification. The Striped Hairstreak is a small brown butterfly (25-35 mm) with two tails on the hind wings. On some specimens a lighter brown patch is present on the dorsal fore wing. The ventral wing surface has an orange submarginal band and a series of thin broken white lines on the discal area.

Life History. Eggs are laid singly on the host plant in fall and overwinter. The following spring the young larvae bore into the buds, eating developing leaves, flowers and fruits. Larvae are light green with a dark dorsal stripe with oblique yellowish green stripes on the sides of the body. Pupae are yellowish brown with a slight red tinge and rusty spots. Larvae feed on a wide variety of plants in the rose family (Rosaceae) and heather family (Ericaceae). Expected hosts in Alberta include Saskatoon (*Amelanchier alnifolia*), Choke Cherry (*Prunus virginiana*) and hawthorn *Crataegus* spp.). Adults perch on the leaves of the host bushes and rarely fly unless disturbed. Flight is rapid and individuals are difficult to follow. The peak flight period in Alberta is in mid-July, with a range from June 10 to August 9. There is one brood per year.

Satyrium liparops fletcheri
Male dorsal

Satyrium liparops aliparops
Male dorsal

Satyrium liparops fletcheri
Female dorsal

Satyrium liparops fletcheri
Female ventral

Amelanchier alnifolia
Saskatoon

181

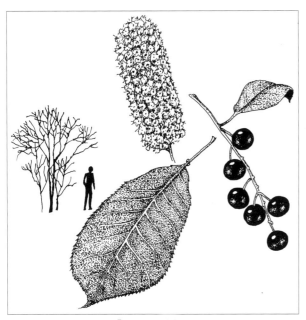

Prunus virginiana
Choke Cherry

Range and Habitat. The Striped Hairstreak ranges across North America, from the Atlantic to the Great Divide, from the Peace River district to Colorado and Florida. In Alberta this butterfly occurs through much of the prairie and aspen parkland regions, both south and central, and in the Peace River region. *Satyrium liparops aliparops* is characterized by the absence of a light brown patch on the fore wing; it occurs in the southern prairies. *Satyrium liparops fletcheri*, which possesses the patch, occurs in the aspen parkland and northern prairies. The Peace River population is undescribed. In Alberta this species was considered rare until it was discovered that adults congregate on Choke Cherry bushes at the heads of ravines and coulees, and along valley sides. Initial observations indicate that large patches of Choke Cherry bushes are required to support a population of this species. The Striped Hairstreak is difficult to observe unless it is disturbed.

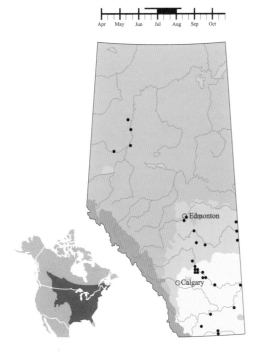

La Crete Ferry on the Peace River, Alberta.   F.A.H. Sperling.

Satyrium saepium (Boisduval, 1852)
Hedgerow Hairstreak

Etymology. The species name comes from the Latin *saepis*, meaning "hedge."

Identification. Dorsally, the wings of the Hedgerow Hairstreak are a uniform rusty brown and the ventral hind wing is without prominent submarginal spots. Ventrally the ground colour of the wings is gray, with a tinge of rust, and the postmedian line is narrow and edged with white.

Life History. This species is often locally abundant. Larvae feed on *Cercocarpus* spp. and tea bush (*Ceanothus* spp.) of which the latter occurs in the Waterton Park to Crowsnest Pass region of Alberta. In Montana, adults fly from mid-July through August.

Range and Habitat. These butterflies occur throughout the western United States including northern Montana (Glacier County) and north into British Columbia. The probability of occurrence in Alberta is high. The Hedgerow Hairstreak should be watched for on dry hill and mountain sides where *Ceanothus* grows in the Waterton Lakes National Park to Crowsnest Pass region.

Satyrium saepium
Female dorsal

Satyrium saepium
Female ventral

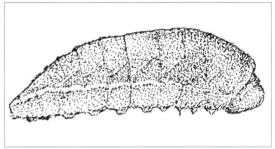
Satyrium saepium larva

Ceanothus sp.
Tea Bush

183

Satyrium sylvinum (Boisduval, 1852)
Sylvan Hairstreak

Satyrium sylvinum
Male dorsal

Satyrium sylvinum
Male ventral

Etymology. From the Latin *sylva* meaning "woods."

Identification. The ventral pattern of spots is similar to that of *Satyrium acadicum*, the Acadian Hairstreak, but the ventral hind wing has smaller discal and submarginal spots. Dorsally the wings are light brown, often with golden tones.

Life History. Larvae are reported to feed on a variety of willows (*Salix* spp.). Adults frequent areas along streams traversing dry regions. In Montana, the butterflies are on the wing from late June through early September.

Range and Habitat. The Sylvan Hairstreak is widespread in the mountain states of the United States from New Mexico and Arizona north to northern Idaho and Montana. In Montana, it has been recorded from Flathead County and is expected in Glacier County.
The probability of occurrence in Alberta is moderate. These butterflies should be watched for along streams in the Waterton Lakes National Park to Crowsnest Pass area.

Salix exigua
Sandbar Willow

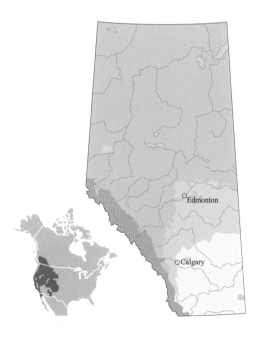

Strymon Hübner, [1818]

Etymology. The genus is named after the river Strymon in northern Greece.

Strymon melinus Hübner, [1818]
Gray Hairstreak
subspecies: *Strymon melinus franki* Field, 1938b

Etymology. The species name is likely from the Greek *melinos*, meaning "ashen," as these butterflies are gray. The subspecies name is a patronym.

Identification. The dorsal wing surface is gray in males and much darker in females. There is an orange spot on the dorsal hind wing near the tail. The ventral wing surface is gray with a thin white and black line extending from the leading edge to the trailing edge.

Life **H**istory. The larvae bore into seeds of a wide variety of plants, mostly in the pea (Leguminosae) and the rose (Rosaceae) families. Despite the impressive list of hosts reported, it is quite uncommon in Alberta. The older larvae may feed externally on leaves. Caterpillars may be green, yellow or brown or multicoloured and are covered with short brown hairs. The pupae overwinter and are dark brown with dark speckles. Adults perch upside down on grass stems during the day. The Gray Hairstreak hilltops and may be encountered along the crest of coulees and ridges, most often in flight. The flight period in Alberta is from May 9 to August 16.

Range and **H**abitat. The Gray Hairstreak is widely distributed from Nova Scotia in the east to Vancouver Island in the west, and south into Central America. Alberta material is difficult to place as we are at the boundary of several subspecies: *Strymon melinus franki* of the Great Plains, *Strymon melinus setonia* McDunnough, of the Great Basin and British Columbia, and *Strymon melinus humuli* (Harris), from New England and the Appalachian Mountains. Alberta specimens are uncommon, poorly defined and appear to be intergrades. The Gray Hairstreak is found mainly in river valleys and badlands in the prairie regions.

Strymon melinus franki
Female dorsal

Strymon melinus franki
Female ventral

Rosa acicularis
Prickly Rose

Subfamily
POLYOMMATINAE
BLUES

Members of the subfamily Polyommatinae are commonly known as blues. Blues are small butterflies with strong sexual colour dimorphism. Males have bluish upper wing surfaces while females have brown wings. Male blues usually patrol in search of mates, in contrast to the perching strategy employed by most coppers and hairstreaks. Caterpillars of many species have glands that produce sugary secretions that are attractive to ants. This benefits the caterpillars as the ants fend off predators and parasites. There are 13 species of blues in Alberta.

Celastrina Tutt, 1906

Etymology. The genus may have been named after the plant *Celastrus*, bittersweet.

Celastrina ladon (Cramer, [1780])
Spring Azure
subspecies: *Celastrina ladon lucia* (W.Kirby, 1837)
Celastrina ladon nigrescens (Fletcher, 1903a)
Purple Azure

Celastrina ladon lucia
Male dorsal

Celastrina ladon lucia
Male ventral

Celastrina ladon lucia
Male dorsal variation

Celastrina ladon lucia
Male ventral variation

Celastrina ladon nigrescens
Male dorsal

Celastrina ladon nigrescens
Male ventral

Etymology. The subspecies names are from the Latin *lucis*, meaning "light" and *nigrescens*, meaning "becoming black."

Identification. The Spring Azure is small with the dorsal wing surface purplish or silvery blue. Some individuals have black apical and marginal bands. The ventral wing surface is grayish brown with darker gray markings. There are no orange or metallic markings. Spots in the centre of the ventral hind wing may be separate or they may coalesce into a single large spot. The subspecies *Celastrina ladon nigrescens* is found in southwestern Alberta and may be distinguished by the greatly reduced ventral markings, white ventral surface, purplish blue dorsal surface and white hind wing fringe. *Celastrina ladon lucia* in contrast has a brownish ventral surface, a silvery-blue dorsal surface and a checkered hind wing fringe. The azures may be distinguished from other gray-coloured blues by the presence of dark marginal markings. This is one of the first species to appear in spring, and is often overlooked.

Life History. Pale green eggs are laid on flower buds. The larvae feed on the flower buds and may be tended by ants. Fully mature larvae are velvety in appearance and come in a variety of colours from yellow-green to pinkish. They have a dark dorsal stripe and oblique lateral greenish stripes. The light yellow-brown pupae have a variety of dark markings.

Caterpillars of *Celastrina ladon* feed on a wide variety of shrubs including tea bush (*Ceanothus* spp.), dogwood, bunchberry (*Cornus* spp.), cranberry (*Viburnum* spp.), bilberry, blueberry, huckleberry, (*Vaccinium* spp.), skunkbush, poison ivy (*Rhus* spp.) and cherry (*Prunus* spp.). Adults are associated with Red Osier Dogwood (*Cornus stolonifera*) in sheltered areas. They perch on leaves, flowers, twigs and the ground, or on Buffalo Berry (*Shepherdia canadensis*). Both sexes are weak fliers and flit through the underbrush. *Celastrina ladon lucia* flies from April 7 to July 6 with peak flight activity in May. *Celastrina ladon nigrescens* is reported on the wing from May 7 through June 12 with peak activity in mid May to early June. There is one brood per year; the pupae of *C. ladon lucia* overwinter, and those of *C. l. nigrescens* are believed to do so.

Range and Habitat. The *Celastrina ladon* complex occurs throughout most of North America. The subspecies *lucia* is found throughout Alberta with the subspecies *nigrescens* occurring locally in the Castle River drainage south of Crowsnest Pass.

Cornus stolonifera
Red Osier Dogwood

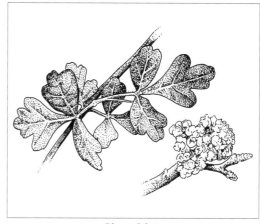

Rhus trilobata
Skunkbush

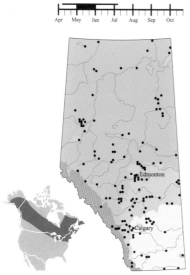

Celastrina ladon lucia

Celastrina ladon nigrescens

187

Euphilotes Mattoni, 1977

Etymology. The name is derived from the Greek prefix *eu* meaning "good" or "true" and *Philotes*, the genus to which the butterflies previously belonged. This name in turn may be derived from the Greek *philos* meaning "friend" and the suffix *tes* meaning "having to do with"; *Euphilotes* thus means " having a true friend."

Euphilotes enoptes (Boisduval, 1852)
Dotted Blue
subspecies: *Euphilotes enoptes ancilla* (Barnes and McDunnough, 1918)

Euphilotes enoptes ancilla
Male dorsal

Euphilotes enoptes ancilla
Male ventral

Euphilotes enoptes ancilla
Female dorsal

Eriogonum flavum
Yellow Umbrella-plant

Etymology. The name *enoptes* appears to be derived from the Greek *en* meaning "in" and a variation of *kopto*, "to cut up." This may refer to the dark markings on the wings being in small pieces, appearing cut up. The subspecific name *ancilla* means "maid servant" in Latin.

Identification. The only other species the Dotted Blue may be confused with is the Acmon Blue, *Plebejus acmon*. The Dotted Blue is distinguished by the lack of metallic scales on the ventral hind wing and positive identification may be made with genitalic dissections of the males. Another character which helps to identify the Dotted Blue is the larger, more block-like spots on the ventral wing surfaces. Marginal scales are checkered in appearance.

Life History. Adults perch on yellow composites and flowers of the umbrella plant (*Eriogonum* spp.) and fly rapidly when disturbed. They may be found along edges of steep and eroding hills near rivers in southern Alberta. No life history accounts are available but it is likely the larvae are similar to those found in California. The last instar larvae are pinkish white with a dorsal brownish stripe. Short white hairs give the larvae a frosted appearance. Known larval host plants are several species of umbrella plant (*Eriogonum* spp.). The main flight period is in early June, and ranges from May 17 to June 30. There is one brood per year; the pupae overwinter.

Range and Habitat. In Alberta, the Dotted Blue is found along the Milk and Oldman rivers but may be expected along the South Saskatchewan River and lower reaches of the Bow River. It also occurs throughout the western United States and southern Saskatchewan.

Apr May Jun Jul Aug Sep Oct

Edmonton

Calgary

Everes Hübner, 1819
TAILED BLUES

Etymology. The genus may have been named after the city of Evere in Belgium, or be a combination of the Latin words *ex*, "out of" and *verus*, "truth."

Everes amyntula (Boisduval, 1852)
Western Tailed Blue
subspecies: *Everes amyntula albrighti* Clench, 1944

Etymology. Boisduval may have coined the species name to compare with that of the Eastern Tailed Blue, *Everes comyntas* (Godart), which in turn may have been named after John Comyn, Lord de Babenoch. The subspecies was named for Dr. C.C. Albright of Great Falls, Montana who provided the type material to Clench.

Identification. This is a small species with tails on the hind wing. The ventral wing surface is light gray with faint spotting and an orange spot at the base of each tail. In males the dorsal side is metallic blue. Specimens from Alberta usually lack black submarginal spots on the dorsal wing surface. The dorsal wing surface of the female is mostly black or dark brown. A significant number of individuals show basal blue scaling. Wing margins in both sexes are white. There is a great deal of variation in size of specimens in our area, but there does not seem to be any correlation with habitat or latitude.

Life History. Pale green eggs are laid singly on flowers of the host plant or on young seed pods. Larvae feed on the seeds in the seed pod and overwinter there. Larvae are variable in colour, ranging from pale to dark green to variations of straw, with pink and maroon maculations. The pupae are tan or gray-green with darker brown bands. Many legumes have been documented as larval hosts including milk vetch (*Astragalus* spp.), loco-weed (*Oxytropis* spp.), clover (*Trifolium* spp.), buffalo bean or golden bean (*Thermopsis* spp.), vetch (*Vicia* spp.) and vetchling or peavine (*Lathyrus* spp.). Many of these legumes occur in Alberta and are likely used as larval hosts. Adults are usually seen perching on leaves of bushes and shrubs in openings and on

Everes amyntula
Male dorsal

Everes amyntula
Male ventral

Everes amyntula
Female dorsal

Everes amyntula
Female ventral

Oxytropis splendens
Showy Loco-weed

189

Vicia americana
Wild Vetch

Thermopsis rhombifolia
Buffalo or Golden Bean

forest edges. They nectar on members of the legume family (Leguminosae) and puddle on hot days. The Western Tailed Blue often rubs its fore and hind wings together when at rest. The flight period in Alberta is recorded from May 9 through August 9 with peak activity in June and July. There is one brood per year.

Range and Habitat. The Western Tailed Blue occurs through most of western North America; in the east it is replaced by the Eastern Tailed Blue, *Everes comyntas*. The Western Tailed Blue is found throughout Alberta, usually near wooded areas. Populations in southern Alberta can be placed in the subspecies *Everes amyntula albrighti* Clench.

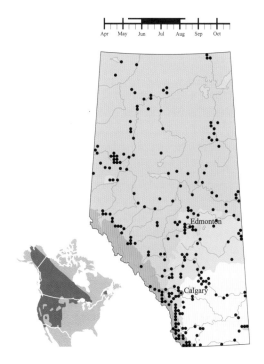

190

Glaucopsyche Scudder, [1871]

Etymology. From the Greek *glaucus* meaning "blue-grey" and Psyche, the companion of Eros in Greek myth, who was sometimes represented as a butterfly.

Glaucopsyche lygdamus (Doubleday, 1841)
Silvery Blue
subspecies: ***Glaucopsyche lygdamus couperi*** Grote, 1873
Glaucopsyche lygdamus oro (Scudder, 1876b)

Etymology. This species was named after Lygdamus, a slave of Cynthia, a mistress of the Roman Propertius. The subspecies was named for William Couper, the collector of the type material on Anticosti Island in the Gulf of St. Lawrence. The subspecies name *oro* may be derived from Latin meaning "to speak."

Identification. The dorsal surface of the wings is blue in males and gray with fewer blue scales in females. The dark edging on the wings is more pronounced in the females. The ventral wing surface is distinctive due to the absence of marginal and submarginal spots and is uniformly light gray with black basal and median spots. The subspecies *oro* is distinguished by the greenish dusting in the basal area of the ventral hind wing. Dirig and Cryan (1991) document the differences between *couperi* and the nominate subspecies *lygdamus*. They suggest these subspecies may be separate species but stop short of a taxonomic pronouncement. Additional research may well support the separation of *lygdamus* and *couperi* at the species level. Should that occur, Alberta populations will be known as *Glaucopsyche couperi*.

Glaucopsyche lygdamus couperi
Male dorsal

Glaucopsyche lygdamus couperi
Male ventral variation

Glaucopsyche lygdamus couperi
Male dorsal variation

Glaucopsyche lygdamus couperi
Male ventral variation

Glaucopsyche lygdamus oro
Female dorsal

Glaucopsyche lygdamus oro
Female ventral

Hedysarum sp.
Sweet Vetch

Life **History.** The Silvery Blue uses a wide variety of larval hosts. Most are legumes, including milk vetch (*Astragalus* spp.), vetch (*Vicia* spp.), sweet vetch (*Hedysarum* spp.) and lupines (*Lupinus* spp.). Larvae feed on flowers and developing seed pods. Ants attend the larvae for the sugary secretions they exude from glands on the tenth abdominal segment. Caterpillars are variable in colour ranging from green to purplish, with a dark dorsal stripe and oblique white dashes. Silvery Blues overwinter as pupae in the leaf litter at the base of the host plant. Adults are weak fliers with males often patrolling in the vicinity of host plants. They are frequent visitors to puddles on hot days. They often perch with folded wings on leaves, flowers or the ground. The Silvery Blue is one of the earlier blues to appear in the spring. The flight period in Alberta is April 4 to August 17 with peak abundance in June and July. There is one brood per year.

Range and **Habitat.** This species is wide-ranging in North America, from the Pacific to the Atlantic and south to Mexico. The subspecies *couperi* occurs throughout most of Alberta, while populations from the extreme south may be best placed in the subspecies *oro*.

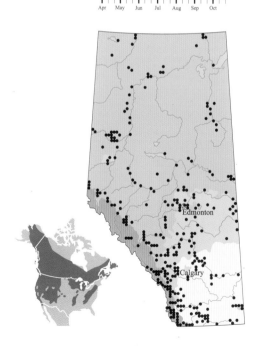

Glaucopsyche lygdamus couperi, near Buffalo Lake, Alberta   C.D. Bird.

Glaucopsyche piasus (Boisduval, 1852)
Arrowhead Blue
subspecies: *Glaucopsyche piasus daunia* (W.H. Edwards, 1871)

Etymology. The species name may be derived from the Latin *pia* meaning "tender, kind." The subspecies name *daunia* may be derived from Daunus, king of Apulia, a region of southern Italy.

Identification. This is a large blue easily distinguished by the prominent white triangular "arrowheads," in the submarginal areas of the ventral hind wings, that point towards the base. The wing margins are clearly checkered. The dorsal wing surface is a metallic violet-blue with dark wing margins that are wider in females.

Life History. The life history of the Arrowhead Blue is not fully documented. In California the larvae are yellowish brown with a dorsal line and marked with other white lines. Other colour phases have been reported. Adults are usually found near patches of lupines (*Lupinus* spp.), the reported larval host plant. The Arrowhead Blue flies from May 24 to July 13 with peak activity in mid-June. There is one brood per year; the pupae overwinter.

Range and Habitat. *Glaucopsyche piasus* is confined to western North America from southern Canada down to New Mexico and Arizona. In Alberta, this Blue is widespread but uncommon in the grasslands of the southern foothills in association with lupines, and in prairie regions east to Saskatchewan.

Glaucopsyche piasus daunia
Male dorsal

Glaucopsyche piasus daunia
Male ventral

Lupinus argentus
Silvery Lupine

193

Lycaeides Hübner, 1819

Etymology. *Lycaeides* may be another name derived from Mt. Lycaeus, a mountain sacred to the Greek god Zeus.

Lycaeides idas (Linnaeus, 1761)
Northern Blue

Lycaeides idas
Male dorsal

Lycaeides idas
Male ventral

Lycaeides idas
Female dorsal

Lycaeides idas
Female ventral

Lathyrus venosus
Purple Peavine

Etymology. Idas in Greek myth was one of the Argonauts and brother of Lynceus who together fought the divine twins Castor and Pollux.

Identification. *Lycaeides idas* is smaller than most of our blues. Both sexes have an orange band that is broken into spots on the ventral surface of both fore and hind wings. Each spot has a metallic gold lining and a black central area. This pattern is similar to that of *Plebejus acmon* and *P. shasta*; however, *P. acmon* has two discal spots on the ventral fore wing, while *P. shasta* has brown rather than black spots on the ventral surface. *Lycaeides melissa* is similar to the Northern Blue in having only one discal spot on the ventral fore wing, but in *idas,* the submarginal band of orange is weakly developed in comparison to that of *melissa*. Female Northern Blues usually have little blue on the dorsal wing surface, while the male is mostly blue. In Alberta, females usually have reduced marginal orange spotting on the dorsal surface. Although male *L. idas* and *L. melissa* can be distinguished only by genitalic characters, females of *L. idas* are often distinct from those of *L. melissa* as the latter possess a more complete orange band.

Life History. The life history of the Northern Blue is incompletely known. Lupines (*Lupinus* spp.) are used as host plants in Colorado, vetch (*Vicia* spp.) and vetchling or peavine (*Lathyrus* spp.) are used in Oregon, while Labrador Tea (*Ledum groenlandicum*), Dwarf Bilberry (*Vaccinium caespitosum*) and other members of the heather family (Ericaceae) are used in eastern North America. Adults are fond of puddling, often congregating by the hundreds on wet patches and seeps. In Alberta, the Northern Blue flies from June 17 to September 12 with peak abundance in July. There is one brood per year; the eggs overwinter.

Range and Habitat. The Northern Blue is widespread through the arctic and subarctic regions south along the Rocky Mountains into the western United States. In Alberta, this butterfly occurs along the mountains and foothills and through the boreal forest region of northern and central Alberta.

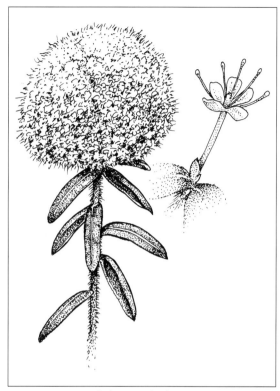

Ledum groenlandicum
Common Labrador Tea

Vaccinium caespitosum
Dwarf Bilberry

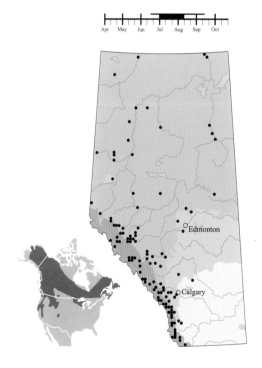

Lycaeides melissa (W.H. Edwards, 1873)
Melissa Blue

Lycaeides melissa
Male dorsal

Lycaeides melissa
Male ventral

Lycaeides melissa
Female dorsal

Lycaeides melissa
Female ventral

Glycyrrhiza lepidota
Wild Licorice

Medicago sativa
Alfalfa

Etymology. In Greek myth Melissa was a nymph who is said to have invented the art of keeping bees.

Identification. The ventral surface of both the fore and hind wings has a marginal orange band in both sexes of *Lycaeides melissa*. The discal spot on the fore wing is absent and there are no metallic scales on the orange band. The dorsal wing surface is metallic blue in males and a dull brown in females. Females also have an orange marginal band on the dorsal sides of both wings. For more detail of similar species, refer to the species account for *Lycaeides idas*.

Life History. Eggs are laid on or near the host plant. Caterpillars feed on leaves and are tended by ants for sweet secretions they produce from their abdominal glands. The mature larvae are usually green and are covered by pale hairs. A wide variety of plants, especially legumes, have been reported, as hosts. These include lupines (*Lupinus* spp.), milk vetch (*Astragalus* spp.), Alfalfa (*Medicago sativa*), loco-weed (*Oxytropis* spp.) and Wild Licorice (*Glycyrrhiza lepidota*). Adults nectar on many kinds of flowers, but most frequently on or near members of the legume family (Leguminosae). The Melissa Blue can be very abundant at times. There appear to be several generations per year with a flight period from May 14 to September 19. The larvae overwinter.

Range and Habitat. *Lycaeides melissa* is wide-ranging across Canada and south into the western and northern states. In Alberta, these butterflies are found across the prairies into the foothills in coulees and river valleys. A population may occur in the Peace River grasslands of west-central Alberta. Two males and one female which appear to be this species were collected by K. Bowman at Wembley (Peace River district) in the 1940s. Genitalia have not been examined and more work is needed to confirm the presence of *melissa* in the Peace River district (Kondla *et al.* 1994).

Plebejus Kluk, 1802
COMMON BLUES

Plebejus (Agriades) Hübner, 1819

Etymology. Possibly from the Latin *agri*, meaning "field."

Plebejus (Agriades) rusticus (W.H. Edwards, 1865)
Rustic Blue
subspecies: ***Plebejus (Agriades) rusticus megalo* (McDunnough, 1927)**
***Plebejus (Agriades) rusticus rusticus* (W.H. Edwards, 1865)**

Etymology. The species epithet *rusticus* is of Latin origin meaning "of or in the country." The subspecies name *megalo* is probably derived from Greek meaning "great, grand, large or big."

Identification. The dorsal wing surface of the males is turquoise to blue, often with a wide brownish margin. Ventrally the surface is variable, with reduced basal markings and a greenish ground colour. The outer half of the ventral hind wing varies from spotless to heavily spotted with the anal angle having an orange spot. Dorsally, the wings of female Rustic Blues are brown with occasional blue scaling. The ventral wing surface is similar to that of males, only darker. This species shows a large amount of geographic variation. In Alberta, the mountain form is darker and more heavily marked and may be assigned to *A. r. megalo*. The prairie form is lighter and more lightly marked and is named *A. r. rusticus*. In the northern portion of Alberta, in the Peace River area, populations similar to prairie *rusticus* can be found northward to Fort Vermilion.

Life History. Different populations of the Rustic Blue use different plants as larval hosts. *Plebejus rusticus rusticus* oviposits on Rock Jasmine (*Androsace chamae-jasme*) in the American Rocky Mountains. Shooting star (*Dodecatheon* spp.) and Diapensia (*Diapensia lapponica*) have also been reported as oviposition sites. Several other plants have been suggested, these being bilberry, blueberry, huckleberry, (*Vaccinium* spp.), Purple Saxifrage (*Saxifraga oppositifolia*) and Fairy

Plebejus rusticus rusticus
Male dorsal

Plebejus rusticus rusticus
Male ventral

Plebejus rusticus rusticus
Female dorsal

Plebejus rusticus rusticus
Female ventral

Plebejus rusticus megalo
Male ventral

Plebejus rusticus megalo
Female ventral

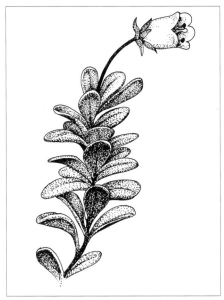

Diapensia lapponica
Diapensia

Candelabra or Pygmy-flower (*Androsace septentrion-alis*). Rustic Blues are strong fliers that frequently move up mountainsides. They are avid puddlers and nectar freely on tall, flowering plants. They perch with wings closed. This species is on the wing from May 4 through September 10. In the mountains, peak flight activity is in July and early August, while on the prairies it is in late May and June. The early stages are not well known. There is one brood per year.

Range and Habitat. This is a wide-ranging species complex with a holarctic distribution. In North America it ranges from Alaska across the arctic islands to Labrador and southward through the Great Plains and Rocky Mountain states reaching Arizona and New Mexico. In Alberta, this butterfly is widespread, with the subspecies *megalo* in the mountain regions and *rusticus* in the prairie and parkland regions. The Rustic Blue inhabits mountain meadows and avidly puddles on damp soil. On the prairies it prefers hillsides and gullies.

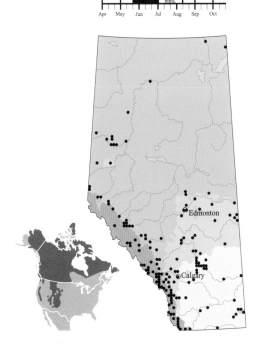

View from Fish Butte, northwest across Bragg Creek (west of Calgary), Alberta.

F.A.H. Sperling.

Plebejus (Icaricia) Nabokov, 1944

Etymology. Icarus was the son of the inventor, Daedalus, in Greek mythology. Despite his father's warning, Icarus flew too close to the sun with waxen wings designed by Daedalus; the wings melted and Icarus fell to his death.

Plebejus (Icaricia) acmon (Westwood and Hewitson, [1852])
Acmon Blue

Etymology. The name may come from the Greek name Acmon, a companion of Aeneas.

Identification. The Acmon Blue is very similar to *Lycaeides melissa* and *Lycaeides idas*. Males and females are gray on the ventral wing surface and have the black spotting typical of other blues. There is a complete orange band with some metallic scaling on the outer edge of the spots. The Acmon Blue has two ventral discal spots that are lacking in the two *Lycaeides* species. The dorsal surface is bright blue on the male and gray on the female; both sexes have an orange band on the hind wing that contains dark spots. Two forms of *Plebejus acmon* occur in Alberta. The prairie form is smaller and more delicately marked while the montane form has stronger, darker markings and looks more like *Lycaeides melissa*.

Life History. Mature larvae from Wyoming are light green with double pink and white lateral stripes. Larval host plants include milk vetch (*Astragalus* spp.), lupines (*Lupinus* spp.), Bird's-foot Trefoil (*Lotus corniculatus*) and umbrella plant (*Eriogonum* spp.). On the prairies the Acmon Blue frequently visits composites growing on hillsides. These butterflies are rapid fliers and are not usually abundant. In the foothills and mountains they are more common and can often be found puddling along roads and paths. In Alberta the Acmon Blue flies from May 8 to August 10 with one specimen reported from August 19. In the mountains there appears to be one generation per year with peak flight activity in July. On the prairies two generations appear with peak flight activity in late May to early June and a second activity peak in late July to early August. The larvae overwinter.

Plebejus acmon
Male dorsal

Plebejus acmon
Male ventral

Plebejus acmon
Female dorsal

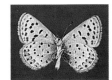
Plebejus acmon
Female ventral

Lotus corniculatus
Bird's-foot Trefoil

199

Eriogonum glabellus
Smooth Fleabane

Range and Habitat. *Plebejus acmon* is distributed throughout the western United States and southwestern Canada eastward onto the Great Plains. In Alberta the butterfly is found in mountain meadows south of Nordegg and in the prairies and parkland south and east of Red Deer. It is most common in the southern mountain foothills in association with open meadows and prairie grasslands.

Astragalus canadensis
Canadian Milk Vetch

Astragalus missouriensis
Milk Vetch

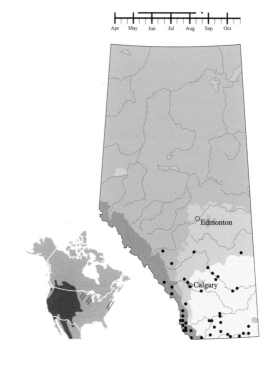

Plebejus (Icaricia) icarioides (Boisduval, 1852)
Icarioides Blue

Etymology. The species name has the same derivation as that of the subgenus, with the addition of the suffix *-oides*, meaning "type of" in Latin.

Identification. *Plebejus icarioides* is a moderately large blue. The dorsal wing surface is blue in the males and brown in the females. The ventral wing surface is gray with black spots surrounded by white scales. Females may be blue dorsally, but in our area they are usually brown. Orange spots and bands are absent. White spots occasionally occur in the centres of the black spots. The Icarioides Blue is easily confused with the smaller species, *Plebejus saepiolus*, but the latter does not have pale rings around the black dots.

Life History. The Icarioides Blue is always closely associated with lupines (*Lupinus* spp.). Over 40 varieties and species of this plant have been reported as larval hosts. Greenish white eggs are laid individually on lupines. The mature larvae are green with indistinct diagonal white bars on each segment. The second instar larvae are reported to be the overwintering stage. Larvae of the Icarioides Blue are tended by ants. In Alberta the adults are on the wing from May 17 to August 22 with peak abundance during June and July. There is one brood per year.

Range and Habitat. *Plebejus icarioides* ranges throughout the western United States and southwestern Canada. In Alberta, the butterfly is found in the mountains from the Bow River south and east onto the southern prairies. Icarioides Blue habitat varies from prairie grasslands to alpine meadows.

Plebejus icarioides
Male dorsal

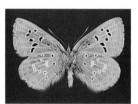
Plebejus icarioides
Male ventral

Plebejus icarioides
Female dorsal

Plebejus icarioides
Female ventral

Apr May Jun Jul Aug Sep Oct

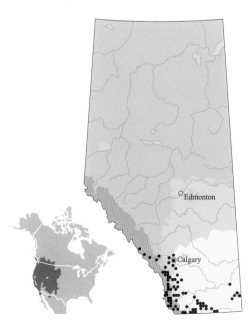

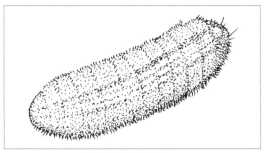
Plebejus icarioides larva

201

Plebejus (Icaricia) shasta (W.H. Edwards, 1862)
Shasta Blue

Plebejus shasta
Male dorsal

Plebejus shasta
Male ventral

Trifolium hybridum
Alsike Clover

Etymology. The name of the butterfly probably comes from Mount Shasta, a volcanic cone in California.

Identification. The Shasta Blue is a small delicate butterfly whose wings quickly become worn from flight. Males are light blue with a hint of a black submarginal band dorsally on both fore and hind wings. Females are brown, with basal blue scaling dorsally. There is a dark spot at the end of the discal cell on the dorsal surface. Ventrally the wing surface has numerous light brown spots and has the appearance of being out of focus. A submarginal orange band is made up of orange spots in conjunction with metallic gold spots. The ventral ground colour is gray.

Life History. Larvae feed on a variety of legumes, most commonly milk vetch (*Astragalus* spp.) but including loco-weed (*Oxytropis* spp.), lupines (*Lupinus* spp.) and clover (*Trifolium* spp.). The Shasta Blue flies from June 2 to August 3 with peak flight activity in late June and early July. There is one brood per year; the larvae overwinter in the egg.

Range and Habitat. The Shasta Blue occurs from California north through the western United States into southern Alberta. Populations are often hard to locate but in the right habitat this species can be quite abundant. Most known populations are from the Red Deer River valley south to the Montana border. A couple of populations are located above treeline in the mountains. Adults are usually found along tops of steep, sparsely vegetated hills and ridges. Along the Red Deer and Oldman rivers, adults perch and nectar on yellow composites at the top of valley walls.

Plebejus (Plebejus) Kluk, 1802

Etymology. The name comes from the Latin *plebeius*, meaning "of the common people" or simply "common."

Plebejus (Plebejus) saepiolus (Boisduval, 1852)
Greenish Blue
subspecies: *Plebejus (Plebejus) saepiolus amica* (W.H. Edwards, 1863b)

Etymology. The name may be from the Latin *saepio*, "to limit," "protect" or "delineate" and *olus*, a diminutive ending. The subspecies name *amica* is Latin meaning "lady friend."

Identification. The dorsal wing surface of males is a light metallic blue while the ventral surface is light gray with many black spots. No orange spots or bands are present on the male. The ventral spots are not surrounded or highlighted by white nor are they very large. There is a complete marginal band. In females the dorsal surface is brown and the ventral surface similar to males, although ground colour tends to be more brownish than gray. Both sexes have the ventral black spotting elongated towards the base of the wing. Both males and females have a grayish brown discal spot on the dorsal fore wing.

Life History. The Greenish Blue lays its eggs on flower heads of several species of clover (*Trifolium* spp.). Larvae feed on the developing flowers and are reported to overwinter and complete development the following year. Larvae occur in two colour phases, red and green. In Alberta, adults fly from May 14 to August 18. There is one brood per year.

Range and Habitat. The Greenish Blue is found across Canada and the western and northern states. Its range may be expanding in eastern Canada, probably the result of cultivation of several species of clover. Most Alberta material can be referred to *Plebejus saepiolus amica*. In Alberta the Greenish Blue can be found almost everywhere and is common wherever clover plants grow. Adults are frequently found nectaring on clovers and other legumes, but on occasion will puddle at seeps and wet patches.

Plebejus saepiolus amica
Male dorsal

Plebejus saepiolus amica
Male ventral

Plebejus saepiolus amica
Female dorsal

Plebejus saepiolus amica
Female ventral

Plebejus saepiolus amica
larva

Apr May Jun Jul Aug Sep Oct

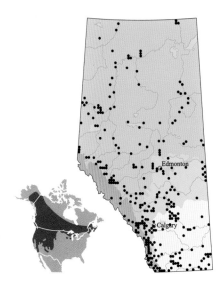

203

Plebejus (Vacciniina) Tutt, 1909

Etymology. Named after the larval host plant genus, *Vaccinium*, which includes Bog Cranberry and Blueberry.

Plebejus (Vacciniina) optilete (Knoch, 1781)
Cranberry Blue
subspecies: *Plebejus (Vacciniina) optilete yukona* (Holland, 1900)

Plebejus optilete yukona
Male dorsal

Plebejus optilete yukona
Male ventral

Vaccinium myrtilloides
Blueberry

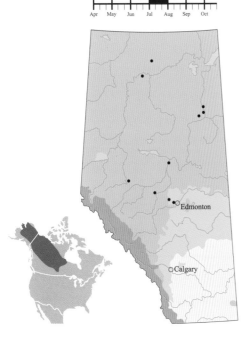

Etymology. The origin of the species name is unclear; it may come from the Latin *optimas* meaning "best" or *optatus* meaning "pleasing," together with the Greek *ilet* meaning "arched" or "wreathed." The subspecies *yukona* is named after Yukon Territory, Canada.

Identification. The dorsal wing surface of Cranberry Blues is metallic blue. The ventral surface is gray with many black spots and a small orange spot on the anal angle of the hind wing. The dorsal wing surface of the female is brown with blue scaling basally.

Life History. Little is known of the immature stages. It has been reported that the larvae feed on Low Bilberry (*Vaccinium myrtillus*). In Alberta, however, Low Bilberry is found in western montane forests and not in the northern locations where the Cranberry Blue occurs. Other species of *Vaccinium* are found in these areas such as Bog Bilberry (*Vaccinium uliginosum*), Bog Cranberry (*Vaccinium vitis-idaea* var. *minus*), Dwarf Bilberry (*Vaccinium caespitosum*) and Blueberry (*Vaccinium myrtilloides*). Adults are on the wing from June 15 to August 12 with peak activity in July. There is one brood per year; the larvae overwinter.

Range and Habitat. This is a northern species ranging from Alaska through the Canadian arctic and northern British Columbia eastward to Manitoba. In Alberta the Cranberry Blue is found north of Edmonton through the boreal forest zone in suitable bog habitats, preferably open bogs. Near Fort McMurray, the highest density of this blue was along an abandoned corduroy road through a lightly forested tamarack bog. They appeared to avoid areas with larger bushes, preferring to fly and land on the ground in a region with Bog Cranberry and Cloudberry (*Rubus chamaemorus*). Other specimens have been found adjacent to bogs and along sand ridges in open Jack Pine forests where Blueberry grows in abundance.

Family NYMPHALIDAE
ANGLEWINGS, FRITILLARIES, CHECKERSPOTS and ADMIRALS

6

Members of the Nymphalidae are commonly called brush-footed butterflies because their fore legs are reduced to non-functional, furry stumps. This is the largest family of butterflies in Alberta with 51 species recorded and two others with ranges that border on our province. Nymphalids are medium-to-large butterflies, typically with an orange background colour to their wings; however, many species have striking blue or mirror-like silver spots. Some of Alberta's most familiar butterflies belong to this group, including the Mourning Cloak (*Nymphalis antiopa*), the anglewings (*Polygonia* spp.) and the fritillaries (*Speyeria* spp.). Nymphalid larvae are generally black and spiny and have host plants in 19 families, from violets (*Viola* spp.) to willows (*Salix* spp.). Our species fall into four subfamilies that are named, in part, for wing characteristics: Nymphalinae (anglewings), Argynninae (fritillaries), Melitaeinae (checkerspots) and Limenitidinae (admirals).

Subfamily
NYMPHALINAE
ANGLEWINGS

There are 15 species of nymphalines in Alberta. The common name for butterflies in this subfamily is anglewings because of the ragged, angled edges of both fore and hind wings. Some of the most cryptic and most strikingly marked nymphalids belong to the Nymphalinae. For example, the under wings of *Polygonia* species camouflage the butterflies as dead leaves or flakes of bark. Species of *Vanessa*, on the other hand, are like beautiful palettes of orange, blue, dark brown and black. One of the best known nymphalines is the Mourning Cloak (*Nymphalis antiopa*). Like many other brush-footed butterflies it overwinters as an adult and is among the first butterflies to grace our province in the spring.

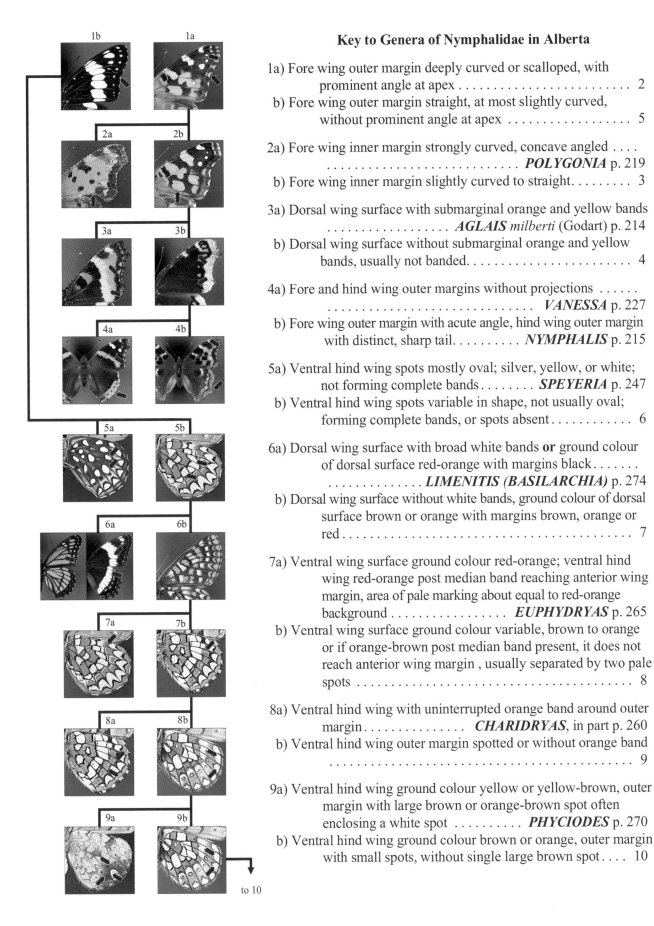

Key to Genera of Nymphalidae in Alberta

1a) Fore wing outer margin deeply curved or scalloped, with prominent angle at apex 2

b) Fore wing outer margin straight, at most slightly curved, without prominent angle at apex 5

2a) Fore wing inner margin strongly curved, concave angled . . . . ***POLYGONIA*** p. 219

b) Fore wing inner margin slightly curved to straight. 3

3a) Dorsal wing surface with submarginal orange and yellow bands . . . . ***AGLAIS*** *milberti* (Godart) p. 214

b) Dorsal wing surface without submarginal orange and yellow bands, usually not banded. 4

4a) Fore and hind wing outer margins without projections . . . . ***VANESSA*** p. 227

b) Fore wing outer margin with acute angle, hind wing outer margin with distinct, sharp tail. . . . . ***NYMPHALIS*** p. 215

5a) Ventral hind wing spots mostly oval; silver, yellow, or white; not forming complete bands . . . . ***SPEYERIA*** p. 247

b) Ventral hind wing spots variable in shape, not usually oval; forming complete bands, or spots absent 6

6a) Dorsal wing surface with broad white bands **or** ground colour of dorsal surface red-orange with margins black. . . . . ***LIMENITIS (BASILARCHIA)*** p. 274

b) Dorsal wing surface without white bands, ground colour of dorsal surface brown or orange with margins brown, orange or red 7

7a) Ventral wing surface ground colour red-orange; ventral hind wing red-orange post median band reaching anterior wing margin, area of pale marking about equal to red-orange background . . . . ***EUPHYDRYAS*** p. 265

b) Ventral wing surface ground colour variable, brown to orange or if orange-brown post median band present, it does not reach anterior wing margin , usually separated by two pale spots 8

8a) Ventral hind wing with uninterrupted orange band around outer margin . . . . ***CHARIDRYAS***, in part p. 260

b) Ventral hind wing outer margin spotted or without orange band 9

9a) Ventral hind wing ground colour yellow or yellow-brown, outer margin with large brown or orange-brown spot often enclosing a white spot . . . . ***PHYCIODES*** p. 270

b) Ventral hind wing ground colour brown or orange, outer margin with small spots, without single large brown spot. . . . 10

to 10

10a) Dorsal fore wing with brown submarginal bands, without brown submarginal spots . . . . ***CHARIDRYAS*** in part p. 260

b) Dorsal fore wing with 1 or 2 submarginal rows of brown spots
. . . . 11

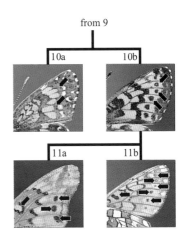

11a) Ventral fore wing with single row of 3 submarginal spots, and cream discal spot contrasting with orange ground colour; large fore wing > 25mm . . . .
. . . . ***EUPTOIETA*** *claudia* (Cramer) p. 245

b) Without above combination; ventral fore wing with either 2 rows of submarginal spots or single row of 5 spots; discal spot not contrasting with ground colour; if submarginal spots indistinct then apex with contrasting yellow and brown patches; smaller fore wing < 25mm . . . .
. . . . ***BOLORIA*** p. 231

Vanessa cardui.

T.W. Thormin.

Key to Species of *Nymphalis* in Alberta

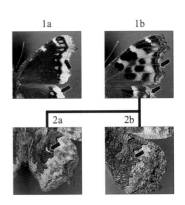

1a) Dorsal wing margin pale cream to yellow . . . .
. . . . *Nymphalis antiopa* (Linnaeus) p. 215

b) Dorsal wing margin brown 2

2a) Ventral hind wing with white "V"- or "J"-shaped mark . . . . . .
. . *Nymphalis vaualbum* (Denis and Schiffermüller) p. 218

b) Ventral hind wing without white mark . . . .
. . . . *Nymphalis californica* (Boisduval) p. 217

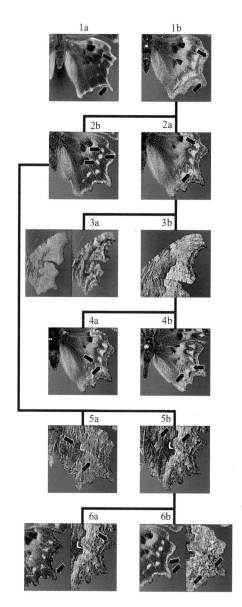

Key to Species of *Polygonia* in Alberta

1a) Dorsal hind wing margin violet. . . . .
. . . . *Polygonia interrogationis* (Fabricius) p. 222
b) Dorsal hind wing margin brown or black 2

2a) Dorsal hind wing submarginal spots diffuse, contiguous or
nearly so, often joining to form partial pale band 3
b) Dorsal hind wing submarginal spots sharply defined, separated
by at least half diameter of spot 5

3a) Ventral wings brown; dorsal hind wing submarginal spots
confluent, forming partial pale band; sexually dimorphic
. . . . *Polygonia satyrus* (W.H. Edwards) p. 225
b) Ventral wings gray; dorsal hind wing submarginal spots slightly
separated; sexual dimorphism not pronounced 4

4a) Dorsal hind wing submarginal spots located in wide brown
band. . . . . . . *Polygonia zephyrus* (W.H. Edwards) p. 226
b) Dorsal hind wing marginal band diffuse, posterior submarginal
spots not in band. . . . .
. . . . *Polygonia oreas* (W.H. Edwards) p. 223

5a) Ventral hind wing uniformly coloured, relatively lighter basally
than following species . . . .
. . . . *Polygonia progne* (Cramer) p. 224
b) Ventral hind wing divided into dark basal area and light outer
area, basal area relatively darker than above species. . . 6

6a) Dorsal wings outer margin uniform black-brown; ventral wings
basal areas nearly black, sharply contrasting with lighter
outer areas, without brown patches; ventral hind wing
submarginal band lacking green scales . . . .
. . . . *Polygonia gracilis* (Grote and Robinson) p. 221
b) Dorsal wings outer margin not uniformly brown, at least tail of
hind wing gray; ventral wings basal area gray to gray-
brown, not as sharply contrasting with lighter outer areas,
often with brown patches; ventral hind wing submarginal
band with green scales . . . .
. . . . *Polygonia faunus* (W.H. Edwards) p. 219

Key to Species of *Vanessa* in Alberta

1a) Dorsal fore wing with orange-red band on dark ground colour
. . . . *Vanessa atalanta* (Linnaeus) p. 228

b) Dorsal fore wing orange band, less well defined, wing base
orange-brown 2

2a) Ventral hind wing submarginal band of blue spots incomplete
. . . . *Vanessa annabella* (Field) p. 227

b) Ventral hind wing submarginal band of blue spots complete. .
. . . . 3

3a) Ventral hind wing with row of 4 to 5 eye spots . . . .
. . . . *Vanessa cardui* (Linnaeus) p. 229

b) Ventral hind wing with 2 large eye spots . . . .
. . . . *Vanessa virginiensis* (Drury) p. 230

Key to Species of *Boloria* in Alberta

1a) Ventral fore wing with single submarginal row of indistinct
spots, wing apex with contrasting patches of yellow and
brown . . . . *Boloria napaea* (Hoffmansegg) p. 243

b) Ventral fore wing with 2 submarginal rows of spots **or** single
row of 5 spots **or** wing apex without colour patches. . . 2

2a) Ventral hind wing marginal spots white or silvered, bright . . 3

b) Ventral hind wing area without white or silver spots, or
washed out, dull 8

3a) Ventral hind wing submarginal spots open and silver- or yellow-
centred. . . . . *Boloria eunomia* (Esper) p. 237

b) Ventral hind wing submarginal spots dark-centred 4

4a) Ventral fore wing marginal spots silvered or white 5

b) Ventral fore wing marginal spots yellow, brown or black . . . 6

5a) Ventral hind wing discal area without black dot. . . . .
. . . . *Boloria freija* (Thunberg) p. 239

b) Ventral hind wing discal area with black dot . . . .
. . . . *Boloria selene* (Denis & Schiffermüller) p. 244

6a) Ventral hind wing discal spots forming a continuous white band
. . . . . . *Boloria astarte* (Doubleday & Hewitson) p. 233

b) Ventral hind wing discal spots not forming a continuous band,
or if continuous, not completely white. 7

7a) Ventral hind wing discal spots yellow or nearly so; **or** ventral
hind wing postmedian area largely lacking white spots
. . . . *Boloria chariclea* (Schneider) p. 235

b) Ventral hind wing discal spots forming a broken band, **and**
ventral hind wing postmedian spots forming a continuous
white band or nearly so. . . . .
. . . . *Boloria freija* (Thunberg) p. 239

to 8

from 2

8a) Fore wing outer margin angled . . . .
. . . . *Boloria bellona* (Fabricius) p. 234

b) Fore wing outer margin evenly curved 9

9a) Ventral hind wing discal sub-costal spot similar in colour to rest of band 10

b) Ventral hind wing discal sub-costal spot distinctly lighter than the rest of the spots 11

10a) Ventral fore wing markings black, edges sharply defined . . . .
. . . . *Boloria epithore* (W.H. Edwards) p. 236

b) Ventral fore wing markings gray-brown, edges indistinct . . . .
. . . . *Boloria alberta* (W.H. Edwards) p. 232

11a) Ventral fore wing markings weak, brown, no distinct black spots . . . . *Boloria improba* (Butler) p. 241

b) Ventral fore wing markings distinct, black 12

12a) Dorsal fore wing spot in discal cell solid . . . .
. . . . *Boloria frigga* (Thunberg) p. 240

b) Dorsal fore wing spot in discal cell circle-like . . . .
. . . . *Boloria epithore* (W.H. Edwards) p. 236

Key to Species of *Speyeria* in Alberta

(** Species marked with a double asterisk are not recorded for Alberta, but have been found just outside the province.)

1a) Ventral hind wing spots cream-coloured not silvered, discal colour reddish brown, one sub-basal discal spot . . . .
. . . . *Speyeria hydaspe* (Boisduval) p. 256

b) Ventral hind wing spots white or silver, discal colour brown, orange brown or greenish brown often with a pale submarginal band, one or two sub-basal spots in discal cell. 2

2a) Dorsal hind wing discal area dark brown contrasting sharply with a wide, pale, submarginal band. . . . .
. . . . *Speyeria cybele* (Fabricius) p. 253

b) Dorsal hind wing discal area not sharply contrasting 3

3a) Ventral hind wing ground colour brown or reddish brown usually with 2 post-basal discal spots in discal cell; usually with 2 or fewer dorsal submarginal spots encircled with dark scales. 4

b) Ventral hind wing with green scales, usually one post-basal discal spot sometimes formed by the fusion of two spots, usually large; usually 4 or more orange submarginal spots encircled with dark scales. 7

4a) Ventral hind wing ground colour dark chocolate brown . . . . .
Speyeria atlantis hollandi (Chermock & Chermock) p. 249

b) Ventral hind wing ground colour red-brown or light red-brown
. . . . 5

to 7   to 5

5a) Dorsal fore wing banding relatively broad, black; ventral
hind wing basal and discal areas red-brown ground colour
darker, with restricted pale yellow patches . . . .
. . . *Speyeria electa beani* (Barnes and Benjamin) p. 249

b) Dorsal fore wing marginal band relatively narrow, black and
orange; ventral hind wing basal and discal areas with
extensive pale yellow patches on red-brown ground
colour 6

6a) Ventral hind wing more brownish; usually two post-basal discal
spots; size smaller, wingspan 50-54 mm; habitat - grasslands
. . . . *Speyeria electa lais* (W.H. Edwards) p. 249

b) Ventral hind wing reddish brown; usually one post-basal discal
spot, if second spot present then it is small; size larger,
wingspan 56-58 mm; habitat - riparian forests, aspen
woodlands and Jack Pine forests . . . .
. . . . *Speyeria aphrodite* (Fabricius) p. 247

7a) Size smaller, wingspan 44-53 mm, ventral hind wing discal and
basal areas ground colour pale creamy yellow to orange-
yellow with gray-green patches . . . .
. . . . *Speyeria mormonia* (Boisduval) p. 257

b) Size larger, wingspan 50-71 mm, wings with green cast, if
small (50-53 mm), then ventral hind wing basal discal and
basal areas ground colour brown, without gray-green
patches 8

8a) Ventral hind wing discal and basal areas green-brown, or gray-
green 9

b) Ventral hind wing discal and basal areas brownish 11

9a) Ventral hind wing ground colour gray-green, submarginal pale
band slightly, if at all, contrasting with ground colour . .
. . . . *Speyeria callippe* (Boisduval) p. 251

b) Ventral hind wing ground colour green-brown, contrasting with
creamy yellow submarginal band. 10

10a) Size smaller, wingspan 60-63 mm; ventral fore wing ground
colour not sharply contrasting, gradually changing from
light orange base to creamy orange apex . . . .
. . . . *Speyeria edwardsii* (Reakirt) p. 254

b) Size larger, wingspan 71 mm; ventral fore wing ground colour
sharply contrasting from orange-red base to creamy yellow
apex. . . . . *Speyeria coronis* (Behr) **p. 252

from 1   from 4

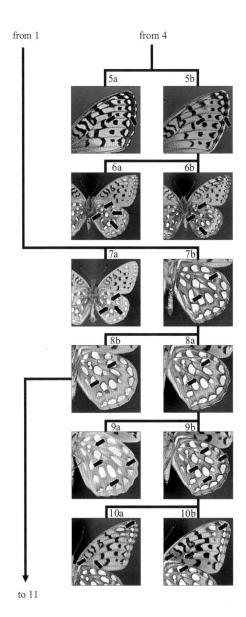

to 11

Wingspan measurement = distance between
arrows x 2

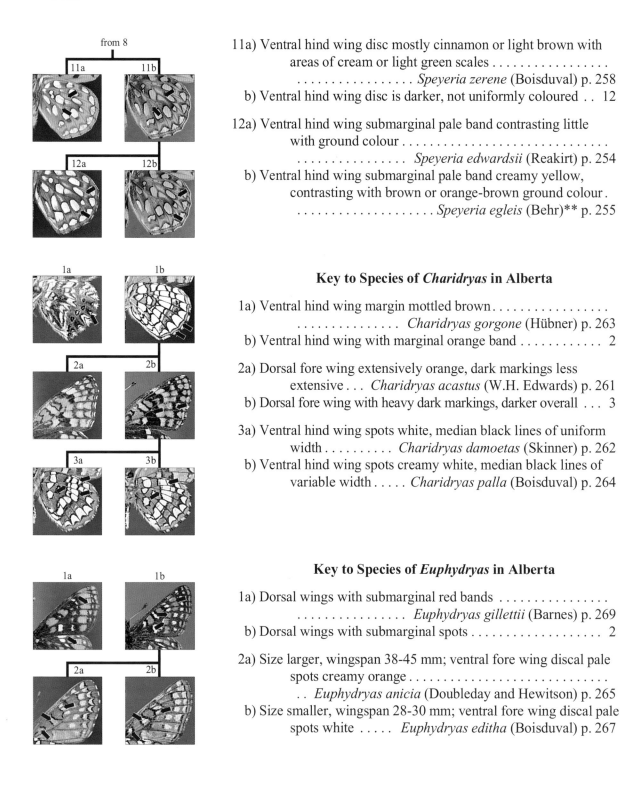

11a) Ventral hind wing disc mostly cinnamon or light brown with areas of cream or light green scales . . . . *Speyeria zerene* (Boisduval) p. 258

b) Ventral hind wing disc is darker, not uniformly coloured . . 12

12a) Ventral hind wing submarginal pale band contrasting little with ground colour . . . . *Speyeria edwardsii* (Reakirt) p. 254

b) Ventral hind wing submarginal pale band creamy yellow, contrasting with brown or orange-brown ground colour . . . . *Speyeria egleis* (Behr)** p. 255

Key to Species of *Charidryas* in Alberta

1a) Ventral hind wing margin mottled brown . . . . *Charidryas gorgone* (Hübner) p. 263

b) Ventral hind wing with marginal orange band 2

2a) Dorsal fore wing extensively orange, dark markings less extensive . . . *Charidryas acastus* (W.H. Edwards) p. 261

b) Dorsal fore wing with heavy dark markings, darker overall . . . 3

3a) Ventral hind wing spots white, median black lines of uniform width . . . . *Charidryas damoetas* (Skinner) p. 262

b) Ventral hind wing spots creamy white, median black lines of variable width . . . . . *Charidryas palla* (Boisduval) p. 264

Key to Species of *Euphydryas* in Alberta

1a) Dorsal wings with submarginal red bands . . . . *Euphydryas gillettii* (Barnes) p. 269

b) Dorsal wings with submarginal spots 2

2a) Size larger, wingspan 38-45 mm; ventral fore wing discal pale spots creamy orange . . . . *Euphydryas anicia* (Doubleday and Hewitson) p. 265

b) Size smaller, wingspan 28-30 mm; ventral fore wing discal pale spots white . . . . . *Euphydryas editha* (Boisduval) p. 267

Key to Species of *Phyciodes* in Alberta

1a) Underside of antennal club black . . . .
. . . . *Phyciodes batesii* (Reakirt) p. 270
 b) Underside of antennal club orange 2

2a) Dorsal fore wing divided by wide median dark line, costal
margin straight to gently curved. . . . .
. . . . *Phyciodes pulchella* (Boisduval) p. 272
 b) Dorsal fore wing not divided or narrowly divided by median
dark line, costal margin gently to strongly curved. 3

3a) Dorsal fore wing brown/black band at base of outer third,
complete; occurs in boreal forest and mountains; female
identified by association with male . . . .
. . . . *Phyciodes tharos* (Drury) p. 273
 b) Dorsal fore wing brown/black band at base of outer third, incomplete or absent; occurs in grasslands; female
identified by association with male . . . .
. . . . *Phyciodes cocyta* (Cramer) p. 271

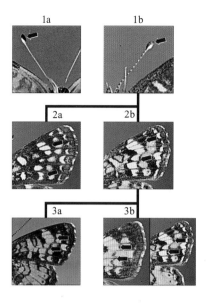

Key to Species of *Limenitis (Basilarchia)* in Alberta

1a) Dorsal hind wing ground colour orange-red, median band
narrow, black . . . .
. . . . *Limenitis (Basilarchia) archippus* (Cramer) p. 275
 b) Dorsal hind wing ground colour black, median band broad,
white 2

2a) Dorsal fore wing apex margin orange-red . . . .
. . . . . *Limenitis (Basilarchia) lorquini* Boisduval p. 277
 b) Dorsal fore wing apex margin black 3

3a) Ventral hind wing basal area brown . . . .
. . . . . . *Limenitis (Basilarchia) arthemis* (Drury) p. 276
 b) Ventral hind wing basal area gray-white with lines . . . .
Limenitis (Basilarchia) weidemeyerii W.H. Edwards p. 278

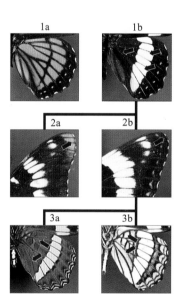

Phyciodes cocyta nectaring on fleabane (*Erigeron* sp.; Compositae), at Clyde, Alberta.   T.W. Thormin.

Aglais Dalman, 1816
TORTOISE SHELLS

Etymology. From the Greek *aglaia* meaning "splendour, beauty." Aglaia was one of the Graces in Greek mythology.

Aglais milberti (Godart, [1819])
Milbert's Tortoise Shell
subspecies: *Aglais milberti milberti* (Godart, [1819])

Aglais milberti milberti
Male dorsal

Aglais milberti milberti
Male ventral

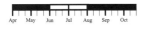

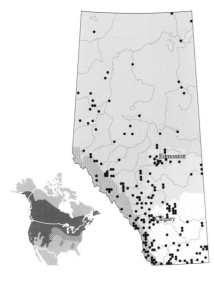

Etymology. This species was named after a friend of Godart. Milbert's collection was deposited in the Museum of Natural History in Paris.

Identification. This bright butterfly is recognized by the band which fades from orange to yellow on the dorsal wing surfaces and the band of blue marginal spots on the dorsal hind wing.

Life History. Eggs are laid in groups on the host plant. Early instars feed gregariously, while older larvae are solitary and feed in folded leaf shelters. Larvae are usually black, finely stippled with white spots, have greenish yellow and orange sides and are covered with branched black spines. Larval hosts are usually nettles (*Urtica* spp.) but the caterpillars may also feed on willows (*Salix* spp.), sunflowers (*Helianthus* spp.) and elms (*Ulmus* spp.). The chrysalids are gray or greenish and are flecked with brown. Like the Mourning Cloak (*Nymphalis antiopa*), adult Milbert's Tortoise Shells over-winter and are sometimes seen flying as early as February during chinooks in southern Alberta. These butterflies are strong fliers and frequently hilltop on mountain peaks, far from breeding habitats. This is one of the earliest butterflies to appear in the spring, with capture dates starting from March 13 and extending to October 19. Peak flight activity is in May and June for the overwintered adults and August and September for the newly emerged adults. There are two broods per year.

Range and Habitat. Milbert's Tortoise Shell occurs through the northeastern and Rocky Mountain states and most of Canada. Three subspecies are described, but they seem to represent clinal variations. Alberta specimens are assigned to *Aglais milberti milberti*, and may be found in or near high elevation forests where nettle occurs. This species is uncommon on the prairies.

Nymphalis Kluk, 1802

Etymology. *Nymphalis* is an adjectival form of *nympha*, "belonging to a fountain." The Greek nymphs were graceful female deities of mountains, trees and water.

Identification. Butterflies of this genus are recognized by the irregular wing margins, the straight trailing margin of the fore wings and the lack of eye spots on the ventral surface. Larvae feed on a wide variety of food plants and have uniform dark appearance and large spines. Many species overwinter as adults and are among the first butterflies seen in the spring. Overwintering adults may be found in crevices, hollow logs and brush piles.

Nymphalis antiopa (Linnaeus, 1758)
Mourning Cloak

Etymology. Antiopa was a daughter of Nycteus and wife of Lycus, king of Thebes.

Identification. This large butterfly is distinguished by the broad, cream-to-yellow-coloured band along the dorsal margin of both fore and hind wings and the interior row of blue spots.

Life History. The Mourning Cloak adult is likely one of the longest-lived butterflies, with a life span of up to ten months. Adult butterflies emerge in July and August. They may feed for a while before finding a suitable shelter until autumn when they again become active. In September and October, adults seek out wintering sites where they remain until the following spring, occasionally emerging in late winter or early spring during warm spells. Overwintered adults mate and females lay eggs in the spring. Eggs are laid in batches on a host, usually willows (*Salix* spp.), poplars (*Populus* spp.) and elms (*Ulmus* spp.). Larvae are communal feeders, often defoliating large branches of trees. Interestingly, larvae have been found feeding on the legume Sainfoin (*Onobrychis viciifolia*) near Lethbridge. It is quite possible that this species uses other hosts that are not recorded in the literature. The mature larvae are black with white marks, a row of dull red spots on the back, and several rows of nymphalid-type spines. Mature larvae often leave their host and wander quite a distance before settling down to pupate. In cities, the tan-coloured pupae are found occasionally hanging from a silk pad by their cremaster under the eaves of houses. The overwintering habit of the adults produces both early and late season

Nymphalis antiopa
Male dorsal

Nymphalis antiopa
Male ventral

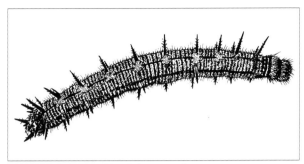

Nymphalis antiopa larva

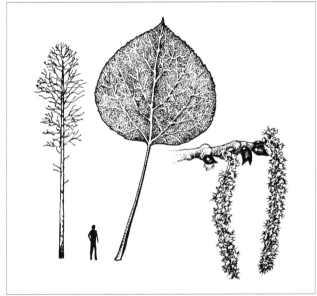

Populus tremuloides
Trembling Aspen

Ulmus americana
American Elm

records ranging from March 23 to December 8! This butterfly may be found flying in every month of the year during warm chinook periods, especially in southern Alberta. Peak flight times are May and June for over-wintered adults and August and September for the new brood about to overwinter. There is one brood per year.

Range and Habitat. The Mourning Cloak is found throughout temperate Europe, Asia and North America from the subarctic to the central Mexican highlands. In Alberta the butterfly can occur most anywhere there are trees and shrubs. The wide range of the larval hosts allows the butterfly to survive in a variety of habitats. On the prairies it is more common along the margins of riparian forests and pond margins with willows (*Salix* spp.) or poplars (*Populus* spp.). Elsewhere adults can be found along trails, in clearings and along the edges of wooded areas.

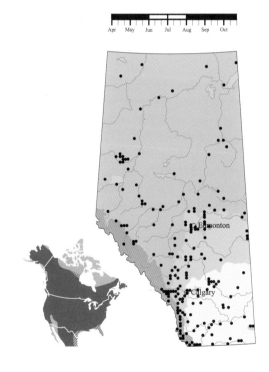

Nymphalis californica (Boisduval, 1852)
California Tortoise Shell

Etymology. The species name *californica* is after the state of California, the type locality.

Identification. A large butterfly, the California Tortoise Shell is orange-brown dorsally with a single black spot on the dorsal margin of the hind wing. Submarginal spots are indistinct and other markings are obscure and dark.

Life History. Larvae are velvety black with yellow dots and the usual nymphalid spines. Larval hosts are various species of tea bush (*Ceanothus* spp.). In Alberta, the host plants occur in the Crowsnest Pass to Waterton Park area where broods are produced in some years. The California Tortoise Shell disperses widely. It is not known if they can overwinter in Alberta. In Alberta, the California Tortoise Shell has been recorded flying from June 10 to October 6 with most flight records in mid-summer.

Range and Habitat. The California Tortoise Shell ranges in western North America from southern Alberta, British Columbia and Saskatchewan southward to California and New Mexico. In Alberta, specimens have been collected north to Edmonton, but are usually found in the southern mountain regions. Two named subspecies occur, *Nymphalis californica californica* and *Nymphalis californica herri* Field, but their status and ranges are uncertain. A subspecies name has not been assigned to the Alberta specimens. Immigrating species tend to intergrade readily as populations shift. The California Tortoise Shell may be found, as an immigrant, almost anywhere. In the Waterton Lakes National Park to Crowsnest Pass area, watch for adults in clearings and along stream beds near dry hills and mountain sides.

Nymphalis californica
Male dorsal

Nymphalis californica
Male ventral

Ceanothus sp.
Tea bush

217

Nymphalis vaualbum (Denis and Schiffermüller, 1775)
Compton's Tortoise Shell
subspecies: *Nymphalis vaualbum j-album* (Boisduval and Le Conte, [1833])

Nymphalis vaualbum j-album
Female dorsal

Nymphalis vaualbum j-album
Male ventral

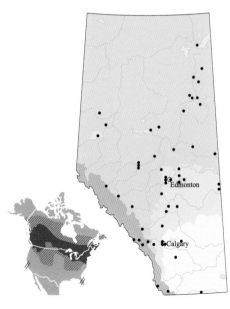

Etymology. From the Greek vau for "V" and the Latin *album* for white, which refers to the "V"-shaped white mark on the ventral hind wing. Neither language had a word for "J," so the character is used to refer to the "J"-shape of the white mark in this subspecies.

Identification. This is a large species easily recognized by the irregular wing margins, and the white "V" or "J" mark on the ventral hind wing. There is a white patch on the dorsal margins of both fore and hind wings.

Life History. In spring, females that overwintered lay eggs in batches on the host plants. The larvae are green and have the typical nymphalid spines. Larval hosts include a variety of trees: Trembling Aspen (*Populus tremuloides*), birch (*Betula* spp.) and willow (*Salix* spp.). Mature larvae may leave the host tree and wander in search of pupation sites. In cities they are observed occasionally crossing sidewalks or streets. Pupae are green with gold-coloured dorsal tubercles. These butterflies have been observed as early as April 10 and as late as October 8. Peak flight periods are in spring (May and early June) and late summer (August and early September). Adults are strong fliers with a fast, erratic flight when disturbed. Adults that overwinter appear early in the spring and die by July. New adults are on the wing in late July but seem to hide until September and October, when they can be observed basking on logs and sunny branches along forest edges. Adults feed freely at sap flows or may be baited with sugar mixtures painted on tree trunks. There is one brood per year.

Range and Habitat. This species occurs in northern Europe, Asia and North America. In North America, it is found through most of Canada from the treeline south into the northern states in the east and south to Colorado in the west. Two subspecies are recognized in Canada, of which *Nymphalis vaualbum j-album* is found in Alberta. These subspecies are known to intergrade in the boreal regions of Canada. The Compton Tortoise Shell is found throughout the forested regions of the province. The adults seem to prefer openings, trails and forest edges.

Polygonia Hübner, 1819
ANGLEWINGS

Etymology. *Polygonia* is derived from the Greek *poly* meaning "many" and *gonia* meaning "angle," and refers to the uneven wing margins of these butterflies.

Identification. Members of the genus have dull, mottled ventral wing surfaces and a jagged, many-angled wing margin. The dorsal surface tends to be more brightly coloured with rust and burnt orange tones and black marks.

Life History. Adult *Polygonia* overwinter under bark, in cracks or in leaf litter. In general, eggs are strongly ribbed, larvae have forked nymphalid-type spines and are highly variable in colour. The pupae are also variable in colour and hang by the cremaster from a silk pad. Pupation sites are often on trees and shrubs. The broken outline of the butterfly wings, when at rest, and the mottled colour pattern make spotting this species difficult as it perches on tree trunks or other broken surfaces.

Polygonia faunus (W.H. Edwards, 1862)
Green Comma
subspecies: *Polygonia faunus arcticus* Leussler, 1935
Polygonia faunus rusticus (W.H. Edwards, 1874)

Etymology. Named after the Roman deity Faunus, god of herds and fields. The Latin rusticus and the Greek *arktikos* refer to "rural" and "northern," respectively.

Identification. The Green Comma is a medium-sized butterfly with a broad, dark brown band on the dorsal fore wings. The wings are mottled brown or gray in the male with a row of greenish spots on the ventral fore wing. Females show either a gray or brown ventral surface and tend to have a more washed-out appearance. Both sexes have a white crescent on the ventral hind wing. The dorsal hind wing has a clear row of orange-brown submarginal spots separated completely from the basal brown of the wing.

 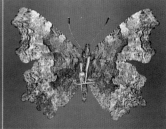

Polygonia faunus arcticus
Male dorsal

Polygonia faunus arcticus
Male ventral

Polygonia faunus rusticus
Male dorsal

Polygonia faunus rusticus
Male ventral

Alnus tenuifolia
Mountain Alder

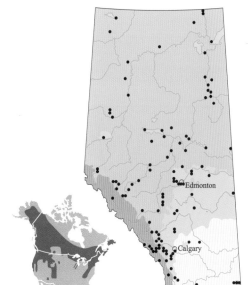

Life History. Adults overwinter and mate in the spring. Females oviposit on the upper sides of leaves. Eggs are green in eastern populations. Mature larvae have complex markings; their colour ranges from yellow to red with a predominantly white dorsal surface and a lateral orange band. They are decorated with transverse black and yellow bands and spots and have mainly white spines, except near the spiracles where they are brown. The pupae are gray-brown and are occasionally marked with green or dark brown. The anterior of the pupae has a forked protuberance and the dorsal surface has many short, pale or silver-tipped projections. Larval hosts include willow (*Salix* spp.), alder (*Alnus* spp.), gooseberry (*Ribes* spp.) and birch (*Betula* spp.). Alberta appears to be an area where subspecies are poorly defined, as specimens have combinations of gray and brown on ventral wing surfaces, unlike the rich brown of *rusticus*. Adults are seen from April 11 to October 5, with peak flight periods in April to May and July to September. Adult Green Commas often congregate around damp spots and sap flows on trees. They are wary and are strong fliers. These butterflies are not easily spotted unless disturbed; they tend to fly short distances before alighting on a tree trunk or branch. There is one brood per year.

Range and Habitat. The Green Comma is distributed from Newfoundland to British Columbia and from near treeline south into the United States along the Appalachian Mountains and Rocky Mountains. The appearance of this species varies clinally across its range. Specimens from Alberta are usually placed in the subspecies *Polygonia faunus rusticus;* however some populations may represent intermediates between *Polygonia faunus rusticus* and the northern form, *Polygonia faunus arcticus*. In the extreme southwest of Alberta the influence of *P. faunus hylas* (W.H. Edwards) is apparent. The Green Comma is found usually in association with spruce (*Picea* spp.) or mixed wood forests.

Polygonia gracilis (Grote and Robinson, 1867)
Hoary Comma

Etymology. The name is derived from the Latin *gracilis* meaning "slender."

Identification. The Hoary Comma is similar to the Zephyr (*Polygonia zephyrus*) except that it shows greater contrast between the basal and marginal areas on the dorsal wing surfaces. There may be blackened patches near the base of the wings. It is not possible to separate *Polygonia gracilis* from *P. zephyrus* in Alberta. *Polygonia gracilis* from eastern Canada has a chocolate-brown basal area on the ventral hind wing which is edged with whitish gray in the marginal area. Specimens from the boreal forest of western Ontario to Alaska are difficult to place as there are two, two-tone phenotypes involved (ventral wings, dark to light gray and dark to light brown). This situation needs further study (Kondla 1992).

Life History. In Alaska the larvae are reported to feed on Wild Red Currant (*Ribes triste*). Adults probably overwinter. There is likely one brood per year.

Range and Habitat. This species is described from Mount Washington in New Hampshire and is found across Canada throughout the boreal forest into the Northwest Territories and Alaska. It ranges south along the Rockies and the mountains of central British Columbia. The Hoary Comma frequents coniferous forests. The map represents a composite of *P. gracilis* and *zephyrus*.

Polygonia gracilis
Male dorsal

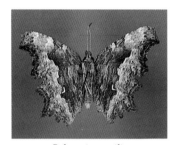

Polygonia gracilis
Male ventral

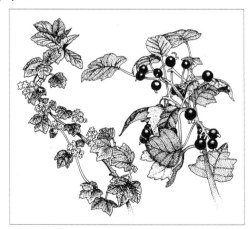

Ribes triste
Wild Red Currant

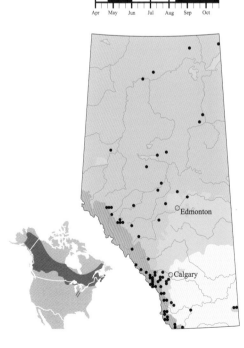

Apr May Jun Jul Aug Sep Oct

Edmonton

Calgary

Polygonia interrogationis (Fabricius, 1798)
Question Mark

Polygonia interrogationis
Ventral view

Polygonia interrogationis larva

Etymology. The species name is derived from the Latin *interrogatio*, for "questioning, inquiring," referring to the ?- shaped mark on the ventral hind wing.

Identification. The Question Mark is the largest species of *Polygonia*. There are two seasonal colour morphs, a dark summer morph and a lighter overwintering form. The summer morph has a mainly black ventral surface. In contrast, the winter morph is rusty orange to brown ventrally, and has slightly longer tails and more violet outlining the hind wings. The colour of the ventral hind wing can vary from the typical, independent of season or sex.

Life History. The bodies and spines of larvae are variable in colour ranging from black to yellow, often with yellow or red lines. Tubercle colour varies from yellow to red and the spines rising from the tubercles may be yellow, red or black. Pupal colour varies from yellow to dark brown. The anterior end of the pupae is notched and there is a prominent thoracic keel. The dorsal surface has metallic spots. In eastern North America, larvae are known to feed on a variety of plants including elm (*Ulmus* spp.) and nettle (*Urtica* spp.). In the east, adults overwinter with some individuals remaining in the north while others migrate south to overwinter. These latter individuals may then migrate north the following spring. Adults are readily attracted to tree sap and rotting fruit. May 14 is the only flight date known for Alberta. In other parts of the range, several broods may be present, with adults of one brood overwintering. Flight begins in the spring and continues with each brood through the summer until September.

Range and Habitat. The Question Mark is found primarily in eastern North America south from southern Ontario and the Maritimes, west into Manitoba and Saskatchewan and south across the Great Plains to Texas. It has been recorded only once in Alberta, at a site near Lloydminster. It is unknown whether the individual was resident or dispersing into Alberta. In eastern North America the Question Mark is found perching on leaves in shrubbery and trees often close to wet areas.

Polygonia oreas (W.H. Edwards, 1869)
Oreas Anglewing
subspecies: *Polygonia oreas silenus* (W.H. Edwards, 1870)

Etymology. The name is derived from *oreias* meaning "mountain nymph" in Greek mythology. The subspecies *silenus* is named after the leader of satyrs in Greek mythology, who constantly pursued nymphs of all sorts.

Identification. Polygonia oreas has areas of white marginal hair on the hind wing, a unique character among Alberta *Polygonia*. In addition, the ventral wing surface of the Oreas Anglewing is dark brown or gray, similar to that of the Gray Comma (*Polygonia progne*), but with a slight separation between the dark basal and lighter marginal areas. The dorsal wing surface is much like that of *Polygonia zephyrus*, the Zephyr.

Life History. The larvae are mainly black and are banded dorsally both anteriorly and posteriorly with a pale yellow line on segments two through five. A white and more-or-less distinct, pale yellow dorsal line extends over segments two and three sometimes to the fourth. Larvae feed on gooseberry (*Ribes* spp.). Flight records in Alberta are from May 21 to July 21, and represent overwintered adults. Flight of the new brood is expected in August and September. There is one brood per year.

Range and Habitat. This species of Anglewing is found from California, north to British Columbia and southern Alberta. Populations in Alberta most resemble *Polygonia oreas silenus*. The eastern limit of this species is unclear and controversial. In Alberta, *Polygonia oreas* has been collected at low elevations in the mountains of the Waterton Lakes National Park to Crowsnest Pass area.

Polygonia oreas silenus
Dorsal

Polygonia oreas silenus
Ventral

Apr May Jun Jul Aug Sep Oct

Ribes hudsonianus
Wild Black Currant

Polygonia progne (Cramer, [1776])
Gray Comma

Polygonia progne
Dorsal

Polygonia progne
Ventral

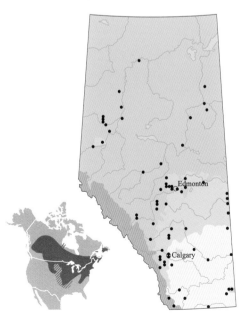

Etymology. The name is derived from Prokne, daughter of Pandion, king of Athens in Greek mythology. She was later changed into a swallow.

Identification. On the dorsal hind wing the black margin is expanded to near the wing base. The wing has relatively small, orange-brown submarginal spots. The ventral fore wing is divided into a dark basal area and a lighter outer area. In contrast, the ventral hind wing is completely dark.

Life History. Eggs of the Gray Comma are light emerald green with seven large vertical ribs that project above the top. Eggs are laid singly, usually on gooseberry (*Ribes* spp.), and hatch in 8 or 9 days. Larvae feed underneath the leaves. There is much variation in larval colour patterns. In mature larvae the head may be orange-brown and the body yellow-brown with dark olive-brown splotches and lines. Black or yellow branched spines cover the head and body. The pupae vary in colour from green to brown or buff and are marked with black or brown. Adults overwinter and breed in the spring. The flight period in Alberta is from April 11 to October 1, with peak flight activity from May to June and August to September. There is one brood per year.

Range and Habitat. The Gray Comma is found from Alaska to Newfoundland in the north, south in the Appalachian Mountains to North Carolina and from Kansas west to Wyoming and Colorado. In Alberta, the Gray Comma occurs throughout forested regions and is usually associated with mixed wood forests. Adults are sighted frequently along roads and in clearings.

Polygonia satyrus (W.H. Edwards, 1869)
Satyr Anglewing
subspecies: *Polygonia satyrus satyrus* (W.H. Edwards, 1869)

Etymology. The species name comes from the Latin Satyrus, a woodland deity represented as a riotous, lascivious, goat-footed man.

Identification. This medium-sized Anglewing is orange-brown on the dorsal surface. The orange submarginal spots on the dorsal hind wing are enlarged and merge into a wide band.

Life History. Satyr Anglewings overwinter as adults and emerge in the spring. They may be seen in late winter during warm periods. Adults feed on sap flows and imbibe water from mud puddles. Eggs are pale green and are laid usually on the underside of leaves. The caterpillars roll leaves into a shelter, and when mature are black with a broad green dorsal stripe. The rows of dorsal and subdorsal spines are greenish white while the lateral rows are black. At present only one host is confirmed, nettle (*Urtica* spp.), but others such as hops (*Humulus* spp.) are suspected. The pupae are light brown with a few darker marks. The Satyr Anglewing is recorded to fly from April 1 to October 14, with peak flight activity in the spring and late summer to early fall. There is one brood per year.

Range and Habitat. The range of the Satyr Anglewing is transcontinental in Canada and south along the mountains to California. In Alberta it is found across the province along river valleys and in forested areas. The subspecies name *Polygonia satyrus satyrus* is applied to Alberta specimens. The Satyr Anglewing is usually associated with woodland habitats where clumps of nettles (*Urtica* spp.) grow, but it can also be found in isolated copses in the prairies. Adults may be attracted to stations baited with sugar and water.

Polygonia satyrus satyrus
Female dorsal

Polygonia satyrus satyrus
Male ventral

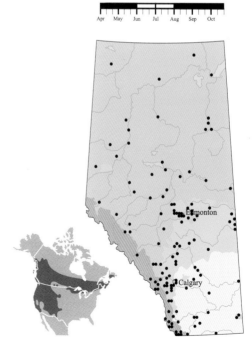

225

Polygonia zephyrus (W.H. Edwards, 1870)
Zephyr

Polygonia zephyrus
Dorsal

Polygonia zephyrus
Ventral

Etymology. The species is named after zephyros, the gentle west wind from Greek mythology.

Identification. The ventral surface is dark gray basally and distinctly lighter gray on the outer half of the wing. Many are brownish gray. Dorsally, the sub-marginal spots form a light band. The Zephyr may be confused with *Polygonia gracilis*, the Hoary Comma.

Life History. As with other *Polygonia* species, adult Zephyrs overwinter. Mating and oviposition occur in the spring. Larvae are black with reddish buff markings that become whitish caudally. The preferred larval host is gooseberry (*Ribes* spp.), but other plants such as elm (*Ulmus* spp.) and *Rhododendron* spp. are used by some populations. Adults are on the wing from April 1 to October 5 with peak flight activity in May to June and August to September. There is one brood per year.

Range and Habitat. The Zephyr is found from Colorado and California north to north-central Alberta and British Columbia. The eastern and western limits of the range of the species are a subject of debate among taxonomists who disagree on the definition of this species. The Zephyr is found in coniferous and mixed wood forests in the boreal forest and the mountain foothills. The map represents a composite of *P. zephyrus* and *gracilis*.

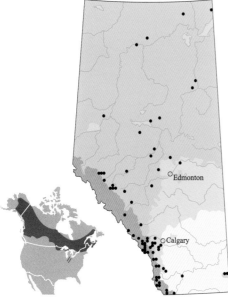

Polygonia zephyrus larva

Vanessa Fabricius, 1807
PAINTED LADIES

Etymology. Vanessa was a mystic divinity of the Orphic rites in ancient Greece.

Identification. This genus has been split on occasion into two genera, *Cynthia* Fabricius and *Vanessa*, then reunited under one name at a later date. We choose the conservative use of the name and use *Vanessa*. Adults are strong fliers and are often seen nectaring at thistles (*Cirsium* spp.) and Alfalfa (*Medicago sativa*). They may be rare or abundant in a given year and most of our species disperse into the province. One of our four species is known to overwinter in Alberta.

Vanessa annabella (Field, 1971)
West Coast Lady

Etymology. Annabella is a woman's proper name.

Identification. The West Coast Lady is a dark brown and orange butterfly similar in appearance to the Painted Lady, *Vanessa cardui*. Unlike *V. cardui*, *V. annabella* has four blue-centred spots, all about the same size, on the dorsal hind wing, and lacks a complete submarginal band of blue spots on the ventral hind wing.

Life History. Immatures of the West Coast Lady are similar to those of the Painted Lady. The spiny caterpillars range in colour from black to light brown and have yellow or orange lines demarcating segments. Larval hosts include mallows (Malvaceae), lupines (*Lupinus* spp.) and nettles (Urticaceae). The flight period for the West Coast Lady in Alberta is from June 13 to October 12. This species is an immigrant, and does not survive Alberta winters. During dispersals it is usually found mixed with immigrants of *Vanessa cardui*. Adults nectar freely on many types of flowers, especially thistles (*Cirsium* spp.).

Range and Habitat. The West Coast Lady ranges in western North America from southern Alberta, British Columbia and Saskatchewan southward to Guatemala. In Alberta, immigrants have been found north to Red Deer. Adults may occasionally be found along roadside ditches, stopping to nectar at flowers during migrations.

Vanessa annabella
Female dorsal

227

Vanessa atalanta (Linnaeus), 1759
Red Admiral
subspecies: *Vanessa atalanta rubria* (Fruhstorfer, 1909)

Vanessa atalanta rubria
Dorsal

Vanessa atalanta rubria
Ventral

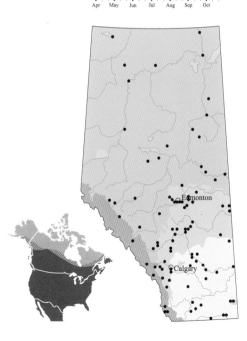

Etymology. Named after Atalante, a virgin huntress in Greek mythology. The subspecies name is from the Latin *ruber*, meaning "red."

Identification. The Red Admiral is easily identified by its large size and the bright orange-red band on a dark background on the dorsal wing surface. No other butterfly in our area shares these characters.

Life History. In Alberta, some Red Admirals are migratory while others hibernate and appear early in the spring. Females lay pale green eggs on the tops of leaves. Young larvae live in leaf shelters, rolling the leaves dorsally. Larvae are solitary. Older larvae make a web nest by tying leaves together. Larvae are variable in colour ranging from blackish to yellow-green with lateral black and yellow stripes. The branched spines that are typical of nymphalid larvae are present. Larval host plants are usually nettles (*Urtica* spp.) but others are also utilized. Pupae range in colour from gray-brown to reddish brown with some black markings and golden tubercles. In some parts of the range pupae may also overwinter. Adults may be found on the wing from May 8 to October 15. Two peaks of activity occur. The first in spring represents overwintered adults and the second in late summer and fall represents the current year's brood before they enter winter diapause. Adults nectar on thistles (*Cirsium* spp.) and Alfalfa (*Medicago sativa*), on which males perch, presumably awaiting females. They will also bask along roadsides in the morning and late afternoon. Males occasionally hilltop. There is one brood per year.

Range and Habitat. The Red Admiral is holarctic in distribution. In North America, it occurs from treeline south to Central America. The North American subspecies is *Vanessa atalanta rubria*. This species is found throughout Alberta. The Red Admiral may occur almost anywhere, often along streams and meadows but is seldom abundant.

Vanessa cardui (Linnaeus, 1758)
Painted Lady

Etymology. *Carduus* is Latin for "wild thistle."

Identification. The Painted Lady is a large, fast-flying butterfly, with mottled orange and dark brown on the dorsal wing surface. It may be recognized by a row of five eye spots on the ventral hind wing of which two are larger than the others and are ringed with black. The complete submarginal band of blue spots on the ventral hind wing separates this species from *Vanessa annabella*, the West Coast Lady.

Life History. Larvae vary in colour from yellow to green. Dark mottling and several rows of spines are present. Larvae live singly and spin loose webs over the host plant. The pupae are usually tan or gray and are usually found on or near the host plant. A wide range of plants from several different families are used as larval hosts. These include species of thistles (Compositae*),* borage (Boraginaceae), mallows (Malvaceae) and peas (Leguminosae). The adults are avid flower visitors, nectaring from such plants as thistles (*Cirsium* spp.) and other composites, Alfalfa (*Medicago sativa*), clovers (*Trifolium* spp.) and various garden flowers. The Painted Lady is not known to overwinter in Alberta and populations here are the product of colonizing immigrants from the south. During peak years they can be one of the most common butterflies in Alberta with several broods but in other years they are totally absent. The first immigrants recorded arrive as early as April 23 and are present until October 24. When they are present, peak flight activity starts in mid-May and continues to early September or the first hard frosts. Individuals seen after late June usually represent offspring of the migrants.

Range and Habitat. The Painted Lady occurs throughout most of North and South America, Europe, Asia and into Africa. During favourable years in the southern United States, enormous populations of Painted Ladies build up, resulting in northward migrations. During these migrations Painted Ladies may be on the move almost everywhere in the province. When breeding, adults are usually associated with fields, gardens and waste areas near thistle patches or nectar sources.

Vanessa cardui
Dorsal

Vanessa cardui
Ventral

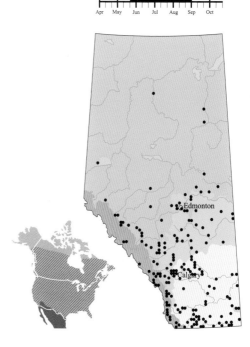

Vanessa virginiensis (Drury, 1773)
American Painted Lady

Vanessa virginiensis
Dorsal

Vanessa virginiensis
Ventral

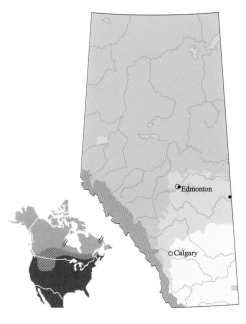

Etymology. The species is named for the state of Virginia, the type locality.

Identification. The American Painted Lady has two very large blue-centred eye spots on the ventral hind wing that dominate the pattern of the wing. The dorsal wing surface is largely mottled orange and dark brown, similar to *Vanessa cardui* and *Vanessa annabella*.

Life History. Eggs of *Vanessa virginiensis* are yellow green and laid on the upper surface of leaves. Larvae are solitary and live in leaf nests. They are multi-coloured with black patches bordered in white, bounded by fine black margins with two white spots in the black. On the first six segments there are four longitudinal rows of black spines that are red at the base. Larval hosts include various composites including cudweed (*Gnaphalium* spp.), pussytoes or everlasting (*Antennaria* spp.) and wormwood or sagebrush (*Artemisia* spp.). The pupae are gray-white and marked with brown often with a greenish tinge. It is unlikely that this species can survive Alberta winters and specimens collected probably disperse from the United States. There are three recorded flight dates for Alberta: July 1, July 19 and September 7.

Range and Habitat. The range is transcontinental in Canada, extending south to South America. This species enters Alberta as an occasional immigrant. The American Painted Lady may be found almost anywhere because of its dispersal ability.

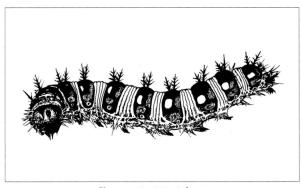

Vanessa virginiensis larva

Subfamily
ARGYNNINAE
FRITILLARIES

Members of the Argynninae are commonly called fritillaries. The scientific name of this subfamily is derived from the Greek *argyros*, meaning "silvery," because of the reflective silvery patches on the ventral hind wings. These spots are especially prominent in *Speyeria* species, which make up eight of the 21 species found in Alberta.

Boloria Moore, 1900
LESSER FRITILLARIES

Etymology. The genus is named after Mt. Bolor, a mountain in Asia.

Identification. There has been some difference of opinion among authorities regarding the generic limits of *Boloria*. The genus has at times been split into three genera; *Boloria*, *Clossiana* and *Proclossiana*. The following table provides evidence in the form of a preponderance of shared derived (synapotypic) features of male genitalia which indicates a close relationship among the genera. Based on the high number of shared characters, the three genera can be considered as a single genus, *Boloria*. *Boloria* species are medium-sized, orange to brown with black-spotted wings, often with silvering on the ventral surface. Eggs are pale green, somewhat conical and covered in a net-like series of ridges. Larvae are dark and spiny. In most species the third instar overwinters, but in others it is the first instar larvae or pupae that overwinter. Pupae are brownish with metallic spots and hang by the cremaster.

Summary of male genitalic character states found in *Boloria*, *Clossiana*, *Proclossiana* and two related genera

Character	Genera				
	Boloria	*Clossiana*	*Proclossiana*	*Issoria*	*Brenthis*
Uncus tip	A: bifid	A: bifid	A: bifid	P: single	A: trifid
Aedeagus base	A: base extended anteriorly	A: base extended anteriorly	A: base extended anteriorly	P: base not extended	P: base not extended
Posterior of aedeagus	A: two-flanged	A: two-flanged	A: two-flanged	P: not flanged	P: not flanged
Endophallic tube	A: bump present	A: bump present	A: bump present	P: bump absent	P: bump absent
Endophallic tube	A: fine teeth	A: fine teeth	A: fine teeth	P: no teeth	P: no teeth
Claspers	A: simple-two prongs	A: simple-two prongs	A: simple-two prongs	A: simple-two prongs	P: simple-one prong
Uncus length	P: wider than long A: short	short to long	A: very long	P: long	P: long
Wings of phallobase	P: simple P: short	P: simple short to large	P: simple A: large	P: simple	P: simple P: short

A = synapotypic (shared derived) character state; P = plesiotypic (ancestral) character state

231

Boloria alberta (W.H. Edwards, 1890)
Alberta Fritillary

Boloria alberta
Male dorsal

Boloria alberta
Male ventral

Etymology. This species was discovered near Laggan, now Lake Louise, and is named after what was then the Territory of Alberta.

Identification. The Alberta Fritillary is medium-sized with muted, diffuse markings. The black spots are smudged on both dorsal and ventral wing surfaces. Silver, white and yellow markings are lacking although some females have a gray dusting on the ventral surface.

Life History. Eggs are laid on White Mountain Avens (*Dryas octopetala*). In several localities adults appear in alternate years, strongly suggesting a two-year life cycle. Edwards, the original collector, indicated that first instar larvae overwinter. Populations are present in Alberta every year. Adults have been collected from June 27 to August 26 and peak flight activity is in mid-July. Adults fly low over windswept ridges and in alpine tundra. Females are often encountered in protected swales below the tops of ridges. Males appear to hilltop on ridges, often seeking the highest or most prominent part of the ridge. Adults will nectar at plants such as Moss Campion (*Silene acaulis*) and mountain avens (*Dryas* spp.).

Range and Habitat. The Alberta Fritillary is restricted almost entirely to Alberta with adjacent populations in Glacier County, Montana, and British Columbia, near the Great Divide. The northernmost known population in Alberta is on Mount Hamell, north of Grande Cache, but the species is expected to range north along the mountains into British Columbia. Another species of *Boloria*, the Polaris Fritillary, *B. polaris* (Boisduval), occurs in northern British Columbia and is also presumed to feed on *Dryas* spp. Competition between these two species may limit their distributions. The Alberta Fritillary is a resident of the high alpine tundra, frequenting barren windswept ridges usually above 2000 m in the north and 2400 m in southern Alberta.

Boloria astarte (Doubleday and Hewitson, [1847])
Astarte Fritillary
subspecies: *Boloria astarte astarte* (Doubleday and Hewitson, [1847])

Etymology. This species is named after Astarte, a Phoenician goddess of fertility and erotic love.

Identification. The Astarte Fritillary is a medium-to-large species with a distinct silvery median band on the ventral hind wing, followed by an orange and then a white postmedian submarginal band. This species is often at the centre of a taxonomic controversy with *Boloria distincta* (Gibson), a similar species found in the mountains of extreme northern British Columbia, Alaska and Yukon Territory. Although found in similar habitats, they differ in intensity of colour and genitalic structures.

Life History. Females deposit eggs on Spotted or Prickly Saxifrage (*Saxifraga bronchialis*), along rock falls, scree slopes and talus fields. Larvae appear to overwinter as first and fourth instars. Flight records start on June 15 and end August 11 with peak activity throughout July. Adults fly every year in Alberta. There is one brood per year. Males hilltop on cliffs and ridges in search of females. Males are strong, wary fliers, and are easily disturbed and blown off ridge tops or over cliffs. Mated females leave the ridges in search of host plants at lower elevations, sometimes following rock-slides and scree slopes below treeline. Both sexes nectar at flowers such as yellow or white mountain avens (*Dryas* spp.) in protected areas along the edges of gullies.

Range and Habitat. The Astarte Fritillary ranges from the mountains of northern British Columbia south through the mountains to Washington and Montana. In Alberta, this species is found on most mountains along the front ranges and expected on most in the main ranges. The habitat of the Astarte Fritillary is high mountain alpine, notably along scree slopes and cliffs. Males tend to congregate at high points.

Boloria astarte astarte
Male dorsal

Boloria astarte astarte
Male ventral

233

Boloria bellona (Fabricius, 1775)
Meadow Fritillary
subspecies: *Boloria bellona jenistae* D. Stallings and Turner, 1946

Boloria bellona jenistae
Male dorsal

Boloria bellona jenistae
Female ventral

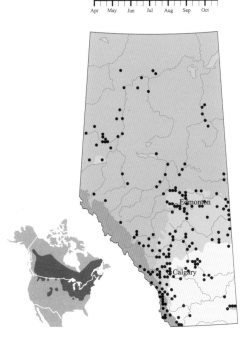

Etymology. The species name is derived from Bellona, goddess of war and sister of Mars in Roman mythology. Stallings and Turner named the subspecies after Mr. and Mrs. Harry E. Jenista.

Identification. The Meadow Fritillary is medium-sized with the brown and black spotted dorsal surface typical of the genus. It is distinguished by the flat apex of the fore wing, which produces a slightly square look to the end of the wing.

Life History. Eggs are laid on violets (*Viola* spp.) and hatch in about 11 days. Early instar larvae are dark and covered with spines. Mature larvae are green with a velvet lateral band. Spines are yellowish brown. Two generations per year are normal. A large, early summer generation is followed by a smaller one later in the season. Summer butterflies have a light reddish hue. Offspring of the summer generation over-winter as third or fourth instar larvae, which resume feeding the following spring and emerge as adults in late May to early June. Adults of this generation are darker. The Meadow Fritillary may be found on the wing for most of the summer. Collection records start on May 8 and finish on September 2 with peak periods from mid-May to early June and again in mid-July to early August. Males patrol for females by flying low to the ground. Flight is not particularly strong or rapid. Adults often feed on members of the daisy family (Compositae).

Range and Habitat. The Meadow Fritillary is found from the Maritimes south to Georgia, west to British Columbia and south to Colorado. There are three subspecies recognized, all of which intergrade with each other. Alberta material is assigned to the subspecies *Boloria bellona jenistae*. The type locality is Rivercourse, Alberta (Kondla, 1994b), but the specimens are not very different from those of eastern North America. It ranges throughout the entire province but is more abundant in parkland habitats. The Meadow Fritillary, as its name implies, is found in meadows and other grassy, open areas, in foothills, aspen parkland and prairie regions.

Boloria chariclea (Schneider, 1794)
Purple Fritillary

Etymology. Unknown.

Identification. The dorsal surface is spotted brown and black and the ventral surface is variable, but always with a dark postmedian submarginal band. There is a purplish tinge on the ventral surface and each marginal triangle has a white bar or spot at its base. Shepard (1994) showed that all American forms of the *Boloria chariclea/titania* complex belong to *Boloria chariclea*.

Life History. Captive females lay eggs on willows (*Salix* spp.), Bistort (*Polygonum viviparum*), scrub birch (*Betula* spp.) and on anything available if its food plants are not present. Eggs hatch in about fourteen days. First instar larvae do not feed and enter directly into wintering diapause. The larvae are gray with dark dorsal and lateral stripes, orange spines and black heads. In eastern Canada, larvae are reported to feed on Arctic Willow (*Salix arctica*), Dwarf Willow (*Salix herbacea*) and Bistort (*Polygonum viviparum*). Flight begins in June with first records June 17 and last record September 9. Most of the flight activity occurs in July. Adults nectar on yellow composite species and *Aster* spp. and are frequently seen drinking at puddles in the mountains. Mating pairs are reluctant to fly when disturbed. There is one brood per year.

Range and Habitat. A Nearctic species, the Purple Fritillary is found in boreal zones in North America. This species is found from New Mexico north to treeline, from Alaska to Newfoundland in the east, south to northern Maine and Minnesota. It is found throughout the province in association with coniferous forests. The Purple Fritillary abounds in meadows and glades in pine and spruce forests in the boreal zone.

Boloria chariclea
Female dorsal

Boloria chariclea
Female ventral

Boloria chariclea
Male ventral

Apr May Jun Jul Aug Sep Oct

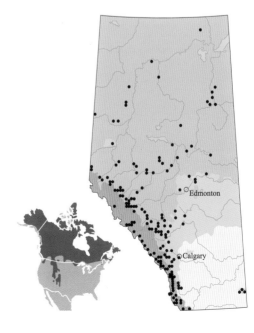

Edmonton

Calgary

235

Boloria epithore (W.H. Edwards, [1864])
Western Meadow Fritillary
subspecies: *Boloria epithore uslui* (Koçak, 1984)

Boloria epithore uslui
Male dorsal

Boloria epithore uslui
Female ventral

Etymology. The butterfly is named after a similar appearing European species, *Boloria thore* Hübner which was named after Thor, Norse god of thunder. The prefix *epi* means "on" or "towards" in Greek.

Identification. The Western Meadow Fritillary is medium-sized with a bright brown and black dorsal surface. The ventral surface lacks silvering and the dark submarginal spots or "chevrons" are bent outwards rather than inwards as in all other Alberta *Boloria*.

Life History. Larvae have been reared on several species of violet (*Viola* spp.). The larvae have a gray ground colour that is darker ventrally and laterally, with gray mid-dorsal lines and a reddish brown lateral stripe. The head is black. The pupae are light brown mottled with white on the head and thorax. Fourth instar larvae overwinter. There is one brood per year. Collecting records indicate flight activity from May 29 to August 5.

Range and Habitat. The range of the Western Meadow Fritillary is from California, north to British Columbia and east to the Rocky Mountain front ranges. Four weakly differentiated subspecies have been described. Alberta material is *Boloria epithore uslui*. The Western Meadow Fritillary is sporadically found in mountain meadows from the Kakwa River basin in the north and more commonly in the Crowsnest Pass to Waterton Lakes National Park area in the southwestern corner of the province. Lush meadows and mountain-sides appear to be home for the Western Meadow Fritillary in Alberta.

Boloria eunomia (Esper, 1787)
Bog Fritillary

subspecies: *Boloria eunomia triclaris* (Hübner, [1821])
Boloria eunomia dawsoni (Barnes and McDunnough, 1916)
Boloria eunomia nichollae (Barnes and Benjamin, 1926)

Etymology. This species is named after Eunomia, a daughter of Zeus, king of the Greek gods. The subspecies *triclaris* is from the Latin *tri* meaning "three" and *clarus*, meaning "distinct, bright"; *dawsoni* was named in honour of Horace Dawson, a butterfly collector in northwestern Ontario; *nichollae* was named after Mary de la Beach-Nicholl, who acquired the first specimen.

Identification. The Bog Fritillary is recognized easily by the round submarginal spots with silver or yellow centres and the almost polygonal silver patches outlined in black on the ventral hind wings.

Life History. Eggs are laid in small groups on smooth-leaved willows (*Salix* spp.). The eggs hatch in seven to eight days with larvae feeding on the ventral leaf surface. Although willows (*Salix* spp.) are a major host plant in Alberta, in other regions of North America, *B. eunomia* uses Bistort (*Polygonum viviparum*) or meadow rue (*Thalictrum* spp.) and in Europe, violets (*Viola* spp.) are reported. When seeds are available, larvae will feed preferentially on them. Larvae in Alberta are black with small white and blue dots. Third and fourth instar larvae are reported to overwinter. There is one brood per year. Flight in Alberta is recorded from May 28 to August 26 with peak activity in June and July.

Boloria eunomia dawsoni
Male dorsal

Boloria eunomia dawsoni
Male ventral

Boloria eunomia nichollae
Female dorsal

Boloria eunomia nichollae
Female ventral

Viola nephrophylla
Bog Violet

237

Salix arctica
Arctic Willow

Range and Habitat. The Bog Fritillary is holarctic in distribution. In North America it occurs from Colorado to the arctic coast, from Alaska in the west to Newfoundland in the east. In eastern North America the Bog Fritillary ranges south to Wisconsin and Minnesota. Many subspecies are recognized in North America. Material from Alberta is intermediate between *Boloria eunomia dawsoni* and *B. e. triclaris,* with closer affinities to *B. e. dawsoni. Boloria eunomia nichollae* is a very dark form from the vicinity of the Columbia Ice Fields. It is possible that this subspecies is a glacial relict. Near Mountain Park, south of Hinton, the light-coloured, low-altitude form appears to intergrade clinally with the darker, high-altitude form. Populations on the Canadian Shield of northeastern Alberta are dark and are different from any described subspecies. In Alberta the Bog Fritillary is widespread throughout the northern half of the province and in the mountains to above treeline. The Bog Fritillary is aptly named, as it frequents wet boggy areas with an abundance of willows. Common places to encounter this butterfly include moist alpine meadows with willows, spruce bogs, and birch, willow and tamarack fens.

Salix exigua
Sandbar Willow

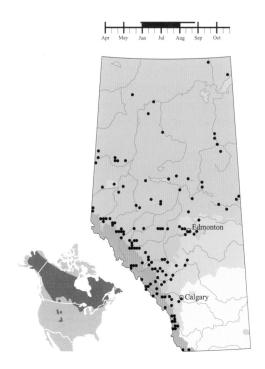

Boloria freija (Thunberg, 1791)
Freija Fritillary
subspecies: *Boloria freija freija* (Thunberg, 1791)

Etymology. The species name is derived from Freya of Norse legend. She was a goddess of love and fertility, daughter of Njord and sister of Frey, and later a wife of Odin.

Identification. The Freija Fritillary's dorsal wing surface has heavy black basal dusting. The ventral surface of the hind wing is heavily silvered in the submarginal area, with a large white or silver triangular patch pointing outward at the end of the discal cell.

Life History. Eggs are deposited on several species of the heather family (Ericaceae) including Common Bearberry or Kinnikinnick (*Arctostaphylos uva-ursi*) and blueberry, bilberry and huckleberry (*Vaccinium* spp.). Eggs hatch in about twelve days. Larvae are brown but lighter dorsally with many spines and a black head. Fourth instar larvae overwinter. There is one brood per year. The Freija Fritillary is found on the wing early in the spring with the first record April 24 and the last specimens recorded on the wing August 3. The greatest flight activity occurs in May. Adults fly low over the ground, females being weaker fliers than males. Both sexes may be seen perching on the food plant or nearby on the ground.

Range and Habitat. The Freija Fritillary is holarctic in distribution. In North America it ranges from Alaska east to Baffin Island and Newfoundland and south to New Mexico and Wisconsin. Specimens from Alberta are assigned to the subspecies *Boloria freija freija*. The Freija Fritillary is found throughout the mountains, foothills and boreal forest regions of Alberta. Clearings in coniferous forests are home to the Freija Fritillary.

Boloria freija freija
Male dorsal

Boloria freija freija
Male ventral

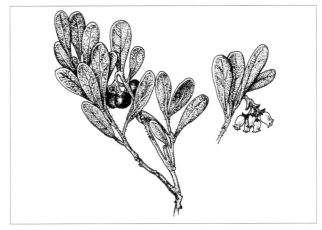
Arctostaphylos uva-ursi
Common Bearberry or Kinnikinnick

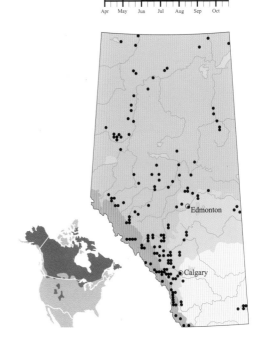

239

Boloria frigga (Thunberg, 1791)
Frigga Fritillary
subspecies: *Boloria frigga saga* (Staudinger, 1861)

Boloria frigga saga
Male dorsal

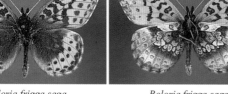

Boloria frigga saga
Male ventral

Boloria frigga saga
Female dorsal

Etymology. This species is named after Frigga, the wife of Odin, and goddess of clouds, sky and conjugal love in Norse mythology. *Saga* is Latin for "fortune teller."

Identification. The Frigga Fritillary is medium-sized with brown and black on both surfaces. There is considerable black basal dusting on the dorsal surface. The ventral hind wing surface has a distinct purplish sheen and a broad silver patch on the dorsal margin. On both surfaces the ground colour is fairly light.

Life History. The female Frigga Fritillary oviposits on willows (*Salix* spp.) and Dwarf Birch (*Betula glandulosa*), on which the larvae feed. Eggs hatch in nine to eleven days and the larvae feed on the underside of leaves at least until the third instar. Late instar larvae overwinter. Adults are rarely observed nectaring. The flight period tends to be quite restricted with peak activity in late May to early July. Capture records are from May 15 to July 26. There is one brood per year.

Range and Habitat. The Frigga Fritillary is a holarctic species. In North America it is found from Baffin Island and the arctic coast of Alaska and Yukon Territory south to Colorado, and east in the boreal forest to Newfoundland and south to northern Wisconsin and Michigan. Alberta specimens are placed in the subspecies *Boloria frigga saga.* The Frigga Fritillary can be found through boreal Alberta in bogs and in the mountains. It inhabits black spruce bogs, swamps, muskeg willow fens and is an occasional visitor to alpine meadows.

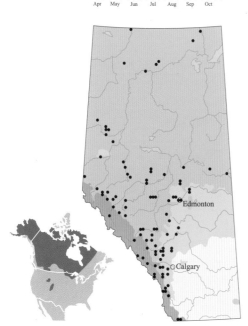

Apr May Jun Jul Aug Sep Oct

Boloria improba (Butler, 1877)
Dingy Arctic Fritillary

Etymology. The species name may be derived from the Latin *improbus*, meaning "not according to the standard"; meaning below standard, poor, or inferior.

Identification. *Boloria improba* is small, brown and dingy with very pale or no silvering on the ventral surface. There is heavy black dusting of scales on the dorsal surface. Markings on the ventral surface are subdued.

Life History. Larvae of the Dingy Arctic Fritillary feed on dwarf willows (*Salix* spp.) in the Alpine zone. Larvae are mottled brown dorsally and lighter below with a darker mid-dorsal stripe and a dark sub-dorsal line edged with a lighter colour. The spines are dark with a reddish hue and the head is black. The pupae are mottled brown with various bumps. First and fourth instar larvae overwinter; elsewhere the situation may differ slightly. There is one brood per year. The recorded flight range is from July 4 to July 28, with peak activity by the second week of July in most years. They nectar on Moss Campion (*Silene acaulis*) and yellow composites. In the barren windswept alpine tundra, the Dingy Arctic Fritillary flies close to the ground to avoid being blown away. Gravid females have difficulty flying.

Boloria improba
Male dorsal

Boloria improba
Male ventral

Boloria improba
Female dorsal

Boloria improba
Female ventral

Adams Lookout, alpine tundra in Willmore Wilderness Park, Alberta.

G.J. Hilchie.

241

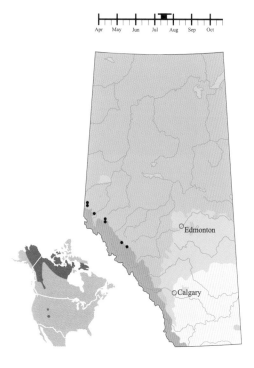

Range and Habitat. This species is holarctic in distribution. In North America, it occurs in arctic tundra west of Hudson Bay and Baffin Island. Colonies are scattered along the Rocky Mountains south to Colorado. There is a controversy over the subspecies of Alberta populations. Populations in Wyoming belong to *Boloria improba harryi* (Ferris). Alberta material is different from it and from arctic populations. They may represent a clinal gradation between *harryi* and *Boloria improba youngi* which is from the Alaska-Yukon border and British Columbia. In Alberta the Dingy Arctic Fritillary is found in local colonies that easily escape detection, even when searched for. Populations have been observed from Southesk Pass in the central mountains of the province, north through Willmore Wilderness Park and adjacent mountains in the Kakwa River basin and north-west along the mountains in British Columbia. The Dingy Arctic Fritillary frequents moist, willow-covered alpine tundra. These willow mat growths occur in depressions and on the lee side of ridges where snow tends to sit a little longer during spring melt. The butter-flies take full advantage of wind eddies while moving about in their habitat. When disturbed, they can be exposed to wind and blown away easily.

Prospect Mountain, Alberta.   T.W. Thormin.

Boloria napaea (Hoffmansegg, 1804)
Napaea Fritillary
subspecies: *Boloria napaea alaskensis* (Holland, 1900)

Etymology. The name is derived from the Napaeae, dell nymphs of Greek mythology.

Identification. The Napaea Fritillary is medium-to-small and recognized by the flattened terminal margin of the hind wing and the bright yellow and silver ventral surface. The dorsal surface is bright orange-brown in males and dusky in females. They have the black spotting typical of this group.

Life History. Oviposition has been observed on Bistort (*Polygonum viviparum*). In Europe the larvae are reported to feed on *Bistorta vivapara*. In North America the life history is poorly known. It is speculated that the larvae pass winter both as first instars and as later instars. In Alberta, adult Napaea Fritillaries have been caught from July 1 to August 5 with peak activity in mid-July. Adults perch on composites and other yellow flowers and have a rapid, low flight. There is one brood per year.

Range and Habitat. The Napaea Fritillary is holarctic in distribution. Some authorities have divided this taxon into *Boloria napaea* in southern Europe and *Boloria alaskensis* in northern Europe, Asia and North America. This division is based on wing characters, but in North America these characters are inconsistent and tend to split arctic from non-arctic forms. *Boloria napaea* occurs from the lower arctic islands to treeline and south to Wyoming. Three subspecies are currently recognized in North America. Alberta material matches most closely *Boloria napaea alaskensis*. It is distributed from the Grande Cache to Willmore Wilderness Park area of Alberta northwest into British Columbia. The Napaea Fritillary flies in moist alpine and subalpine meadows near treeline, in areas rich with flowers.

Polygonum viviparum
Bistort

Boloria napaea alaskensis
Male dorsal

Boloria napaea alaskensis
Male ventral

243

Boloria selene (Denis and Schiffermüller, 1775)
Silver-bordered Fritillary
subspecies: *Boloria selene atrocostalis* (Huard, 1927)

Boloria selene atrocostalis
Female dorsal

Boloria selene atrocostalis
Female ventral

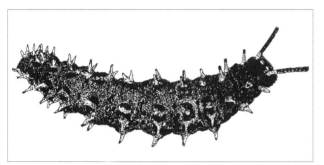

Boloria selene atrocostalis larva

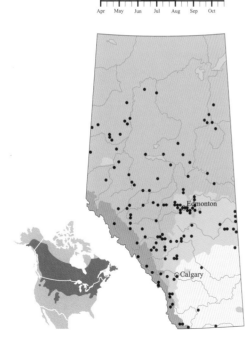

Etymology. The species name is from Selene, the Greek goddess of the moon.

Identification. The dorsal surface is bright orange-brown with black spots and little or no basal dusting. The ventral surface has bright silver marginal spots and a postmedian submarginal band. There is a distinctive black-centred silver spot just basal to this band.

Life History. Eggs are usually laid on violets (*Viola* spp.), but may be deposited on other plants nearby. Eggs hatch in about nine days. Mature larvae have two large tufts of setae behind the head and are covered with spines. Pupae are dark to light brown with dorsal rows of sharp conical tubercles on the abdomen. These butterflies have a lazy type of flight until disturbed. They nectar frequently and perch on prominent twigs and flowers. The larvae overwinter; there is one brood per year. The Silver-bordered Fritillary flies from May 25 to August 27 with peak flight activity from early-to-mid-June to late July.

Range and Habitat. The Silver-bordered Fritillary is holarctic in distribution. In North America it ranges from Alaska south to New Mexico, through the Rocky Mountain states and across southern Canada and the northern United States to the maritime provinces and North Carolina. Many subspecies have been described from North America, with most representing ends and midpoints of clines. We were unable to assign a subspecies name that represents specimens from Alberta adequately, although extreme east-central populations have been assigned to *Boloria selene atrocostalis* (Kohler 1977). In Alberta, the Silver-bordered Fritillary is found in the aspen parkland and boreal zones. It occurs sporadically in undisturbed bogs and marshes, but may be abundant in moist aspen groves and disturbed bogs.

Euptoieta Doubleday, 1848

Etymology. In Greek *euptoietos* means "easily scared."

Identification. Butterflies of this genus are largely tropical and poorly studied. Six species are known from South America, with two species ranging north into Central and North America. The genus *Euptoieta* is usually placed in the Argynninae, but lacks some of the characters which help to define the subfamily. In some respects they may be more closely related to Heliconiinae, another nymphalid subfamily. *Euptoieta* spp. lack the silvering found on most argynnines; in the male genitalia, the unsclerotized area on the tegumen of the uncus is missing; and structure of the aedeagus and valvae is different. Both North American species are migratory and often travel great distances.

Euptoieta claudia (Cramer, [1775])
Variegated Fritillary

Etymology. This species may refer to any one of several Roman emperors named Claudius.

Identification. The dorsal surface of the Variegated Fritillary is brown and black like other fritillaries and exhibits a fairly clear separation between basal and marginal areas producing a distinctive pattern. The ventral wing surface is mixed mottled brown without silvering. The Variegated Fritillary has a distinctive pointed apex of the fore wing.

Life History. The caterpillar is reddish orange with longitudinal rows of black spines and alternating white and black dorsal patches. Two white stripes running along each side are periodically interrupted with black. The pupae are iridescent pearly white and marked with dark brown patches and points. Larvae feed on host plants from a wide range of families, including several species of violet (*Viola* spp.), stonecrop (*Sedum* spp.), Purslane (*Portulaca oleracea*) and others. The Variegated Fritillary is an immigrant that periodically enters Alberta. There is no evidence that this species overwinters, as it appears intolerant of temperatures below freezing in any life stage. Fresh specimens from local broods may appear any time from July through September. Records show specimens collected from June 4 to October 14. Adults are rapid fliers, nectaring at composites and other flowers.

Euptoieta claudia
Male dorsal

Euptoieta claudia
Male ventral

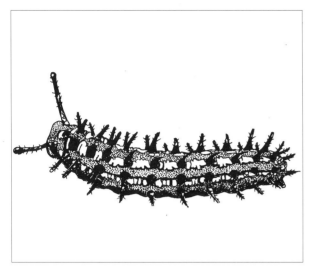

Euptoieta claudia larva

Range and Habitat. Year-round resident populations of the Variegated Fritillary are found in the southern United States and south through the tropics and subtropics of the Americas. As an immigrant, it is found from southern and central Canada through all of the United States into Central and South America to Argentina. In Alberta, dispersing individuals have been collected as far north as Fort McMurray, but are more commonly found in the southern prairie grasslands. *Euptoieta claudia* appears to favour habitats such as meadows, grasslands, fields and road allowances.

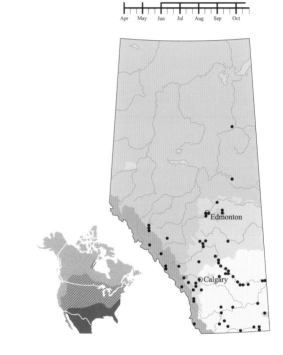

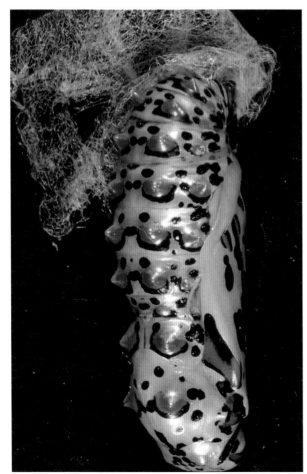

Pupa of *Euptoieta claudia*.   J. Scott.

Portulaca oleracea
Purslane

Speyeria Scudder, [1871]
GREATER FRITILLARIES

Etymology. *Speyeria* was named in honour of Adolph Speyer (1812-1892), a German lepidopterist.

Identification. Fritillaries are medium-to-large and characterized by brown ground colour, black spotting on the ventral fore wing and silvery spots on the ventral hind wing (lacking on some species). A dorsal unsclerotized area on the male genitalia is similar to the condition seen in members of *Boloria*, the lesser fritillaries. On the male genitalia, the aedeagus has a spiny "tongue" and a line of teeth at the inside base of the valvae.

Larvae look like those of a typical temperate nymphalid. In most species, the larvae feed on violets (*Viola* spp.). Adults are strong, swift fliers. Most species nectar on a variety of flowers, including thistles (*Cirsium* spp.) and bergamot (*Monarda* spp.). Males typically emerge from the pupae before the females.

Speyeria aphrodite (Fabricius, 1787)
Aphrodite Fritillary
subspecies: *Speyeria aphrodite manitoba* (Chermock and Chermock, 1940)

Etymology. This species is named after Aphrodite, the Greek goddess of love and beauty who sprang from the foam of the sea. The subspecies is named after the province of Manitoba.

Identification. The Aphrodite Fritillary is a large butterfly, often confused with the Atlantis Fritillary (*Speyeria atlantis*). Males are easily recognized because they lack the thickened black dorsal wing veins of the Atlantis Fritillary. Females have a dark reddish basal area on the fore wing that is reduced or absent in the Atlantis Fritillary. Many Aphrodite Fritillaries have orange or brown basal areas similar to those on the Great Spangled Fritillary (*S. cybele*) however they are not as bright in the former species.

Speyeria aphrodite manitoba
Male dorsal

Speyeria aphrodite manitoba
Male ventral

Speyeria aphrodite manitoba
Female dorsal

Speyeria aphrodite manitoba
Female ventral

Life History. The larvae are very similar to those of the Great Spangled Fritillary. Pupae are reddish brown or gray with mottling and black stripes. In the east, several species of violets (*Viola* spp.) are utilized as host plants. First instar larvae overwinter. Adult butterflies may be found patrolling edges of forests, road allowances and cutlines. They nectar occasionally on Alfalfa (*Medicago sativa*), bergamot (*Monarda* spp.) and yellow composites. The Aphrodite Fritillary has been observed from June 17 to August 25. Peak flight activity is in late July to early August. There is one brood per year.

Range and Habitat. The Aphrodite Fritillary is wide-ranging, from Georgia and Tennessee north to the Maritimes and Quebec, west to British Columbia and south in the Rocky Mountains to Colorado. One subspecies, *Speyeria aphrodite manitoba*, is recognized in Alberta. Intergrades with *Speyeria aphrodite ethne* (Hemming) occur in the southern prairies of Alberta. The Aphrodite Fritillary is an inhabitant of riparian forests, aspen woodlands, Jack Pine forests and native prairie grassland.

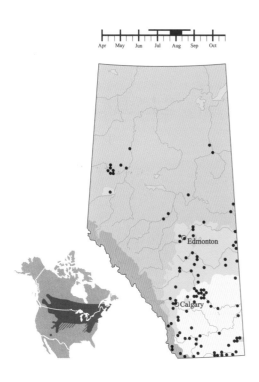

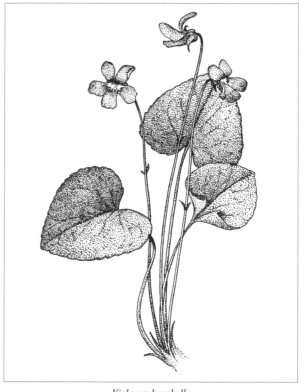

Viola nephrophylla
Bog Violet

Speyeria atlantis complex
Atlantis Fritillary
Speyeria atlantis (W.H. Edwards, 1862)
subspecies: *Speyeria atlantis hollandi* (Chermock and Chermock, 1940)

Speyeria electa (W.H. Edwards, 1878)
Northwestern Fritillary
subspecies: *Speyeria electa beani* (Barnes and Benjamin, 1926)
Speyeria electa lais (W.H. Edwards, 1884)

Etymology. Atlantis is derived from the name of the mythical lost continent of the Atlantic Ocean. Two of the subspecific names seem to be patronyms, *hollandi* most likely after W.J. Holland, a well known American lepidopterist; *beani* after T.E. Bean, a lepidopterist who collected extensively in the Lake Louise area. The name *electa* is most likely derived from the Greek Electra, considered to be the daughter of Atlas. *Lais* refers to two Greek courtesans.

Identification. Recent checklists and most books recognize one species in the *Speyeria atlantis* complex. Howe (1975) recognized separate eastern and western species and Klassen *et al.* (1989) agreed with this approach for Manitoba populations. We concur with the comment make by Moeck (1957): "...we cannot escape the uneasy thought that possibly there has been misde-termination of one or more valid species, now lumped in the complex." In Alberta it is quite clear that there are two distinct species lumped together as *Speyeria atlantis*. It is less clear just what names are correct to use according to the rules of nomenclature. This is due to uncertainty in American populations and whether or not *hollandi* is a species or a subspecies in relation to *atlantis*. The two species that occur in Alberta are: (1) a smaller butterfly with a reddish disc; and (2) a larger butterfly with a chocolate to blackish brown disc. The names used are *S. electa beani* and *S. atlantis hollandi*, respectively, following Howe (1975), Klassen *et al.* (1989) and Kondla (1992). Prior literature contains little information on the differences between these taxa. Forms of *S. atlantis hollandi* and *S. aphrodite* are frequently confused in the boreal forest of Alberta, Saskatchewan and Manitoba as well as in other parts of their range where populations are sympatric. *Speyeria* species, subspecies and populations are notoriously

Speyeria atlantis hollandi
Female ventral

Speyeria electa beani
Female ventral

Speyeria electa lais
Female ventral

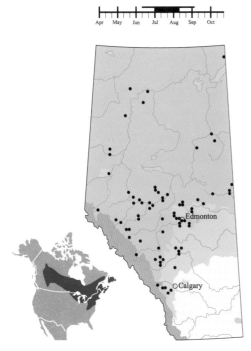

Speyeria atlantis hollandi

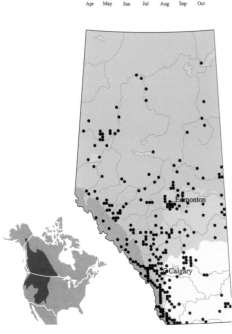

Speyeria electa

variable from one location to another. Consequently, descriptions and comparisons are valid only over defined parts of species ranges with similar ecological characteristics. Given the phenotypic, phenological and ecological differences between *S. electa beani* and *S. atlantis hollandi*, it makes good biological sense to treat them as separate species. Taxa with the scope of differences described herein, with extensive sympatry and with no published data to support the occasional allegation of hybridization, are normally accorded species status. In Alberta, the Atlantis Fritillary is morphologically variable. It is similar to the Aphrodite Fritillary (*S. aphrodite*) and Northwestern Fritillary (*S. electa*) but is duller and more heavily marked than either of these species. *S. atlantis hollandi* is larger (fore wing 30 mm, 32.5 mm) than *S. electa beani*. The discal area is dark, chocolate to blackish brown and the markings on the fore wing are wider. Ventrally, the hind wing margin is narrower and paler, the marginal silver triangles are generally larger and more broadly capped with blackish brown, the hind wing disc has areas with greenish-blue scales, the median silver spots are strongly bordered with dark spots and the hind wing submarginal band is crossed by dark veins. Dorsally, the marginal band is broader and mostly black. In the males the dorsal fore wing veins have broad black scaling.

Life History. Eggs are laid where violets (*Viola* spp.), the reported larval host plants, will grow in the spring. First instar larvae overwinter. Larvae are dark brown dorsally and lighter below. Many spines have orange on them. The pupae are brown with lighter transverse bands on the abdomen, somewhat mottled in appearance. Adults of *atlantis* are on the wing from June 10 through September 3 with peak flight activity in July and early August. Adults of *electa* are on the wing from May 20 to September 22 with main flight activity in late June and July. Adults patrol forest edges and fly up and down cutlines. They readily nectar at yellow composites. There is one brood per year.

Range and Habitat. The Atlantis Fritillary ranges from the Maritimes and New England states, south in the Appalachian Mountains to Virginia, west across the northern states and southern Canada to British Columbia and south in the Rocky Mountains to Arizona and New Mexico.

Speyeria callippe (Boisduval, 1852)
Callippe Fritillary
subspecies: *Speyeria callippe calgariana* (McDunnough, 1924)

Etymology. In Latin, Callippus is a man's name. The subspecies name is derived from Calgary, the city near the type locality of Pine Creek.

Identification. The Callippe Fritillary is highly variable over its range; however, in Alberta, it is relatively uniform. The ground colour of the dorsal wing surface is light orange and dark brown and the ventral surface has many large silver spots. In this respect, it is similar to the Edwards' Fritillary (*Speyeria edwardsii*) except that adult *S. callippe* are smaller and the ventral surface is lighter green, or almost grayish in some specimens. Silver spots in the postmedian submarginal band are elongated. Androconia are present in males. Females have a brighter red-brown patch at the base of the ventral fore wing. *S. c. calgariana* has a light greenish ventral hind wing disc.

Life History. Eggs are laid near dried-up violets (*Viola* spp.). The blue prairie violet (*Viola* sp.) is the favourite host plant in Alberta. First instar larvae overwinter and feed on new vegetation in the spring. The larvae are gray with a dark dorsal line and dark patches at the base of the spines. The head is black. Male Callippe Fritillaries patrol bluffs and hill tops. Females usually nectar on plants such as Alfalfa (*Medicago sativa*) along roadsides. This species has been recorded from June 6 to September 17 with peak flight activity in late June and July.

Range and Habitat. The Callippe Fritillary occurs from southern Manitoba south to Colorado and west to the Pacific coast. In Alberta the subspecies *Speyeria callippe calgariana* is widespread from Edmonton southwards across the prairies. Butterflies of this species in the Crowsnest Pass are more similar to *Speyeria callippe semivirida* (McDunnough) which occurs from British Columbia to northeastern California.

Speyeria callippe calgariana
Male dorsal

Speyeria callippe calgariana
Female ventral

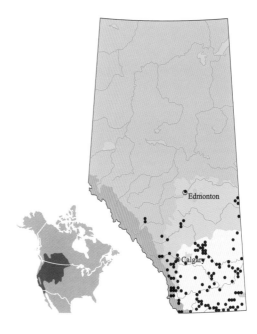

Speyeria coronis (Behr, 1864)
Coronis Fritillary

Etymology. The species name may be from the Latin *corona* meaning "crown."

Identification. *Speyeria coronis* is a large butterfly that is easily confused with *Speyeria aphrodite* and *Speyeria zerene*. On the hind wing of *S. coronis*, the silver spots are distinctly rounded, whereas they are more pointed in *S. aphrodite*, which also has more elongate discal spots (see page 259). The Coronis Fritillary is typically larger than the Zerene Fritillary.

Life History. In Montana, this butterfly is on the wing from late May through mid-August.

Range and Habitat. *Speyeria coronis* occurs throughout much of the western United States from Nebraska and South Dakota to the Pacific and north to northern Montana (Toole County). Taxonomic confusion with other species also obscures information on the limits of this butterfly's range. The probability of occurrence in Alberta is high. *Speyeria coronis* should be watched for on shrubby hillsides in southern Alberta.

Speyeria coronis
Female dorsal

Speyeria coronis
Female ventral

Speyeria cybele (Fabricius, 1775)
Great Spangled Fritillary
subspecies: *Speyeria cybele leto* (Behr, 1862)
Speyeria cybele pseudocarpenterii (Chermock and Chermock, 1940)

Etymology. The Great Spangled Fritillary is named after Cybele, a Greek earth goddess. Leto was another Greek goddess, and the mother of the deities Apollo and Artemis. The subspecies is from *pseudo,* meaning "false or deceptive," hence similar to *carpenterii.*

Identification. Our largest fritillary is easily recognized by the solid brown basal area on the dorsal surface. The ventral surface also has a darker basal area. Females are larger and more heavily marked than males. *Speyeria cybele leto* is recognized by the reduced submarginal spots on its ventral hind wing and the pale, almost white, dorsal appearance of the females.

Life History. Eggs are laid on or near violets (*Viola* spp.). Larvae hatch and overwinter without feeding, until the following spring, and are nocturnal feeders. The mature caterpillars are black dorsally, chocolate-brown ventrally and covered with black spines that are yellow at the base. There is a pair of transverse dots between each dorsal pair of spines. Pupal colour is variable, dark brown and mottled with red-orange or light brown. Both males and females patrol edges of forests, road allowances and seismic cut lines. They nectar at a variety of flowers: composites, Alfalfa (*Medicago sativa*), bergamot (*Monarda* spp.), thistles (*Cirsium* spp.) and milkweed (*Asclepias* spp.). Flight dates have been recorded from June 14 to September 8. Peak flight activity is in July. There is one brood per year.

Range and Habitat. The Great Spangled Fritillary ranges from coast to coast in Canada and the United States, from Georgia to California in the south and British Columbia to the Maritimes in the north. Two subspecies are represented in Alberta, *S. c. leto* of southern Alberta and the foothills westward into British Columbia, and *S. c. pseudocarpenterii* of the Great Plains region. These two subspecies intergrade along the eastern slopes of the Rocky Mountains. The Great Spangled Fritillary is associated with grasslands and open areas, including prairie coulees, edges of riparian forests, meadows, edges of pasture land and cutlines in coniferous forests.

Speyeria cybele leto
Female dorsal

Speyeria cybele pseudocarpenterii
Female dorsal

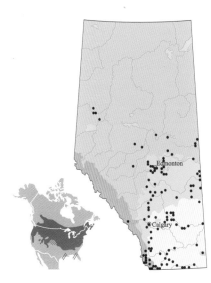

Speyeria edwardsii (Reakirt, 1866)
Edwards' Fritillary

Speyeria edwardsii
Male dorsal

Speyeria edwardsii
Male ventral

Apr May Jun Jul Aug Sep Oct

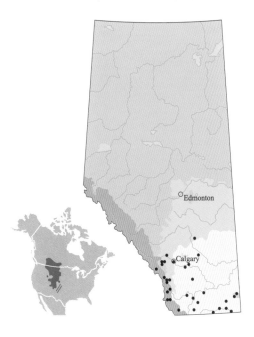

Etymology. This species is named in honour of W.H. Edwards.

Identification. Edwards' Fritillary is large with two rows of light brown spots on a darker brown background on the dorsal wing surface. Ventrally, the hind wing is heavily silvered between the silver spots. Ventral hind wing veins are distinctly brown. The wings are more pointed in this species than in most other *Speyeria*. Males have androconia on the fore wings and there is often a greenish shade to the hind wings.

Life History. Eggs are usually laid in August near locations where violets (*Viola* spp.) will grow in the spring. First instar larvae overwinter and feed on the new growth of violets the following spring. Larvae are yellow and gray with a black median line. Several different colours (black and white, gray-green and yellow) are present around the base of the spines. The head is brownish black and lighter posteriorly. The pupae are a mottled brownish yellow with gray on the abdomen and a dark jagged strip at the anterior edge of each abdominal segment. In Colorado, Edwards' Fritillary is reported to feed on Yellow Prairie Violet (*Viola nuttalli*). Adults have been observed nectaring at Alfalfa (*Medicago sativa*). *Speyeria edwardsii* appears to be relatively long-lived, as flight records extend from May 30 to September 12. One brood is present per year. Peak flight activity is in mid-June to late July

Range and Habitat. Edwards' Fritillary is found on the Great Plains of North America from Manitoba, Saskatchewan and Alberta in the north, to Nebraska and Colorado in the south. In Alberta, this species occurs in the southern portion of the province including the foothills and Cypress Hills. It may be encountered in riparian forests, meadows and clearings.

Speyeria egleis (Behr, 1862)
Egleis Fritillary

Etymology. The origin of *egleis* is obscure.

Identification. This species is most likely to be confused with *Speyeria callippe*. The ventral hind wing disc is olive-green; the ventral fore wing basal area is slightly orange whereas this orange flush is quite pronounced on other *Speyeria*. The dorsal surface is fairly dark but not diffuse or smoky and is usually a two-tone orange colour that is dull in comparison with the bright orange of *S. callippe* and other Alberta *Speyeria*.

Life History. The flight period in Montana is late May to the end of August.

Range and Habitat. *Speyeria egleis* has a similar but more extensive range than that of *S. coronis* and has been recorded from Montana in every county that borders Alberta. The probability of occurrence in Alberta is high; it has likely been collected here but misidentified. The Egleis Fritillary frequents roadsides, meadows and stream banks. It should be expected in southern Alberta.

Speyeria egleis
Male dorsal

Speyeria egleis
Male ventral

Speyeria egleis
Female dorsal

Speyeria egleis
Female ventral

255

Speyeria hydaspe (Boisduval, 1869)
Hydaspe Fritillary
subspecies: *Speyeria hydaspe sakuntala* (Skinner, 1911a)

Speyeria hydaspe sakuntala
Male dorsal

Speyeria hydaspe sakuntala
Female ventral

Etymology. This species may be named after the Hydaspes River of India, a tributary of the Indus. The origin of *sakuntala*, however, is obscure.

Identification. The Hydaspe Fritillary may be recognized by the purplish basal colour and wide band between the rows of silver spots on the ventral hind wing.

Life History. Larvae are nearly black and lack a dorsal stripe. Dorsal spines are black and lateral spines are yellowish orange darkening to brown at the base. Like other *Speyeria*, first instar larvae overwinter. Host plants are several species of violets (*Viola* spp.). Hydaspe Fritillaries have been observed from June 20 to September 7 with peak flight activity in late July and early August. Adults are strong fliers and are often seen nectaring on yellow composites. There is one brood per year.

Range and Habitat. The Hydaspe Fritillary is found from southern Alberta and British Columbia, south through the Rocky Mountain states to New Mexico. In Alberta, the species is found in the southern mountain and foothill regions. Seven subspecies are recognized, most of which are geographically isolated from each other. Alberta material is referred to *Speyeria hydaspe sakuntala*. The Hydaspe Fritillary may be seen in mountain meadows, clearings and along roads.

Speyeria mormonia (Boisduval, 1869)
Mormon Fritillary
subspecies: *Speyeria mormonia eurynome* (W.H. Edwards, 1872a)

Etymology. This species may be named after the early Mormon settlers of Utah and Nevada. The subspecies may be from the Greek *euryno*, meaning "to make broad."

Identification. Our smallest fritillary is highly variable, often without the silver spotting that characterizes other members of this genus. It has crisp black markings on the dorsal wing surfaces that are narrow compared to other *Speyeria*. The ground colour on both wing surfaces is usually light, although it can be quite dark in specimens from the northern Rocky Mountains.

Life History. Larvae probably feed on violets (*Viola* spp.). One larva, collected at 2158 m at Horn Ridge in the Torrens River area, was over 243 m above treeline, where there were no violets. Alpine Poppy (*Papaver kluanensis*), Moss Campion (*Silene acaulis*), Mountain Avens (*Dryas octopetala*), vetches (Leguminosae) and saxifrages (*Saxifraga* spp.) were the major plant species in the area, so we suspect an alternate host was being used. The larvae are almost black with a broad pale mid-dorsal stripe. The spines are lighter in colour. First instar larvae are reported to overwinter. Favourite nectar sources are thistles (*Cirsium* spp.) in southern Alberta, bergamot (*Monarda* spp.) in central regions and legumes (Leguminosae) in the mountains and foothills. Adults fly strongly when disturbed. The Mormon Fritillary has been observed from June 2 to September 24. At low elevations peak activity is in early July, while at higher elevations peak flight is in late July to mid-August. There is one brood per year.

Range and Habitat. Mormon Fritillaries range from Alaska, south along the Rocky Mountains to Colorado and central California and east to Manitoba with strays reported from Minnesota. Alberta material is difficult to place; many specimens from mountainous regions are similar to both *S. m. opis* (W.H. Edwards) and *S. m. bischoffii* (W.H. Edwards). *S. m. eurynome* is the name associated with specimens from the boreal region and most of the Rocky Mountain region. It occurs throughout much of boreal Alberta and the mountain and foothill areas. Habitats vary from prairie grassland, mixed forest in the foothills, forest openings and along water courses in the mountains to alpine meadows.

Speyeria mormonia eurynome
Male dorsal

Speyeria mormonia eurynome
Male ventral

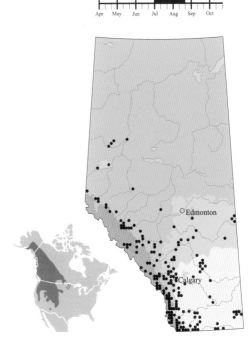

Speyeria zerene (Boisduval, 1852)
Zerene Fritillary
subspecies: *Speyeria zerene garretti* (Gunder, 1932b)

Speyeria zerene garretti
Male dorsal

Speyeria zerene garretti
Female ventral

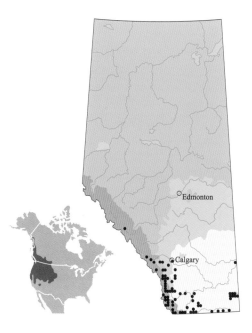

Etymology. This species name is derived from the Latin *zerena*, meaning "to parch or dry up," in reference to the dry southern California habitat in which the butterfly was first collected. The subspecies was named after C. Garrett, collector of the type specimens.

Identification. The Zerene Fritillary is large with dorsal and ventral surfaces of the fore wing having bold, wide, black markings. Females are quite dark, more black than orange. Males have androconia. The ventral surface has silvered spots, with little silvering outside the spots. The basal area of the ventral wing surface is a darker brown than the wing margins. Silvered spots of the submarginal band are more round than triangular. *Speyeria zerene* is likely to be confused with *S. coronis* in southern Alberta and Montana east of the Rocky Mountains. The table on the following page lists characters that help distinguish between these two species.

Life History. The larvae have a dark mid-dorsal line and dark blackish patches near the bases of the spines. A ventral eversible gland is present. First instar larvae overwinter. Violets (*Viola* spp.) are larval host plants. The Zerene Fritillary has been collected from June 8 to September 19. Peak flight activity is in July and August with egg-laying in August. Males use a hilltopping strategy to find females. There is one brood per year.

Range and Habitat. The Zerene Fritillary ranges from southwestern Saskatchewan west to the Pacific coast and south to California and Nebraska. In Alberta, the subspecies is *Speyeria zerene garretti*, which is found from Jasper south along the mountains and foothills. The Zerene Fritillary is found in clearings and meadows of the mountains and foothills (including the Cypress Hills) and riparian forests extending out onto the prairies.

Differentiation Between *Speyeria zerene* and *Speyeria coronis*

Speyeria zerene

Speyeria zerene garrettii
Female ventral

Speyeria coronis

Speyeria coronis
Female ventral

Creamy/dull yellow ventral hind wing submarginal band usually with some suffusion of cinnamon or light brown scales.

Slightly smaller (in series).

Ventral hind wing marginal triangles boldly capped by cinnamon brown scales.

Ventral hind wing submarginal band invaded proximally by cinnamon brown spots in most individuals.

Ventral hind wing disc dark cinnamon or light brown with areas on some individuals suffused with yellow or greenish scales.

Brighter straw yellow ventral hind wing submarginal band with no suffusion of darker scales (except in females which may have some dusting of dark scales).

Slightly larger (in series).

Ventral hind wing marginal triangles with ghost caps of pale green.

Ventral hind wing submarginal band invaded proximally by light green ghost spots; this, plus the previous character, make the submarginal band look wider than that of *S. zerene*.

Ventral hind wing disc light yellowish brown or greenish brown.

Subfamily
MELITAEINAE
CHECKERSPOTS

Members of this subfamily are commonly called checkerspots because of the squarish, black-outlined white patches on the ventral wing surfaces of most species (e.g., *Charidryas* and *Euphydryas* spp.). These markings are not as striking in the genus *Phyciodes*, whose members are instead called crescents because of the conspicuous white crescent-shaped spot on the ventral hind wing. There are 11 species of melitaeines in Alberta.

Euphydryas anicia at Castle River falls, Alberta.   G.J. Hilchie.

Charidryas Scudder, 1871
CHECKERSPOTS

Etymology. The generic name is composed of two Greek roots, *charis* meaning "delight" and *dryas* meaning "wood nymph."

Identification. *Charidryas* species have smooth wing margins and both dorsal and ventral wing surfaces are checkered orange and black. There can be substantial black dusting of the basal region of the dorsal wing surfaces, or it can be lacking. There is a clear orange marginal band in three of our four species and a distinct cream- or silver-coloured median band on the ventral surface.

The classification of this group of species is subject to considerable variation, as some lepidopterists split them into as many as three genera. In our more conservative classification we use *Charidryas* for the Alberta species.

Checkerspots reach their greatest diversity in the tropics, with modest numbers in the southwestern United States. Only a few species reach north into Alberta.

Charidryas acastus (W.H. Edwards, 1874)
Acastus Checkerspot

Etymology. Acastus was the son of Pelias, king of Thessaly.

Identification. The Acastus Checkerspot is medium-sized with bright silvery-white spotting on the ventral wing surface and a uniform orange and black checkering on the dorsal wing surface. This species is most similar to *Charidryas palla*, the Northern Checkerspot, but lacks the cream-coloured ventral spotting and two-toned orange ground colour on the dorsal surface typical of *C. palla*.

Life History. Eggs are laid in groups and the larvae feed communally until the third instar. Mature larvae are solitary. *Charidryas acastus* larvae, which are similar to those of *C. palla* are black with orange spots below the spiracles and have shiny black spines with fine white spots. Larvae outside Alberta feed on a variety of plants, including rabbit-brush (*Chrysothamnus* spp.), *Aster* spp. and *Machaeranthera* spp. In Alberta, larvae are known to feed on *Machaeranthera canescens*. Adults nectar at thistles (*Cirsium* spp.) and a variety of other flowers. They readily perch on the ground and small shrubs. Flight is strong and swift. Adults have been recorded from May 8 to September 5 with peak flight activity in late June through July. The larvae are believed to overwinter.

Range and Habitat. *Charidryas acastus* ranges from New Mexico and California north to Alberta and Saskatchewan. In Alberta, it occurs on the prairies. The Acastus Checkerspot favours badlands-type terrain along rivers and coulees in southern Alberta.

Charidryas acastus
Female dorsal

Charidryas acastus
Female ventral

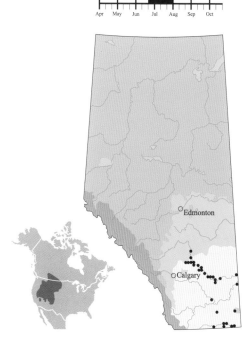

261

Charidryas damoetas (Skinner, 1902)
Rockslide Checkerspot
subspecies: *Charidryas damoetas damoetas* (Skinner, 1902)

Charidryas damoetas damoetas
Male dorsal

Charidryas damoetas damoetas
Male ventral

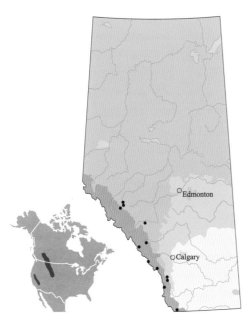

Etymology. Damoetas is the name of a shepherd in Latin and Greek.

Identification. The Rockslide Checkerspot is medium-sized with a heavy basal dusting of black making it look dingy. The ventral hind wing has regular black bands, particularly the submarginal band. It is easily confused with the larger Northern Checkerspot (*Charidryas palla*) but is found in a different habitat.

Life History. Oviposition is reported on Fleabane (*Erigeron leiomerus*) and Alpine Goldenrod (*Solidago multiradiata*). The life cycle is biennial with the larvae overwintering. Adults fly over rocky terrain and alight with open wings to sunbathe. They nectar on flowers above and below rockslides. The flight period in Alberta is from June 27 to August 5 with peak activity in July.

Range and Habitat. Rockslide Checkerspots occur from southern Alberta and British Columbia, south to Colorado along the Rocky Mountains and Colorado massif. A disjunct population is found in the Sierra Nevada Mountains. In Alberta it is found in the mountains south of the Athabasca River. Alberta material is placed with the nominate subspecies, *Charidryas damoetas damoetas*. The Rockslide Checkerspot is associated with scree slopes and rockslides in the mountains. Adults may be observed easily where creeks, railroads and roadways cut across rockslide areas.

Solidago multiradiata
Alpine Goldenrod

Charidryas gorgone (Hübner, 1810)
Gorgone Checkerspot
subspecies: *Charidryas gorgone carlota* (Reakirt, 1866)

Etymology. We are not certain if the species was named after Gorgons, daughter of Forkys, king of the sea in Greek mythology, or the Gorgons, three monstrous sisters, the most famous of whom was Medusa. The subspecies name may be a patronym.

Identification. The Gorgone Checkerspot is small and recognized by the sinuous nature of the silvery submarginal and median bands of the ventral hind wing. The dorsal surface is a checkered orange and black with white marginal checkering.

Life History. Outside of Alberta, larvae are reported to feed communally on many composites including *Aster* spp. and sunflowers (*Helianthus* spp.). Larvae are spiny with black heads and yellow bodies with black lateral and dorsal stripes. The pupae are mottled gray. In Alberta the Gorgone Checkerspot is known to fly from May 6 to July 15. Peak flight activity is in June. There is one brood per year; the larvae overwinter.

Range and Habitat. The Gorgone Checkerspot ranges from Alberta in the north, south and east across the Great Plains to the Mississippi Valley, with isolated populations scattered through the Appalachian Mountains. This butterfly is found on the prairies of south and central Alberta and in the Peace River grasslands. Alberta material is referred to *Charidryas gorgone carlota*. The Gorgone Checkerspot is a resident of open areas, primarily prairie grasslands. It is seldom abundant.

Charidryas gorgone carlota
Male dorsal

Charidryas gorgone carlota
Male ventral

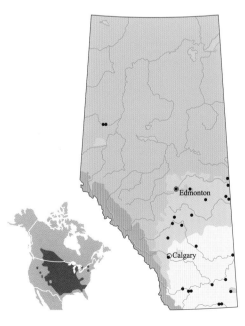

Helianthus rhomboideus
Rhombic-leaved Sunflower

Aster laevis
Smooth Aster

Charidryas palla (Boisduval, 1852)
Northern Checkerspot

Charidryas palla
Female dorsal

Charidryas palla
Female ventral

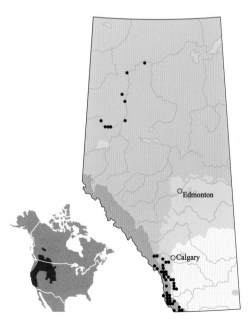

Etymology. The name comes from *palla*, a long wide upper garment of Roman ladies that was held together by broaches.

Identification. The Northern Checkerspot is medium-sized and may be separated from the Pearly Checkerspot (*Charidryas acastus*) and the Rockslide Checkerspot (*C. damoetas*) by the two-tone ground colour on the dorsal wing surfaces. Ventrally, the light bands are cream or yellow. Material from the Peace River district is lighter and more faded with cream-coloured areas enlarged and the ground colour on both surfaces lighter.

Life History. Larvae of the nominate subspecies in California are black and spiny with orange and white spots. Larval hosts are composites, *Aster* spp., fleabane (*Erigeron* spp.), rabbit-brush (*Chrysothamnus* spp.) and others. Adults may be seen sunning on composite flowers in mountain meadows. In southern Alberta, *C. palla* flies from June 19 to August 6 with peak activity in late June through July. Limited collections in the north show flight activity from June 10 to June 22. There is one brood per year; the larvae overwinter.

Range and Habitat. Northern Checkerspots are found in all the western mountain states and provinces except Alaska. Many populations appear isolated and have been given many subspecies names. Howe (1975) applied the subspecies name *calydon* (Holland) to all Rocky Mountain material including specimens from Alberta, but many populations are not phenotypically *calydon*. *C. palla* is found in the mountains and north to Fort Vermilion in the Peace River district. This checkerspot may be seen in mountain meadows and on the prairies of the Peace River area.

Charidryas palla
male dorsal

Charidryas palla
male ventral

Euphydryas Scudder, [1871]
CHECKERSPOTS

Etymology. The name is derived from the Greek *euphys*, meaning "shapely, comely" and *dryas*, meaning "wood nymph."

Identification. *Euphydryas* species are small-to-medium-sized butterflies. The genus has been split into a number of genera in recent years, but in our opinion the changes have not been justified. We recognize one genus whose species are characterized by the relatively smooth wing margins, pointed fore wing and the presence of distinct orange bands on the dorsal wing surfaces and the ventral hind wing. They are bright orange and black on both surfaces. Species in our area are montane to alpine, with one species found in the Cypress Hills.

Euphydryas anicia (Doubleday, [1847])
Anicia Checkerspot
subspecies: *Euphydryas anicia anicia* (Doubleday, [1847])

Etymology. The name is derived from *anicianus*, adjective; pertaining to Anicius, named after him.

Identification. The Anicia Checkerspot is medium-sized with rounded, oblong fore wings and the dorsal surface banded with brick red and cream in the centre. The ventral fore wing has a weak cream-coloured sub-marginal band that usually deteriorates towards the trailing edge. Many specimens are difficult to distinguish from Edith's Checkerspot (*Euphydryas editha*) except by genitalic dissection. In general, though, Edith's Checkerspot is smaller and more "banded" on the dorsal wing surfaces.

Euphydryas anicia anicia
Male dorsal

Euphydryas anicia anicia
Male ventral

Life History. Larvae are reported to feed on beard-tongue (*Penstemon* spp.), paintbrush (*Castilleja* spp.) and members of the plantain family (Plantaginaceae) and the borage family (Boraginaceae). Adults are weak fliers. They are seen frequently sunning on roadsides where they puddle at damp spots. They nectar on yellow flowers. These butterflies have an extended flight period reflecting elevation-related differences in development and emergence times. Flight records are from May 17 to September 11, with most in June and July. There is one brood per year; the larvae overwinter.

Euphydryas anicia anicia
Female dorsal

265

Euphydryas anicia anicia
Female ventral

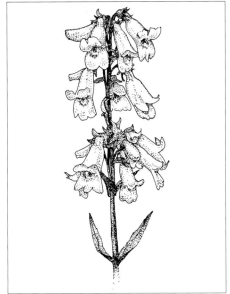

Penstemon gracilis
Lilac-coloured Beard-tongue

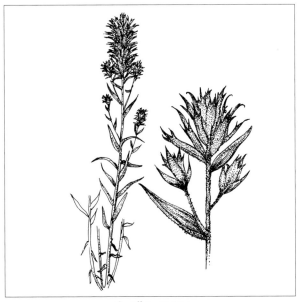

Castilleja miniata
Indian Paint-brush

Range and Habitat. The Anicia Checkerspot is distributed from central Alaska and the Yukon Territory south in the mountains of western North America to Arizona and New Mexico. Alberta material is *Euphydryas anicia anicia*. In Alberta, it occurs in the mountain and foothill regions and the Cypress Hills. In the mountains, the Anicia Checkerspot rarely strays above treeline. *Euphydryas anicia anicia* was presumably described from specimens collected at Rock Lake, Alberta. Whether or not *E. anicia* is a species distinct from *E. chalcedona* (Doubleday) has been the subject of some debate in the literature. Brussard *et al.* (1989) reported that, on the basis of gel electrophoresis of some western populations, the two should be viewed as conspecific with *chalcedona* the senior name. The populations they studied were in Oregon and Colorado, about 1000 and 1400 km from the type locality in Alberta. Consequently, we decline to follow their taxonomic recommendation pending confirmation using specimens from Alberta populations and those linking the populations they studied.

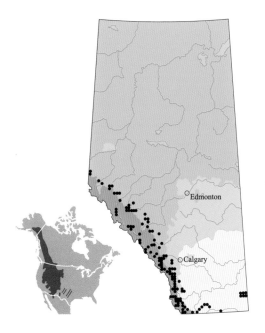

Euphydryas editha (Boisduval, 1852)
Edith's Checkerspot
subspecies: ***Euphydryas editha beani*** (Skinner, 1897)
Euphydryas editha near ***hutchinsi*** McDunnough, 1928a

Etymology. The name is from Edith, a woman's proper name. The subspecies is also a patronym, from Thomas Bean of Laggan, now Lake Louise, Alberta. The subspecific name hutchinsi is a patronym from R.E. Hutchins, the collector of the holotype and an active collector in Montana in the 1920s.

Identification. Edith's Checkerspot is small and morphologically similar to the Anicia Checkerspot. It may be distinguished by its small size and the duskier appearance of the ventral surface. In *E. editha*, the ventral fore wing has two clear white spots in the discal cell and one below it. *Euphydryas editha hutchinsi* is larger than *E.e. beani* and looks radically different. It is placed here only for the sake of conformance with the literature. The only evidence for conspecificity is genitalic and this is not conclusive.

Life History. Larvae are black with black and white stripes and are speckled with white and orange. Larvae overwinter during the final instar. The number of instars appears to be variable. Many host plants are reported, including plantain (*Plantago* spp.), paintbrush (*Castilleja* spp.), owl-clover (*Orthocarpus* spp.) and lousewort (*Pedicularis* spp.). Adults fly strongly and low over the ground. They perch on composites and forget-me-nots (*Myosotis* spp.). Adults have been observed from June 20 to August 12, with peak flight activity in July. There is one brood per year.

Range and Habitat. Edith's Checkerspot is found in the mountains of Alberta and in the Cypress Hills south to Mexico. Twenty geographically isolated subspecies are commonly recognized. Alberta material from the mountains is given the name *Euphydryas editha beani*. The subspecies "near *hutchinsi*" is found in the Cypress Hills. This checkerspot frequents alpine tundra and dry mountain meadows at higher elevations.

Euphydryas editha beani
Male dorsal

Euphydryas editha beani
Male ventral

Orthocarpus luteus
Owl-clover

Plantago major
Common Plantain

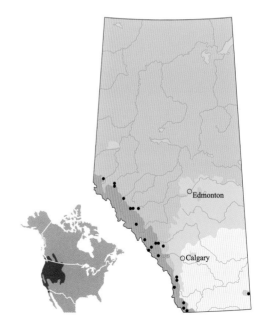

Differentiation Between
Euphydryas editha near *hutchinsi* and *Euphydryas anicia*

Euphydryas editha nr. *hutchinsi*
Male dorsal

Euphydryas anicia
Male dorsal

Euphydryas editha nr. *hutchinsi*
Male ventral

Euphydryas anicia
Male ventral

Euphydryas editha near *hutchinsi*	*Euphydryas anicia*
Pale areas mostly dull white.	Pale areas mostly creamy white.
Fore wing more rounded.	Fore wing more pointed.
Smoothly banded (i.e., regular curvature of spot bands).	Irregularly banded.
Ventral fore wing whitish, little red.	Ventral fore wing mostly red.
Generally smaller but much variation.	Larger.
Dorsal fore wing with two substantial white submarginal bands.	Dorsal fore wing with innermost submarginal band pale and wide, outermost submarginal band narrow and mostly reddish.
Ventral hind wing pale median band and orange post-median band separated by double black lines that in some individuals form a thick black line*.	Ventral hind wing pale median band and orange post-median band separated by single black line (although some females are more like *hutchinsi* in this character).

*NOTE:
This character also helps to separate *beani* from *anicia*.

Euphydryas gillettii (Barnes, 1897)
Gillett's Checkerspot

Etymology. This species was named after Clarence P. Gillett, who was an entomologist at Colorado State University, Fort Collins, Colorado from 1891 to his death in 1941.

Identification. Gillett's Checkerspot is medium-sized with a wide reddish-orange submarginal band on the dorsal and ventral surfaces.

Life History. Yellow eggs are deposited on Bracted Honeysuckle (*Lonicera involucrata*), snowberry (*Symphoricarpos* spp.) and Heliotrope (*Valeriana occidentalis*). Larvae overwinter in the third or fourth instar, resuming development the following spring. Fifth instar larvae are dingy yellow with a lateral brown stripe, white spiracular stripes, and a lemon-yellow mid-dorsal stripe. Tubercles are black. Adults tend to be weak fliers and feed and perch on yellow composites. Gillett's Checkerspot flight records are from June 16 to August 7 with most records in late June and July. There is one brood per year.

Range and Habitat. Gillett's Checkerspot is found from Nordegg south in the mountains of Alberta to Wyoming and Idaho. This species prefers mountain meadows and clearings. Alberta is one of only a few places this species is commonly encountered. Lepidopterists visit Alberta from across North America to collect this species.

Euphydryas gillettii
Female dorsal

Euphydryas gillettii
Female dorsal

Symphoricarpos occidentalis
Buckbrush

Lonicera involucrata
Bracted Honeysuckle

Phyciodes Hübner, 1819
CRESCENTSPOTS

Etymology. The generic name may be from the Greek *phykos*, meaning "painted" or "covered with cosmetics."

Identification. This genus is composed of bright black and orange butterflies of small-to-medium size with a white crescent-shaped mark at the margin of the ventral hind wing.

Phyciodes batesii (Reakirt, 1865)
Tawny Crescent
subspecies: *Phyciodes batesii lakota* Scott, 1994

Phyciodes batesii
Male dorsal

Phyciodes batesii
Male ventral

Phyciodes batesii
Female dorsal

Apr　May　Jun　Jul　Aug　Sep　Oct

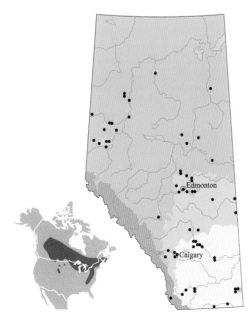

Etymology. This butterfly was named for Henry W. Bates, 1820-1892, an assistant secretary of the Royal Geographical Society, and the lepidopterist after whom Batesian Mimicry became known. The subspecies was named after the Lakota Indians.

Identification. The Tawny Crescent is a small orange-brown butterfly with wide black dorsal margins and black lines crossing the dorsal orange areas. Below, the fore wing has a black patch on the hind margin and black patches near the costa and outer edge. The underside of the hind wing is yellowish orange with some brown; females more frequently have a white and brown mixture.

Life History. Eggs are laid in batches on the undersides of leaves. First and second instar larvae live communally in webs on the host plant. Third instar larvae overwinter. Various species of *Aster* are used as larval host plants. The pupae are brown, often with a pinkish tinge, with a broad pale stripe on the back. Adults have been found on the wing from June 6 to July 29, with peak activity in the last half of June. There is one brood per year.

Range and Habitat. The Tawny Crescent occurs in north-central North America, from northeastern British Columbia east to Ontario and Quebec and southeast to Nebraska with isolated populations in the eastern states. In Alberta, it occurs in the Peace River region with scattered records in the boreal forest north to about 57°, and in suitable habitats throughout the aspen parkland and prairie. It is generally found in mesic habitats. In the north, these are deciduous forests, sand dune areas and breaks of the Peace River. In the south, favoured habitats are wooded and shrubby river valleys and coulees, and aspen groves and shrubby areas in the aspen parkland.

Phyciodes cocyta (Cramer, 1777)
Northern Pearl Crescent

Etymology. The name of this species is derived from "cocytus," a river of the lower world.

Identification. The Northern Pearl Crescent is small (fore wing 16-20 mm) and coloured orange and black with broad black borders. Females are darker than males. The underside is yellowish orange and the ventral hind wing has a darker brown patch that encompasses the crescent mark. It can be distinguished from the similar Pearl Crescent (*P. tharos*) by its larger size, wide, solid black upper wing margin and more extensive orange areas on the upper side of the fore wing. For many years this species was confused with *P. tharos* and has been treated in the literature as *P. tharos*, *P. morpheus* (Fabricius), *P. pratensis* (Behr) and *P. tharos* "type B." Scott (1994) has clarified the nomenclature.

Life History. The eggs are pale green and are laid in clusters on leaves of *Aster* spp. Larvae are chocolate brown with cream markings. Pupae are cream with brownish streaks. Adults freely nectar on *Aster* spp. and goldenrod (*Solidago* spp.). The species is single-brooded; larvae overwinter. Adults fly from May 17 to September 1, with peak activity in June and July, depending on latitude, elevation and seasonal variations in climate.

Range and Habitat. The Northern Pearl Crescent ranges across the northern forested areas of North America and south along the Rocky Mountains to Arizona and New Mexico. In Alberta, this species occurs throughout the forested areas and in a few grassland locations. Northern Pearl Crescents are found in shrubby areas, moist grasslands near trees, poplar forests and at lower elevations in the mountains.

Phyciodes cocyta
Male dorsal

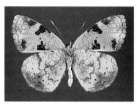

Phyciodes cocyta
Male ventral

Phyciodes cocyta
Female dorsal

Phyciodes cocyta
Female ventral

Apr May Jun Jul Aug Sep Oct

Aster laevis
Smooth Aster

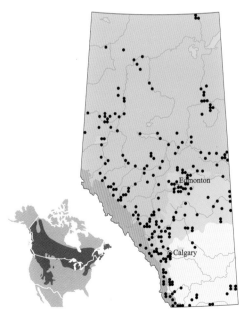

Phyciodes pulchella (Boisduval, 1852)
Field Crescent

Etymology. The species name is derived from a latin adjective meaning "cute little."

Phyciodes pulchella
Male dorsal

Phyciodes pulchella
Male ventral

Phyciodes pulchella
Female dorsal

Phyciodes pulchella
Female ventral

Identification. The Field Crescent is small, black and orange and similar to the Tawny Crescent (*P. batesii*), but with more black on the dorsal wing surfaces. Females often have yellowish orange patches on the dorsal wing surface but these are uniformly orange in males. The ventral fore wing has fewer and smaller black patches. The male ventral hind wing is yellowish orange with a vague marginal brown patch containing a light crescent. The female ventral hind wing is most often checkered white and brown. This species has been listed in contemporary works under the name *P. campestris* (Behr) and *P. pratensis*. Scott (1994) has clarified the nomenclature.

Life History. Eggs are pale yellow to green and laid on the undersides of leaves. Larvae feed on *Aster* spp. and are blackish brown with black heads. Pupae are creamy brown with mottling and dorsal bumps. Adults nectar on *Aster* spp. but also use a variety of other nectar sources, especially ragwort (*Senecio* spp.). The flight period is June 15 to August 30. Field Crescents are most abundant in July. There is one brood per year; the larvae overwinter.

Range and Habitat. The Field Crescent is found through most of western North America from Alaska and Yukon Territory south into Mexico and east to Kansas. In Alberta, this is essentially a mountain butterfly, with some records from fringe areas of the boreal forest, cool uplands along the American border east of the mountains and a single wind-blown stray from Lethbridge. This species occurs in most mountain habitats at all elevations, although it is most abundant in open coniferous forest, meadows, and other non-forested sites.

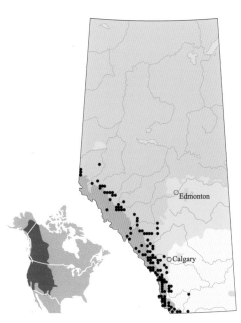

Phyciodes tharos (Drury, [1773])
Pearl Crescent

Etymology. The origin of this name is obscure. It may be from the Greek word *theros*, meaning "summer."

Identification. The Pearl Crescent is small (fore wing 14-18 mm), orange and black with black borders. Unlike the similar Northern Pearl Crescent (*P. cocyta*), this species has narrow black lines crossing the orange of the dorsal fore wing. The black marginal band of the dorsal hind wing contains a conspicuous, pale, wavy band.

Life History. The pale green eggs are laid in clusters on the underside of leaves of various *Aster* spp. Larvae are chocolate-brown with cream markings. Pupae are creamy tan with brownish streaks. Adults may be found from May 3 to August 28. The long flight period, in any Alberta locality regardless of seasonal conditions, suggests that this species is multi-brooded. Populations in the eastern United States are multi-brooded, with a summer generation as short as 35 days. In the fall, under the influence of short day length and cooling temperatures, third instar larvae enter diapause and overwinter, resuming development the following spring.

Range and Habitat. The range of the Pearl Crescent is essentially eastern North America with extensions west into the Great Plains of southern Canada. In Alberta the Pearl Crescent is found on the dry prairies north to the Battle River. This butterfly is widespread in prairie grasslands, especially in brushy areas along streams, coulees and riparian woodland.

Phyciodes tharos
Male dorsal

Phyciodes tharos
Male ventral

Phyciodes tharos
Female dorsal

Phyciodes tharos
Female ventral

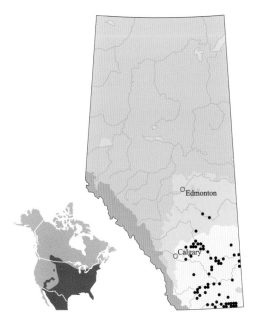

273

Subfamily
LIMENITIDINAE
ADMIRALS

Members of this subfamily are commonly called admirals. We have four species of *Limenitis* in Alberta, all in the subgenus *Basilarchia*. The best known of these is the Viceroy, *Limenitis (Basilarchia) archippus*, which mimics the poisonous Monarch butterfly, *Danaus plexippus* (Danaidae).

Limenitis Fabricius, 1807

Limenitis (Basilarchia) Scudder, [1871]
ADMIRALS

Etymology. *Limenitis* may be derived from the Latin *limus* meaning "an apron trimmed with purple," and *itus* meaning "a movement or departure." In Latin, *basilaris* means "regal."

Identification. Members of this genus are strong and rapid fliers. They are distinguished by the white band on the dorsal surface, with the exception of *Limenitis (Basilarchia) archippus*, a famous mimic of the Monarch butterfly. This characterization works well in Alberta, but not for North America or the rest of the world. This genus has been affected by the recent taxonomic upheaval attempting to make North American classification conform with European classification.

Species boundaries in this genus are weak, and when two species are found in the same area there is considerable interbreeding. This produces individuals that either do not fit any of the species characterizations, or fit two at the same time. In Alberta, such hybrids have been found between *Limenitis (Basilarchia) arthemis* and *L. lorquini*, and between *L. arthemis* and *L. weidemeyerii*. Hybrid zones occur in the Crowsnest Pass area and along the American-Canadian border in the Milk River valley.

Limenitis archippus on buckbrush
(*Symphoricarpos* sp.; Caprifoliaceae) at
Writing-On-Stone Provincial Park, Alberta.

T.W. Thormin.

Limenitis (Basilarchia) archippus (Cramer, [1776])
Viceroy
subspecies: *Limenitis (Basilarchia) archippus archippus* (Cramer, [1776])

Etymology. Archippus was a Greek poet or comedian. The common name reflects its mimicry of the Monarch (*Danaus plexippus*); a viceroy is a stand-in for a monarch.

Identification. The Viceroy is large, orange and black and easily confused with the Monarch. It can be recognized by the presence of a black band across the wings from front to back on the dorsal surface, about two-thirds of the way down the wing. Northern populations are slightly darker than those found in the south.

Life History. Spherical pale green eggs are laid singly. Overwintering larvae construct a leaf-tip shelter. Mature larvae lack spines. Larval colour varies from green to brown. Pupae are black or brown with white on the abdomen. The dorsal portion is raised with a large spatulate protuberance projecting from the anterior dorsal abdomen. Larval host plants are usually willow (*Salix* spp.), poplar (*Populus* spp.) and cherry (*Prunus* spp.). The Viceroy may be found in Alberta from June 13 to August 12, with most adults flying in July. Adults nectar on thistles (*Cirsium* spp.) and Alfalfa (*Medicago sativa*). There is one brood per year.

Range and Habitat. The Viceroy ranges from Nova Scotia in the east, west to Alberta and from the Northwest Territories in the north, south to Florida and California. Specimens from Alberta are placed in *Limenitis (B.) archippus archippus*. Studies conducted on the relationship between the Viceroy and the Monarch show that a level of protection from predators is achieved in areas where both the toxic model, the Monarch, and the more palatable mimic, the Viceroy, occur in close proximity. Birds learn colour patterns and tend to avoid eating anything that looks like a Monarch. Monarchs are less common farther north, so northern Viceroy populations do not have a model to mimic. In these areas a colour shift may occur as seen in the dark phase of the Viceroy found in northern Alberta. For further discussion on the Monarch, see page 312. The Viceroy may be found in open habitats, such as roadways, meadows and edges of fields. Usually the shrubs and trees that serve as larval host plants are nearby.

Limenitis archippus archippus
Male dorsal

Limenitis archippus archippus
Male ventral

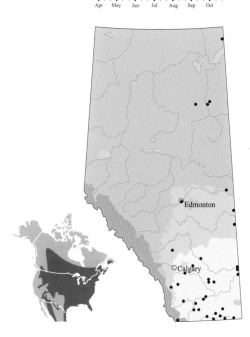

Limenitis (Basilarchia) arthemis (Drury, [1773])
White Admiral
subspecies: *Limenitis (Basilarchia) arthemis rubrofasciata* (Barnes and McDunnough, 1916)

Limenitis arthemis rubrofasciata
Male ventral

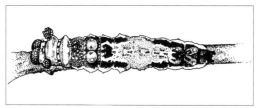

Limenitis arthemis rubrofasciata larva

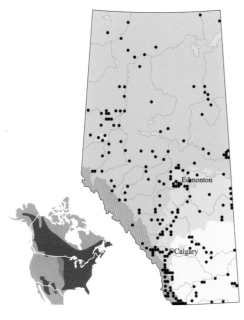

Etymology. Arthemis was a Greek goddess who was represented as a huntress and associated with the moon. The subspecies name is a combination of the Latin *ruber* meaning "red" and *fasciatus* meaning "bundled."

Identification. The White Admiral is a large butterfly that is almost entirely black and white. It can be differentiated from *Limenitis lorquini* and *L. weidemeyerii* by the lack of both apical red patches on the dorsal fore wing and extensive brown markings on the ventral surface.

Life History. The round, pale green eggs are laid singly on leaves of the host. Larvae and pupae are similar in appearance to those of the Viceroy. The larvae, especially in early instars, resemble bird droppings on the host plant's leaves. The partly grown larvae overwinter in a leaf shelter, and resume feeding and developing the following spring. The pupae are light-coloured with a large projection from the back. Larval food plants include birch (*Betula* spp.), Trembling Aspen (*Populus tremuloides*), poplar (*Populus* spp.) and willow (*Salix* spp.). Males patrol forest edges and coulees. Both sexes puddle actively. Adults are strong fliers, but prefer to glide and flutter. In Alberta, adults have been collected from May 23 to September 9. Peak flight occurs in late June and July. There is one brood per year.

Range and Habitat. These butterflies range across Canada from the treeline south to Michigan, Manitoba and North Dakota. *Limenitis arthemis* has been grouped with *L. a. astyanax* (Fabricius) in recent years because of a large zone of intergradation in the eastern United States. This form is largely purple on the dorsal surface, and is found in the eastern United States, south to Florida and west to Colorado. Boundaries between subspecies are obscure in these cases, and poorly understood in others. Most Alberta material is referred to *L. a. rubrofasciata*. Hybrids of *L. arthemis* and *L. lorquini* are found in the mountain passes and valleys of the Crowsnest and Castle river drainages in southwestern Alberta. Hybridization also occurs with *L. weidemeyerii* in other localities. These butterflies may be observed puddling after a rain or cruising along forest edges.

Limenitis (Basilarchia) lorquini Boisduval, 1852
Lorquin's Admiral
subspecies: *Limenitis (Basilarchia) lorquini burrisoni* Maynard, 1891

Etymology. Named after Lorquin, an early collector in California. The subspecies name is probably a patronym.

Identification. Lorquin's Admiral is easily recognized by the presence of a reddish apical patch on the dorsal fore wing, sometimes also present on the ventral fore wing. There is a broad white band across the wings on both surfaces.

Life History. Pale green eggs are laid singly on host plants. The young larvae feed for a while, then make a leaf shelter and spend the winter as partially grown larvae. Larvae and pupae are morphologically similar to other species of the subgenus *Basilarchia*. Larval hosts include willow (*Salix* spp.), poplar (*Populus* spp.), Trembling Aspen (*Populus tremuloides*), and cherry (*Prunus* spp.). Adults patrol roadsides, creeks and cut lines. Adults have been collected from June 20 to September 8. Peak flight activity occurs in July.

Range and Habitat. Lorquin's Admiral is found from southwestern Alberta to Vancouver Island, south to Baja California. Two subspecies are recognized but their status and relationship are unclear. Alberta specimens are assigned to *Limenitis (B.) lorquini burrisoni*. It is found in the Crowsnest, Castle River and Waterton areas. Many specimens are hybrids with *Limenitis arthemis*. Lorquin's Admiral frequents meadows and stream beds near deciduous trees.

Limenitis lorquini burrisoni
Female dorsal

Limenitis lorquini burrisoni
Female ventral

Populus balsamifera
Balsam Poplar

277

Limenitis (Basilarchia) weidemeyerii (W.H. Edwards, 1861)
Weidemeyer's Admiral
subspecies: *Limenitis (Basilarchia) weidemeyerii oberfoelli* (F.M. Brown, 1960)

Limenitis weidemeyerii oberfoelli
Male dorsal

Limenitis weidemeyerii oberfoelli
Male ventral

Apr May Jun Jul Aug Sep Oct

Etymology. This species was named after Edwards' friend J.W. Weidemeyer. The subspecies was named after James Oberfoell, collector of the type specimens.

Identification. Weidemeyer's Admiral is a large species recognized easily by the extensive white patches on the ventral surface of the hind wing and the lack of an apical red patch on the dorsal fore wing. It superficially resembles the White Admiral (*L. arthemis*), but differs in having more white scaling at the base of the wing.

Life History. The life history is similar to that of the two preceding species. Greenish eggs are laid singly on a leaf, the larvae hatch, feed for a while then make a leaf shelter where they spend the winter as third instars. Development resumes the following spring. Larvae and pupae look like those of other *Limenitis* species. Larval hosts include willow (*Salix* spp.), poplar (*Populus* spp.) and other trees. Oviposition has been observed on Saskatoon (*Amelanchier alnifolia*) near Writing-On-Stone Provincial Park in southern Alberta. The limited number of records indicates a flight period from June 7 until July 22. Most flight activity occurs in late June and early July. There is one brood per year.

Range and Habitat. Weidemeyer's Admiral is distributed throughout the southwestern United States, north to southern British Columbia and along the Milk River in southern Alberta. Alberta specimens belong to *Limenitis (B.) weidemeyerii oberfoelli*. It is found in riverine forests and coulee bottoms.

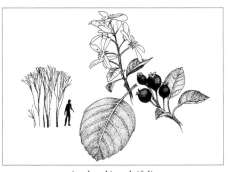

Amelanchier alnifolia
Saskatoon

7

Family SATYRIDAE
SATYRS, WOOD NYMPHS, MEADOW BROWNS and RINGLETS

This family is often included as a subfamily of the Nymphalidae. Like nymphalids, satyrids have fore legs that are reduced to stumps; however, they can be recognized by conspicuously swollen vein bases in the fore wings in all genera except *Enodia* and *Oeneis*. Most satyrids are an undistinguished dull gray or brown, with eye spots (ocelli) along the wing margins. The egg is subconical or barrel-shaped. Satyrid larvae feed on grasses or sedges. Many species develop slowly, taking two years or more to mature. In most species, winter is passed in the larval stage (mature or immature). Most adult satyrids do not wander far from the larval habitat and prefer sap flows and rotting fruit to floral nectar. Male *Enodia* and *Oeneis* tend to use a perching strategy to find mates, while males of other genera patrol. There are 19 species in Alberta, and two species whose ranges border our province.

Cercyonis pegala at Erskine, Alberta.   C.D. Bird.

Subfamily
ELYMNIINAE

There are only two species of this subfamily in Alberta. Unlike most of the other satyrids in our province, *Enodia anthedon* and *Satyrodes eurydice* have numerous distinct eye spots on the dorsal and ventral surfaces of both fore and hind wings. Both species frequent wet grassy areas.

Key to Genera of Satyridae in Alberta

(** Species marked with a double asterisk are not recorded for Alberta, but have been found just outside the province)

1a) Fore wing with subcosta, cubitus and anal veins weakly swollen 2

b) Fore wing with veins strongly swollen at base 5

2a) Eyes hairy; ventral hind wing with 6 or more ocelli 3

b) Eyes naked; ventral hind wing with 5 or fewer ocelli 4

3a) Ventral wing ocelli smaller, spots about 3 times diameter of pupil, hind wing slightly scalloped . . . .
. . . . *SATYRODES* eurydice (Johansson) p. 284

b) Ventral wing ocelli larger, spots 4 times diameter of pupils, hind wing more strongly scalloped . . . .
. . . . *ENODIA* anthedon A.H. Clark p. 283

4a) Dorsal wings with cream-coloured band, ocelli present on fore wing only. . . . .
. . . . *NEOMINOIS* ridingsii (W.H. Edwards) p. 310

b) Dorsal wings without cream-coloured band, ocelli usually present on both fore and hind wings . . . . *OENEIS* p. 299

5a) Subcosta, cubitus and anal veins strongly swollen at base; dorsal surface pale, orange to yellow *COENONYMPHA* p. 288

b) At least one but not all of subcosta, cubitus or anal veins strongly swollen at base; darker, black, gray, brown often with orange or rust. 6

6a) Hind wing scalloped; ventral fore wing ocelli large in subapical (M1) and cubitus cell (Cu1) . . . . . *CERCYONIS* p. 285

b) Hind wing margin smoother; ventral fore wing with or without ocelli, when present, largest are in M1 and M2. . . . .
. . . . *EREBIA* p. 291

Oeneis alberta at Nose Hill, Calgary, Alberta.   T.W. Thormin.

Key to Species of *Oeneis* in Alberta

1a) Fore wing without ocelli, other markings weak or apparently absent, black to dark brown, often somewhat translucent, alpine to subalpine rocky areas . . . .
. . . . *Oeneis melissa* (Fabricius) p. 306
b) Ocelli present or absent on fore wing or ventral hind wing distinctly banded or both 2

2a) Ventral hind wing striated, lacks a median band, 4 ocelli usually present on each fore and hind wing . . . .
. . . . *Oeneis uhleri* (Reakirt) p. 309
b) Ventral hind wing not marked as above, ocelli 0-3 on fore wing 0-2 on hind wing, median band often present 3

3a) Light orange-brown covering more than 75% of dorsal wing area; large; fore wing greater than 23 mm 4
b) Darker colour, more earth tones, browns and grays, or smaller wingspan than above 5

4a) Larger, fore wing greater than 28 mm, usually with 2 ocelli, hind wing with 1 ocellus. . . . .
. . . . *Oeneis macounii* (W.H. Edwards) p. 305
b) Smaller, fore wing less than 28 mm, usually with 4-6 ocelli, hind wing usually with 1-2 ocelli . . . .
. . . . *Oeneis chryxus* (Doubleday) p. 301

5a) Veins on ventral hind wings usually outlined with white scaling, median band usually strongly contrasting basally 6
b) Veins on ventral hind wings lacking light scaling 7

6a) Ventral fore wing usually with 1 to 3 ocelli and hind wing with 1; discal cell with many dark markings . . . .
. . . . *Oeneis alberta* Elwes p. 299
b) Ventral fore wing usually lacking ocellus; no ocellus on hind wing; discal cell with few markings; ventral hind wing band more sharply defined . . . .
. . . . *Oeneis taygete* Geyer p. 308

7a) Light gray to brown, often washed out in appearance; ocelli reduced or absent. . . *Oeneis polixenes* (Fabricius) p. 307
b) Dorsal wings are darker, brownish with orange-brown scaling around ocelli, fore wing with 2-4 ocelli, hind wing with 1 ocellus, greater than 23 mm . . . .
. . . . *Oeneis jutta* (Hübner) p. 303

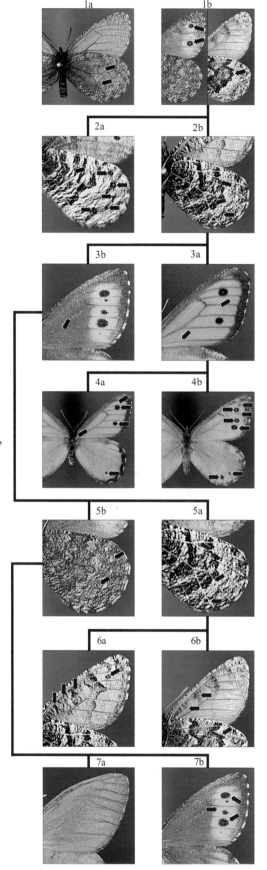

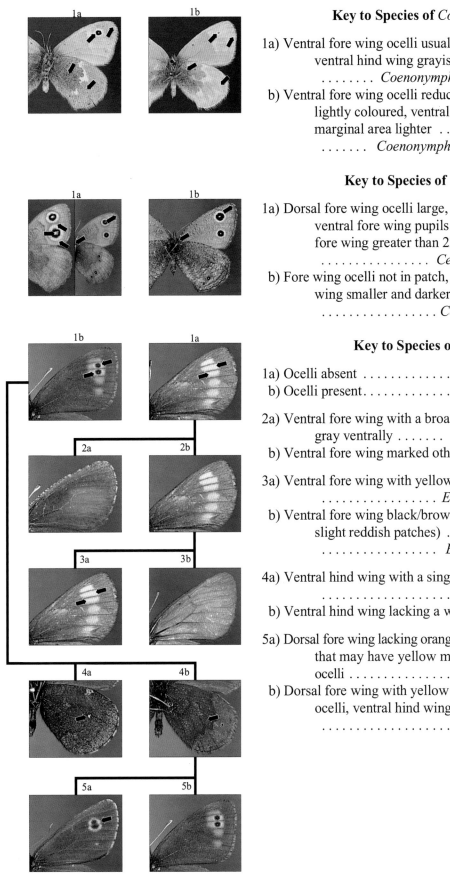

Key to Species of *Coenonympha* in Alberta

1a) Ventral fore wing ocelli usually distinct, wing margins grayish, ventral hind wing grayish . . . .
. . . . *Coenonympha inornata* W.H. Edwards p. 288

b) Ventral fore wing ocelli reduced, paler, wing margin cream, lightly coloured, ventral hind wing grayish basally with marginal area lighter . . . .
. . . . *Coenonympha ochracea* W.H. Edwards p. 290

Key to Species of *Cercyonis* in Alberta

1a) Dorsal fore wing ocelli large, may be surrounded by pale area; ventral fore wing pupils may have pale blue scales, or fore wing greater than 23 mm . . . .
. . . . *Cercyonis pegala* (Fabricius) p. 287

b) Fore wing ocelli not in patch, pupil never with blue scales, fore wing smaller and darker . . . .
. . . . *Cercyonis oetus* (Boisduval) p. 285

Key to Species of *Erebia* in Alberta

1a) Ocelli absent 2

b) Ocelli present. 4

2a) Ventral fore wing with a broad reddish flush, mottled with light gray ventrally . . . . *Erebia discoidalis* (Kirby) p. 293

b) Ventral fore wing marked other than above 3

3a) Ventral fore wing with yellow-orange postmedian bars. . . . . .
. . . . *Erebia theano* (Tauscher)** p. 298

b) Ventral fore wing black/brown without discrete spots (rarely slight reddish patches) . . . .
. . . . *Erebia magdalena* Strecker p. 295

4a) Ventral hind wing with a single white spot in discal area . . . .
. . . . *Erebia disa* (Thunberg) p. 291

b) Ventral hind wing lacking a white spot 5

5a) Dorsal fore wing lacking orange or yellow band, two ocelli present that may have yellow margins, ventral hind wing lacking ocelli . . . . *Erebia rossi* Curtis** p. 297

b) Dorsal fore wing with yellow or orange band or spots, 2 to 5 ocelli, ventral hind wing with ocelli. . . . .
. . . . *Erebia epipsodea* Butler p. 294

Enodia Hübner, 1819

Etymology. The name may be derived from the Greek *enodios*, "of the road," or *enodis*, meaning "smooth."

Enodia anthedon A.H. Clark, 1936
Northern Pearly Eye
subspecies: *Enodia anthedon borealis* A.H. Clark, 1936

Etymology. Anthedon was a community in ancient Greece.

Identification. The Northern Pearly Eye may be confused with the Pearly Eye, *Enodia portlandia* (Fabricius), where their ranges overlap in the eastern United States. It can be distinguished from the other Elymniinae in Alberta, *Satyrodes eurydice*, by the darker brown wings, larger eye spots and more angulate margin of the hind wing.

Life History. The eggs are greenish, short and barrel-shaped, and are laid singly on host grasses. Young larvae overwinter and mature the following summer. Mature larvae have greenish yellow heads with red-tipped horns and a yellowish green body with green and yellow stripes. The cleft tail is tipped in pink. Pupae are green to blue-green with the head and edges of the wing pads cream-coloured. In Alberta, known flight dates are June 29 to July 10. There is one brood per year.

Range and Habitat. This is a species of transition areas near the southern limit of the boreal forest. It occurs from Nova Scotia west through central Saskatchewan to Lac La Biche, Alberta. The Northern Pearly Eye should be watched for in east-central Alberta in poplar woods near streams and lakes.

Enodia anthedon borealis
Male dorsal

Enodia anthenodon borealis
Male ventral

Satyrodes Scudder, 1875

Etymology. The generic name is derived from the Greek *satyros*, or "satyr," a goat-legged woodland deity partial to drinking wine and chasing nymphs.

Satyrodes eurydice (Johansson, 1763)
Eyed Brown
subspecies: *Satyrodes eurydice eurydice* (Johansson, 1763)

Satyrodes eurydice eurydice
Male dorsal

Satyrodes eurydice eurydice
Male ventral

Apr May Jun Jul Aug Sep Oct

Etymology. Eurydice was the wife of the musician Orpheus in Greek mythology.

Identification. *Satyrodes eurydice* is a creamy brown, medium-sized butterfly (wingspan 41-51 mm) with four to five submarginal ocelli on the fore wing and six ocelli on the hind wing. Ventrally, it is lighter brown, with white-centred ocelli bordered by two yellow rings.

Life History. Eggs are laid on sedges (*Carex* spp.). The caterpillars feed and overwinter partially grown. Mature larvae are slender and striped lengthwise with yellow, tan and dark green stripes. The head bears horns with red markings. The green pupae are often suspended from sedges. There is normally only one generation per year but the adults emerge over much of the summer. This butterfly has a low, weaving, floppy flight. Adults seldom stray from the sedge marsh. In Alberta, recorded flight dates are June 12 to July 6.

Range and Habitat. The subspecies *Satyrodes eurydice eurydice* is found primarily east of the 100th meridian, and is widespread in eastern Canada and the United States. Its range enters Alberta along the northeastern boundary with Saskatchewan and extends north to Great Slave Lake. The Eyed Brown has been collected near Lloydminster. The subspecies *Satyrodes eurydice fumosus* Leussler occurs to the south in the United States (Nebraska). The Eyed Brown is found in wet meadows, sedge marshes and fens.

Subfamily
SATYRINAE

Almost all of Alberta's satyrids belong to this subfamily. Satyrines have fewer, less distinct eye spots but are otherwise similar in appearance to members of the Elymniinae. There are 17 species in Alberta, with two additional species and one subspecies whose ranges may extend into our province.

Cercyonis Scudder, 1875
WOOD NYMPHS

Etymology. *Cercyon* is named after Kerkyon, the robber killed by Theseus, in Greek mythology.

Identification. The bases of the fore wing veins in *Cercyonis* species are swollen, as they are in most other satyrines except *Neominois* and *Oeneis*. The outer margins of the hind wings are strongly scalloped, although this may be less obvious in worn specimens.

Cercyonis oetus (Boisduval, 1869)
Dark Wood Nymph

Etymology. The species name may come from the Greek *oitos*, meaning "doom" or "fate."

Identification. The Dark Wood Nymph is similar in appearance to the Common Wood Nymph, *Cercyonis pegala*, but is smaller (wingspan 39-44 mm). Wings are an even, dark brown dorsally, with one or two ocelli on the fore wing. The ventral fore wing has two ocelli, the apical one being larger with a white pupil and haloed with a yellow to cream border. The second ocellus is smaller, sometimes without a pupil, and is closer to the wing margin. A faint marginal band may be present. The ventral hind wing appears frosted and has a marginal band. There are two to five submarginal ocelli, usually with pupils, but without halos. The subspecies name *charon* (W.H. Edwards) is applied to the uniformly dull individuals found from Colorado (type locality) north into western Idaho and edging into Montana. The subspecies *phocus* (W.H. Edwards) (type locality British Columbia), currently in synonymy under *C. oetus sylvestris* (W.H. Edwards), is characterized by extremely dark fore wings, typical of many montane

Cercyonis oetus
Male dorsal

Cercyonis oetus
Male ventral

Cercyonis oetus
Female dorsal

Cercyonis oetus
Female ventral

C. oetus from Alberta. Grassland inhabitants are paler and more similar to *C. oetus charon*. None of the subspecies satisfactorily describes the Alberta specimens.

Life History. The Dark Wood Nymph has barrel-shaped, lightly sculptured eggs. Larvae are reported to feed on various grasses, including bluegrass (*Poa* spp.). The first instar larvae diapause over the winter and resume feeding in the spring. Mature larvae are characterized by a dark green dorsal stripe narrowly edged with white. Pupae are green to brown with dark brown striations. Adult Dark Wood Nymphs can be found on flowers along roadside ditches and other grassy areas in southern Alberta. The adults do not range much above 1500 m in the foothills and mountains. The species appears to have one generation per year, but the adults have a scattered emergence ranging from June 5 through September 13, with most on the wing from late July to early August.

Range and Habitat. There are four widespread subspecies in western Canada and the United States, but only *Cercyonis oetus charon* enters our area. Its range extends from Colorado through Montana into Alberta. The Dark Wood Nymph is common in the prairie region of Alberta and is distributed locally in low elevation grasslands in the mountains.

Poa pratensis
Kentucky Bluegrass

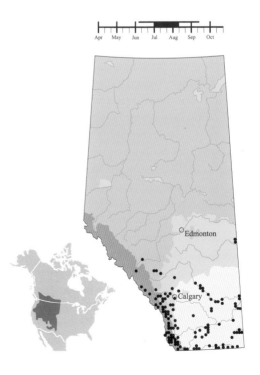

Cercyonis pegala (Fabricius, 1775)
Common Wood Nymph
subspecies: *Cercyonis pegala ino* Hall, 1924

Cercyonis pegala ino
Male ventral

Etymology. The species name is a combination of the Greek *pege*, meaning "well" or "fountain," and the suffix *-al* meaning "belonging to." Ino was a Greek sea goddess.

Identification. The Common Wood Nymph is medium-to-dark brown with a wingspan of 42 to 52 mm. Females are generally larger and paler than males. The ventral fore wing has two white-centred ocelli haloed with a pale yellow ring. The halos may touch and fuse into a yellow patch, especially in females. There are white centres to the ocelli in less than 25% of Alberta specimens. The rest of the wing is tan brown, darker basally, with dark striations below a submedian band. The hind wing may have no ocelli or several small ones.

Cercyonis pegala ino
Female ventral

Life History. Eggs are laid on or scattered around host plants. The cream-coloured eggs are larger than those of *C. oetus* and are barrel-shaped with longitudinal ribbing. The first instar larvae overwinter. Pupae are green with white or yellow longitudinal stripes. Host plants include many grasses, oats (*Avena* spp.), needle grass (*Stipa* spp.), and some sedges (*Carex* spp.). These butterflies are fond of visiting flowers such as thistle (*Cirsium* spp.) and Alfalfa (*Medicago sativa*), and sometimes gather at mud puddles. The main flight period is July to early August but ranges from June 9 to September 7. There is one brood per year.

Range and Habitat. *Cercyonis pegala* is a widespread species, ranging across southern Canada and the United States. It is highly variable and may represent a complex of closely related sister species. Thirteen or more subspecies are recognized, depending on the authority. *Cercyonis pegala ino* is found in suitable habitats on the Canadian prairies, and in Montana and Wyoming. The type locality for *Cercyonis pegala ino* is Calgary, Alberta. In contrast to its common name, the Common Wood Nymph is usually encountered in grasslands often far from wooded areas. They are seen regularly along roads and fields. They fly in grassy openings of the sand dunes in the northern boreal forest and appear to have invaded agricultural land in central Alberta and the river valleys to the south.

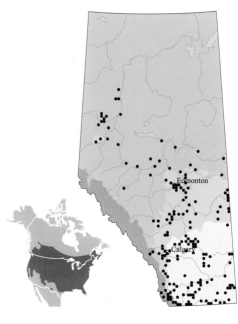

Coenonympha Hübner, 1819
RINGLETS

Etymology. The generic name is a combination of the Greek words *koinos*, meaning "common" and *nymph*, a minor female deity of wood or water.

Identification. Ringlets are relatively uniform in appearance and size (wingspan 25-45 mm). In general, there is a single ocellus on the fore wing and zero to nine on the hind wing. Colours vary from white through ochre and brown. The taxonomy of the group is not clear, as there may be a few highly polymorphic species or complexes of sibling species. In Alberta there are two forms that we treat as separate species.

Coenonympha inornata W.H. Edwards, 1861
Inornate Ringlet
subspecies: *Coenonympha inornata benjamini* McDunnough, 1928

Coenonympha inornata benjamini
Male dorsal

Coenonympha inornata benjamini
Male ventral

Coenonympha inornata benjamini
Female ventral

Etymology. From the Latin *in* meaning "not," and *ornatus* meaning "decorated, adorned," hence, "unadorned, plain." The subspecies is named in honour of F.H. Benjamin.

Identification. The Inornate Ringlet has one black ocellus with a small white pupil on the ventral fore wing. The apex of the wing is off-white, with the remainder fawn-yellow. The ventral hind wing is darker, frosted with white scales, and has small irregular white-to-cream-coloured patches (median band) in the discal region. There are occasionally additional eye spots along the anal lateral borders. Dorsally the ringlet is a more uniform colour on both fore and hind wings. The ocellus on the fore wing is muted. Wingspan ranges from 30 to 35 mm. One white Inornate Ringlet was found near Kinsella.

Life History. The yellow eggs are laid on or near the host plants. Mature larvae are olive-to-tan with darker longitudinal stripes. The brown head is covered with fine hair. Larval hosts elsewhere are reported to be various grasses and, less commonly, sedges (*Carex* spp.). Larvae have been reared on Kentucky Bluegrass (*Poa pratensis*) in captivity. Inornate Ringlets overwinter as partially mature larvae. The translucent brown-to-green pupae have darker striping on the wing pads and are usually suspended from grass. Adults emerge in late spring and fly through mid-summer. A wandering, bouncing flight makes moving butterflies easy to spot.

They are not avid flower visitors, however, and their colouring makes them difficult to locate when at rest hanging from tall stalks of grass. In Alberta, there may be two or more generations per year with flight times ranging from May 9 to October 30. The peak flight period is from late May to early August.

Range and Habitat. The Inornate Ringlet ranges from Alberta east to Labrador and south into Montana, the Dakotas, Saskatchewan and Manitoba. Brown (1961) believed that *Coenonympha inornata benjamini* was a Pleistocene hybrid of *Coenonympha inornata* and *Coenonympha ochracea*. The type locality for *C. inornata benjamini* is Waterton Lakes, Alberta. The Inornate Ringlet can be found in most grasslands in the province, but is uncommon at higher elevations. North American distribution map is a composite of *Coenonympha inornata* and *ochracea* species complex.

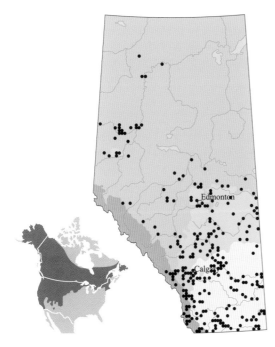

Carex douglasii
Douglas Sedge

Coenonympha inornata attacked by the Flower Spider (*Misumena vatia* (Clerck); Thomisidae) on groudsel (*Senecio* sp.; Compositae) at the Wagner Natural Area, Alberta.

T.W. Thormin.

289

Coenonympha ochracea W.H. Edwards, 1861
Ochreous Ringlet
subspecies: *Coenonympha ochracea mackenziei* Davenport, 1936

Coenonympha ochracea mackenziei
Male dorsal

Coenonympha ochracea mackenziei
Male ventral

Etymology. The species name is from the Latin *ochraceus* meaning "coloured pale yellow." The subspecies was named after the District of Mackenzie, Northwest Territories, or the Mackenzie River, whose names refer to the explorer Alexander Mackenzie.

Identification. The Ochreous Ringlet is similar to the Inornate Ringlet, but its ventral wing surface is darker, more grayish olive with the hind wing median band often complete. Submarginal eye spots (zero to six) on the ventral hind wing are more commonly present. The dorsal wing surface is a brighter ochre colour. There is speculation that *Coenonympha ochracea mackenziei* is a subspecies of *C. inornata* rather than of *C. ochracea*.

Life History. The life cycle is unknown for *Coenonympha ochracea mackenziei* but is expected to be similar to that of *Coenonympha inornata* with larval hosts being grasses. The single recorded flight date in Alberta is June 23.

Range and Habitat. The Ochreous Ringlet appears to be a resident of the Rocky Mountain states from Montana south to New Mexico and Arizona. There is one subspecies in the Northwest Territories in the vicinity of Great Slave Lake. The type locality of the northern subspecies *Coenonympha ochracea mackenziei* is Nyarling River, Northwest Territories. It ranges south into northern Alberta. The Ochreous Ringlet occupies northern grasslands and clearings. North American distribution is a composite of *Coenonympha ochracea* and *inornata* species complex.

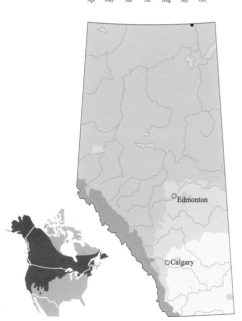

Erebia Dalman, 1816
ALPINES

Etymology. Erebos was the son of Chaos and Darkness in Greek mythology; hence *erebennus* means "dark" in Greek.

Identification. This is a largely arctic and alpine genus, hence the common name for these butterflies. They are small-to-medium-sized dark brown butterflies, often with orange-haloed ocelli on the wings. Four species occur in Alberta and two others range near our province.

Erebia disa (Thunberg, 1791)
Disa Alpine
subspecies: *Erebia disa mancinus* Doubleday, [1849]

Etymology. The species name may be derived from the Greek *deisa* meaning "moistness, filth," perhaps referring to the moist, dirty look of the bog habitat of the Disa Alpine. The subspecies name may come from the Latin *mancus* meaning "maimed, infirm, imperfect," perhaps referring to this butterfly's habit of dropping from flight as if injured.

Identification. The Disa Alpine is a medium-sized black butterfly (wingspan 40-46 mm). The fore wings have three or four ocelli that are fringed with orange. The dorsal surface is paler in the discal region and darker towards the wing margins. Ventrally, the apical corner of the fore wing is dusted with white scales. The wing fringes have alternating dark and light patches, while the hind wing dorsal surface is uniform dark brown. The ventral wing surface has one white discal smudge.

Life History. Little is known about the immatures of the Disa Alpine. Based on food preferences of other members of *Erebia*, larvae probably feed on grasses or sedges (*Carex* spp.). Larvae probably overwinter. Adult *Erebia disa* may be flushed when disturbed from their roosts in mature black spruce (*Picea mariana*) and tamarack (*Larix laricina*) bogs. The stunted trees allow patches of sunlight to shine on the ground, making the dark colours of this butterfly difficult to follow as it flies through the black, lichen-festooned branches. Disa Alpines have been observed puddling on the road up Shunda Mountain, near Nordegg. The main flight period of the adults is mid-June ranging from May 28 to July 23. There is one brood per year.

Erebia disa mancinus
Male dorsal

Erebia disa mancinus
Male ventral

Erebia disa mancinus
Female dorsal

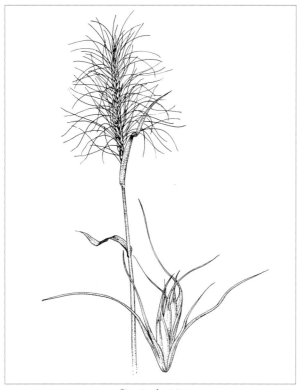

Sitanion hystrix
Squirreltail

Calamagrostis canadensis
Marsh Reed Grass

Range **and Habitat.** The range of the Disa Alpine is circumpolar. In North America, it is found from Alaska east in coniferous forests to western Ontario. Three sub-species are recognized in North America with *Erebia disa mancinus* having the broadest range. The type locality for *E. d. mancinus* is near Rock Lake, Alberta. In Alberta, *Erebia disa mancinus* is found in the mountains from Spray Lakes north and eastward in the boreal forest. It is usually associated with black spruce (*Picea mariana*) and tamarack (*Larix laricina*) bogs. In the mountain region, strays may be found on mountain tops and flying through Lodgepole Pine (*Pinus contorta*) forests although they normally prefer open boggy forests.

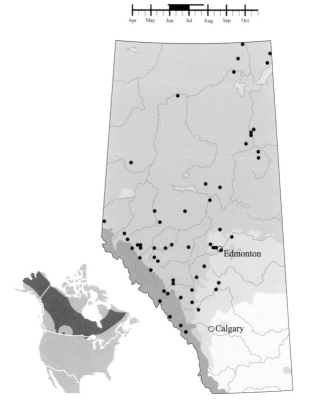

Erebia discoidalis (W. Kirby, 1837)
Red-disked Alpine
subspecies: *Erebia discoidalis mcdunnoughi* dos Passos, 1940

Etymology. In Greek *diskos* means "a disc" and the suffix *-oid* means "resembling." The subspecies was named after James McDunnough, an early Lepidopterist in Canada.

Identification. This is an early spring alpine. Its wingspan ranges from 25 to 44 mm. The dorsal fore wing discal area is reddish brown; the wing margins are brown and lack ocelli. The ventral costal margin is mottled with brown and white, and the distal margin is dusted with white scales. The discal area is reddish brown. The dorsal hind wing is brown while the ventral surface is lightly mottled and darker basally, giving the wing a grizzled appearance.

Life History. Single, barrel-shaped eggs are laid low on host plants. Larvae hatch in 9-11 days. The cream-coloured larvae are covered with short setae. A dark diagonal stripe is present on most segments starting high on the anterior margin and descending ventrally to the posterior margin. Larvae have been reared on lawn grass clippings (including *Poa* spp.). Weak silk webbing has been associated with mature larvae. In Manitoba, larvae are reported to feed on the grass *Poa canbyi*; elsewhere it is speculated that larval hosts are other grasses or sedges (*Carex* spp.). The Red-disked Alpine may be seen flying in clearings and meadows over the previous year's dried grass. The main flight period is May to early June (range April 1 to August 21). In May, this butterfly can be found at low elevations in central and southern Alberta. By early June it is present in the mountains and far north. There is one brood per year and the larvae are believed to overwinter.

Range and Habitat. The Red-disked Alpine ranges from central Asia across arctic and boreal North America eastward into Quebec. *E. d. mcdunnoughi* occurs in Alaska, Yukon Territory, east into Saskatchewan and south to northern Montana. In Alberta the Red-disked Alpine is widespread in boreal, parkland and montane forest meadows and is always associated with moisture. It is found early in the spring in open grassy areas in the parklands, fens in the boreal forest, and valley floor grasslands in the mountains.

Erebia discoidalis mcdunnoughi
Male dorsal

Erebia discoidalis mcdunnoughi
Male ventral

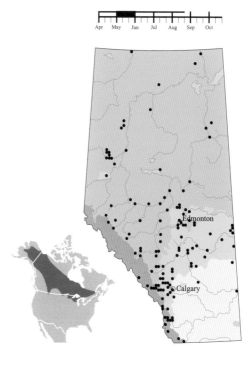

293

Erebia epipsodea Butler, 1868
Common Alpine
subspecies: ***Erebia epipsodea epipsodea*** Butler, 1868
Erebia epipsodea freemani Ehrlich, 1954

Erebia epipsodea freemani
Male dorsal

Erebia epipsodea freemani
Male ventral

Erebia epipsodea freemani
Female dorsal

Erebia epipsodea freemani
Female ventral

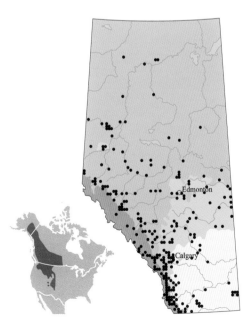

Etymology. The species name may come from the Greek *epipsavo* meaning "to touch lightly." The second subspecies was named in honour of Tom Freeman.

Identification. The Common Alpine is a variable species with a wingspan of 38 to 44 mm. The fore wing is brown with three to four white-centred ocelli in the submarginal area that are surrounded by orange to red patches. The hind wings are brown with three to four white-centred ocelli that are sometimes reduced to small dots. The ocelli are usually surrounded by orange to rust patches but these may also be greatly reduced.

Life History. The chalky white eggs are laid on thick-bladed grasses. Larvae overwinter partially grown and complete development the following spring. The mature larvae are green with dark green dorsal and lateral stripes. The pupae, which are often located at the base of grass tufts, are spotted with blotches of yellow and brown and have light stripes outlining wing venation. The lazy flight and relative abundance of the Common Alpine make these butterflies easy to observe. Adults are on the wing for most of the summer (range May 6 to October 11). There is one brood per year.

Range and Habitat. The Common Alpine occurs throughout western North America. *Erebia epipsodea epipsodea* (type locality: Rock Lake, Alberta) ranges from Colorado north through the mountains of Alberta, while *E. e. freemani* (type locality: Lloydminster, Alberta) is found in eastern Alberta and Saskatchewan. Assignment of the Alberta populations to *epipsodea* or *freemani* is usually difficult. The possible influence of the arctic *E. e. remingtoni* Ehrlich and the British Columbian *E. e. hopfingeri* Ehrlich further complicates the picture. Most Alberta specimens fall between *epipsodea* and *freemani* and no distinct subspecies boundaries have been observed. For now, the montane specimens are assigned to *E. e. epipsodea* and the lowland prairie and parkland specimens to *E. e. freemani*. The Common Alpine may be found in moist meadows with lush grass, from alpine sites to short grass prairies. They are more abundant in the parkland and foothill meadows.

Erebia magdalena Strecker, 1880
Magdalena Alpine
subspecies: *Erebia magdalena saxicola* Hilchie, 1990

Etymology. The species name may be biblical, from Mary Magdalene, a reformed prostitute healed by Jesus Christ. This may be an allusion to the blackness of both Mary Magdalene's previous character and the blackness of the butterfly. On the other hand, the species may have been named in honour of a female friend of the discoverer. The subspecies name is derived from the Latin *saxum* meaning "rock" and the suffix *-icola*, "inhabitant," thus "rock inhabiting."

Identification. The Magdalena Alpine is perhaps the most nondescript of our butterflies. It is dark brown to black and completely devoid of markings. A dusting of white scales is present on the ventral wing surface of some specimens, both on the fore wing apex and hind wing discal areas. The wingspan ranges from 51 to 64 mm. This species may be confused with the Melissa Arctic (*Oeneis melissa*) which occurs in the same habitat; however, the wings of *Erebia magdalena* are opaque whereas the wings of *Oeneis melissa* are translucent and usually have bands of spots on the hind wings.

Life History. The round, cream-coloured eggs are laid under rocks near food plants. The larvae hatch in about seven days. Larval hosts are various alpine grasses. Under laboratory conditions the larvae will feed on Kentucky Bluegrass (*Poa pratensis*), creeping fescue (*Festuca* spp.) and Barley (*Hordeum vulgare*). Their growth rate indicates that at least one year, perhaps two or more, is required to reach maturity. Mature larvae overwinter. Pupation occurs the following spring and lasts about seven days. The pupae are short, ovoid, brown-coloured and lack a cremaster. Pupation occurs on the ground, probably under a rock. No silk has been observed associated with the pupae. Males patrol ridges and rock fields in bright sunshine. Courtship takes place during midday and oviposition ensues shortly after. Females fly lower on the mountain, near the breeding sites. Some flower visitation occurs but most of the time is spent basking. Flight is lazy unless the butterfly is disturbed, then it becomes fast and erratic. Loose rock, steep slopes and cliffs often make pursuit difficult. Adults are observed flying from July 1 through August 1 with most activity in mid-July.

Erebia magdalena saxicola
Female dorsal

Erebia magdalena saxicola
Female ventral

Erebia magdalena saxicola
Male ventral

Range and Habitat. The Magdalena Alpine is known from alpine regions of northern New Mexico, Utah, Colorado, Wyoming, southern Montana, the Willmore Wilderness area of Alberta and the McBride area of British Columbia. A related species, *Erebia mackinleyensis* Gunder is found in Alaska and Yukon Territory. In Alberta, this butterfly is associated with black, lichen-covered rocks and barren alpine ridges in the company of other high-altitude butterflies. Frost polygons with vegetated centres appear to be the breeding habitat.

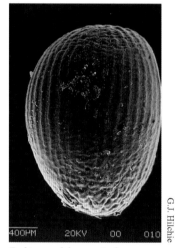

Erebia magdalena saxicola egg.
Scanning electron micrograph.

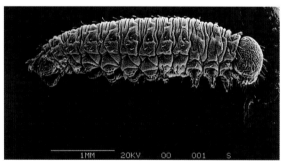

Erebia magdalena saxicola first instar larva
Scanning electron micrograph.

G.J. Hilchie.

Erebia magdalena saxicola larva

G.J. Hilchie.

Erebia magdalena saxicola pupa

G.J. Hilchie

Erebia rossii (Curtis, 1835)
Ross' Alpine

Etymology. The species name is presumably a patronym in honour of arctic explorer Captain John Ross.

Identification. This species is similar to the Common Alpine, *Erebia disa*, but is banded and lacks the white spot on the ventral hind wing.

Life History. No confirmed records for Alberta are available, although Gregory (1975) lists the species for the province.

Range and Habitat. Ross' Alpine is known from the Northwest Territories, northern British Columbia and Manitoba. The southernmost recorded locality is Caribou Pass, British Columbia. This butterfly is a resident of open bogs and subarctic areas. In Alberta, suitable open bog and wet alpine habitat occurs in the Rocky Mountains of the Willmore Wilderness Park area, the Caribou Mountains and the extreme northwestern part of the province.

Erebia rossii
Male dorsal

Erebia rossii
Male ventral

Mount Torrens area, north of
Willmore Wilderness Park, Alberta.

G.J. Hilchie.

297

Erebia theano (Tauscher, 1809)
Theano Alpine

Erebia theano
Male dorsal

Erebia theano
Male ventral

Erebia theano
Female dorsal

Erebia theano
Female ventral

Etymology. In Greek, *thea* means "an aspect."

Identification. The Theano Alpine is smaller than the average North American *Erebia*. This species has squarish orange to orange-red wing patches that often form bands.

Life History. Eggs, weakly ribbed with reddish brown spots, are laid on dead grass or sedge leaves, but willow (*Salix* spp.) may also be used. The larvae are tan with a dark brown mid-dorsal stripe and three dark brown stripes on each side. Two winters are passed in the larval stage with pupation occurring in the second spring. Adults can be expected from mid-July to early August.

Range and Habitat. The Theano Alpine is easily missed, as it tends to have very localized populations. Populations are recorded from the Beartooth Plateau region of Montana, Wyoming, Colorado and the Summit Lake area of northern British Columbia. The species is widely distributed through Alaska, Yukon Territory and the Northwest Territories eastward to northern Manitoba. A report (Ehrlich 1958) of *Erebia theano* in Alberta is assumed to be incorrect. A specimen labelled "Calgary, N.W. Ter. VI/24" in the American Museum of Natural History was located; however, there are no indications that the species occurs in the vicinity of Calgary. There is a low probability that a population of *Erebia theano* will be located in Alberta. Potential sites are remote alpine and subalpine meadows of the Willmore Wilderness Park and adjacent mountain regions.

Edmonton

Calgary

Oeneis Hübner, 1819
ARCTICS

Etymology. The genus may be named after Oeneus, king of an ancient city in western Greece, who is described as the first man to grow grapes.

Identification. The common name of this genus is fitting for a group of butterflies found mainly in the far north and high alpine habitats. Arctics are medium-to-large species with orange or brown, almost translucent, wings. Eye spots may be present or absent. There are eight species in Alberta, and one subspecies that is also likely to occur in the province.

Oeneis alberta Elwes, 1893
Alberta Arctic
subspecies: *Oeneis alberta alberta* Elwes, 1893

Etymology. This species was named after the region from which the type specimen was collected, near Calgary, District of Alberta, Northwest Territories, now the Province of Alberta. The type locality is near the mouth of Fish Creek.

Identification. The Alberta Arctic is a medium-sized butterfly (wingspan 35-43 mm), small for the genus, with a gray or gray-brown dorsal surface. There is a clear median band on the ventral hind wing and relatively few ocelli. Veins on the ventral hind wing are outlined in gray. Specimens from the Peace River region are larger, darker and more strongly marked on the ventral surface. Females are larger than males and have darker markings.

Oeneis alberta alberta
Male dorsal

Oeneis alberta alberta
Male ventral

Oeneis alberta alberta
Female dorsal

Oeneis alberta alberta
Female ventral

Vulpia octoflora
Six-weeks Fescue

Life History. In the Peace River area, cream-coloured eggs are laid on or near the ends of grass blades. The barrel-shaped eggs have shallow vertical ribs. In other areas, grasses, including fescue (*Festuca* spp.), are also reported as larval hosts. The reddish brown larvae hatch in about 30 days. They have longitudinal stripes, lack visible setae and have cleft posteriors. Fifth instars over-winter as prepupae. Pupation occurs early in the spring, during snow melt. Pupae rest loosely in the grass near the ground. Adult males perch and patrol in their efforts to locate mates. Males may defend loosely defined terri-tories and have a tendency to hilltop. Flight is usually short and rapid. Mating pairs do not fly and may be picked up by hand. Females oviposit and fly in late afternoon. The Alberta Arctic flies early, starting April 16 and occasionally going to July 3. Peak flight activity is in May.

Range and Habitat. *Oeneis alberta* is found in the grasslands of Alberta, including a disjunct population in the Peace River region, and British Columbia, south and east into Manitoba, North Dakota, and Montana. Isolated populations occur in Arizona, New Mexico, and Colorado. The Alberta Arctic is found on natural short- and mixed-grass prairies in southern Alberta and in the Peace River district. Adults may be abundant on hilltops and ridges, but do not nectar.

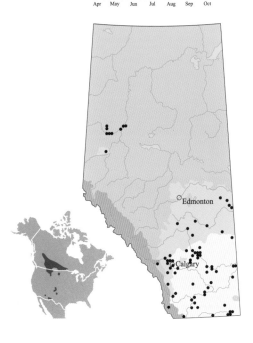

Oeneis alberta at Wintering Hills, Alberta.   J.H. Acorn.

Oeneis chryxus (Doubleday, [1849])
Chryxus Arctic
subspecies: *Oeneis chryxus caryi* Dyar, 1904
Oeneis chryxus chryxus (Doubleday, [1849])

Etymology. The species name may be derived from the Greek *chrysos* meaning "gold," in reference to the golden amber colour of the dorsal wing surface. The second subspecies was named in honour of Merritt Cary, who collected the type material in 1903.

Identification. *Oeneis chryxus* is a large species with rather pointed fore wings, usually with few spots. Dorsal wing colouration is bright golden orange. The median band on the ventral hind wing is prominent, with much contrast between the ground colour and the markings on the band. Males have a prominent patch of androconial scales on the dorsal fore wing.

Life History. The white, ridged, subconical eggs are laid on trees above the larval food plants (Scott 1992). Larvae feed then overwinter. Larval foods reported are sedges and grasses; Pyle (1981) speculated that *Festuca idahoensis* is used in Washington. Scott (1992) reported various sedges (*Carex* spp.) as food plants in Colorado. Mature larvae are furry and tan-coloured with brown lateral and ventral stripes and a dark head. The dark-coloured pupae are located at the base of grass clumps. Males patrol territories on open hillsides, paths and gullies and also perch on prominent twigs, logs or rocks. These butterflies often nectar at yellow flowers. Females are usually seen near nectaring and oviposition sites. The Chryxus Arctic flies from May 23 to August 16 with peak activity in July. Peak activity for *Oeneis chryxus caryi* is in June. There is one brood per year.

Range and Habitat. *Oeneis chryxus* ranges from Alaska to eastern Canada and south in the west along the mountains to California and New Mexico. Two subspecies occur in Alberta. *Oeneis chryxus chryxus* (type locality: near Rock Lake, Alberta) is found in the mountains from Alaska south through Alberta to New Mexico. *Oeneis chryxus caryi* ranges through the northern boreal forest of Alberta east across Saskatchewan and Manitoba. *Oeneis c. chryxus* inhabits spruce and pine forests in the mountains. Males appear to be resident along gullies, paths and edges of meadows. *O. c. caryi* is found in open pine forests.

Oeneis chryxus chryxus
Male dorsal

Oeneis chryxus chryxus
Male dorsal

Oeneis chryxus chryxus
Female dorsal

Oeneis chryxus chryxus
Female ventral

Oeneis chryxus caryi
Male dorsal

Oeneis chryxus caryi
Male ventral

Oeneis chryxus caryi
Female dorsal

Oeneis chryxus caryi
Female ventral

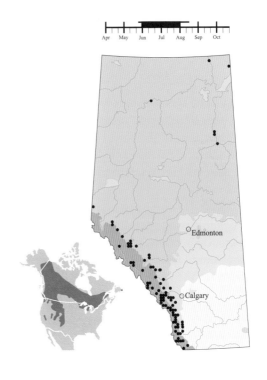

Oeneis chryxus chryxus at Oldman River,
Alberta.

T.W. Thormin.

Oeneis jutta (Hübner, 1805-1806)
Jutta Arctic
subspecies: *Oeneis jutta chermocki* Wyatt, 1965
Oeneis jutta ridingiana Chermock and Chermock, 1940

Etymology. The species is probably named after the old Danish state of Jutland (the type locality is in Lapland — northern Sweden, Norway and Finland) or *jutta* may be a proper name equivalent to Jane or Joan. The first subspecies was named in honour of the Chermock brothers, collectors and butterfly researchers. The second was named after the Riding Mountains of Manitoba.

Identification. *Oeneis jutta* is a large, gray-brown butterfly mottled with black on the underside. The median band on the ventral hind wing is faint, the dorsal surface is grayish, often with some brown at the fore wing apex. On females, this brown patch is often well developed. The dark spots on the dorsal wing surface are surrounded by a light orange band. There are one or two ocelli on the ventral fore wing. Males have a prominent androconial patch on the dorsal fore wing.

Life History. Eggs are barrel-shaped and ribbed. Larvae of eastern populations in Michigan feed on cotton grass (*Eriophorum* spp.), sedges (*Carex* spp.) and rushes (*Juncus* spp.), and on other grasses in Europe. Pyle (1981) speculated that the host in the Pacific Northwest may be cotton grass. Ted Pike has observed oviposition on cotton grass and reared larvae to second instar on it. Males perch on prominent objects, usually twigs and stems, most often in sunny areas. Searching for mates usually lasts several days and males have a number of favoured perches; the experienced observer can often find these and spot the male without disturbing him. If a good photo opportunity is missed, set up and wait; the males are territorial and will return in about 15 minutes. Females appear to fly randomly through the bog in their search for mates and oviposition sites. The Jutta Arctic also occurs in fens, in dune areas of the boreal forest, and in the mountains; males spend a good deal of time in the surrounding pine forest. The Jutta Arctic flies from May 28 to August 12. Peak flight activity is from early June through mid-July. There is one brood per year; the larvae overwinter.

Oeneis jutta chermocki
Male dorsal

Oeneis jutta chermocki
Female dorsal

Oeneis jutta chermocki
Female ventral

303

Eriophorum veridi
Cotton Grass

Range and Habitat. The Jutta Arctic is holarctic in distribution. In North America, it is found from Newfoundland to Alaska, from treeline in the north to Michigan (east) and Colorado (west) in the south. Much confusion surrounds separation and identification of the eight current subspecies. In Alberta, *Oeneis jutta chermocki* was described from the Banff area; this name applies to the darker form found in the montane areas. The lighter boreal form appears closest to *Oeneis jutta ridingiana*, but may be influenced by intergradation with a subspecies found in Alaska (*O. j. alaskensis* Holland). Hooper (1973) reported the occurrence of *O. j. ridingiana* in the Cypress Hills of southwestern Saskatchewan; it should be watched for on the Alberta side. This butterfly is found in black spruce bogs in the boreal forest, fens, and in northern montane regions. In the southern mountains, *Oeneis jutta* adults may be found along edges of fens and pine forests. Adults are usually found in more dense, but stunted, stands of trees.

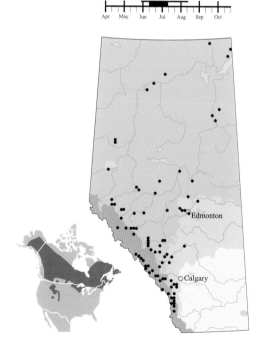

Bog with cotton grass (*Eriophorum* sp.; Cyperaceae) at Bistcho Lake, northwestern Alberta.

A.T. Finnamore.

Oeneis macounii (W.H. Edwards, 1885)
Macoun's Arctic

Etymology. The species was named after John Macoun, a botanist and collector of the type specimen, who was important in the biological exploration of western Canada.

Identification. Macoun's Arctic is our largest *Oeneis*. They are bright gold dorsally with a few dark ocelli and dark wing margins. There is a distinct median band on the ventral hind wing.

Life History. The life history of Macoun's Arctic is undescribed. Larval hosts are likely to be grasses or sedges (*Carex* spp.). Males are known to hilltop. In the mountains, these butterflies can be collected every year but boreal forest populations apparently fly in odd-numbered years. Both sexes are strong fliers, but have a slow, gliding flight until alarmed. These butterflies tend to fly along forest edges and clearings, darting into the forest when disturbed. Males may perch on prominent shrubs in forest openings. Both sexes bask on roads or patches of sandy ground and are rarely seen nectaring. The peak flight period is mid-June (flight range May 28 to August 17).

Range and Habitat. Macoun's Arctic is distributed across northern British Columbia, east through Ontario and Michigan. In Alberta, this species occurs in the northern half of the province southwards in the mountains and foothills to Kananaskis Provincial Park. In the northern part of this butterfly's range, it is found in pine and aspen forests and on hilltops near these areas. In the foothills, Macoun's Arctic is found in dry mixed forests.

Oeneis macounii
Male dorsal

Oeneis macounii
Male ventral

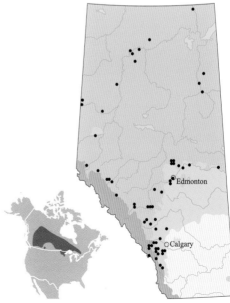

305

Oeneis melissa (Fabricius, 1775)
Melissa Arctic
subspecies: *Oeneis melissa beanii* Elwes, 1893

Oeneis melissa beanii
Female dorsal

Oeneis melissa beanii
Female ventral

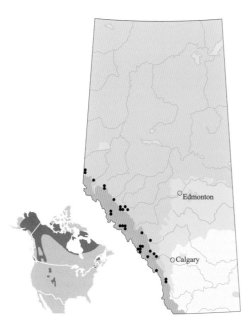

Etymology. In Greek, *mellis* means "honey"; however, the species name may also be derived from the feminine proper name. The subspecies was named in honour of Thomas Bean, who collected in Alberta before the end of the 19th century.

Identification. The Melissa Arctic is a dark gray or black, medium-sized butterfly and lacks any significant markings. There are no eye spots and the medial band on the ventral hind wing is faint or absent. Although it is similar to the Magdalena Alpine (*Erebia magdalena*), *Oeneis melissa* can be recognized by its more translucent wings and the flecked or slightly mottled undersides.

Life History. The subconical eggs are grayish white. Both the larvae and pupae overwinter. The mature larvae are green or brownish with dark heads and longitudinal stripes. The brown pupae are often located underneath rocks. Adults perch on rocks where their cryptic colouration allows them to blend with the substrate. The wings are normally held upright when basking in the sun. Males tend to hilltop and are very aware of intruders. When disturbed, these butterflies fly strongly, often over the edge of a cliff. The Melissa Arctic flies from June 27 to August 24 with peak activity in July and early August. There is one brood per year.

Range and Habitat. This butterfly is commonly found in rocky habitats above treeline in North America. It ranges from New Hampshire north to Labrador, west through the Canadian arctic and down the Rocky Mountains to Colorado. The type locality for the Albertan subspecies *Oeneis melissa beanii* is near Lake Louise (formerly Laggan), Alberta. This butterfly inhabits scree slopes, cliff edges and fields above treeline. Males are usually found on the tops of mountains with females flying at slightly lower elevations. Black, lichen-covered rocks are often associated with their mountaintop habitat.

Oeneis polixenes (Fabricius, 1775)
Polixenes Arctic
subspecies: *Oeneis polixenes brucei* (W.H. Edwards, 1891)

Etymology. Polyxene, the daughter of Priam and Hecuba, was betrothed to Achilles, hero of the battle of Troy. The subspecies was named in honour of David Bruce, a mural painter from Brockport, New York, and a resident of Colorado in the 1890s. Bruce provided W.H. Edwards with many specimens.

Identification. The Polixenes Arctic is medium-sized (wingspan 43-46 mm) and usually soft-brown in colour. Veins on the ventral hind wing are not lined with a contrasting colour of scales. Ocelli are usually absent. The medial band on the ventral hind wing is usually distinct, but few other markings are present.

Life History. The barrel-shaped eggs are white and heavily sculptured. Larvae may mature in their first year or overwinter, thus producing erratic emergences from one year to the next. They are light brown with darker longitudinal stripes. The larval hosts are various alpine grasses. Pupae are brown and stout. Adults are usually slow fliers, making short, skipping flights. Males tend to perch rather than patrol for females. This species has not been observed at flowers. The Polixenes Arctic flies from June 24 to August 7 with peak flight activity in July. There is one brood per year.

Range and Habitat. In North America, the Polixenes Arctic is found at or near treeline. There are currently six subspecies recognized, which range from an isolated population in Maine to populations across the Canadian arctic and down the Rocky Mountains to Colorado. The Albertan subspecies is *Oeneis polixenes brucei*. In Alberta, *O. p. brucei* is found above treeline in the mountains and from Fort Vermilion north in the boreal forest. Adults can be expected in moist to dry alpine meadows, usually in areas with exposed gravel patches. In the subarctic, this butterfly may also be seen in open bogs.

Oeneis polixenes brucei
Male dorsal

Oeneis polixenes brucei
Male ventral

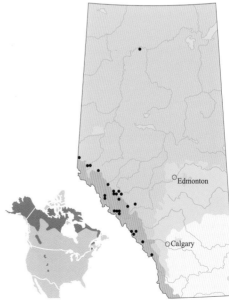

307

Oeneis taygete Geyer, [1830]
White-veined Arctic

subspecies: *Oeneis taygete edwardsi* dos Passos, 1949

Oeneis taygete edwardsi
Male dorsal

Oeneis taygete edwardsi
Male ventral

Etymology. The origin of *taygete* is unknown. The subspecies was named in honour of William H. Edwards (1822-1909) of West Virginia who contributed to the early study of North American butterflies.

Identification. The White-veined Arctic is distinguished by its small size (wingspan 36-42 mm) relative to other species in this genus. Ventral hind wing veins are lined with gray or white scales. A dark line extends from the leading edge to the trailing edge of both wings.

Life History. The life history is unknown, but is speculated to be similar to other *Oeneis* in larval appearance and food preferences, (i.e., grasses or sedges [*Carex* spp.]). Adults fly low over alpine meadows, often perching on tall grass stems. Basking on the ground is done with the wings folded. When startled, these butterflies tend to fly erratically, often up or down slopes. The flight period for this species is June 18 to July 29. Peak flight activity occurs in late June and early July.

Range and Habitat. The White-veined Arctic is holarctic in distribution. Populations of *O. taygete* occur in Maine, across the Canadian Arctic to Alaska and down the Rocky Mountains to Colorado. In Alberta, *Oeneis taygete edwardsi* is found in the mountains south to Nordegg. This species is usually associated with the lush alpine meadows just above treeline. Strays may be found up to the summit.

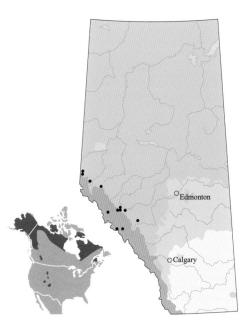

Oeneis uhleri (Reakirt, 1866)
Uhler's Arctic
subspecies: ***Oeneis uhleri varuna*** (W.H. Edwards, 1882)

Etymology. The species was named in honour of Philip Reese Uhler (1835-1913), librarian at the Museum of Comparative Zoology at Harvard University. The subspecies may be derived from the Latin *varus* meaning "grown inward, bent," or from Varuna, a powerful Hindu god.

Identification. *Oeneis uhleri* is brown, medium-sized, with a pronounced row of black spots near the outer edges of both surfaces of the wings. The dorsal surface is a gray-brown and the ventral surface is slightly lighter in most specimens. The ventral surface of the hind wing has no distinct band, but is covered with fine stripes of black and gray.

Life History. The white eggs are barrel-shaped, with shallow ridges running from one end to the other. They are laid on or near the tips of grass blades. Larvae hatch in about 20 days. They are light tan or gray throughout their lives and lack visible setae. Before pupation, larvae have a series of dark longitudinal stripes and a slightly cleft posterior. Third instar larvae overwinter then pupate in late May. Males perch or patrol in search of mates. Flight is usually erratic and may continue for 20 to 30 m before settling. Females hide in the grass until afternoon when they start flying and ovipositing. When perching on grass or the ground, these butterflies use lateral basking to maximize the warming effect of the sun. The adults have not been observed nectaring. They normally fly in late May and early June (range May 1 to August 26), although alpine populations usually emerge in early August, more than two months after the prairie populations. There is one brood per year.

Range and Habitat. *Oeneis uhleri varuna*, is widespread in the grasslands of southern and central Alberta through Saskatchewan and Manitoba and the northern United States. A population of slightly larger and more brightly marked *O. uhleri* is found in the Peace River grasslands of northwestern Alberta. Uhler's Arctic is found in many of the fescue (*Festuca* spp.) and needle grass (*Stipa* spp.) grasslands in the province. Strays may be found in old hay fields and pastures.

Oeneis uhleri varuna
Male dorsal

Oeneis uhleri varuna
Male ventral

Apr   May   Jun   Jul   Aug   Sep   Oct

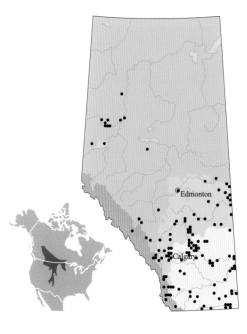

309

Neominois Scudder, 1875

Etymology. The generic name comes from the Greek prefix *neo* meaning "new" and *Minois*, a genus of Eurasian butterflies.

Neominois ridingsii (W.H. Edwards, 1865)
Ridings' Satyr
subspecies: *Neominois ridingsii minimus* Austin, 1986

Neominois ridingsii minimus
Male dorsal

Neominois ridingsii minimus
Male ventral

Bouteloua gracilis
Blue Grama Grass

Apr May Jun Jul Aug Sep Oct

Edmonton

Calgary

Etymology. The species was named in honour of James Ridings, an early collector of butterflies in the Rocky Mountains and a contemporary of W.H. Edwards. The subspecies name denotes the small size of this subspecies relative to other members of the species.

Identification. Ridings' Satyr is medium-sized (wingspan 35-40 mm) and tan to gray-brown with two white-centred ocelli on the fore wing. An irregular gray to white submarginal band bisects the hind wing giving it a striated appearance. Females are slightly smaller than males.

Life History. The white, barrel-shaped, faintly sculptured eggs are laid on grasses and other plants. Larvae feed on grasses, including Blue Grama Grass (*Bouteloua gracilis*). The last instar larvae are olive-coloured with several dark longitudinal stripes. The immature larvae overwinter and resume development the following spring. The green or brown pupae may be suspended or hidden in the leaf litter at the base of grass tussocks. Most adults encountered are flushed from their roosts in the grass. They fly rapidly for a short distance, then disappear back into the grass. Adults are on the wing in early summer. Flight dates range from June 11 to July 23 in Alberta, with the peak flight period in late June and early July.

Range and Habitat. *Neominois ridingsii* is found on the western Great Plains west to California. In Canada, its range extends from southern Manitoba west into south-central Alberta and north to Saskatoon, Saskatchewan. In Alberta the butterfly frequents native fescue and mixed-grass prairies, often near river valleys, coulees and sand dunes.

8

Family **DANAIDAE**
MILKWEED BUTTERFLIES

Most butterflies in this family are tropical to subtropical. There are three species in the genus *Danaus* that occur in North America. One species, the Monarch, migrates into Alberta. Larvae of most danaid species feed on plants in the Asclepiadaceae, the milkweeds, and the Solanaceae, the potato, tomato and nightshade family. Like the nymphalids, milkweed butterflies have reduced fore legs, but lack scales on their antennae. Males have scent patches on their hind wings. For additional reading on the family, see Ackery and Vane-Wright (1984).

Danaus Kluk, 1802
MONARCH and QUEENS

Etymology. Danaus was a mythical king of Argos in ancient Greece.

Danaus plexippus
Male dorsal

Danaus plexippus (Linnaeus, 1758)
Monarch

Danaus plexippus
Female dorsal

Danaus plexippus
Female ventral

Etymology. Plexippos was one of the fifty sons of Aegyptus, the brother of Danaus in Greek mythology.

Identification. One of our largest butterflies, the Monarch has a wingspan of 8 to 10 cm. Dorsally, the wings are orange with a double row of white spots in the black wing margins. Veins are bordered with black. Ventrally, the pattern is repeated, except that the hind wings are a paler orange. The male has a scent patch on the dorsal hind wing. The antennae are uniformly black. The only species with which the Monarch may be confused is the Viceroy (*Limenitis archippus*). The Viceroy is smaller, has a single row of spots in the margin, a longitudinal narrow black medial band on the hind wing, and scales on the antennae. Details of the apical area of the fore wing also differ.

Life History. The Monarch has perhaps the best documented life history of the butterflies. The pale green, conical eggs are laid on 14 species of milkweed (*Asclepias* spp.) and occasionally on dogbane (*Apocynum* spp.) and green milkweed (*Acerates* spp.). In Alberta, Showy Milkweed (*Asclepias speciosa*) is used as the primary larval host. Due to the Monarch's migratory habits, the breeding areas in the province vary from year to year. During most years, breeding populations can be found along the lower reaches of the Bow River south of Brooks. The Monarch has been known to breed as far north as Edmonton using Low Milkweed (*Asclepias ovalifolia*) found scattered along the banks of the North Saskatchewan River. The larvae are green, striped with black and yellow bands, and have two fleshy filaments both anteriorly and posteriorly. The Monarch requires 20 to 30 days to develop from egg to adult under favourable conditions. Adults may emerge up until the first hard frosts in September. They nectar on almost any flower visited by butterflies, but milkweed flowers are noted favourites. Adults have been observed on the wing in Alberta from June 1 through August 25. The early dates represent spring migrants and the later records are the offspring of the migrants.

Much research has been done on the benefits derived by insects which utilize plant-produced chemicals for their own protection. Monarch larvae feed on milkweeds, sequestering toxic cardiac glycosides from the plants in their bodies. Both larval and adult Monarchs are toxic to birds and other vertebrates. Not all milkweed plants produce significant amounts of the toxin leaving some individuals more palatable to birds. Insect predators and parasitoids appear less deterred by the chemicals as parasitism of up to 75% of larvae has been reported from one locality. In Alberta, tachnid flies have been reared from field-collected Monarch larvae. The Viceroy, a palatable species, mimics the Monarch to obtain protection from predators. Its range in Alberta extends beyond that of the Monarch. Protection through mimicry may occur even when the Monarch is not present, as most birds migrate and overwinter within the range of the Monarch. For more detailed reading on the Monarch, see Urquhart (1960).

Range and Habitat. One subspecies is recorded for North America, *Danaus plexippus plexippus*. This subspecies ranges from Mexico north through the United States into southern Canada. The Monarch is noted for its yearly migrations, moving south to winter in Mexico and California, then migrating north in the spring. They colonize milkweed patches along the way and reach Alberta in late May to early June. Migrants have been sighted as far north as Lac La Biche. Adult Monarchs can be found almost anywhere in the course of their migrations. Breeding usually occurs along river banks and irrigation ditches, where patches of milkweed can be found.

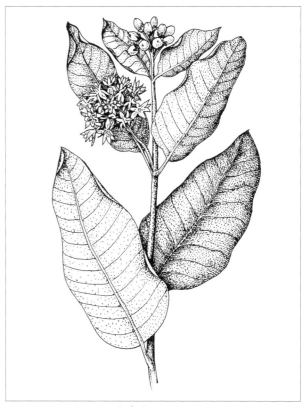

Asclepias speciosa
Showy Milkweed

Danaus plexippus larva

Glossary

abdomen: the last body section on an insect, holding most of the internal organs and bearing the external genitalia.

adult: the final life stage of an insect, usually possessing wings and capable of reproduction.

alpine: referring to the zone above treeline in mountainous regions.

alpines: common name of butterflies of the genus *Erebia* (Satyridae: Satyrinae).

admirals: common name of some butterflies in the genera *Limenitis* and *Vanessa* (Nymphalidae: Limenitidinae and Nymphalinae).

androconia: specialized scented scales on the wings of some male butterflies.

anglewings: common name of butterflies in the genus *Polygonia* (Nymphalidae: Nymphalinae).

antennae: paired, filamentous sensory structures on an insect's head.

apex: (plural **apices**) front tip of a butterfly's fore wing.

author: person who described and named a new taxon (e.g., species, subspecies); the author's name is often placed after the name of the taxon he or she described.

basal: part of a structure closest to the body.

blues: common name for butterflies in the subfamily Polyommatinae of the family Lycaenidae.

boreal: referring to northern areas dominated by coniferous trees.

butterfly: day-flying members of the Order **LEPIDOPTERA** possessing clubbed antennae; more specifically, those with antennae that do not have drawn-out hooks or points at their tips.

Canadian National Collection: Agriculture Canada's insect collection, housed on the Central Experimental Farm in Ottawa.

caterpillar: the larva, a worm-like, juvenile life stage of insects in the Order **LEPIDOPTERA**.

cell: an area of wing membrane between veins.

cline: a gradient of morphological or physiological change shown by a group of related organisms, usually correlated with an environmental or geographical transition (e.g., an altitudinal cline in wing colour in *Colias* butterflies).

colony: a localized breeding group of butterflies.

composites: plants in the daisy family (Compositae).

conifers: cone-bearing, usually evergreen trees (e.g., pine, spruce, fir).

coppers: common name of butterflies in the subfamily Lycaeninae of the family Lycaenidae.

coulee: a ravine formed by streams (often temporary ones) typical of grassland areas in southern Alberta.

cremaster: a group of tiny hooks at the tip of the pupal abdomen, used to anchor the insect during pupation.

crucifer: a plant in the mustard family, Cruciferae.

deciduous: refers to trees that lose their leaves before winter, in contrast to evergreens.

diagnosis: a set of characteristics used to recognize a particular taxon (e.g., species, genus).

diapause: a period of dormancy between periods of activity (e.g., hibernation).

discal cell: the major cell in the butterfly wing, located in the centre of the wing close to its base.

discoidal cell: another term for **discal cell** (see above).

distal: part of a structure farthest from the body.

distribution: the area in which a certain taxon (e.g., species) is found.

diurnal: active during the day.

dorsal: the side facing up, e.g., when a butterfly is resting on the ground with its wings spread, the dorsal surface of the wings is uppermost.

elfin: common name for butterflies in the genus *Incisalia* (Lycaenidae: Heclinae).

entomologist: one who practises **entomology**, the study of insects.

eversible: something that can be turned inside out.

eye spot: eye-shaped spot on butterfly wings, often complete with highlights and a central pupil-like dot.

flight period: time of year when adults of a given butterfly species are likely to be found.

flyway: flight paths commonly taken by butterflies, often paralleling features like ravines, coulees, or animal trails.

fore wing: the front wing of an insect.

form: a genetic variant within a population (e.g., the black form of *Papilio zelicaon*).

frenulum: the spine (in males) or bristles (in females) arising from the base of the hind wing and extending beneath the fore wing used to unite the wings in flight.

genus: the taxonomic level immediately above the species level (e.g., there are two Alberta species in the genus *Glaucopsyche*: *G. piasus* and *G. lygdamus*). The plural of genus is **genera**.

ground colour: the background colour of a butterfly's wing (e.g., *Neophasia menapia* has black markings on a white ground colour).

hilltop: hilltopping is an activity performed by butterflies in many taxa, in which males gather at geographical prominences to wait for passing females.

hind wing: the back wing of an insect.

holarctic: having a geographic distribution across the northern parts of North America, Asia and Europe.

host plant: plant species on which caterpillars of a given species feed, and on which egg-laying occurs.

hybrid: offspring of a mating between two different species; the phenomenon is termed **hybridization**.

instar: a life stage of an insect between moults. Butterflies pass through many larval (i.e., caterpillar) instars.

intergrade: the result of a cross between two subspecies.

larva: the immature stage of an insect. In the Order **LEPIDOPTERA**, larvae are also called caterpillars.

legumes: plants in the pea family (Leguminosae).

Lepidoptera: an order of insects including butterflies, skippers and moths.

locality: a specific geographic location in which a species is found.

macrolepidoptera: a category of the Order **LEPIDOPTERA** that includes butterflies, skippers and large moths.

marbles: common name of butterflies in the genus *Euchloe* (Pieridae: Anthocharinae).

microlepidoptera: a category of the Order **LEPIDOPTERA** that includes small moths.

migrant: a species incapable of sustaining a population in a given location (e.g., because winter is too harsh) and so is present in that area only because it migrates in from a stable source populations.

montane: referring to mountainous areas below the treeline.

morphology: physical structure of an organism.

moth: typically nocturnal member of the Order **LEPIDOPTERA** possessing filamentous or feathery antennae.

muskeg: northern bog composed mainly of sphagnum moss.

nectar: a verb meaning to feed on nectar from flowers.

nocturnal: active during the night.

nominate subspecies: refers to a subspecies that contains the original type specimen of a species and therefore has the same name as the specific epithet (e.g., *Euchloe ausonides ausonides*).

ocellus: (plural **ocelli**) another term for **eye spot** (see above).

osmeteria: a pair of smelly eversible tubes located near the head of caterpillars in the family Papilionidae.

oviposition: the laying of eggs.

palp: small appendage located at the base of the proboscis in adult lepidopterans.

parental species: the two pure species whose mating produces hybrids.

parnassians: common name of butterflies in the subfamily Parnassiinae of the family Papilionidae.

patrolling: the continuous flight of male butterflies when searching for females.

patronym: a scientific name derived from the name of a person (e.g., *Colias alexandra*).

phenology: timing of life cycle events.

polymorphism: phenomenon in which multiple forms (typically colour forms) occur in a single species.

population: a group of potentially interbreeding members of a given species.

priority: the rule that the first name given to a taxon (e.g., genus, species) is the official name.

proboscis: the long tube through which adult **LEPIDOPTERA** suck fluids.

proximal: part of a structure closest to the body.

puddle: a verb meaning to congregate at puddles or wet patches of soil to imbibe fluids.

pupa: the typically immobile stage between the final larval instar and the adult insect.

reticulanum: a hook, loop, or specialized scales attached to the underside of the fore wings near the base, to receive the frenulum.

ringlet: common name of butterflies in the genus *Coenonympha* (Satyridae: Satyrinae).

riparian: referring to things located on the banks of a river (e.g., riparian vegetation).

satellite spot: small spot located next to a larger one on a butterfly's wing.

scales: flattened, colourful hairs that cover the wings of **LEPIDOPTERA**.

scree: accumulation of loose stones and pebbles at the base of a hill.

sibling species: species that are each other's closest relatives and are often difficult to distinguish morphologically.

skipper: day-flying member of the Order **LEPIDOPTERA** possessing clubbed antennae with tips drawn out into points or hooks.

species: a group of individuals capable of successfully interbreeding.

species group: a group of closely related species that is not assigned to an official taxonomic level (e.g., the *Papilio machaon* species group).

specific epithet: the part of a species' name that explicitly denotes that species (e.g., in *Danaus plexippus* the specific epithet is *plexippus*).

sphragis: a pouch-like structure at the tip of the abdomen of mated female Parnassians, secreted by the male during mating.

spiracles: breathing holes on the thorax and abdomen of an insect

stigma: a patch of specialized scented scales found on the wings of many male butterflies.

subalpine: referring to areas slightly lower in altitude than alpine zones.

subapical: slightly below the apex, or tip.

submarginal: the area located just inside the outer margins of both the fore and hind wings.

subspecies: morphologically distinctive populations of a given species.

sulphurs: common name of butterflies in the subfamily Coliadinae of the family Pieridae.

swale: a low-lying, usually wet stretch of land.

Swallowtails: common name of butterflies in the subfamily Papilioninae of the family Papilionidae.

synonym: when a taxon (e.g., species, subspecies) has been described and named several times, each name is called a synonym. The oldest name is the senior synonym and more recent ones are junior synonyms. Almost invariably, the senior synonym is the valid name. A list of all names in the literature is called a **synonymy**.

talus: rock debris at the base of a cliff or mountainside.

taxon: a group of organisms given a proper scientific name (e.g., the family Papilionidae of the Order **LEPIDOPTERA**).

taxonomy: the classification of organisms. Someone who engages in taxonomy is a **taxonomist**.

thecla spot: a small blue and red spot near the base of the hind wing tails of *Satyrium* butterflies (Satyridae: Theclinae).

thorax: the middle of the three body parts of an insect, bearing legs and wings.

tubercle: a fleshy bump or protuberance.

tundra: a treeless plain in arctic and subarctic regions characterized by permanently frozen subsoil.

type locality: the place where the type specimen for which a new taxon was described was first found.

umbellifers: plants belonging to the carrot family (Umbelliferae).

uncus: the terminal dorsal plate in the male butterfly's genitalia.

vein: a hard, thickened line in the wing of an insect.

ventral: the side facing downwards, e.g., when a butterfly has its wings spread, the ventral side is lowermost.

whites: common name of butterflies in the subfamily Pierinae of the family Pieridae.

Bibliography

Ackery, P.R. 1973. A list of the type specimens of *Parnassius* (Lepidoptera: Papilionidae) in the British Museum (Natural History). *Bulletin of the British Museum of Natural History Entomology* **29**:1-35.

Ackery, P.R. and R.I. Vane-Wright. 1984. Milkweed butterflies: their cladistics and biology. British Museum (Natural History), London. 425 pp.

Acorn, J. H. 1976. Pages from an insect watcher's notebook. *Edmonton Naturalist* **4**:193-195.

___ 1993. Butterflies of Alberta. Lone Pine Publishing, Edmonton, Alberta.

Acorn, J. H. and E. Savoy. 1994. The first official butterfly counts in Alberta. *Alberta Naturalist* **24**:11-12.

Acorn, J. H. and T. W. Thormin. 1976. Faunal observations for the Edmonton area: Spring 1976. Part III -Butterflies. *Edmonton Naturalist* **4**:179-182.

Adler, P.H. and D.L. Pearson. 1982. Why do male butterflies visit mud puddles? *Canadian Journal of Zoology* **60**:322-325.

Allen, P. 1974. Observation of a Mourning Cloak butterfly (*Nymphalis antiopa*). *Calgary Field Naturalist* **5**:204.

Anderson, R. L. 1959. New distributional records for two species of Lepidoptera. *Proceedings of the Seventh Annual Meeting of the Entomological Society of Alberta*, pp. 8-9.

___ 1960. A collecting trip to the Nordegg area July 4 and 5, 1960. *Proceedings of the Eighth Annual Meeting of Entomological Society of Alberta*, pp. 14-16.

___ 1974. New butterflies for the city of Calgary. *Calgary Field Naturalist* **5**:208-209.

Anonymous. 1978. Plants and animals seen on a CFN's annual bus trip on June 4, 1978 (day trip to Buffalo Lake). *Calgary Field Naturalist* **10**:63-64.

Arnold, R.A. 1985. Geographic variation in natural populations of *Speyeria callippe* (Boisduval) (Lepidoptera: Nymphalidae). *Pan-Pacific Entomologist* **61**:1-23.

Austin, G.T. 1986. A review of the Satyrinae genus *Neominois*, with descriptions of three new subspecies. *Bulletin of the Allyn Museum* **107**:1-27.

Barnes, W. 1897. Some new species and varieties of Lepidoptera from the Western United States. *The Canadian Entomologist* **29**:39-42.

Barnes, W. and F.H. Benjamin. 1923. A new race of *Brenthis* from Colorado (Lepid.). *The Canadian Entomologist* **55**:146.

___ 1926. Notes on diurnal Lepidoptera with additions and corrections to the recent "List of Diurnal Lepidoptera". *Bulletin of the Southern California Academy of Sciences* **25**:88-98.

Barnes, W. and J. McDunnough. 1916. Some new races and species of North American Lepidoptera. *The Canadian Entomologist* **48**:221-226.

___ 1917. Checklist of the Lepidoptera of Boreal America. Herald Press. Decatur, Illinois. 22 pp.

___ 1918. Contributions to the natural history of the Lepidoptera of North America. Decatur **4**(2):61-208.

Battrum, M. V. (Compiler) 1977-1979. Natural History observations - other than birds. *Calgary Field Naturalist* **9**:60-62; **9**:102-106; **9**:134-137 (1977); **9**:157-159; **10**:35-36; **10**:59-62; **10**:83-95; **10**:125-132; **10**:154-162 (1978); **11**:19-20; **11**:43-49 (1979).

Bean, T.E. 1890, 1893, 1894. The butterflies of Laggan N.W.T.; account of certain species inhabiting the Rocky Mountains in Latitude 51°25'[N]. *The Canadian Entomologist* **22**:94-99; **22**:126-132 (1890); **25**:145-149 (1893); **6**:155-156 (1894).

___ 1893. Food plants of *Grapta zephyrus*. *Entomological News* **4**:220-221.

___ 1895. A comparison of *Colias hecla* with *Colias meadii* and *Colias ellis*. *Psyche* **7**:219-229.

Behr, H.H. 1862. Our Californian Argynnides. *Proceedings of the California Academy of Natural Sciences* **2**:172-177.

___ 1863. On Californian Lepidoptera. III. *Proceedings of the California Academy of Natural Sciences* **3**:84-93.

___ 1864. *In*: W.H. Edwards, Notes on the Argynnides of California. *Proceedings of the Entomological Society of Philadelphia* **3**: 434-436.

___ 1866. Description of a new species of *Chrysophanus*. *Proceedings of the Entomological Society of Philadelphia* **6**:208.

___ 1869. Description of a new genus of Pieridae, and certain new species of butterflies from California. *Transactions of the American Entomological Society* **2**:303-304.

Belicek, J., N. Kondla and T. Kral. 1989. The European Skipper: New to Alberta. *Alberta Naturalist* **19**:36-37.

Beutenmüller, W. 1898. Revision of the species of *Euchloe* inhabiting America north of Mexico. *Bulletin of the American Museum of Natural History* **10**:235-248.

Billberg, G.J. 1820. Enumeratio insectorum in Museo Billberg. Gadel, Stockholm. **4**:1-138.

Bird, C.D. 1973a. Early spring butterflies in the city of Calgary. *Calgary Field Naturalist* **4**:199-200.

_____ 1973b. Late spring butterflies in the city of Calgary. *Calgary Field Naturalist* **4**:227-229.

_____ 1973c. Spring 1973 migration of the painted lady butterfly into Alberta. *Calgary Field Naturalist* **5**:5-7.

_____ 1973d. Summer butterflies in the city of Calgary. *Calgary Field Naturalist* **5**:8-9.

_____ 1973e. New or hypothetical butterflies for Calgary. *Calgary Field Naturalist* **5**:58-61.

_____ 1973f. New butterflies for Calgary. *Calgary Field Naturalist* **5**:107-108.

_____ (ed.) 1973g. Five "Natural Areas" in the city of Calgary. A report prepared by a committee of the Calgary Field Naturalists' Society. 272 pp.

_____ (Compiler) 1973-1976. Natural history observations - other than birds. *Calgary Field Naturalist* **5**:199-200 (1973); **6**:96-102, **6**:129-130, **6**:213-214, **6**:364-368 (1974); **7**:58-72, **7**:138-140, **7**:159-160, **7**:186-188 (1975); **7**:314-316, **8**:26-32, **8**:51-52 (1976).

_____ 1974a. More new butterflies for Calgary. *Calgary Field Naturalist* **5**:209-210.

_____ 1974b. Further notes on the butterflies and skippers of Calgary. *Calgary Field Naturalist* **5**:247.

_____ 1974c. A calendar of the butterflies and skippers of Calgary. *Calgary Field Naturalist* **5**:275-277.

_____ (ed.) 1974d. Natural areas 1973. A report prepared by the natural areas committee of the Calgary Field Naturalists' Society. 245 pp.

_____ 1975a. Checklist of the butterflies of the natural areas in Calgary. Pp. 175-177 *in*: Sherrington, P. (ed.) A popular guide to the natural areas of Calgary. *Calgary Field Naturalists' Society*.

_____ 1975b. Rhopalocera in the N.B. Sanson collection. *Journal of the Lepidopterists' Society* **30**:201-206.

_____ 1975c. Moths, skippers and butterflies in the Yamnuska natural area. Pp. 22-27 *in*: Yamnuska, introductory studies of a natural area with proposals for its protection and use. Bow Valley Naturalists: Banff.

_____ 1975d. A calendar of the butterflies and skippers of Banff National Park, Alberta. *Naturalist* **5**:71-75.

_____ 1975e. A revised calendar of the butterflies and skippers of Calgary. *Calgary Field Naturalist* **6**:312-314.

_____ 1975f. A calendar of the butterflies and skippers of the alpine area of Plateau Mountain. *Alberta Naturalist* **5**:26-28.

_____ 1977. The lichens, bryophytes, and butterflies of the proposed park in the Kananaskis Lakes area. Unpublished report for Parks Planning and Design Branch; Alberta Recreation, Parks and Wildlife, Edmonton. 76 pp.

_____ 1978. R.J. Fitch 1886-1961. *Blue Jay* **36**:174-176.

_____ 1979a. The question mark - another "eastern" butterfly new to Alberta. *Alberta Naturalist* **9**:66.

_____ 1979b. Paul F. Bruggemann, 1890-1974. *Blue Jay* **37**:195-197.

_____ 1982. Endangered species/habitats-butterflies. *Alberta Naturalist* **12**:50-52.

Bird, C.D. and E. Cooley. (Compilers) 1973. Natural history observations. Part 2. Species other than birds. *Calgary Field Naturalist* **5**:120-132, 176-180, 203-204.

Bird, C.D. and C.D. Ferris. 1979. Type locality of *Epidemia dorcas florus* (Lepidoptera: Lycaenidae). *The Canadian Entomologist* **111**:637-639.

Bird, C.D. and A.M. Harper. 1980. F.H. Wolley-Dod, Alberta's leading pioneer lepidopterist. *Alberta Naturalist* **10**:49-55.

Bird, C.D., G.J. Hilchie, N.G. Kondla, W.W. Smith, E. Kuyt, J.R. Ryan and T.W. Thormin. 1982. Butterflies of northeastern Alberta. *Blue Jay* **40**:141-153.

Bird, C.D. and N.G. Kondla. 1974. Some skippers and butterflies from Dinosaur Provincial Park, Alberta. *Blue Jay* **32**:87-88.

Bird, C.D., V. Lang and C. Robinson. (Compilers) 1973. Natural History observations. *Calgary Field Naturalist* **5**:17-44.

Bird, C.D., W.G. McKay, V. Lang and B. Danielson. (Compilers) 1973. Natural History observations. *Calgary Field Naturalist* **4**:206-218.

Bird, C.D. and E. Sangster. (Compilers) 1974-1975. Natural History observations other than birds. *Calgary Field Naturalist* **6**:45-58 (1974); **7**:97-112 (1975).

Bird, C.D. and W.W. Smith. 1979. The hobomok skipper - another "eastern" species in Alberta. *Alberta Naturalist* **8**:158-159.

Boisduval, J.A. 1832-1843. Icones historiques des Lépidoptères d'Europe, nouveaux ou peu connus. Collection avec figures coloriées des Papillons d'Europe nouvellement découverts. Ouvrage formant le complément de tous les auteurs iconographes. Roret, Paris.

_____ 1852. Lépidoptères de la Californie. *Annales de la Société Entomologique de France* **2**(10):275-324.

___ 1869. Lépidoptères de la Californie. *Annales de la Société Entomologique de Belgique* **12**:5-94.

Boisduval, J.A. and J. Leconte. 1829-1842. Histoire générale et iconographie des Lépidoptères et des Chenilles de l'Amérique septentrionale. Roret, Paris.

Boisduval, J.A., J.A. Rambur and Ad. de Graslin. 1832-1843. Collection iconographique et historique des Chenilles d'Europe, ou descriptions et figures des Chenilles d'Europe, avec l'histoire de leurs métamorphoses et des applications à l'agriculture. Roret, Paris.

Borror, D.J., C.A. Triplehorn and N.F. Johnson. 1989. An introduction to the study of insects. 6th Edition. Saunders College Publishing, Toronto.

Bowman, K. 1919. Annotated checklist of the macrolepidoptera of Alberta. Alberta Natural History Society, Red Deer. 16pp.

___ 1921a. Annotated checklist of the macrolepidoptera of Alberta. Additions, 1919. *The Canadian Entomologist* **53**:13-14.

___ 1921b. Annotated checklist of the macrolepidoptera of Alberta. Additions, 1920. *The Canadian Entomologist* **53**:211-212.

___ 1923. Annotated checklist of the macrolepidoptera of Alberta. Additions, 1921. *The Canadian Entomologist* **55**:71-72.

___ 1924. Annotated checklist of the macrolepidoptera of Alberta. Additions. *The Canadian Entomologist* **56**:189-191.

___ 1928. Additions to annotated checklist of the macrolepidoptera of Alberta. *The Canadian Entomologist* **60**:117-118.

___ 1934. Annotated checklist of the macrolepidoptera of Alberta, additions and corrections. *The Canadian Entomologist* **66**:131-132.

___ 1938. Additions and corrections to checklist of the macrolepidoptera of Alberta. *The Canadian Entomologist* **70**:260-261.

___ 1942. A note on *Colias eurytheme* Bdv., with description of a new race (Lepidoptera, Pieridae). *The Canadian Entomologist* **74**:25.

___ 1944. Additions and corrections to checklist of the macrolepidoptera of Alberta. *The Canadian Entomologist* **76**:191-192.

___ 1951. An annotated list of the Lepidoptera of Alberta. *Canadian Journal of Zoology* **29**:121-165.

Britten, H.B. and P.F. Brussard. 1992. Genetic divergence and the Pleistocene history of the alpine butterflies *Boloria improba* (Nymphalidae) and the endangered *Boloria acrocnema* (Nymphalidae) in western North America. *Canadian Journal of Zoology* **70**:539-548.

Brower, L.P. 1958. Larval food plant specificity in butterflies of the *Papilio glaucus* group. *Lepidopterists' News* **12**:103-114.

___ 1959. Speciation in butterflies of the *Papilio glaucus* group. I. Morphological relationships and hybridization. *Evolution* **13**:40-63.

Brown, F.M. 1953a. Taxonomic notes on *Oeneis uhleri* Reakirt (Lepidoptera, Satyridae). *American Museum Novitates* No. 1625. 26 pp.

___ 1953b. The subspecies of *Oeneis alberta* (Lepidoptera, Satyridae). *American Museum Novitates* No. 1626. 21 pp.

___ 1955. Studies of Nearctic *Coenonympha tullia* (Rhopalocera, Satyridae), *Coenonympha tullia inornata* Edwards. *Bulletin of the American Museum of Natural History* **105**:359-410.

___ 1960. A badlands subspecies of *Limenitis weidemeyerii* Edwards (Lepidoptera, Nymphalidae). *American Museum Novitates* No. 2018. 6 pp.

___ 1965. The types of the nymphalid butterflies described by William Henry Edwards. Part I. Argynninae. *Transactions of the American Entomological Society* **91**:233-350.

___ 1969. The types of the lycaenid butterflies named by William Henry Edwards. Part II. Lycaenidae. *Transactions of the American Entomological Society* **95**:161-179.

___ 1970. The types of the lycaenid butterflies named by William Henry Edwards. Part III. Plebejinae. With four neotypes established by John C. Downey. *Transactions of the American Entomological Society* **96**:353-433.

___ 1971. The Arrowhead Blue, *Glaucopsyche piasus* Boisduval (Lycaenidae: Plebejinae). *Journal of the Lepidopterists' Society* **25**:240-246.

___ 1973. The types of the pierid butterflies named by William Henry Edwards. *Transactions of the American Entomological Society* **99**:29-118.

Brown, F.M. and L.D. Miller. 1977. The types of the hesperiid butterflies named by William Henry Edwards. Part II, Hesperiidae: Hesperiinae, Section I. *Transactions of the American Entomological Society* **103**:259-302.

Brown, F.M., D. Eff and B. Rotger. 1957. Colorado Butterflies. Denver Museum of Natural History. Denver, Colorado. 368 pp.

Brussard, P.F., J.F. Baughman, D.D. Murphy, P.R. Ehrlich and J. Wright. 1989. Complex population differentiation in checkerspot butterflies (*Euphydryas* spp.). *Canadian Journal of Zoology* **67**:330-335.

Bryant, O. 1935. Notes on the diurnal Lepidoptera of the Canadian arctic. Collected by Owen Bryant in the summers of 1929 to 1932. III: Notes on the species. *Bulletin of the Brooklyn Entomological Society* **30**:115-118.

Bryk, F. 1935. Lepidoptera Parnassiidae pars ii (subfam. Parnassiinae). *Das Tierreich*, part 65. 790 pp.

Bryk, F. and C. Eisner. 1935. Kritische revision der Gattung *Parnassius* unter benutzung des materials der Kollektion Eisner. *Parnassiana* **3**:47-62.

Burns, J.M. 1964. Evolution in skipper butterflies of the genus *Erynnis*. *University of California Publications in Entomology* **37**:1-216.

_____ 1990. *Amblyscirtes*: problems with species, species groups, the limits of the genus, and genus groups beyond - a look at what is wrong with the Skipper classification of Evans (Hesperiidae). *Journal of the Lepidopterists' Society* **44**:11-27.

_____ 1994a. Genitalia at the generic level: *Atrytone* restricted, *Anatrytone* resurrected, new genus *Quasimellana* - and Yes! We have no *Mellanas* (Hesperiidae). *Journal of the Lepidopterists' Society* **48**:*273-337.*

_____ 1994b. Split skippers: Mexican genus *Poanopsis* goes in the *origenes* group - and *Yvretta* forms the *rhesus* group - of *Polites* (Hesperiidae). *Journal of the Lepidopterists' Society* **48**:24-45.

Butler, A.G. 1868. Catalogue of Diurnal Lepidoptera described by Fabricius in the collection of the British Museum. London, Printed by Order of the Trustees.

_____ 1877. Description of a new species of *Argynnis* from Arctic America. *Entomologist's Monthly Magazine* **13**:206.

Butler, A.G. and W.F. Kirby. 1893. List of insects collected by Miss Elizabeth Taylor in western North America in the summer of 1892. *Annals and Magazine of Natural History*, Series 6, **12**:11-21.

Byers, J.R., B.T. Roth, R.D. Thomson and A.K. Topinka. 1984. Contamination of mustard and canola seed by frass of painted lady caterpillars, *Vanessa cardui* (Lepidoptera: Nymphalidae). *The Canadian Entomologist* **116**:1431-1432.

Cadbury, J.W. 1937. Lepidoptera collected in northern British Columbia by Miss Josephine de N. Henry. Part I - Rhopalocera. *Proceedings of the Academy of Natural Sciences of Philadelphia* **89**:387-413.

Carde, R.T., A.M. Shapiro and H.K. Clench. 1970. Sibling species in the *eurydice* group of *Lethe* (Lepidoptera: Satyridae). *Psyche* **77**:70-103.

Cary, M. 1907. On the diurnal Lepidoptera of the Athabaska and Mackenzie region, British America. *Proceedings of the United States National Museum* **31** no. 1488:425-457.

Case, J.W. (Compiler) 1976. Natural History observations - other than plants and birds and mammals. *Calgary Field Naturalist* **8**:103-106, 132.

_____ 1980. A report of a goldenrod spider preying on pearl crescent. *Blue Jay* **38**:14.

Case, J.W. and C.D. Bird. 1977. Butterflies and skippers of west-central Alberta. *Blue Jay* **35**:208-219.

CFNS Butterfly Study Group and T. Pike. 1990. The butterflies of the Cross Nature Conservancy. *Pica* **10**:13-18.

Chang, V.C.S. 1963. Quantitative analysis of certain wing and genitalia characters of *Pieris* in western North America. *Journal of Research on the Lepidoptera* **2**:97-125.

Chermock, F. H. 1929. Notes on North American Lepidoptera. *Bulletin of the Brooklyn Entomological Society* **24**:20-21.

Chermock, F.H. and R.L. Chermock. 1940. Some new diurnal Lepidoptera from the Riding Mountains and the Sand Ridge, Manitoba. *The Canadian Entomologist* **72**: 81-83.

Clark, A.H. 1932. The forms of the common Old World swallow-tail butterfly (*Papilio machaon*) in North America, with descriptions of two new subspecies. *Proceedings of the United States National Museum* **81**, no. 2934. 15 pp.

_____ 1936. Notes on the butterflies of the genus *Enodia* and description of a new fritillary from Peru. *Proceedings of the United States National Museum* **83**, no. 2983:251-259.

Clench, H.K. 1944. Two new subspecies of *Everes comyntas* Godart (Lepidoptera, Lycaenidae). *Journal of the New York Entomological Society* **52**:59-61.

_____ 1963. *Callophrys* (Lycaenidae) from the Pacific northwest. *Journal of Research on the Lepidoptera* **12**:151-160.

Clench, H.K. and L.D. Miller. 1980. *Papilio ladon* Cramer vs. *Argus pseudargiolus* Boisduval and Le Conte (Lycaenidae): a nomenclatorial nightmare. *Journal of the Lepidopterists' Society* **34**:103-119.

Clench, H.K. and P.A. Opler. 1983. Studies on Nearctic *Euchloe*. Part 8. Distribution, ecology, and variation of *Euchloe olympia* (Pieridae) populations. *Annals of the Carnegie Museum* **52**:41-54.

Collins, N.M. and M.G. Morris. 1985. Threatened swallowtail butterflies of the world. International Union for Conservation of Nature and Natural Resources, Gland, Switzerland. 402 pp.

Commonwealth Scientific and Industrial Research Organization. 1991. The insects of Australia. Volume II. 2nd Edition. Cornell University Press, Ithaca, New York.

Comstock, J.A. 1924. Butterflies of California. *Bulletin of the Southern California Academy of Sciences* **23**:18-20.

_____ 1940. Notes on the early stages of *Euphydryas gillettii* Barnes. *Bulletin of the Southern California Academy of Sciences* **39**:111-113.

Comstock, W.P. 1913. A new North American butterfly in the family Lycaenidae. *Bulletin of the Brooklyn Entomological Society* **8**:33-36.

Cook, J.H. 1906, 1907. Studies in the genus *Incisalia* II. *Incisalia augustus*. *The Canadian Entomologist* **38**:214-217; **39**:145-149.

Cook, J.H. and F.E. Watson. 1907. A new butterfly of the genus *Incisalia*. *The Canadian Entomologist* **39**:202-204.

Cooley, E. and C.D. Bird. (Compilers) 1973. Natural history observations. Part 2. Species other than birds. *Calgary Field Naturalist* **5**:73-96, 152-156.

Coolidge, K.R. 1908. The North American species of the genus *Erebia* (Lepidoptera). *Entomological News* **19**:73-75.

Cramer, P. 1775-1780. De uitlandsche kapellen voorkomende in de drie waereld-deelen Asia, Africa en America, by een verzameld en beschreeven door den Heer Pieter Cramer. - Onder deszelfs opzigt allen naar het leven getekend, in het koper gebragt, en met natuurlyke koleuren afgetekend. Baalde, Amsterdam.

Criddle, N. 1921. The entomological record 1920. *Annual Report of the Entomological Society of Ontario*. **51**:72-90. **52**:57-70; **55**:89-106.

_____ 1922. The entomological record 1921. *Annual Report of the Entomological Society of Ontario*. **52**:57-70.

_____ 1925. The entomological record 1924. *Annual Report of the Entomological Society of Ontario*. **55**:89-106.

Criddle, N. and C.H. Curran. 1923. The entomological record, 1922. *Annual Report of the Entomological Society of Ontario 1922*. **53**:76-90.

Cross, F.C. 1937. Butterflies of Colorado. *Proceedings of the Colorado Museum of Natural History* **16**:1-28.

Curtis, J. 1835. Description of the insects brought home by Commander James Clark Ross second voyage. *Appendix of Natural History* **4**:61-80.

Curtis, N.S. and C.D. Ferris. 1985. A review of *Colias meadii* W.H. Edwards with a description of a new subspecies from Idaho (Pieridae: Coliadinae). *Bulletin of the Allyn Museum* **91**:1-9.

Dalman, J.W. 1816. Försök till systematisk uppställning af Sveriges Fjärilar. *Vetensk. Acad. Handl.* **37**:48-101, 199-225.

Danks, H.V. and R.G. Foottit. 1989. Insects of the boreal zone of Canada. *The Canadian Entomologist* **121**:625-690.

Davenport, D. 1936. A new American *Coenonympha* (Lepidoptera, Satyridae). *The Canadian Entomologist* **68**:79-80.

_____ 1941. The butterflies of the satyrid genus *Coenonympha*. *Bulletin of the Museum of Comparative Zoology, Harvard College* **87**:1-138.

Denis, M. and I. Schiffermuller. 1775. Verzeichniss der Schmetterlinge der Wiener Gegend.

Dion, Y.-P. 1994. Extension de l'aire de répartition connu de *Colias canadensis* Ferris (Lepidoptera: Pieridae) en Alberta. *Fabreries* **19**:45-46.

Dirig, R. and J.F. Cryan. 1991. The status of Silvery Blue subspecies (*Glaucopsyche lygdamus lygdamus* and *G.l.couperi*: Lycaenidae) in New York. *Journal of the Lepidopterists' Society* **45**:272-290.

Dodge, G. 1874. *Hesperia Pawnee*. New species. *The Canadian Entomologist* **6**:44-45.

Dornfeld, E.J. 1980. The butterflies of Oregon. Timber Press. Forest Grove, Oregon.

dos Passos, C.F. 1938. Some new subspecies of North American Lycaenidae (Lepidoptera). *The Canadian Entomologist* **70**:45-48.

_____ 1940. A new subspecies of *Erebia discoidalis* Kirby (Rhopalocera: Satyridae). *American Museum Novitates* No. 1053. 2 pp.

_____ 1943. Some new subspecies of *Incisalia* from North America (Lepidoptera, Lycaenidae). *American Museum Novitates* No. 1230. 5 pp.

_____ 1949. The distribution of *Oeneis taygete* Geyer in North America with descriptions of new subspecies (Lepidoptera, Satyridae). *American Museum Novitates* No. 1399. 21 pp.

_____ 1958. The satyrid butterflies of northwestern North America (Lepidoptera: Satyridae). *Proceedings of the Tenth International Congress of Entomology* (1956) **1**:673-691.

_____ 1964. A synonymic list of the Nearctic Rhopalocera. *Lepidopterists' Society Memoir* No.1. 145 pp.

_____ 1970. A revised synonymic catalogue with taxonomic notes on some Nearctic Lycaenidae. *Journal of the Lepidopterists' Society* **24**:26-38.

dos Passos, C.F. and L.P. Grey. 1947. Systematic catalogue of *Speyeria* (Lepidoptera, Nymphalidae) with designation of types and fixations of type localities. *American Museum Novitates* No. 1370. 30 pp.

_____ 1955. A new name for *Argynnis lais* Edwards (Lepidoptera, Rhopalocera). *Journal of the New York Entomological Society* **63**:95-96.

Doubleday, E. 1841. Description of a new North American *Polyommatus*. (*P. lygdamus*). *Entomologist* pp. 209-211.

Doubleday, E., J.O. Westwood and W.C. Hewitson. [1847]. The genera of diurnal Lepidoptera, comprising their generic characters, a notice of their habits and transformation and a catalogue of species in each genus; illustrated with 86 plates by W.C. Hewitson. Longman, London. Vol. 1 (1846-1850).

Downey, J.C. and W.C. Fuller. 1961. Variation in *Plebejus icarioides* (Lycaenidae) I. Food plant specificity. *Journal of the Lepidopterists' Society* **15**:34-42.

Drury, D. 1773. Illustrations of natural history, wherein are exhibited upwards of two hundred and forty figures of exotic insects, according to their different genera; very few of which have hitherto been figured by any author, being engraved and coloured from nature, with the greatest accuracy, and under the authors own inspection, on fifty copper-plates; with a particular description of each insect etc. White, London.

Dufrane, A. 1939. Lycaenidae. *Bulletin et Annales de la Société Entomologique de Belgique* **79**:289-292.

Dyar, H.G. 1904. Two new forms of *Oeneis* Hübner. *Proceedings of the Entomological Society of Washington* **6**:142.

Edwards, H. 1881. On some apparently new forms of Diurnal Lepidoptera. *Papilio* **1**:50-55.

Edwards, W.H. 1861-1862. Description of Diurnal Lepidoptera found within the limits of the United States and British America. *Proceedings of the Academy of Natural Sciences of Philadelphia* **13**:160-164 (1861); 54-58, 221-226 (1862).

_____ 1863a. Description of Diurnal Lepidoptera found within the limits of the United States and British America. *Proceedings of the Academy of Natural Sciences of Philadelphia* **15**:14-22.

_____ 1863b. Descriptions of Diurnal Lepidoptera found within the limits of the United States and British America. *Proceedings of the Entomological Society of Philadelphia* **2**:14-22, 78-82.

_____ 1864. Description of certain species of diurnal Lepidoptera found within the limits of the United States and British North America. *Proceedings of the Entomological Society of Philadelphia* **2**:501-507.

_____ 1865. Description of certain species of diurnal Lepidoptera found within the limits of the United States and British North America. *Proceedings of the Entomological Society of Philadelphia* **4**:201-204.

_____ 1869. Descriptions of new species of Diurnal Lepidoptera found within the United States. *Transactions of the American Entomological Society* **2**:369-376.

_____ 1870. Descriptions of new species of Diurnal Lepidoptera found within the United States. *Transactions of the American Entomological Society* **3**:10-22.

_____ 1871. Descriptions of new species of North American Butterflies. *Transactions of the American Entomological Society* **3**:266-277.

_____ 1872a. Descriptions of new species of Diurnal Lepidoptera found within the United States. *Transactions of the American Entomological Society* **4**:61-70.

_____ 1872b. Synopsis of North American butterflies. American Entomological Society, Philadelphia. 52 pp.

_____ 1873. Descriptions of new species of Diurnal Lepidoptera found within the United States. *Transactions of the American Entomological Society* **4**:343-348.

_____ 1874. Descriptions of new species of Diurnal Lepidoptera found in North America. *Transactions of the American Entomological Society* **5**:13-19, 103-111.

_____ 1877. Lepidoptera of the Big Horn Mountains. *Field and Forest* **3**:48.

_____ 1878. Descriptions of new species of North American Lepidoptera. *Field and Forest* **3**:115-119, 142-144.

_____ 1879. Descriptions of new species of North American butterflies; also notes upon certain species. *The Canadian Entomologist* **11**:81-89.

_____ 1881a. Descriptions of new species of Diurnal Lepidoptera found within the United States. *Transactions of the American Entomological Society* **9**:1-8.

_____ 1881b. Description of a new species of *Chrysophanus*. *Transactions of the Kansas Academy of Science* **7**:69-70.

_____ 1882. Description of the preparatory stages of *Grapta interrogationis* Fabricius. *The Canadian Entomologist* **14**:201-207.

_____ 1883. Descriptions of new species of North American butterflies. *The Canadian Entomologist* **15**:209-211.

_____ 1884. Notes upon *Colias christina* Edwards and *C. astraea* Edwards. *Papilio* **4**:30-34.

_____ 1885. Description of a new species of *Chionobas* from British America. *The Canadian Entomologist* **17**:74-75.

_____ 1890a. Notes on *Erebia epipsodea* Butler. *The Canadian Entomologist* **22**:48-52.

_____ 1890b. Description of a new species of *Argynnis* from Canada. *The Canadian Entomologist* **22**:113-114.

_____ 1891a. Description of a new species of *Erebia*, and notes on the so-called *Chionobas bore* of Colorado. *The Canadian Entomologist* **23**:31-33.

    1891b. Description of a new species of *Argynnis* from Alberta Territory. *The Canadian Entomologist* **23**:198-199.

    1892. Miscellaneous notes on butterflies, larvae, etc. *The Canadian Entomologist* **24**:49-56, 105-111.

    1893. Notes on *Chionobas subhyalina* Curtis. *The Canadian Entomologist* **25**:137-139.

    1894. On *Chionobas alberta* Elwes. *The Canadian Entomologist* **26**:192.

    1897. The butterflies of North America. 3rd series. Houghton Mifflin and Co., Boston and New York.

Eff, D. (Coordinator) 1950. Rocky Mountains - New Mexico, Utah, to Alberta. Pp. 93-96 *in:* The field season summary of North American Lepidoptera for 1950. *Lepidopterists' News* **4**:85-107.

    (Coordinator) 1962-1978. Season's summary. Zone 3 Rocky Mountains Area: Alberta, Wyoming, Utah, Colorado and New Mexico. *News of the Lepidopterist's Society* **3**:4-7 (1962); **3**:5-7 (1965); **3**:6-7 (1966); **3**:6-8 (1967); **3**:9-11 (1968); **3**:8-10 (1969); Season's summary, Zone 3. Alberta, Wyoming, Utah, Colorado and New Mexico. **2**:3-6 (1972); **2**:6-9 (1973); **2**:4-6 (1974); **2-3**:4-7 (1975); **2**:4-7 (1976); **2**:5-8 (1978).

Ehrlich, P.R. 1954. Two new subspecies of *Erebia epipsodea* Butler (Lepidoptera: Satyridae). *Journal of the Kansas Entomological Society* **27**:80.

    1955. The distribution and subspeciation of *Erebia epipsodea* Butler (Lepidoptera: Satyridae). *University of Kansas Science Bulletin* **37**:175-194.

    1958. Problems of Arctic-Alpine insect distribution as illustrated by the butterfly genus *Erebia* (Satyridae). *Proceedings of the Tenth International Congress of Entomology* (1956) **1**:683-686.

Ehrlich, P.R. and A.H. Ehrlich. 1961. How to know the butterflies. Wm. C. Brown Company, Dubuque. 262 pp.

Eisner, C. 1957. Parnassiana nova, XII-XVII. Kritische Revision der Gattung *Parnassius* (Fortzetzung 9). *Zoologische Mededelingen* **35**:79-111.

    1977. Parnassiana nova 52. The genus *Parnassius* Latreille in William H. Howe's "The Butterflies of North America" (1975). *Zoologische Mededelingen* **52**:213-216.

Eitschberger, U. 1981. Die nordamerikanischen Arten aus der *Pieris napi-bryoniae-* Gruppe (Lep., Pieridae). *Atalanta* 11:366-371.

    1983. Systematische Untersuchungen am *Pieris napi-bryoniae-* Komplex. *Herbipoliana* 1.1 and 1.2.

Elliot, J.M. and A. Kawazoé. 1983. Blue butterflies of the *Lycaenopsis grais* group. British Museum (Natural History). 309 pp.

Ellis, S.L. 1973. Field observations on *Colias alexandra* Edwards (Pieridae). *Journal of the Lepidopterists' Society* **28**:114-125.

Elwes, H.J. 1893a. *Argynnis astarte. The Canadian Entomologist* **25**:186.

    1893b. *In*: Elwes, H.J. and J. Edwards. A revision of the genus *Oeneis. Transactions of the Entomological Society of London* 1893 Part XV:457-481.

    1894. Some little known species of *Oeneis. The Canadian Entomologist* **26**:336.

Emmel, J.F. and O. Shields. 1979. Larval food plant records for *Papilio zelicaon* in the western United States, and further evidence for the conspecificity of *P. zelicaon* and *P. gothica. Journal of Research on the Lepidoptera* **17**:56-67.

    1978. The biology of *Plebejus (Icaricia) shasta* in the western United States (Lycaenidae). *Journal of Research on the Lepidoptera* **17**:129-140.

Emmel, J.F. and T.C. Emmel. 1963. Larval food plant records for six western Papilios. *Journal of Research on the Lepidoptera* **1**:191-193.

Emmel, J.F., O. Shields and D.E. Breedlove. 1970. Larval foodplant records for North American Rhopalocera. Part 2. *Journal of Research on the Lepidoptera* **9**:233-242.

Emmel, T.C. 1969. Taxonomy, distribution and biology of the genus *Cercyonis* (Satyridae). I. Characteristics of the genus. *Journal of the Lepidopterists' Society* **23**:165-175.

Esper, E.J. 1787. Die (Europäischen) Schmetterlinge in Abbildungen nach der Natur mit Beschreibungen.

Evans, W.H. 1953. A catalogue of the American Hesperiidae indicating the classification and nomenclature adopted in the British Museum (Natural History). Part II (groups B,C,D). Pyrginae, Section 1. British Museum (Natural History), London. 178 pp.

    1953. A catalogue of the American Hesperiidae. Part III. Pyrginae, Section 2. British Museum (Natural History), London. 246 pp., 53 pl.

    1955. A catalogue of the American Hesperiidae. Part IV. Hesperiinae and Megathyminae. British Museum (Natural History), London. 499 pp., 88 pl.

Fabricius, J.C. 1775. Systema Entomologiae sistens Insectorum classes, ordines, genera, species, adjectis synonymis, locis, descriptionibus, observationibus. Flensburgi et Lipsiae, Korte. 832 pp.

____ 1787. Mantissa Insectorum sistens eorum species nuper detectas adjectis characteribus genericis, differentiis specificis, emendationibus, observationibus. Hafniae, Proft. 348 pp.

____ 1793. Entomologia systematica emendata et aucta, secundum classes, ordines, genera, species, adjectis synonymis, locis, observationibus, descriptionibus. Hafniae, Proft. 487 pp.

____ 1798. Supplementum Entomologiae systematicae. Hafniae, Proft et Storch. 572 pp.

____ 1807. Systema Glossatorum. Nicht publicirt. In der Bibliothek von Hr. Dohrn in Stettin gedruckt vorhanden.

Felder, C. 1862. Verzeichnis der von den Naturforschern der Novara gesammelten Macrolepidopteren. *Verhandlungen Zoologische-Botanische Gesellschaft in Wein* **12**:473-496.

Felder, C. and R. Felder. 1859. Lepidopterologische Fragmente. *Wiener Entomologische Monatsschrift* **3**:263-273.

Ferris, C.D. 1970. A new subspecies of *Plebejus* (*Icaricia*) *shasta* from Wyoming (Lepidoptera, Lycaenidae). *Entomological News* **81**:203-207.

____ 1972. Notes on certain species of *Colias* (Lepidoptera: Pieridae) found in Wyoming and associated regions. *Bulletin of the Allyn Museum* **5**:1-23.

____ 1973. A revision of the *Colias alexandra* complex (Pieridae) aided by ultraviolet reflectance photography with designation of a new subspecies. *Journal of the Lepidopterists' Society* **27**:57-73.

____ 1974. Distribution of Arctic-Alpine *Lycaena phlaeas* L. (Lycaenidae) in North America with designation of a new subspecies. *Bulletin of the Allyn Museum* **18**:1-13.

____ 1975. A note on *Oeneis melissa* (Fabricius) in the western United States (Satyridae). *Journal of Research on the Lepidoptera* **14**:213-215.

____ 1976a. A proposed revision of non-arctic *Parnassius phoebus* Fabricius in North America (Papilionidae). *Journal of Research on the Lepidoptera* **15**:1-22.

____ 1976b. Revisionary notes on *Plebejus* (*Icaricia*) *shasta* (Edwards). *Bulletin of the Allyn Museum* **36**:1-16.

____ 1977. Taxonomic revision of the species *dorcas* Kirby and *helloides* Boisduval in the genus *Epidemia* Scudder (Lycaenidae: Lycaeninae). *Bulletin of the Allyn Museum* **45**:1-42.

____ 1979. Biochemical studies of the larval hosts of two species of *Lycaena* Fabricius (Lycaenidae). *Journal of Research on the Lepidoptera* **17**:27-32.

____ 1981. A new subspecies of *Colias alexandra* W.H. Edwards and notes on *Colias hecla* Lefèbvre (Pieridae: Coliadinae). *Bulletin of the Allyn Museum* **63**:1-12.

____ 1982. Revision of North American *Colias hecla* Lefèbvre (Pieridae: Coliadinae). *Bulletin of the Allyn Museum* **71**:1-19.

____ 1984. Overview of *Clossiana improba* (Butler) in North America with a description of a new subspecies from Wyoming (Nymphalidae: Argynninae). *Bulletin of the Allyn Museum* **89**:1-7.

____ 1985. Revision of *Colias boothii* Curtis, *Colias thula* Hovanitz and *Colias nastes* Boisduval in North America (Pieridae, Coliadinae). *Bulletin of the Allyn Museum* **96**:1-51.

____ 1987. A revision of the North American *Salix*-feeding *Colias* species (Pieridae: Coliadinae). *Bulletin of the Allyn Museum* **112**:1-25.

____ 1988a. Revision of several North American Leguminosae-feeding *Colias* species, with description of a new subspecies (Pieridae: Coliadinae). *Bulletin of the Allyn Museum* **116**:1-28.

____ 1988b. Revision of the North American Ericaciae [sic]-feeding *Colias* species (Pieridae: Coliadinae). *Bulletin of the Allyn Museum* **122**:1-34.

____ 1989. Supplement to: A Catalogue/Checklist of the Butterflies of America North of Mexico. *The Lepidopterists' Society Memoir* No. 3. 103 pp.

____ 1993. Reassessment of the *Colias alexandra* group, the legume-feeding species, and preliminary cladistic analysis of the North American *Colias* (Pieridae: Coliadinae). *Bulletin of the Allyn Museum* **138**:1-91.

Ferris, C.D. and F.M. Brown. (eds.) 1981. Butterflies of the Rocky Mountain states. University of Oklahoma Press, Norman. 442 pp.

Ferris, C.D. and M.S. Fisher. 1973. *Callophrys* (*Incisalia*) *polios* (Lycaenidae): distribution in North America and description of a new subspecies. *Journal of the Lepidopterists' Society* **27**:112-118.

Ferris, C.D. and D.R. Groothuis. 1970. A new subspecies of *Boloria eunomia* (Nymphalidae) from Wyoming. *Journal of Research on the Lepidoptera* **9**:243-248.

Field, W.D. 1936. Three new butterfly races (Lepidoptera: Nymphalidae, Lycaenidae). *Entomological News* **47**:121-124.

Field, W.D. 1938a. A new race of *Lycaena mariposa* (Reakirt) (Lepidoptera, Lycaenidae). *The Pan-Pacific Entomologist* **14**:142-143.

326

___ 1938b. New forms and subspecies of North American Libytheidae and Lycaenidae. *Journal of the Kansas Entomological Society* **11**:124-133.

___ 1971. Butterflies of the genus *Vanessa* and of the resurrected genera *Bassaris* and *Cynthia* (Lepidoptera: Nymphalidae). *Smithsonian Contributions to Zoology* no. 84:1-105.

Field W.D., C.F. dos Passos and J.H. Masters. 1974. A bibliography of the catalogues, lists, faunal and other papers on the butterflies of North America north of Mexico arranged by State and Province (Lepidoptera: Rhopalocera). *Smithsonian Contributions to Zoology* No. 157, 104 pp.

Fisher, B.M. (Compiler) 1977. Natural history observations - other than birds. *Calgary Field Naturalist* **8**:179-180, 266.

Fletcher, J. 1886. Lists of Lepidoptera collected by Mr. J.B. Tyrrell in 1884 and 1885, and Mr. D.B. Dowling in 1886. Pp. 167-168 *in:* Tyrrell, B. Annual Report, Geological Survey of Canada.

___ 1893. [Book Notice]. The Butterflies of North America third series, part 13. *The Canadian Entomologist* **25**:86-87.

___ 1902. Entomological record 1901. *Annual Report of the Entomological Society of Ontario.* **32**:99-108.

___ 1903a. Descriptions of some new species and varieties of Canadian butterflies. *Transactions of the Royal Society of Canada* **9**(4):207-216.

___ 1903b. Entomological record 1902. *Annual Report of the Entomological Society of Ontario.* **33**:57-101.

___ 1905. Entomological record 1904. *Annual Report of the Entomological Society of Ontario.* **35**:56-78.

___ 1908. Entomological record 1907. *Annual Report of the Entomological Society of Ontario.* **38**:113-133.

___ 1909. Entomological record 1908. *Annual Report of the Entomological Society of Ontario.* **39**:99-116.

___ 1908. Mountain sprites. *Ottawa Naturalist* **21**:225-231.

Forbes, W.T. 1936. The *persius* group of *Thanaos* (Lepidoptera, Hesperiidae). *Psyche* **43**:104-113.

___ 1944. The genus *Phyciodes* (Lepidoptera, Nymphalinae). *Entomologica Americana* **24**:139-206.

Freeman, H.A. 1943. New Hesperioidea, with notes on some others from the United States (Lepidoptera, Rhopalocera). *Entomological News* **54**:72-77.

Freeman, T.N. 1938. A new race of *Incisalia niphon* Hbn. with notes on *Strymon acadica* Edwards (Lepidoptera, Lycaenidae). *The Canadian Entomologist* **70**:246-248.

___ 1939. Notes on the distribution of *Plebeius aquillo* Bdv. with the description of a new race from Manitoba (Lepidoptera, Lycaenidae). *The Canadian Entomologist* **71**:178-180.

___ 1958. The distribution of arctic and subarctic butterflies. *Proceedings of the Tenth International Congress of Entomology* (1956) **1**:659-672.

___ 1972. A correlation of some butterfly distributions with geological formations. *The Canadian Entomologist* **104**:443-444.

Fruhstorfer, H. 1909. Neue *Limenitis* Rassen. *Internationale entomologische Zeitschrift Guben* **3**:94-95.

Gadd, B. 1986. Handbook of the Canadian Rockies. Corax Press. Jasper, Alberta. 876 p.

Gall, L.P. and F.A.H. Sperling. 1981. A new high altitude species of *Boloria* from southwestern Colorado (Nymphalidae), with a discussion of phenetics and hierarchial decisions. *Journal of the Lepidopterists' Society* **34**:230-252.

Gautreau, E.J. and J.C.E. Melvin. 1974. Forest insects collected in Waterton National Park 1948-1971. Northern Forestry Centre, Canadian Forestry Service Report NOR-X-120. Edmonton. 37 pp.

Geddes, J. 1853. List of diurnal Lepidoptera collected in the Northwest Territory and the Rocky Mountains. *The Canadian Entomologist* **15**:221-223.

___ 1884a. List of diurnal Lepidoptera collected in the Northwest Territory and the Rocky Mountains during season of 1883, with localities. *The Canadian Entomologist* **16**:56-57.

___ 1884b. List of diurnal Lepidoptera collected in the Northwest and the Rocky Mountains season of 1884, with localities. *The Canadian Entomologist* **16**:224.

___ 1885a. *Euptoieta claudia. The Canadian Entomologist* **17**:60.

___ 1885b. Rocky Mountain butterflies. *The Canadian Entomologist* **17**:120.

___ 1887. Notes on the genus *Argynnis* whilst alive in the imago state. *The Canadian Entomologist* **19**:230-235.

___ 1889. Notes for collectors visiting the prairies and Rocky Mountains. *The Canadian Entomologist* **21**:57-58.

Geiger, H.J. and A. Scholl. 1985. Systematics and evolution of holarctic Pierinae (Lepidoptera): An enzyme electrophoretic approach. *Experientia* **41**:24-29.

Geiger, H. and A.M. Shapiro. 1986. Electrophoretic evidence for speciation within the nominal species *Anthocharis sara* Lucas (Pieridae). *Journal of Research on the Lepidoptera* **25**:15-24.

___ 1992. Genetics, systematics and evolution of holarctic *Pieris napi* species group populations (Lepidoptera, Pieridae). *Zeitschrift für Zoologisches Systematik und Evolutionsforschung* **30**:100-122.

Gerould, J.H. 1923. Inheritance of white wing colour a sex-limited (sex controlled) variation in yellow pierid butterflies. *Genetics* **8**:495-551.

Geyer, C. [1830]. *In*: J. Hübner. Zuträge zur Sammlung exotischer Schmetterlinge. Verfasser, Augsburg.

Gibson, A. 1911. The entomological record for 1910. *Annual Report of the Entomological Society of Ontario* **41**:101-120.

___ 1912. The entomological record for 1911. *Annual Report of the Entomological Society of Ontario* **42**:89-112.

___ 1913. The entomological record for 1912. *Annual Report of the Entomological Society of Ontario* **43**:113-140.

___ 1916. The entomological record for 1915. *Annual Report of the Entomological Society of Ontario* **46**:194-230.

___ 1917. The entomological record for 1916. *Annual Report of the Entomological Society of Ontario* **47**:137-171.

___ 1918. The entomological record for 1917. *Annual Report of the Entomological Society of Ontario* **48**:99-127.

___ 1919. The entomological record for 1918. *Annual Report of the Entomological Society of Ontario* **49**:97-123.

Gibson, A. and N. Criddle. 1920. The entomological record 1919. *Annual Report of the Entomological Society of Ontario 1919* **50**:112-134.

Gifford, S.M. and P.A. Opler. 1983. Natural history of seven hairstreaks in coastal North Carolina. *Journal of the Lepidopterists' Society* **37**:97-105.

Gillham, N.W. 1954. The taxonomic identity of *Melitaea* (*Athaliaeformia*) *mayi* Gunder (Lepidoptera, Nymphalidae). *Psyche* **61**:16-19.

___ 1956. Geographic variation and the subspecies concept in butterflies. *Systematic Zoology* **5**:110-120.

Godart, J.B. [1819]. [Article] Papillon. Encyclopédie Méthodique, vol **9**.

Goodpasture, C. 1973. Biology and systematics of the *Plebejus* (*Icaricia*) *acmon* group (Lepidoptera: Lycaenidae). I. Review of the group. *Journal of the Kansas Entomological Society* **46**:468-485.

___ 1974. Food plant specificity in the *Plebejus* (*Icaricia*) *acmon* group (Lepidoptera: Lycaenidae). *Journal of the Lepidopterists' Society* **28**:53-63.

Gregory, W.W. 1975. Checklist of the butterflies and skippers of Canada (Lepidoptera). *Lyman Entomological Museum and Research Laboratory, Memoir* No. 3. 44 pp.

___ 1983. A revised checklist of the butterflies and skippers of Canada. *Lyman Entomological Museum and Research Laboratory, Memoir* No. 14. 39 pp.

Grey, L.P. 1951. The subspeciation of *Speyeria atlantis. Lepidopterists' News* **5**:31-35.

Grey, L.P. and A.H. Moeck. 1962. Notes on overlapping subspecies. I . An example in *Speyeria zerene* (Nymphalidae). *Journal of the Lepidopterists' Society* **16**:81-97.

Grey, L.P., A.H. Moeck and W.H. Evans. 1963. Notes on overlapping subspecies. II. Segregation in the *Speyeria atlantis* of the Black Hills (Nymphalidae). *Journal of the Lepidopterists' Society* **17**:129-147.

Griffiths, A.J.F. and F.R. Ganders. 1983. Wildflower Genetics. Flight Press, Vancouver, British Columbia. 215 pp.

Griffiths, G.C.D. and D. E. Griffiths. 1980. Preliminary insect survey of the Clifford E. Lee Nature Sanctuary (Alberta) during 1980. Clifford E. Lee Nature Sanctuary Management Committee. 99 pp.

Grote, A.R. 1872. On a new checkered *Hesperia. The Canadian Entomologist* **4**:69-70.

___ 1873. On the butterflies of Anticosti. *Bulletin of the Buffalo Society of Natural Sciences* **1**:185.

Grote, A.R. and C.T. Robinson. 1867. Notes of the Lepidoptera of America. No. 1. *Annals of the Lyceum of Natural History (New York)* **8**:432-466.

Grum-Grshimaïlo, G.F. 1895. Lepidoptera palaearctica nova III. *Horae Societatis Entomologicae Rossicae* **29**:290-293.

Gunder, J.D. 1928. Additional transition forms (Lepid., Rhopalocera). *The Canadian Entomologist* **60**:162-168.

___ 1929a. New butterflies and sundry notes (Lepidoptera, Rhopalocera). *Bulletin of the Brooklyn Entomological Society* **24**:325-332.

___ 1929b. The genus *Euphydryas* Scudder of boreal America (Lepidoptera, Nymphalidae). *Pan-Pacific Entomologist* **6**:1-8.

___ 1932a. A few new butterflies (Lepidoptera, Rhopalocera). *Pan-Pacific Entomologist* **8**:123-127.

___ 1932b. New Rhopalocera (Lepidoptera). *The Canadian Entomologist* **64**:276-284.

Guppy, C.S. 1984. Alpine melanism in the butterfly *Parnassius phoebus* F. (Lepidoptera: Papilionidae). M.Sc. thesis, University of British Columbia. 158 pp.

___ 1986. Geographic variation in wing melanism of the butterfly *Parnassius phoebus* F. (Lepidoptera: Papilionidae). *Canadian Journal of Zoology* **64**:956-962.

___ 1989. Evidence for genetic determination of variation in adult size and wing melanism of *Parnassius phoebus* F. *Journal of the Lepidopterists' Society* **43**:148-151.

Hagen, R.H., R.C. Lederhouse, J.L. Bossart and J.M. Scriber. 1991. *Papilio canadensis* and *P. glaucus* (Papilionidae) are distinct species. *Journal of the Lepidopterists' Society* **45**:245-258.

Hall, G.C. 1924. Notes on *Polygonia j-album, Cercyonis alope, Phyciodes tharos, Heodes epixanthe* and *Euphydryas gillettii*. *Journal of the New York Entomological Society* **32**:109-111.

Hallworth, B. (ed.) 1988. Nose Hill: A popular guide. Calgary Field Naturalists' Society, 133 pp.

Hardy, G.A. 1959. On the life history of *Incisalia eryphon* (Lycaenidae) on southern Vancouver Island. *Journal of the Lepidopterists' Society* **13**:70.

Harper, A.M. 1979. A bibliography of Alberta entomology: 1883 to 1977. Alberta Agriculture, Edmonton. 101 pp.

Harris, T.W. 1829. American turnip butterfly. *New England Farmer* **7**:402.

_____ 1862. A report on the insects of Massachusetts, injurious to vegetation. 3rd edition. Andere Ausgabe, New York. 640 pp.

Harvey, D.T. and T.A. Webb. 1981. Ants associated with *Harkenclenus titus, Glaucopsyche lygdamus* and *Celastrina argiolus* (Lycaenidae). *Journal of the Lepidopterists' Society* **34**:372.

Hayes, J.L. 1980. Some aspects of the biology of the developmental stages of *Colias alexandra* (Pieridae). *Journal of the Lepidopterists' Society* **34**:345-352.

Hemming, F. 1935. Notes on seventeen genera of Rhopalocera. *Stylops* **4**:1-3.

Hewitson, W.C. 1867. Illustrations of Diurnal Lepidoptera (Part 1 Lycaenidae).

Higgins, L.G. 1953. Butterfly collecting in the U.S.A. *The Entomologist* **86**:207-210.

_____ 1960. A revision of the melitaeine genus *Chlosyne* and allied species (Lepidoptera: Nymphalinae). *Transactions of the Royal Entomological Society of London* **112**:381-475.

Hilchie, G.J. 1990. Classification, relationships, life history and evolution of *Erebia magdalena* Strecker (Lepidoptera: Satyridae). *Quaestiones Entomologicae* **26**:665-693.

Hoffmansegg, J.C. Graf von. 1804. Alphabetisches Verzeichniss zu J. Hübners Abbildungen der Papilionen mit den beigefugten vorzuglichsten Synonymen. *Illigers Magazin* **3**:181-206.

Holland, W.J. 1888. Captures made while travelling from Winnipeg to Victoria, B.C. *The Canadian Entomologist* **20**:89-92.

_____ 1898. The Butterfly Book. Doubleday, Page and Co., Garden City, New York. 2nd edition 1918), 382 pp.

_____ 1900. Alaska Insects. *Entomologist's Newsletter* **11**:381-389, 416-423.

_____ 1903. The Moth Book. Doubleday, Page and Co.,Garden City, New York. 479 pp.

Hooper, R.R. 1967. New butterfly records for Saskatchewan and Alberta. *Blue Jay* **25**:83-84.

_____ 1973. The Butterflies of Saskatchewan: A field guide. Saskatchewan Museum of Natural History, Regina. 216 pp.

_____ 1986. Revised checklist of Saskatchewan Butterflies. *Blue Jay* **44**:154-163.

Hovanitz, W. 1944. The ecological significance of the color phases of *Colias chrysotheme* in North America. *Ecology* **25**:45-60.

_____ 1949. Increased variability in populations following natural hybridization. Pp. 339-355 *in*: Genetics, Palaeontology and Evolution. G.L. Jepson, E. Mayr and G.G. Simpson (eds.). Princeton University Press, Princeton. 474 pp.

_____ 1950a. The biology of *Colias* butterflies. I. The distribution of the North American species. *Wasmann Journal of Biology* **8**:49-75.

_____ 1950b. The biology of *Colias* butterflies. II. Parallel geographical variation of dimorphic color phases in North American species. *Wasmann Journal of Biology* **8**:197-219.

_____ 1951. The biology of *Colias* butterflies. III. Variation of adult flight in the Arctic and Subarctic. *Wasmann Journal of Biology* **9**:1-9.

_____ 1962a. The distribution of the species of the genus *Pieris* in North America. *Journal of Research on the Lepidoptera* **1**:73-83.

_____ 1962b. The origin of a sympatric species in *Colias* through the aid of natural hybridization. *Journal of Research on the Lepidoptera* **1**:261-274.

_____ 1965. *Colias christina - alexandra* intergradation. *Journal of Research on the Lepidoptera* **4**: cover illustration with caption.

Hovanitz, W. and V.C.S. Chang. 1962. The effect of various food plants on survival and growth rate of *Pieris*. *Journal of Research on the Lepidoptera* **1**:21-42.

Howe, W.H. (ed.) 1975. The butterflies of North America. Doubleday and Co., Garden City, New York. 632 pp.

Huard, V.A. 1929. *In*: L. Provancher and V.A. Huard. Faune entomologique de la province de Québec. Sixième ordre. *Le Naturaliste Canadien* **56**:9-21, 37-46, 57-71.

Hübner, J. 1805, 1806. Sammlung europäischer Schmetterlinge. Verfasser, Augsburg. 1796-1841.

_____ 1810, 1821. Sammlung exotischer Schmetterlinge. Verfasser, Augsburg. 1806-1824.

_____ [1818]. Zuträge zur Sammlung exotischer Schmetterlinge. Verfasser, Augsburg. 1818-1837.

_____ 1819, 1823. Verzeichniss bekannter Schmetterlinge. Verfasser, Augsburg. 431 pp. 1816-1826.

Iftner, D.C. 1983. A new food plant record for *Chlosyne gorgone carlota* (Reakirt) (Nymphalidae). *Journal of the Lepidopterists' Society* **37**:80-81.

Ives, W.G.H. and H.R. Wong. 1988. Tree and shrub insects of the prairie provinces. Northern Forestry Centre, Canadian Forestry Service Report NOR-X-297. Edmonton. xi+327 pp.

Janz, L.J. 1990. A fortunate bit of collecting. *News of the Lepidopterists' Society* 1990, No. 2. 37 pp.

Johansson, B. 1763. *In*: C. Linnaeus. Centuria Insectorum rariorum. *Amoen. Acad.* **6**:384-415.

Johnson, K. 1978. Specificity, geographic distributions and foodplant diversity in four *Callophrys* (*Mitoura*) (Lycaenidae). *Journal of the Lepidopterists' Society* **32**:3-19.

_____ 1992. The Palearctic "elfin" butterflies (Lycaenidae, Theclinae). *Neue Entomologische Nachrichten* 29. 141 pp.

Johnson, K. and G. Balogh. 1977. Studies in the Lycaeninae (Lycaenidae). 2. Taxonomy and evolution of the nearctic *Lycaena rubidus* complex with description of a new species. *Bulletin of the Allyn Museum* **43**:1-62.

Kendall, R.O. 1964. Larval food plants for 26 species of Rhopalocera (Papilionidae) from Texas. *Journal of the Lepidopterists' Society* **18**:129-157.

_____ 1965. Larval food plants and distribution notes for 24 Texas Hesperiidae. *Journal of the Lepidopterists' Society* **19**:1-33.

_____ 1966. Larval food plants and distribution notes for 3 Texas Hesperiidae. *Journal of the Lepidopterists' Society* **20**:229-232.

Kirby, W. 1837. Fauna boreali-Americana or the Zoology of the northern parts of British America, containing descriptions of the objects of natural history collected on the late northern land expeditions, under command of Captain Sir John Franklin by John Richardson. Longman , London **4**:39-325.

Kirby, W.F. 1884. On a copy of "Peale's Lepidoptera Americana" in the library of the zoological department of the British Museum. *Papilio* **4**:103-104.

Klassen, P., A.R. Westwood, W.B. Preston and W.B. McKillop. 1989. The butterflies of Manitoba. Manitoba Museum of Man and Nature, Winnipeg. 290 pp.

Klots, A.B. 1930. Diurnal Lepidoptera from Wyoming and Colorado. *Bulletin of the Brooklyn Entomological Society* **25**:147-170.

_____ 1935. A new *Colias* from South Dakota (Lepidoptera: Pieridae). *American Museum Novitates* No. 767:1-2.

_____ 1939. *Brenthis aphirape* (Hübner) in North America, with a new record of the species from Maine (Lepidoptera, Nymphalidae). *Bulletin of the Brooklyn Entomological Society* **34**:259-264.

_____ 1940. New butterfly subspecies from Wyoming (Nymphalidae, Pieridae). *American Museum Novitates* No. 1054:1-6.

_____ 1951. A Field Guide to the Butterflies of North America, East of the Great Plains.Houghton Mifflin Co., Boston. 349 pp.

Kluk, K. 1802. Zwierzat domowych i dzikich osobliwie krajowych. *Warszawa* **4**.

Knoch, A.W. 1781. Beitrage zur Insectengeschichte. Vol 1:10-98. Schwickert, Leipzig .

Kocak, A.O. 1984. Notes on the names published in "A catalogue checklist of the butterflies of America north of Mexico" by L.D. Miller and F.M. Brown in 1981. *Priamus* **3**:93-97.

Kohler, S. 1977. Revision of North American *Boloria selene* (Nymphalidae) with description of a new subspecies. *Journal of the Lepidopterists' Society* **31**:243-268.

Kondla, N.G. 1977. A preliminary resource assessment of the proposed Drumheller Provincial Park. Unpublished report for Parks Planning and Design Branch; Alberta Recreation, Parks and Wildlife, Edmonton. 31pp.

_____ 1979. Skippers and butterflies of a prairie farm. *Alberta Naturalist* **9**:71-75.

_____ 1981a. Skippers and butterflies of a disjunct aspen parkland area in Alberta. *Blue Jay* **39**:4-12.

_____ 1981b. Type localities of the Badlands Old World Swallowtail in Alberta. *Blue Jay* **39**:144.

_____ 1983. Additional records of skippers and butterflies from Dinosaur Provincial Park. *Alberta Naturalist* **13**:152-157.

_____ 1985. Skippers and butterflies of a boreal forest sand dune area in Alberta. *Alberta Naturalist* **15**:42-48.

_____ 1986. Skippers and butterflies of the Kootenay Plains, Alberta. *Alberta Naturalist* **16**:11-14.

_____ 1991. A discussion on the correct status of *Colias eurytheme alberta*. *Utahensis* **6**:44-45.

_____ 1992. An update on the butterflies of the Redwater sand dunes. *Alberta Naturalist* **22**:10-17.

_____ 1993. The *Colias alexandra* complex in Alberta. *Alberta Naturalist* **23**:57-61.

___ 1994a. Type localities of *Colias christina* and *Oeneis chryxus caryi*. *Utahensis* (in press).

___ 1994b. Clarification of some butterfly type localities. *Utahensis* (in press).

___ 1995. Sulphur butterflies of the *Colias alexandra* complex in Alberta. *Blue Jay* **53**:15-27.

Kondla, N.G. and C.D. Bird. 1979. The skippers and butterflies of Kananaskis Provincial Park Alberta. *Blue Jay* **37**:73-85.

Kondla, N.G., E.M. Pike and F.A.H. Sperling. 1994. Butterflies of the Peace River Region of Alberta and British Columbia. *Blue Jay* **52**:71-90.

Kondla, N.G. and C. Schmidt. 1991. Fall emergence of *Plebejus rusticus*. *Alberta Naturalist* **21**:50.

Kondla, N.G., T.W. Thormin and T. Pike. 1981. Oslar's roadside skipper in Alberta. *Alberta Naturalist* **11**:15-16.

Lang, B.V. and C.D. Bird. (Compilers) 1973. Natural history observations. *Calgary Field Naturalist* **4**:240-254.

Latreille, P.A. 1804. Mehrere Artikel im Dictionnaire d'Histoire naturelle do Deterville.

___ 1824. *In*: Olivier, Latreille, Le Peletier de Saint Fargeau, Serville et Guérin. Encyclopédie Méthodique. Histoire Naturelle. Insectes. Paris. 1789-1825.

Leblanc, A. 1985. Les lycenides (Lepidoptera: Lycaenidae) du Québec. Fabreries Supplément 4. 66 pp.

Le Conte, J.E. 1833. Histoire générale et iconographie des Lépidoptères et des Chenilles dr l'Amérique septentrionale. Roret, Paris.

Lederer, J. 1852. Versuch die europäischen Lepidopteren in moglichst naturliche Reihenfolge zu stellen. *Verhandlungen der Zoologisch-botanischen Gesellschaft in Wien* **2**:14-54.

Leech, H.B. 1946. Flights of *Nymphalis californica* Bdv. in British Columbia and Alberta in 1945. *The Canadian Entomologist* **77**:203.

Leussler, R.A. 1935. Notes on the diurnal Lepidoptera of the Canadian arctic collected by Owen Bryant in the summers of 1929-1932. II. *Bulletin of the Brooklyn Entomological Society* **30**:42-62.

___ 1938. An annotated list of the butterflies of Nebraska, with the description of a new species (Lepidoptera: Rhopalocera). *Entomologist's Newsletter* **49**:3-9.

Lindsey, A.W. 1942. A preliminary revision of *Hesperia*. *Denison University Bulletin Journal of the Science Laboratory* **37(1-2)**:1-50.

Linnaeus, C. 1758. Systema Naturae per regna tria naturae secundum classes, ordines, genera, species, cum characteribus, differentiis, synonymis, locis. ed. decima reformata. Laur. Salvii, Stockholomiae. 823 pp.

___ 1761. Fauna Suecica sistens animalia Sueciae regni: quadrupedia, aves, amphibia, pisces, insecta, vermes distributa per classes, et ordines, genera et species, cum differentiis speciorum, synonymis autorum nominibus incolarum, locis habitationum, descriptionibus insectorum. Laur. Salvii, Stockholmiae. 578 pp.

Linter, J.A. [1878]. Entomological contributions. *Report of the New York State Cabinet Natural History* **30**:117-254.

Looman, J. and K.F. Best. 1979. Budd's Flora. Research Branch, Agriculture Canada Publication 1662.

Lucas, H. 1852. Description de nouvelle espèces de Lépidoptères appartenant aux collections entomologiques du Musée de Paris. *Revue Magasine Zool.* (2)**4**:128-141, 324-343.

Lyman, H.H. 1892. *Pamphila manitoba* Scudder, and its varieties. *The Canadian Entomologist* **24**:57-59.

___ 1896. Notes on the preparatory stages of *Erebia epipsodea* (Butler). *The Canadian Entomologist* **28**:274-278.

MacNeil, C.D. 1964. The skippers of the genus *Hesperia* in western North America with special reference to California (Lepidoptera: Hesperiidae). *University of California Publications in Entomology* 35, 230 pp.

Manz, M. 1989. Naturalist guide to Bisset Woods. *The Edmonton Naturalist* **17**:9-29.

Martin, J.E.H. 1977. The insects and arachnids of Canada. Part 1. Collecting, preparing and preserving insects, mites, and spiders. Canada Department of Agriculture Publication 1643. 182 pp.

Masters, J.H. 1968a. Ecological and distributional notes on *Erebia disa* (Satyridae) in central Canada. *Journal of Research on the Lepidoptera* **7**:19-22.

___ 1968b. R.J. Fitch's list of Saskatchewan butterflies. *Blue Jay* **26**:194-199.

___ 1969. An unusual nomenclatural problem regarding *Oeneis jutta* (Lepidoptera: Satyridae). *Bulletin of the Association of Minnesota Entomologists* **3**:23-24.

___ 1970a. Concerning *Colias eurytheme alberta* Bowman (Pieridae). *Journal of Research on the Lepidoptera* **9**:97-99.

___ 1970b. Concerning *Colias christina mayi* Chermock and Chermock. *Journal of Research on the Lepidoptera* **9**:227-232.

___ 1972. A new subspecies of *Lycaeides argyrognomon* (Lycaenidae) from the eastern Canadian Forest Zone. *Journal of the Lepidopterists' Society* **26**:150-154.

___ 1974a. The proper subspecific name for *Speyeria aphrodite* (Nymphalidae) in southwest Manitoba. *Journal of the Lepidopterists' Society* **28**:100-102.

___ 1974b. Biennialism in *Oeneis macounii* (Satyridae). *Journal of the Lepidopterists' Society* **28**:237-242.

___ 1975. Variation in *Colias alexandra christina* Edwards (Pieridae) in southwest Manitoba. *Journal of Research on the Lepidoptera* **4**:149-157.

Mattoni, R.H.T. 1977. The Scolitantidini I: Two new genera and a generic rearrangement (Lycaenidae). *Journal of Research on the Lepidoptera* **16**(4):223-242.

Mattoon, S.O., R.D. Davis and O.D. Spencer. 1971. Rearing techniques for species of *Speyeria* (Nymphalidae). *Journal of the Lepidopterists' Society* **25**:247-256.

Maynard, C.J. 1891. Manual of the North American butterflies. Boston.

McCabe, T.L. and R.L. Post. 1977. Skippers (Hesperoidea) of North Dakota. North Dakota Insects Publication No. 11. North Dakota State University. 69 pp.

McDunnough, J.H. 1920. Notes on the life-history of *Phyciodes batesi* Reakirt (Lepidoptera). *The Canadian Entomologist* **52**:56-59.

___ 1922. Notes on the Lepidoptera of Alberta. *The Canadian Entomologist* **54**:134-141.

___ 1924. Some new Canadian Argynnid races. *The Canadian Entomologist* **56**:42-43.

___ 1927. The Lepidoptera of the Seton Lake region, British Columbia. *The Canadian Entomologist* **56**:152-162.

___ 1928a. A new *Euphydryas* (Lepidoptera). *The Canadian Entomologist* **60**:248-249.

___ 1928b. Notes on Canadian diurnal Lepidoptera. *The Canadian Entomologist* **60**:266-275.

___ 1932. Notes on some diurnal Lepidoptera figured in Holland's revised Butterfly Book. *The Canadian Entomologist* **64**:267-270.

___ 1934. Notes on Canadian diurnal Lepidoptera. *The Canadian Entomologist* **66**:81-87.

___ 1936a. On the identity of a so-called race of *Parnassius smintheus* from Manitoba. *The Canadian Entomologist* **65**:43.

___ 1936b. A critical review of the treatment of the North American *Parnassius* species by Felix Bryk in *Das Tierreich* Part 65. *The Canadian Entomologist* **68**:216-225.

___ 1937. Critical notes on the Canadian species of the genus *Erebia* (Lepid.). *The Canadian Entomologist* **65**:14-15.

___ 1939. A new race of *Papilio* belonging to the *machaon* complex. *The Canadian Entomologist* **68**:43.

___ 1940. The Argynnids of the Cariboo region of British Columbia (Lepid.). *The Canadian Entomologist* **72**:23-25.

McGugan, B.R. 1958. Papilionidae to Arctiidae. Volume I. Forest Lepidoptera of Canada recorded by the forest insect survey. Canada Department of Agriculture publication 1034. 76 pp.

Mead, T.L. 1878. Description of two new Californian butterflies. *The Canadian Entomologist* **10**:196-199.

Menetries, E. 1855. Enumeratio corporum animalium Musei imperialis academiae scientiarum Petropolitanae. Classis Insectorum. Ordo Lepidopterorum. Petropoli. Lipsiae, Voss. 102 pp.

Michener, C.D. and C.F. dos Passos. 1942. Taxonomic observations on some North American *Strymon* with descriptions of new subspecies. (Lepidoptera: Lycaenidae). *American Museum Novitates* no. 1210. 7pp.

Miller, L.D. and F.M. Brown. 1951. A Catalogue/Checklist of the Butterflies of America North of Mexico. *The Lepidopterists' Society, Memoir* no. 2. 280 pp.

___ 1979. Studies in the Lycaeninae (Lycaenidae) 4. The higher classification of the American coppers. *Bulletin of the Allyn Museum* **51**:1-30.

Moeck, A.H. 1957. Geographic variability in *Speyeria*. A 1975 reprint by Entomological Reprint Specialists of a paper presented to and sponsored by the Milwaukee Entomological Society. 48 pp.

Moore, F. 1900. *Lepidoptera incica*. **4**:137-260.

Moss, E.H. 1983. Flora of Alberta. 2nd ed., revised by J.G. Packer. University of Toronto Press, Toronto. 687 pp.

Myres, M.T. 1985. A southward return migration of painted lady butterflies, *Vanessa cardui*, over southern Alberta in the fall of 1983, and biometeorological aspects of their outbreaks into North America and Europe. *Canadian Field-Naturalist* **99**:147-155.

Nabokov, V. 1943. The nearctic forms of *Lycaeides* Hübner. (Lycaenidae, Lepidoptera). *Psyche* **50**:87-99.

___ 1944. Notes on the morphology of the genus *Lycaeides* (Lycaenidae, Lepidoptera). *Psyche* **51**:104-138.

___ 1949. The nearctic members of the genus *Lycaeides* Hübner (Lycaenidae, Lepidoptera). *Bulletin of the Museum of Comparative Zoology* **101**:479-541.

Nelson, R.W. 1985. Southward migration of painted ladies in Alberta and British Columbia. *Blue Jay* **43**:7-15.

Neumoegen, B. 1890. New beauties from near and far. *Entomologica Americana* **6**:61-64.

Newcomer, E.J. 1963. The synonymy, variability and biology of *Lycaena nivalis*. *Journal of Research on the Lepidoptera* **2**:271-280.

Nicholl, Mrs. [de la B.]. 1906. Butterfly collecting in Canada, 1904. *Annual Report of the Entomological Society of Ontario* 1905 **36**:70-80.

Nordstrom, W.R. 1976. A resource assessment and development capability of the Cold Lake study area. Unpublished report for Parks Division; Alberta Recreation, Parks and Wildlife, Edmonton. 148 pp.

Oberhauser, K.S. 1988. Male monarch butterfly spermatophore mass and mating strategies. *Animal Behaviour* **36**:1384-1388.

Ochsenheimer, F. 1808. Die Schmetterlinge von Europa.

Oliver, C.G. 1978. Experimental hybridization between the nymphalid butterflies *Phyciodes tharos* and *P. campestris montana*. *Evolution* **32**:594-601.

___ 1979a. Experimental hybridization between *Phyciodes tharos* and *P. batesii*. (Nymphalidae). *Journal of the Lepidopterists' Society* **33**:6-20.

___ 1979b. Genetic differentiation and hybrid viability within and between some Lepidoptera species. *American Naturalist* **114**:681-694.

___ 1980. Phenotypic differentiation and hybrid breakdown within *Phyciodes "tharos"* (Lepidoptera: Nymphalidae) in the northeastern United States. *Annals of the Entomological Society of America* **73**:715-721.

Opler, P.A. 1966. Studies on Nearctic *Euchloe*. Part 4. Type data and type locality restrictions. *Journal of Research on the Lepidoptera* **5**:190-195.

___ 1968. Studies on Nearctic *Euchloe*. Part 5. Distribution. *Journal of Research on the Lepidoptera* **7**:65-86.

___ 1974. Studies on Nearctic *Euchloe*. Part 7. Comparative life histories, hosts and the morphology of immature stages. *Journal of Research on the Lepidoptera* **13**:1-20.

___ 1992. A field guide to eastern butterflies. Houghton Mifflin and Company, Boston. 396 pp.

Opler, P.A. and G.O. Krizek. 1984. Butterflies east of the Great Plains. An illustrated natural history. John Hopkins University Press, Baltimore. 294 pp.

Osborne, C. 1976. Report on gun club slough. *Calgary Field Naturalist* **7**:253-257.

Ovenden, L. and J. Peters. 1974. An ecological survey of Moose Lake Provincial Park. Unpublished report for Parks Division; Alberta Lands and Forests, Edmonton. 72 pp.

Pallas, P.S. 1771. Reisen durch verschiedene Provinzen des Russischen Reiches in den Jahren 1768-1774. Akadem. Buchhandl., Petersburg.

Peregrine Research and Documentation Ltd. 1977. Report on the vertebrate fauna of Kananaskis Provincial Park. Unpublished report for Parks Planning and Design Branch; Alberta Recreation, Parks and Wildlife, Edmonton. Volume 2:1- 405.

Perkins, E.M. and W.C. Meyer. 1973. Revision of the *Boloria epithore* complex, with description of two new subspecies (Nymphalidae). *Bulletin of the Allyn Museum* **11**:1-23.

Perkins, E.M. and S.F. Perkins. 1966. A new race and discussion of the *Boloria epithore* complex (Nymphalidae). *Journal of the Lepidopterists' Society* **20**:103-117.

Peters, J. and L. Ovenden. 1974. An ecological survey of the Vermilion Provincial Park. Unpublished report for Parks Division; Alberta Lands and Forests, Edmonton. 80 pp.

Petersen, B. 1964. Monarch butterflies are eaten by birds. *Journal of the Lepidopterists' Society* **18**:165-169.

Philip, K.W. (Coordinator) 1974. Zone 8: Far north: Alaska and northern Canada. *In*: The 1973 field season summary. *News of the Lepidopterists' Society* (**2**):14-16.

Pike, E.M. 1972. Some butterflies of Alberta. *Teen International Entomology Group Newsletter* **7**:7-10.

___ 1978. Origin of tundra butterflies in Alberta, Canada and their significance in the study of refugia of Wisconsin age. M.Sc. thesis, University of Alberta. 137 pp.

___ 1979. A critique of the genus *Boloria* (Nymphalidae) as represented in the "Butterflies of North America", with corrections, additions and key to species. *Journal of Research on the Lepidoptera* **18**:153-166.

___ 1980. Origin of tundra butterflies in Alberta. *Quaestiones Entomologicae* **16**:555-596.

___ [1986?]. *Limenitis weidemeyerii* or Weidemeyer's Admiral in Canada. Report for World Wildlife Fund Canada. 10 pp.

Pinel, H.W. 1983. Skippers and butterflies of the Indian Grave Campground area, Alberta. *Blue Jay* **41**:71-77.

___ 1985. Skippers and butterflies of Crimson Lake Provincial Park, Alberta. *Blue Jay* **43**:155-159.

___ 1988. Skippers and butterflies of Bow Valley Provincial Park Alberta. *Alberta Naturalist* **18**:7-10.

___ 1990. Northern Pearly Eye - new for Alberta. *Blue Jay* **48**:197-199.

Pinel, H.W. and N.G. Kondla. 1985. Skippers and butterflies of the Police Coulee area, Alberta. *Blue Jay* **43**:213-223.

Pinel, H.W. and N.G. Kondla. 1995. Butterflies and skippers of Plateau Mountain, Alberta. *Blue Jay* **53**:28-41.

Platt, A.P. 1983. Evolution of North American admiral butterflies. *Bulletin of the Entomological Society of America* **29**:10-22.

Police Point Interpretive Centre. 1990. Butterflies of Medicine Hat. Check List. 2 pp.

Porter, W.B. and J.D. Lousier. 1975. An entomological reconnaissance of Syncrude lease #17 and its environs. Environmental Research Monograph 1971-1. Syncrude Canada. 71pp.

Pratt, G.F., D.M. Wright and G.R. Ballmer. 1991. Multivariate and phylogenetic analyses of larval and adult characters of the *editha* complex of the genus *Lycaena* (Lepidoptera:Lycaenidae). *Journal of Research on the Lepidoptera* **30**:175-195.

Pratt, G.F., D.M. Wright and H. Pavulaan. 1994. The various taxa and hosts of the North American *Celastrina* (Lepidoptera:Lycaenidae). *Proceedings of the Entomological Society of Washington* **96**:566-578.

Pyle, R.M. 1981. The Audubon Society Field Guide to North American Butterflies. Chanticleer Press Inc., New York. 916 pp.

Rambur, J.R. 1840. Faune entomologique de l'Andalousie. Artus Bertrand, Paris. Pp. 213-304.

Reakirt, T. 1865. Descriptions of some new species of *Eresia*. *Proceedings of the Entomological Society of Philadelphia* **5**:224-227.

___ 1866. Coloradian Butterflies. *Proceedings of the Entomological Society of Philadelphia* **6**:122-151.

Reist, J.D. 1979. *Callophrys niphon* (Lycaenidae) in Alberta with notes on the identification of *C. niphon* and *C. eryphon*. *Journal of the Lepidopterists' Society* **33**:248-253.

Remington, C.L. 1968. Suture-zones of hybrid interaction between recently joined biotas. *Evolutionary Biology* **2**:321-428.

Remington, P.S. 1952. Collecting along the Alaska highway. *Lepidopterists' News* **61**:103-106.

___ 1955. Interspecific relationships of two rare swallowtail butterflies, *Papilio nitra* and *Papilio hudsonianus*, to other members of *Papilio machaon* complex. *American Philosophical Society, Yearbook* 1955,:142-146.

Roland, J. 1978. Variation in spectral reflectance of alpine and arctic *Colias* (Lepidoptera: Pieridae). *Canadian Journal of Zoology* **56**:1447-1453.

___ 1981. The adaptive value of melanism in alpine *Colias* butterflies (Lepidoptera: Pieridae). M.Sc. thesis, University of British Columbia. 114 pp.

___ 1982. Melanism and diel activity of alpine *Colias* (Lepidoptera: Pieridae). *Oecologia* **53**:214-221.

Rothschild, W. and K. Jordan. 1906. A revision of the American Papilios. *Novitates Zoologicae, Tring.* **13**:411-753.

Ryan, J.K. and G.J. Hilchie. 1980. Report on an ecological survey of terrestrial insect communities in the AOSERP study area. Prepared for the Alberta Oil Sands Environmental Research Program, by McCourt Management Ltd. AOSERP Report 115. 202 pp.

Schneider, D.H. 1794. Neuestes Magazin für die Liebhaber der Entomologie. Struck, Stralsund. Pp. 513-640.

Schrank, F. von P. 1801. Fauna Boica. Ingolstadt, Landshut, Nurnberg. Vol. 2. 374 pp.

Scopoli, J.A. 1777. Introductio ad historiam naturalem, sistens genera lapidum, plantarum et animalium etc. Gerele, Pragae. Pp. 406-444.

Scott, J.A. 1973. Population biology and adult behaviour of the circumpolar butterfly *Parnassius phoebus* (Papilionidae). *Entomologica Scandinavica* **4**:161-168.

___ 1974. Mate-locating behavior of butterflies. *American Midland Naturalist* **91**:103-117.

___ 1975. Mate locating behavior of western North American butterflies. *Journal of Research on the Lepidoptera* **14**:1-40.

___ 1978. The identity of the Rocky Mountain *Lycaena dorcas - helloides* complex (Lycaenidae). *Journal of Research on the Lepidoptera* **17**:40-50.

___ 1979. Geographic variation in *Lycaena xanthoides*. *Journal of Research on the Lepidoptera* **18**:50-59.

___ 1981. New Papilionoidea and Hesperioidea from North America. *Papilio* (New Series) **1**:1-12.

___ 1982. Book Review: Butterflies of the Rocky Mountain states by C.D. Ferris and F.M. Brown (eds.). *Journal of Research on the Lepidoptera* **20**:58-64.

___ 1984. A review of *Polygonia progne* (*oreas*) and *P. gracilis* (*zephyrus*) (Nymphalidae), including a new subspecies from the southern Rocky Mountains. *Journal of Research on the Lepidoptera* **23**:197-210.

___ 1986a. The Butterflies of North America: A Natural History and Field Guide. Stanford University Press, Stanford. 583 pp.

___ 1986b. Larval hostplant records for butterflies and skippers (mainly from western United States), with notes on their natural history. *Papilio* (New Series) **4**:1-37.

___ 1992. Hostplant records for butterflies and skippers (mostly from Colorado) 1959-1991, with new life histories and notes on oviposition, immatures, and ecology. *Papilio* (New Series) **6**:1-171.

___ 1994. Biology and systematics of *Phyciodes* (*Phyciodes*). *Papilio* (New Series) **7**:1-120.

Scott, J.A. and P.A. Opler. 1974. Population biology and adult behaviour of *Lycaena xanthoides*. *Journal of the Lepidopterists' Society* **29**:63-66.

Scriber, J.M. 1982. Food plants and speciation in the *Papilio glaucus* group. Pp. 307-314 *in:* Proceedings of the 5th International Symposium on Insect-Plant Relationships. Pudoc, Wageningen.

___ 1983. Evolution of feeding specialization, physiological efficiency, and host races in selected Papilionidae and Saturniidae. Pp. 373-412 *in:* Variable Plants and Herbivores in Natural and Managed Systems. Denno, R.F. and M.S. McClure (eds.). Academic Press, New York. 717 pp.

___ 1986. Origins of the regional feeding abilities in the tiger swallowtail butterfly: ecological monophagy and the *Papilio glaucus australis* subspecies in Florida. *Oecologia* **71**:94-103.

___ 1988. Tale of the tiger: Beringial biogeography, binomial classification and breakfast choices in the *Papilio glaucus* complex of butterflies. Pp. 241-301 *in:* Chemical Mediation of Coevolution. Spencer K.C. (ed.). American Institute of Biological Sciences, Academic Press, New York. 609 pp.

Scudder, G.G.E. 1979. The nature and strategy of species. Pp. 533-547 *in:* Canada and its insect fauna. Danks, H. V. (ed.). *Memoirs of the Entomological Society of Canada* No. 108. 573 pp.

Scudder, S.H. 1861. Notice of some North American species of *Pieris*. *Proceedings of the Boston Society of Natural History* **8**:178-185.

___ 1862. On the genus *Colias* in North America. *Proceedings of the Boston Society of Natural History* **9**:103-111.

___ 1863. A list of the butterflies of New England. *Proceedings of the Essex Institute* **3**:161-179.

___ 1870. *Eudamus bathyllus* Harris = *E. Pylades*. *Proceedings of the Boston Society of Natural History* **13**:207.

___ 1871. A systematic revision of some of the American butterflies, with brief notes on those known to occur in Essex County, Mass. *Report of the Peabody Academy of Science* **4**:24-82.

___ 1874. The species of the Lepidopterous genus *Pamphila*. *Memoirs of the Boston Society of Natural History* **2**:341-353.

___ 1875. Synonymic list of the butterflies of North America, north of Mexico. *Bulletin of the Buffalo Society of Natural Sciences* **2**:233-269.

___ 1876a. Synonymic list of the butterflies of North America, north of Mexico. *Bulletin of the Buffalo Society of Natural Sciences* **3**:98-129.

___ 1876b. The North American Blue butterflies of the genus *Nomiades*. *The Canadian Entomologist* **8**:21-24.

___ 1879. *In*: W.H. Edwards. Description of a new species of *Pamphila*. *The Canadian Entomologist* **11**:238-239.

___ 1888-1889. The butterflies of the eastern United States and Canada, with special reference to New England. 3 vols., xi + 1956 pp., 3 coloured maps and 89 lithographed plates (of which 36 are partly or fully colored). S.H. Scudder: Cambridge, Massachusetts.

Scudder, S.H. and E. Burgess. 1870. On asymmetry in the appendages of hexapod insects, especially as illustrated in the Lepidopterous genus *Nisoniades*. *Proceedings of the Boston Society of Natural History* **13**:282-306.

Shapiro, A.M. 1974. A salt marsh population of *Lycaena helloides* (Lepidoptera:Lycaenidae) feeding on *Potentilla* (Rosaceae). *Entomological News* **85**:40-44.

Shapiro, A.M. and R.T. Carde. 1970. Habitat selection and competition among sibling species of satyrid butterflies. *Evolution* **24**:48-54.

Shepard, J.H. (unpublished). Maps of Butterflies of British Columbia.

___ 1964. The genus *Lycaeides* in the Pacific northwest. *Journal of Research on the Lepidoptera* **3**:25-36.

___ 1984. Type locality restrictions and lectotype designations for the "Rocky Mountain" butterflies described by Edward Doubleday in "The Genera of Diurnal Lepidoptera" (1847-1849). *Quaestiones Entomologicae* **20**:35-44.

___ 1994. The correct name for the *Boloria chariclea/titania* complex in North America (Lepidoptera: Nymhalidae). Pp. 727-730 *in*: Systematics of western North American butterflies. T.C. Emmel (ed.). Mariposa Press, Gainesville. 859 pp.

Shepard, J.H., S.M. Shepard, and T.R. Manley. 1994. A revision of the *Parnassius phoebus* complex in North America (Lepidoptera: Papilionidae). Pp. 717-726 *in*: Systematics of western North American butterflies. T.C. Emmel (ed.). Mariposa Press, Gainesville. 859 pp.

Sheppard, P.M. 1965. The Monarch butterfly and mimicry. *Journal of the Lepidopterists' Society* **19**:227-230.

Shields, O. 1965. *Callophrys* (*Mitoura*) *spinetorum* and *C.* (*M.*) *johnsoni*, their known range, habits, variation and history. *Journal of Research on the Lepidoptera* **4**:233-250.

Shields, O. and J.C. Montgomery. 1966. The distribution and bionomics of Arctic-Alpine *Lycaena phlaeas* subspecies in North America. *Journal of Research on the Lepidoptera* **5**:231-242.

Shields, O., J.F. Emmel and D.E. Breedlove. 1970. Butterfly larval food plant records and a procedure for reporting food plants. *Journal of Research on the Lepidoptera* **8**:21-36.

Skinner, H. 1897. Notes on Rhopalocera, with descriptions of new species and varieties. *The Canadian Entomologist* **29**:154-156.

_____ 1899. Notes on butterflies, with descriptions of new species. *Entomologist's Newsletter* **10**:111-113.

_____ 1902. A new species of *Melitoea*. *Entomologist's Newsletter* **13**:304.

_____ 1906. A new variety of *Papilio rutulus* Baird. *Entomological News* **17**:379.

_____ 1908. *Argynnis astarte*, Doubl.-Hew. *The Canadian Entomologist* **40**:14-15.

_____ 1911a. A new *Argynnis* and a new *Parnassius* (Lep.). *Entomological News* **22**:108.

_____ 1911b. *Colias nastes streckeri* Gr. Grum-Grshimaïlo. *Entomological News* **22**:231.

_____ 1916. The genus *Parnassius* in America (Lep.). *Entomological News* **27**:210-216.

Smith, M.E. 1953. More butterflies from Alaska and the Highway. *Lepidopterists' News* **7**:123-126.

Smith, W.W. 1976. Butterflies of Cold Lake, Gregoire Lake, Red Lodge, Bow Valley and Beauvais Lake Provincial Parks and the Hillard's Bay area of Lesser Slave Lake (May - September, 1976). Unpublished report for Parks Planning and Design Branch; Alberta Recreation, Parks and Wildlife, Edmonton. 13 pp.

Smith, W.W. and C.D. Bird. 1977. Some butterflies and skippers from the Milk River-Lost River area of southern Alberta. *Blue Jay* **35**:15-18. Errata. *Blue Jay*. **35**:77.

Spalding, D.A. (ed.) 1980. A Nature Guide to Alberta. *Provincial Museum of Alberta Special Publication* No. 5. Hurtig, Edmonton. 368 pp.

Sperling, F.A.H. 1986. Evolution of the *Papilio machaon* species group in western Canada. M.Sc. thesis, University of Alberta. 285 pp.

_____ 1987. Evolution of the *Papilio machaon* species group in western Canada (Lepidoptera). *Quaestiones Entomologicae* **23**:198-315.

_____ 1990. Natural hybrids of *Papilio* (Insecta: Lepidoptera): poor taxonomy or interesting evolutionary problem? *Canadian Journal of Zoology* **68**:1790-1799.

_____ 1991. Mitochondrial DNA phylogeny, speciation and hostplant coevolution of *Papilio* butterflies. Ph.D. thesis, Cornell University. Ithaca, New York. 132 pp.

_____ 1993a. Mitochondrial DNA phylogeny of the *Papilio machaon* species group (Lepidoptera: Papilionidae). *Memoirs of the Entomological Society of Canada* **165**:233-242.

_____ 1993b. Mitochondrial DNA variation and Haldane's rule in the *Papilio glaucus* and *P. troilus* species groups. *Heredity* **71**:227-233.

_____ 1993c. Twenty-seven years of butterfly observations at Fish Butte, Alberta. *Blue Jay* **51**:132-137.

_____ 1994. Sex-linked genes and species differences in Lepidoptera. *Canadian Entomologist* **126**:807-818

Sperling, F.A.H. and P.P. Feeny. 1995. Umbellifer and composite-feeding in *Papilio* species: phylogenetic frameworks and constraints on caterpillars. Pp. 199-208 *in*: Swallowtail Butterflies: Their Ecology and Evolutionary Biology, J.M. Scriber, Y.Tsubaki and R.C. Lederhouse, (eds.). Scientific Publishers, Inc., Gainsville, FL

Sperling, F.A.H. and R.G. Harrison. 1994. Mitochondrial DNA variation within and between species of the *Papilio machaon* group of swallowtail butterflies. *Evolution* **47**:408-422.

Sperling, F.A.H. and N.G. Kondla. 1991. Alberta swallowtails and parnassians: natural history, keys and distribution. *Blue Jay* **49**:183-192.

Stallings, D.B. and J.R. Turner. 1946. New American butterflies. *The Canadian Entomologist* **78**:134-137.

Stanford, R.E. 1977. Rocky Mountain butterfly distribution maps. Denver, Colorado. 39 pp.

_____ (Coordinator) 1980-1990. Season Summary. Zone 3 (Rocky Mountains) : Alberta, Montana, Wyoming, Utah, Colorado and New Mexico. *News of the Lepidopterists' Society* (**2**):15-18 (1980); (**2**):15-20 (1981); (**2**):16-21(1982); (**2**):16-22 (1983) ; (**2**):18-23 (1984); - Zone 4 (Rocky Mountains): Alberta, Montana, Wyoming, Utah, Colorado and New Mexico. (**2**):18-23 (1985); (**2**):17-26 (1986); (**2**):18-26 (1987); (**2**):20-24 (1988); (**2**):18-21 (1989); (**3**):45-48 (1990).

_____ 1985. Rocky Mountain butterfly distribution maps. 4th edition. Published privately, Denver, Colorado. 43 pp.

_____ 1991. *Thymelicus lineola* (European Skipper) in western North America (Hesperiinae, Hesperiidae, Lepidoptera). *Utahensis* **6**:43, 48.

Stanford, R.E. and P.A. Opler. 1993. Atlas of Western USA Butterflies. Published privately. 275 pp.

Still, G.N., V.B. Patterson and J.C.E. Melvin. 1974. Forest insects collected in Banff National Park 1948-1971. Northern Forest Research Centre, Canadian Forestry Service, Edmonton. Report NOR-X-104. 37 pp.

Stoll, C. 1790. Supplementband zu Cramers Papillons exotiques. Graevius, Amsterdam. 184 pp.

Staudinger, O. 1861. Reise nach Finmarken. Macrolepidoptera. *Stettiner Entomologische Zeitung* **22**:325-404.

Strecker, F.H. 1880. Descriptions of some new species and varieties of North American Lepidoptera. *Bulletin of the Brooklyn Entomological Society* **3**:33-36

———— 1885. Description of a new *Colias* from the Rocky Mountains, and an example of polymelanism in *Samia cecropia*. *Proceedings of the Academy of Natural Sciences of Philadelphia* **37**:24-27.

———— 1900. Lepidoptera, Rhopaloceres and Heteroceres, indigenous and exotic. Supplement No. 3, Reading. 4 to:13-37.

Strong, W. and K. Leggatt. 1981. Ecoregions of Alberta. Alberta Energy and Natural Resources. 64 pp.

Susut, J.P. and J.C.E. Melvin. 1974. Forest insects collected in Jasper National Park 1948-1971. Northern Forest Research Centre, Canadian Forestry Service, Edmonton.. Report. NOR-X-107. 30 pp.

Tauscher, A.M. 1809. Lepidopterorum Russiae indigenorum observationes sex. *Memoirs Société Nationale Moscou* **1**:207-212.

Thormin, T.W. 1977. The butterflies of Beaverhill Lake. *Edmonton Naturalist* **5**:160-163.

———— 1988. Annotated list of the butterflies (Lepidoptera) of Bistcho Lake. Pp. 83-84 *in*: The Natural History of Bistcho Lake, northwestern Alberta. W.B. McGillivray and R.I. Hastings, (eds.). *Provincial Museum of Alberta, Natural History Occasional Paper* No. 10.

———— 1990. Annotated list of the butterflies (Lepidoptera) of Andrew Lake. Pp. 63-64 *in* The Natural History of Andrew Lake, northeastern Alberta W.B. McGillivray and R.I. Hastings, (eds.). *Provincial Museum of Alberta, Natural History Occasional Paper* No. 12.

Thormin, T.W. and J.H. Acorn. 1976. Faunal observations: 1975 - Butterflies. *Edmonton Naturalist* **4**:113-116.

Thormin, T.W., N.G. Kondla and C.D. Bird. 1980. Further records of skippers and butterflies from the Milk River - Lost River area of southeastern Alberta. *Blue Jay* **38**:5-10.

Thormin, T.W. and M. White. 1977. Field trips to Cardinal Divide. *Edmonton Naturalist* **5**:6-8.

Thornhill, R. and J. Alcock. 1983. The Evolution of Insect Mating Systems. Harvard University Press, Cambridge, Mass.

Thunberg, C.P. 1791. Dissert. Entomol. sistens insecta Suecica. Edman, Upsaliae **2**:25-46.

Tietz, H.M. 1972. An index to the described life histories, early stages and hosts of the macrolepidoptera of the continental United States and Canada. Vol. 1. Allyn Museum of Entomology, Sarasota, Florida.

Tilden, J.W. and A.C. Smith. 1986. A Field Guide to the Western Butterflies. Houghton Mifflin and Co., Boston. 370 pp, 48 colour plates.

Troubridge, J.T. and D.K. Parshal. 1988. A review of the *Oeneis polixenes* (Fabricius) (Lepidoptera: Satyrinae) complex in North America. *The Canadian Entomologist* **120**:677-696.

Tutt, J.W. 1906. A study of the generic names of the British Lycaenides and their close allies. *Entomological Record* **18**:129-132.

———— 1909. A natural history of the British butterflies. London **3**:1-410.

Tyler, H.A. 1975. The swallowtail butterflies of North America. Naturegraph Publishers, 192 pp.

Tyler, H.A., K.S. Brown and K.H. Wilson. 1994. Swallowtail butterflies of the Americas. A study in biological dynamics, ecological diversity, biosystematics and conservation. Scientific Publishers Inc., Gainesville. 376 pp.

Urquhart, F.A. 1960. The Monarch Butterfly. University of Toronto Press, Toronto. 361 pp.

Vane-Wright, R.I. and M. Boppré. 1993. Visual and chemical signalling in butterflies: functional and phylogenetic perspectives. *Philosophical Transactions of the Royal Society of London* (B). **340**:197-205.

Van Veen, N.W. 1960. Collecting data for 1960 for Lepidoptera from southeastern Alberta. *Proceedings of the Eighth Annual Meeting of the Entomological Society of Alberta,* pp. 16-17.

———— 1961. Collecting data for 1961 for Lepidoptera from southeastern Alberta. *Proceedings of the Ninth Annual Meeting of the Entomological Society of Alberta*, pp. 12-13.

Verity, R. 1905-1911. [1908]. Rhopalocera palaearctica. Papilionidae et Pieridae. Roger Verity: Firenze. 86+368 pp., 2+12+72 pls. (some in color).

Wallis, C. 1976. Milk River Canyon resource evaluation. Unpublished report, Parks Planning and Design Branch; Alberta Recreation, Parks and Wildlife, Edmonton. 122 pp.

Wallis, C. and C.R. Wershler. 1984. Kazan Upland Resource Assessment. Unpublished report for Public Lands Division, Alberta Energy and Natural Resources, Edmonton. 81 pp. + maps.

Warren, B. 1924. A new European skipper. *Transactions of the Entomological Society of London* pp. 56-57.

Warren, B.C.S. 1936. Monograph of the genus *Erebia*. British Museum (Natural History), London. 407pp., 104 pls.

———— 1961. The androconial scales and their bearing on the question of speciation in the genus *Pieris* (Lepidoptera). *Entomologisk Tidskrift* **82**:121-148.

——— 1963. The androconial scales in the genus *Pieris*. 2. The nearctic species of the *napi* group. *Entomologisk Tidskrift* **84**:1-4.

——— 1965. On the nearctic species of the *bryoniae* and *oleracea* groups of the genus *Pieris*. *Entomologist's Record* **80**:61-66.

——— 1968. On the nearctic species of the *bryoniae*- and *oleracea*- groups of the genus *Pieris*. *Entomologist's Record* **80**:61-66.

Watson, F.E. and W. P. Comstock. 1920. Notes on American Lepidoptera with descriptions of new varieties. *Bulletin of the American Museum of Natural History* **42**:447-457.

Watt, W.B. 1968. Adaptive significance of pigment polymorphisms in *Colias* butterflies. I. Variation of melanin pigment in relation to thermoregulation. *Evolution* **22**:437-458.

Wershler, C.R. 1980. South Writing-On-Stone natural history inventory. Unpublished report for Parks Division; Alberta Recreation and Parks, Edmonton. 54 pp.

Weseloh, C., C.D. Bird and L. McKeane. 1974. Natural history observations. *Calgary Field Naturalist* **5**:285-296.

Westwood, J.O. and W.C. Hewitson. 1852. Vol. 2, pp. 251-534. *In*: The Genera of Diurnal Lepidoptera etc. E. Doubleday. Longman, London.

White, R.R. and M.C. Singer. 1974. Geographical distribution of hostplant choice in *Euphydryas editha* (Nymphalidae). *Journal of the Lepidopterists' Society* **28**:103-107.

Whitehouse, F.C. 1918. A week's collecting on Coliseum Mountain, Nordegg, Alta. *The Canadian Entomologist* **50**:1-7.

——— 1919. F.H. Wolley-Dod. *The Canadian Entomologist* **51**:239-240.

Williams, C.B. 1970. The migrations of the Painted Lady butterfly, *Vanessa cardui* (Nymphalidae), with special reference to North America. *Journal of the Lepidopterists' Society* **24**:157-175.

Wolley-Dod, F.H. 1907. Notes on *Chrysophanus hypophlaeas* and its allies, with description of new species. *The Canadian Entomologist* **39**:169-171.

Wyatt, C.W. 1965. Zwei neue Formen von holarktischen Tagfaltern. *Zeitschrift Wiener Entomologische Geseluschaft* **50**:69-71.

Index

B

bairdii brucei, Papilio (Papilio) 99
Basilarchia
    see *Limenitis (Basilarchia)*
batesii, Phyciodes 213, 270, 272
batesii lakota, Phyciodes 270
bellona, Boloria 15, *210*, 234
bellona jenistae, Boloria 234
Blue
    Acmon 188, 199
    Arrowhead 193
    Cranberry 15, 204
    Dotted 15, 188
    Eastern Tailed 189, 190
    Greenish 203
    Icarioides 180, 201
    Melissa 196
    Northern 194, 195
    Rustic 15, 197
    Shasta 202
    Silvery 191, 192
    Western Tailed 189, 190
Blue Copper 156
Blues 149, 186
    Common 197
    Tailed 189
Bog Fritillary 237, 238
Boloria 207, 231, 247
    acrocnema 13
    alaskensis 243
    alberta 6, 17, *210*, 232
    astarte 5, 15, 17, *209*, 233
    astarte astarte 233
    bellona 15, *210*, 234
    bellona jenistae 234
    chariclea 209, 235
    chariclea/titania complex 235
    distincta 233
    epithore 210, 236
    epithore uslui 236
    eunomia 209, 237
    eunomia dawsoni 237, 238
    eunomia nichollae 8, 237, 238
    eunomia triclaris 237, 238
    freija 209, 239
    freija freija 239
    frigga 15, 17, *210*, 240
    frigga saga 240

improba 13, 17, *210*, 241
improba harryi 242
improba youngi 242
key to species 209
napaea 17, *209*, 243
napaea alaskensis 243
polaris 232
selene 209, 244
selene atrocostalis 244
thore 236
todii jenistae 9
Branded Skippers 53
Brenthis 231
Broad-winged Skippers 80
Bronze Copper 164
Brown, Eyed 284
Brown Elfin 172

C

Cabbage Butterfly 15, 18, 19, 24, 111, 119, 120, 121, 122
California Tortoise Shell 18, 217
California White 123, 126
californica, Nymphalis 18, *207*, 217
californica californica, Nymphalis 217
californica herri, Nymphalis 217
callippe, Speyeria 211, 251, 255
callippe calgariana, Speyeria 7, 9, 251
Callippe Fritillary 251
Callophrys 167
    affinis 151, 168
    sheridanii 151, 168, 169
    sheridanii sheridanii 169
campestris, Phyciodes 272
Canada Sulphur 135
canadensis, Colias 114, 135
canadensis, Papilio (Pterourus) 15, *94*, 105, 106, 108, 109
Canadian Tiger Swallowtail 15, 105, 106, 108, 109, 110
cardui, Vanessa 18, *209*, 227, 229, 230
Carterocephalus 78
    palaemon 56, 78
    palaemon mandan 78
catullus, Pholisora 55, 86

Celastrina 186
    ladon 15, *153*, 186, 187
    ladon lucia 5, 186, 187
    ladon nigrescens 13, 186, 187
centaureae, Pyrgus 54, 87, 90
centaureae freija, Pyrgus 87, 88
centaureae loki, Pyrgus 87, 88
Cercyonis 280, 285
    key to species 282
    oetus 282, 285, 286, 287
    oetus charon 285, 286
    oetus phocus 285
    oetus sylvestris 285
    pegala 282, 285, 287
    pegala ino 9, 287
cesonia, Zerene 113, 133, 148
chalcedona, Euphydryas 266
Chalceria
    see *Lycaena (Chalceria)*
chariclea, Boloria 209, 235
Charidryas 206, *207*, 260
    acastus 212, 261, 264
    damoetas 212, 262, 264
    damoetas damoetas 262
    gorgone 18, *212*, 263
    gorgone carlota 263
    key to species 212
    palla 17, 18, *212*, 261, 262, 264
    palla calydon 264
Checkered Skipper 89
Checkered White 24, 123, 124, 125
Checkerspot
    Acastus 261
    Anicia 15, 18, 265, 266, 267
    Edith's 265, 267
    Gillett's 269
    Gorgone 18, 263
    Northern 17, 18, 261, 262, 264
    Pearly 264
    Rockslide 262, 264
Checkerspots 205, 260, 265
christina, Colias 5, 15, *113*, *114*, 134, 136, 137, 138
christina christina, Colias 136
Christina Sulphur 15, 136
chrysotheme, Colias 138
Chryxus Arctic 15, 301
chryxus, Oeneis 5, 15, *281*, 301
chryxus caryi, Oeneis 8, 301, 302
chryxus chryxus, Oeneis 301